CONCERNS OF A CONSERVATIVE DEMOCRAT

Foreword by
John Wesley Snyder AND
Dean Acheson

Notes by Eugene P. Trani

Concerns of
a Conservative
Democrat

by Charles Sawyer

Carbondale and Edwardsville
SOUTHERN ILLINOIS UNIVERSITY PRESS

Feffer & Simons, Inc.
London and Amsterdam

To Margaret, mother of my children

Copyright © 1968 by Southern Illinois University Press

Foreword

JOHN WESLEY SNYDER

DEAN ACHESON

OUR COLLEAGUE in the Cabinet of President Truman, Charles Sawyer, Secretary of Commerce, 1948–53, has here given us his story, the life of a self-made Ohio Yankee. He calls himself a conservative Democrat and in Ohio that can be pretty conservative. But here we have to take him with a grain of salt. Later on he gives us a clue as to what he means by "conservative." He believed in Democratic doctrine—and under Mr. Truman we all knew what that was—but he did not share the view of many "that the businessman was a God-given whipping boy." With that qualification the joint authors of this foreword agree also. All of us in the Cabinet knew who the whipping boys were. We were—perhaps, not God-given, but certainly popularly chosen. Charlie took his share of the knocks and, fairly enough, does not miss the chance to give a few back where he believes the record to have been garbled, misstated, or fabricated.

This story of an active, adventurous, and successful life is told in the forthright style of a healthy extrovert, without self-analysis, regrets about might-have-beens, or nagging self-depreciation. Charles Sawyer is and was a vigorous activist. He made his way in the law, went to World War I, came back to more law, politics, and business; and to war a second time as Ambassador to wartorn Belgium. Then came a second return to a more important position in law, politics, and business,— even the hazards of building a sports stadium in Cincinnati— before his call to the Cabinet in Washington. His excellent memory and sharp observation spice the narrative with lively and amusing anecdotes.

Charles Sawyer was a good team player and colleague. Loyal and able, he did his full share of the common task and carried his full share of the burdens. Friends from all the varied stages of his life will enjoy reliving it with him and will catch some of his hearty joy in doing so. We wish his book a fair wind and good luck.

Preface

WHY DO people write books? For a variety of reasons; and sometimes apparently for no reason at all.

As for me, I began this effort for my children. As it went on, I found myself indulging a weakness of advancing years. It is pleasant to reminisce, or exhibit, in the words of Ben Franklin, "the inclination so natural to old Men, to be talking of themselves and their own past Actions."

As I reminisced I was from time to time amused at the changes in my thinking, but I also enjoyed discovering a certain consistency in many of my beliefs. Even as a City Councilman I had felt that public officials make too small an effort to apply common sense to their assignments. From that early post to my final assignment in Washington I saw that theory vindicated. Many officials quickly surround themselves with an aura of greatness, or superiority, and then get wordy and pompous. I found that matter-of-fact dealing produced a good response from the average citizen in Ohio, royalty in Belgium or Congressmen in Washington.

vii

I had always been fairly independent politically but I became more independent and less partisan as time went on. In Washington I decided, some thought foolishly, to forget politics. I did not claim to know much about politics but had experience, in greater variety and volume than most officials there, and was not frightened by political threats. I knew how unimportant most of them were. Even where they were important, as in my unqualified defense of business, I ignored them. My defense of business was not popular then nor is it today. Most people regard business and businessmen at best as a necessary evil. They have not faced objectively the picture of what their lives would be if business were to be done away with.

Businessmen are not perfect—but they are not ogres or beasts—they are like the rest of us, with one qualification; they are more timid, beaten down by government investigation, supervision, suppression and attack—they seem to be afraid to present their case vigorously.

A glaring example is their failure to emphasize one important consideration: they represent millions of American citizens—the shareholders, men and women, who outnumber the members of organized labor and probably on the average enjoy a smaller income. They permit the idea to circulate that labor leaders represent human beings and they represent avarice. I do not quarrel with the leaders of labor—they are doing what they should. I do suggest that the leaders of industry should be equally zealous in presenting the case for other human beings, the real owners of American business.

As to my concerns, they have changed. I, like everyone else, have, as life went on, been worried about one thing or another—but, especially in later years, I have tried to differentiate between things which are irritating, things which are alarming, and things which are portentous. In my last chapter I have undertaken to emphasize the real ones.

As I conclude this narrative, I feel that the ideas which I

undertook to express as a public official are as sound today as they were then. This may be regarded by some as an arrogant attitude but, as my fellow Cabinet members indicated, perhaps with a touch of irony, in the Foreword, I am not given to nagging self-depreciation.

CHARLES SAWYER

Cincinnati, Ohio
June 3, 1968

Contents

xi

List of Illustrations

CONCERNS OF A CONSERVATIVE DEMOCRAT

1 *Yankee from Ohio*

THIS IS the story of a conservative northern democrat.[1] I would not have been called "conservative" during my younger years. But in time I developed the characteristics of a true New England Yankee—thrift, a respect for the lessons of the past, a restrained idealism which allows for change and reform, and a belief in the old-fashioned virtues. These qualities were strong in my father, Edward Milton Sawyer, who came from Maine, and in my mother, Caroline Butler, who was born in Stamford, Connecticut.

Most of my earliest memories are of New England, for I spent almost every boyhood summer in Maine. My father enjoyed the teacher's privilege of a long vacation. He would bring his family back from Ohio to the farm in the foothills of the White Mountains where my grandfather, Amos Knight Sawyer, a gentle and hardworking soul, wrested a living from the flinty soil. We would go by train to New York, then take the boat to Boston. We looked forward with trepidation to Block Island Channel, where the water was always rough. From Boston, by another boat, we would go to Portland and spend two or three days there, visiting cousins, going out to

3

Cape Elizabeth, Peak's Island, and Cushing's Island, fishing for "cunners" off the rocks, swimming in the frigid waves at Old Orchard Beach, and nosing around the fish-smelling wharves.[2]

My mother's forebears were lawyers, preachers, and professors (one of them at Yale) but my father's forebears were sailors, and one of them, Uncle Manson, was still living. On one of these trips my father took me to visit Uncle Manson in Portland. His house was near the docks and very old. He was a small man, with mutton-chop whiskers and weather-beaten skin, retired after many voyages around the world. As he told of his travels and showed his collection of curios, I was a fascinated listener. Once he had bought a winning ticket on the Louisiana Lottery. It had paid a large sum of money—perhaps equivalent to three hundred thousand dollars today. With my great-great-uncle, however, it went as easily as it had come; the only remnant of this windfall was a house in Auburn, Maine, where my father was born.

From Portland, we traveled by train to Bridgeton Junction and then, by narrow gauge, to Ingall's Station, a small frame building deep in the pine woods. The train was so small that a tall man could look over the cars and almost see over the engine. We would climb out on the platform and, as the train puffed off into the distance, stand and drink in the utter silence of the woods. There would be my grandfather, waiting with his horse and wagon. In high good humor we would clamber aboard with our bags and drive two miles to the farm.

It was not a large place, perhaps one hundred acres, enclosed by stone fences. I recall only one crop—hay, and I have a vivid recollection of mowing and carting in bulging loads of it. There was always something to do. We would go up into the foothills for blueberries, carrying enormous pails which were soon filled. Occasionally I fished for trout in the little black streams or "brooks," which ran through the meadows. Sometimes I walked several miles to a modest peak called Mount

Pleasant and climbed the mountain to its summit. Sometimes I was allowed to help dynamite rocks. We would drill a hole in the rock, insert several sticks of dynamite, touch it off, and haul the broken pieces away on a sledge. The rock crop was almost as regular as the hay. No matter how often or thoroughly the land was cleared, the rocks would soon come up again.[3] I had my own rifle and shotgun and hunted small game. Uncle Albert, my father's brother, was an expert shot and sometimes took me to nearby lakes for fishing and shooting. On one of these trips I shot a loon, whose stuffed carcass I remember seeing around the house for many summers.[4]

My grandparents were "pious"; nothing prevented their church attendance, nor ours. Every Sunday morning we would put on our Sunday clothes, climb into the old surrey, and ride three miles to East Denmark where the farmers of the countryside and their wives would arrive at the little church, after driving by a few "sinners" who sat indifferently on their porches. The congregation would stand outside gossiping briefly and then enter the church. I recall nothing of the service except my grandmother's voice. Shortly after a hymn began everyone else became silent. Her voice was rich and strong and filled the little church. It could be heard afar through the open windows.

These trips to Maine instilled in me a lasting love for New England—the brooks, the lakes, the stone fences, the smell of the pine woods, the mountains—and for the people. Many times I thought of going back and in October 1962 I did so. My wife and I motored up into the mountains from Boston. I could scarcely wait to get my first glimpse of these long-remembered scenes. We came to East Denmark where the church had stood. On one corner had been a grocery store, on another the post office. But as we drove by this spot nothing was familiar—the grocery store, the post office, and the church were gone. Everything I remembered had vanished. Finally I found an old sand road leading back to my grandfather's farm.

My car could not go through—so I walked the two miles. The scene was strange and unfamiliar. The fields were overgrown with scrub pine and birch. The once intriguing farmhouse, long unoccupied and abandoned, had collapsed. The farm itself had become the home of deer, moose, bear, and other wild animals.

My grandfather had owned another farm near East Denmark. Its large, long, New England farmhouse, built so one could pass from house to barn even in the heaviest winter snow, was no longer there. A woman nearby said it had burned down when "lightnin" struck it. At the spot was a small modern house owned by two women from New York who had purchased it from an artist. I drove to a site said to be the final resting place of my grandmother, Maria, whose burial I had witnessed many years before. I could find no headstone or marker for her grave.

I should not have gone back—but as we drove off in the late afternoon, with the setting sun behind us, I could still see in my mind's eye all the pleasure-filled scenes of my boyhood.

I am a grandson of New England, not a son. I was born at Tusculum, near the site of the first Cincinnati settlement where some of my mother's ancestors had landed on the north bank of the Ohio River.[5] The family moved several times in and around Cincinnati before settling in the suburb of Madisonville. It is difficult to know which of my earliest experiences I really recall and which were later told to me; but I think I remember a few. When I was five years old, I came trudging home one afternoon with a fishing pole over my shoulder. I had no fish and the fishhook was caught in the seat of my pants.

I was on occasion the butt of jokes. Once, after a heavy rain, an older lad suggested that I stand under a small tree and shake it hard. My mother had just dressed me in clean, starched clothes. With my white collar, flowing necktie, and button-up jacket, I must have looked a tempting picture of innocence. I shook the tree with all my might. The result was predictable. Some time later the same boy asked to see what would happen if I poked a stick into a round, white hornets' nest. The hornets flew out and did what came naturally. I quickly left the scene, well stung, but wiser. Shortly thereafter I was locked in a shed by older boys who taunted me by pushing the key through the keyhole. As I took hold, it was quickly jerked back. My finger was drawn into the keyhole and torn open. I still have the scar. It has served as a reminder that one should not grasp too quickly what appear to be attractive opportunities.

I did not always get the worst of it. Near us lived some larger boys who bullied me incessantly. One day, as I was riding proudly down the street on a bicycle given me at Christmas, two of these boys overtook me and tried to take my new possession away. I thereupon exhibited a primal instinct —this was my property and I did not intend it to get away from me. I reacted with uncontrollable fury and surprising strength. I kept the bicycle. That night the boys' father came to our house to complain about the beating I had given his sons.

My parents were retiring but determined and hard-working schoolteachers, interested in books and scholarship. They were deeply religious, and I can still see my father starting for church on Sunday morning with the family Bible under his arm. I also remember watching for him in the late afternoon as he came home from his teaching. At a distance all I could see was his hat moving up and down over an intervening fence. This fascinated me—at that time I read, or had read to me, a hair-raising story from the *Youth's Companion* in which a gorilla had killed a man, put on his felt hat, and was seen coming through a cornfield with only the bobbing hat in sight. My younger brother George was not a robust child; I played most rough games with other boys. However, we were very fond of each other. I would occasionally bully him, but when my father or mother would punish me for this, George would immediately turn on them and defend me with great energy.

We lived simply. There was no servant or maid. New clothes were rare, especially for my brother, who usually wore the ones I had outgrown. We had no money for luxuries other than our trips to Maine. Since my father could give me no spending money, I undertook to earn my own. Among other chores I carried milk on an extended neighborhood route. On occasion I picked up money in other ways. When I was ten, my mother took me to Cincinnati to see the Fall Festival Parade, in which my father was to ride a white horse and lead one of the school divisions. Shortly after we were seated, high up on the bank of seats, a woman without a seat appeared and asked if she could find one among us. I volunteered to sell her mine for two dollars. My mother said: "Are you sure you don't want to stay up here where you can see well?" I said: "No, I prefer the two dollars." The woman gave me the money and I walked down to the ground. Within a short time I had climbed up the back of the seat bank and was about as close to my mother as I had been before. When she saw me she said: "You gave up your good seat—now you go back down." My mother permitted nothing that even looked like cheating and made me stay on the ground until the parade ended. My scholarship was good but my conduct apparently was not. On one report card, every subject—reading, spelling, language, arithmetic, geography, writing, music, United States history, composition—was graded "excellent" but "Deportment" was marked "poor." Strangely enough, I recall no misconduct unless one might so regard the ringing of the village fire-alarm bell and watching from a safe distance as the volunteer firemen rushed to the nonexisent blaze. This I do remember.

I resolved at an early date to do anything I felt afraid to do. When I was very young I jumped off a bridge with an open umbrella, hoping it would drop me down gently. I was well banged-up; but I had done what I was afraid to do. I took part in many sports, but excelled in none. During one football game against a neighboring high school, I engaged in pointed altercation with an opposing player. Shortly thereafter, while I was lying on my back, he jumped on my stomach with both feet. I was out of the game and for some time thereafter suffered continuous pain. My parents were greatly concerned. When my father offered to buy me a shotgun if I would play no more football, I accepted the offer.

My interests and ambitions were changing. I began to read voraciously. I read a few novels, some books on travel, many biographies, and almost anything about Napoleon. I was also fascinated by Theodore Roosevelt, followed his career closely and read everything he wrote; one of my favorite books was *The Winning of the West*.[6] I still recall my excitement when I saw him in person at Music Hall in Cincinnati. Probably because of my worship of Roosevelt and his advocacy of the "strenuous life," I decided to learn to box. From my meager savings, I paid for a membership in the Cincinnati YMCA, where I took lessons from a pug named Gus Bezenah. I was well beaten up on several occasions. I remember coming home one night on the streetcar with my face bloody and bruised, a horrifying and bewildering spectacle to the other passengers. When I was sixteen, Congressman William B. Shattuc, of the First Congressional District of Ohio, appointed me as an alternate to Annapolis.[7] I took and passed the examinations. But the original applicant also passed and was admitted. My naval career was at an end. The successful candidate went on to become a famous dirigible pilot during World War I.

It had been assumed that I would go to college, even though my father's circumstances were straitened. I had thought of Yale. However, I was urged by a friend to try Oberlin College where he was a student. This might be the proper point at which to say that I went to Oberlin because I was enchanted by its liberal attitude toward educating women and its vigorous and dedicated crusades for Negro rights; but this would not be true.[8] I went there because it was cheaper, and because my mother hoped I would learn to play the pipe organ at Oberlin's fine Conservatory of Music. I never studied the organ, but did sing in the large church choir.

I was eighteen when I climbed on the train headed for college, the first time I had been away from home alone. Oberlin was then a small Midwest college town, undistinguished except for broad streets and beautiful trees. Many of the original brick buildings were still standing and in use. The houses where students lived were mostly old residences. Only after the Oberlin windfall from Charles Hall did its great building program begin.[9] At the first freshman rally I was chosen cheerleader. At the same rally appeared another freshman (at least he claimed to be one) of forbidding appearance, dressed in black tights, and offering to take on anyone who would box with him. I volunteered to take the punishment. To the surprise of everyone I got the best of him. Throughout my college career I continued to box and fought many bouts with a man named Zerker, a heavyweight who had once been a sparring partner of Jim Jeffries. Zerker weighed one hundred pounds more than I did (I weighed only 132 at that time). Several times he knocked me cold although he tried not to hurt me, for I was the only one who would box with him. Once or twice I succeeded in knocking him down. Boxing was my only sport. I did little else athletically, other than to attend the required gym classes.

During my first year I determined to complete the four-year course in three years, well aware that this would involve extra hours of work and study during the summer. I was not an outstanding student but did well in all my courses except German, where my low grade prevented my securing a Phi Beta Kappa key. I was fortunate enough to have one great teacher—Charles Henry Adams Wager. Small and frail, he bulked large in the classroom. He had infinite charm, spoke and wrote with impeccable style, and exercised a powerful influence upon the students who packed his English classes. I spent long hours in his study, discussing Chaucer and Shakespeare and all manner of things. Stimulated by his ideas of greatness and beauty in literature, I became even more of a reader than before. During one summer in Oberlin I was reading a book a day, from which I developed some eye trouble.

My three-year schedule gave me little time for campus activities. I was, however, associate editor of the Oberlin *Review*, the college paper, and took part in several oratorical contests, none of which I won. I wrote many papers for classroom work, for my own edification, and for possible publication, and among others, a paper on the "Siege of Saragossa," another on Theodore Roosevelt, a lengthy essay on Alexander Hamilton and the Federalist Party; and an extended paper on State Government in Indiana.[10] During my senior year I participated in the Republican Mock Convention. It was not until some years later that Oberlin became broad-minded enough to hold a Democratic Mock Convention. I nominated William Howard Taft in typically extravagant political oratory. I pointed out Taft's many accomplishments and then in conclusion declaimed, "His enemies say he is an echo of Roosevelt. Can 300 pounds be an echo? Can you call that mountain of manhood a reverberation?"

In those days automobiles were a rarity. None of us had ridden in one. I enjoyed walking and did much of it. Many times my friends and I walked ten or twelve miles to the town of Vermilion, on Lake Erie. We would spend the night on the shore, curled up in the blankets which we had carried with us.

I had almost no money of my own, and my father and mother practiced rigid economies to keep me in college. What money I had came from odd jobs, including waiting at table. Once when Oberlin was about to play a football game at Ohio State I decided to try to increase my income. I had never made a bet and had no business betting five dollars, or even one; but I knew that our team would win. This was my chance to replenish my exchequer; I bet twenty-five dollars. You have guessed it—Oberlin lost! I never gambled again at college, nor for years thereafter.

Although it was necessary for me to study in the summer, I tried to earn some money during what vacation was left. One year my roommate and I undertook to sell libraries throughout the Middle West. We would enter a town, approach a drugstore, or any store where there was room for library shelves, and arrange to set up a library. Memberships were solicited at two dollars per person, permiting the contributor to take out any book for a period of one week. After a few days had passed, we faced the appalling realization that one man had made our endeavor hopeless. His name was Andrew Carnegie. Every town had a Carnegie library, where all sorts of books could be borrowed at no cost whatever.[11] We soon ran out of money and were forced to hitchhike our way home.

As my college days were about to end, I had no clear picture of my future. During my days in Madisonville, as I made small deposits in the Building Association, I tried to imagine myself as a banker. Sometimes I had looked at politics with interest. However, I most fancied myself as the owner of a newspaper. I would take on the habits of a country squire, ride and hunt in the afternoons, meet with leading citizens and write moving editorials in the evening, slowly accumulate this world's goods and play a more and more important part in the life of the community—and even beyond. In the late spring of my senior year I discussed this ambition with my roommate, who soon began to share my enthusiasm. A few weeks before graduation I learned that a weekly newspaper was for sale in Lamro, South Dakota. After long discussion and with some concern, we arranged to buy it for $1,500. We were excited. But two days before commencement I received a telegram from the owner stating that a "cash customer" had appeared and he regretted that the paper was not for sale to us.[12] My college course had ended; graduation was at hand; I had no prospects for the future.

Within a day, however, things changed. I was approached by President King who said that Oberlin had received from the Cincinnati Law School the offer of a one-year scholarship.[13] As I was the only senior from Cincinnati, perhaps I would be interested. I still wanted to run a newspaper; but it was necessary for me to reappraise my situation. I had never intended to be a lawyer; but I had finished the four years of college in three years and was entitled to one year to experiment. I decided to accept the scholarship. My three years at Oberlin had passed quickly, but the next three moved even faster. I found a liking for the law, and finished each year near the top of my class. My days were filled with work and study, with little time for fun. Although my scholarship lasted only one year, I managed to arrange free tuition for my last two years by becoming the law school secretary and librarian. I joined the debating team and competed for every prize the school offered. Happily, I won some of them, although the rewards were not magnificent—one hundred dollars was the top prize.

These winnings were important, for I was in constant need of money. I had accepted no help from my father after my second year in college. Although I had been elected a director of a building association, the modest fee of three dollars for each weekly meeting was not enough to live on. Since both my parents had been teachers, it was easy for me to decide to earn money by teaching. The Cincinnati night high schools offered an opportunity. The history examination dealt specifically with my favorite subject—Napoleon. I received a perfect grade in that test and passed all the others and was given my teacher's certificate. The salary was twelve dollars a week—three nights at four dollars a night. I taught for several years, enjoyed it immensely and became fond of my students, many of whom were older than I. They worked during the day, came to class tired, and fought off sleep in the classroom. I, too, was tired when class was over.

Between my second and third year at the law school, I became a salesman for the West Disinfecting Company. My job was to travel through Ohio and sell a product called "Chloronaptholeum," a heavy disinfectant, used principally in toilets. For this I received a salary of twelve dollars a week plus ten dollars for expenses. My first trip was through western Ohio where I went from house to house and tried to sell one can of this product to each housewife. I was reasonably successful, but as I sat alone one night and reviewed my situation, I had an idea. When I returned to Cincinnati after two weeks, I approached the manager and asked if he would pay a good commission if I took no salary. This was agreeable. I then asked if I could receive an additional commission if he paid me nothing for expenses. He wondered how I would live and I told him I had saved the twenty-four dollar salary I had already received. He agreed to pay me a total commission of fifteen per cent. I then asked if he had a territory where no salesman had ever gone. He said that no one had traveled up the Ohio River for several years, and I could take that territory. I began my trip. My idea had been to sell the product in bulk. As I traveled up the river, from town to town, I called on no housewives. Instead I called upon county commissioners and school boards. They bought my "Chloronaptholeum" by the barrel. I returned in four weeks, having earned $400. The manager hesitated to pay me this enormous sum; but I had the orders. He was so impressed that he offered me a job at fifty dollars a week—in those days a substantial income. However, I turned him down. I now had no wish to be anything but a lawyer.

My ambition, however, did not end with the law. I had been intrigued by Theodore Roosevelt's statement that he wanted to be a politician because politicians were the ruling class. At an

early age I entered politics. Politics is a disease. Some men
suffer only a mild attack, some eventually conquer it. In my
case for many years it was chronic. There are two types of
politician: those who work in the organization, and those who
run for office. I was both. I was not even old enough to vote
when I became a precinct committeeman, a foot soldier of the
party. Years later Harry Truman told me that he valued my
political advice because I was the only member of his Cabinet
who had ever polled a precinct. While still in law school, I was
in the midst of my first political battle. I tried to prevent the
annexation of Madisonville, my home town, by the neighboring metropolis of Cincinnati. I wrote to the mayor of Madisonville, John Dittgen, and suggested a campaign to keep our
town from being swallowed by its enormous neighbor. Dittgen
was also a printer and we would publish a newspaper, the
Madisonville Citizen. I outlined my plan:

A motto—We can always go in; we can never get out.

Also, of course, articles in each issue on much-mooted topics like
the water works; the water itself; our streets; the sewer question;
the tax problem; the folly of letting Cincinnati get the advantage
of our excessively high tax duplicate; the possible loss of our high
school,—etc.

If the campaign gets hot, a personal column where we can pay our
respects to our friends, the enemy.[14]

When I called, the mayor was enthusiastic and we started at
once to put my plan into action. During the campaign I
undertook to speak at a meeting of the opposition. I was
hooted down—but used the *Citizen* to strike back.

What, among all their sarcasm and bitterness, is the sum of their
charge against me? —It is that I am a young man. I do not deny it.
There are some things which one cannot conceal, and youth is
among them. It is a common misfortune. Those gentlemen were
probably young once themselves.

Dittgen and I were at the print shop every night until very late. We set up and printed four copies of the *Madisonville Citizen*.[15] I personally wrote all the editorials and most of the articles. When we had not received enough "letters to the editor" from leading citizens, I entered a few of my own—anonymously. I was brash and combative and probably not too persuasive—but I was having the time of my life. We lost the fight and Madisonville was annexed to Cincinnati, but I had tasted blood.

In 1911, just twenty-four and a law school senior, I decided to run for the City Council of Cincinnati, although a few months earlier I had not even been a resident of Cincinnati. I proceeded to organize a "spontaneous demand" that I represent the Democratic party in the Second Ward. My Republican opponent was a popular German. The Ward was normally Republican and his friends put up a hard fight, including the effort to label me a "total abstainer." I was not a total abstainer, although my parents were. According to family legend my mother's father had died from too much drinking, and my father shared the sentiment of many devoted churchworkers that drinking was a sin. In this, my first essay for public office, I campaigned hard, but relied heavily upon Henry T. Hunt. He had been the prosecutor of Hamilton County and was running for Mayor of Cincinnati on a "good government" platform. My literature was a card:

Mr. Voter:
    Henry T. Hunt will be the next Mayor of this City; but his success in the housecleaning business will be seriously impaired if he plays a lone hand. Mr. Hunt should have a Council which will aid, instead of one which will impede and embarrass him. If you believe that the time has come to make a change, do a good job and put in a Democratic Council as well as a Democratic Mayor.[16]

The local Madisonville paper was kind enough to advocate my election.

This is The Man. Why Sawyer Should be Elected. He has lived all
his life in this town. We have had opportunity to know him well.
His record is clean. He will be active in furthering the interests of
this ward. He will not confine his activities to drawing his salary.
He is well able to handle himself before a public body and he has
a knowledge of municipal affairs and municipal law which will
make him a valuable man in Council.[17]

This campaign was a success. Upon my election, the Cincinnati *Enquirer* noted: "Councilman from Second Ward, youngest to ever occupy seat, is strictly a product of Cincinnati." [18]
They apparently had forgotten that a few months before I had
protested bitterly becoming a citizen of their city.

All of these activities went on while I was still in law school.
About the middle of my senior year I was approached by a
former judge who conducted a quiz-class, preparing law students for the bar examinations. He asked if I would be willing
to join his class for a fee of thirty-five dollars. I replied that I
would try to go it alone, and told my father that if, after three
years in law school, I was not able to pass the bar examination,
I had better become a farmer and plow corn. My father then
told me the story of the young man who had seen in the sky in
big letters—PC. He was sure this was a message to him to
"Preach Christ"; his father disagreed: "It means Plow
Corn."

The bar examination was given in Columbus and lasted two
days. My brother George was then a student at Ohio State
University. To save the two dollars for a hotel room, I spent
two nights with him. On the second night I went to bed early I
had experienced two full days and was very tired. But as I was
about to fall asleep I began to review my answers. Suddenly I
thought of one which was wrong. As I lay there worrying, I
thought of a number of other wrong answers. I jumped out of
bed, turned on the lights, and began to read anything I could
find—mostly magazines. My mind was keyed up, far beyond
normal. For the first and the only time in my life I could read

a whole page at a time. After about an hour and a half, during which I read practically everything in the room, I went back to bed and to sleep. I was sure I had failed the examination; but it could not be helped. I had relatives in Syracuse, New York, and went there for a few days to await the outcome. If I passed, I planned to go from there to Columbus where the successful candidates would be sworn in. The day before the ceremonies I received a telegram from my father telling me that I had received first place in the examination with a grade of 92.7. My success was probably partly due to my decision to write as legibly as possible. I had marked many papers as a teacher and knew what a good impression was made when it was easy for the teacher to read the answers.

I traveled to Columbus that night and the next morning was sworn in. I was now a lawyer.

2 Beginnings

My LAW practice began in 1911. I was twenty-four.
The day after I was sworn in I purchased a desk for eight
dollars, rented a small room in downtown Cincinnati, and
waited for clients to flock to my office. They didn't. I had been
offered positions in two big Cincinnati law firms but had
turned them down. I was very confident and not too wise.
After some few days had passed, my first client walked in—a
boyhood friend sued by a tailor whom he would not pay because the clothes did not fit. I was able to settle for a small
part of the tailor's claim and my friend continued to wear the
suit.

For some time there was no other client at my door. I was,
however, not wholly unoccupied; I had already begun to participate in politics and was involved in my first business ventures. Before graduation from law school, another student and
I almost purchased a haberdashery store. I can still remember
taking the inventory of neckties and collars (then detachable)
and other items which the store contained. Next I was approached by a man who had discovered a wonderful fat-reduc-
ing ointment. The trick was to rub it on in a certain way. After

19

a modest preliminary investment I learned, as might be imagined, that there was nothing to it. Then I conceived the idea of building houses. I had saved $400 and put this amount, plus what I could borrow from a building and loan association, into my first and last real-estate deal. Shortly after the cellar of my first house was dug, it became obvious that the contractor had ignored the law of gravity. Water did not run from my cellar into the street; it ran from the street into my cellar. This mistake was remedied and the house went up. A beautiful job of plastering proved too tempting to the boys of the neighborhood; the white walls were soon covered with dirty words. After a second whitewashing the doors and windows were put in and locked, and the house was ready for occupancy. I sold it to a hard-working young carpenter of twenty-seven with a wife and two children. He was to make weekly payments both to the building association and to me. He made his payments faithfully for six months. Then he lost his job. He could pay nothing and I did not have the heart to put him and his family out into the street. Although the venture was far from profitable, I began a second house. We managed to avoid our earlier mistakes, but I was unable to dispose of this one for sometime. After several months I sold both houses at a small profit. It had been a valuable experience, but I decided that real estate was not for me.

Meanwhile, I had become an Assistant Secretary of the Ohio Chamber of Commerce and was an active member of the Cincinnati City Council.[1] In the new Council I had been made Chairman of the Sewer Committee, and dealt with the building, repair, and location of all the sewers in the city. This gave me a close acquaintance with the various parts of Cincinnati that was helpful when I later campaigned as a candidate for mayor. I tried hard to take care of the various needs of my constituents: putting a gas light on a street corner; placing a waterplug in front of a certain house; removing a telephone pole from the entrance to a Catholic Church; installing a drinking fountain; extending a gas main; repairing a sidewalk; putting lights on dark streets; rerouting a streetcar line. These were a few of my projects. I learned to get along with Mike Mullen, the Republican boss, who had ruled the City Council for years. A politician of the old school, a big, tough, dominating Irishman, he knew every voter by name. One year the returns from his Eighth Ward showed three Democratic and 870 Republican votes. He was supposed to have said: "One Democrat and two mistakes." Although political opponents, we became fond of each other. Years later, when I was at Camp Sherman, he came all the way up to Chillicothe to bring me a box of cigars.

In 1912 I attended the Democratic National Convention at Baltimore. Our Ohio candidate was Governor Judson Harmon. There were other candidates—William Jennings Bryan, Champ Clark, and Woodrow Wilson. Bryan made an impassioned address in his usual style, but the great speech of the Convention was delivered by Newton D. Baker. He, along with a few other Ohio delegates, had refused to support Governor Harmon and was promoting the candidacy of Woodrow Wilson. His speech was dramatic, colorful, and emotional. I still recall the remark of Mrs. J. Borden Harriman who was sitting next to me while Baker spoke. As he finished she turned and said: "That is the finest speech I ever heard." It certainly was of great help to Wilson. But I took no part in the convention proceedings. I was an alternate, really no more than a spectator, yet I was on the scene and saw things which were not shown in the minutes.[2] Even today, with television, not everyone can see what goes on outside the convention hall. Here in Baltimore I walked into a dining room one evening and found some delegates from Cincinnati. They had lost interest in the convention, but were greatly interested in getting a drink. One big German banged his beer glass on the table and demanded: "What the hell do we care who's our president. What we want to know is where's our waiter went."

After two years I ran for re-election. This time I was opposed by an older lawyer. Again I campaigned vigorously. I had become friendly with Republicans throughout my ward and many of them supported me, some openly. I carried every precinct, including my opponent's, where I beat him two to one.[3] Henry Hunt had been of help to me in my first campaign, but I won this one on my own. In fact, Hunt was not re-elected. During this second term, I was recognized as the Democratic leader of Council and important enough to be consulted by the party bigwigs.

Meanwhile, my solitary law practice had ended. A few months after I opened my office, I was approached by Judge Alberto C. Shattuck, an Oberlin graduate just finishing a term on the Cincinnati Superior Court, who asked me to become his partner. I was greatly complimented and accepted his offer. Our relationship was a most happy one; but after two years I realized that he was too conservative for me.[4] I liked and admired him, but the tempo was very slow. We parted—the best of friends.

Through my activities in the Cincinnati City Council I had become acquainted with John Weld Peck, later a Federal District Court Judge, and in 1913 I became associated with his firm of Peck, Shaffer, and Peck. Almost at once I was extremely busy. My principal activity was the examination of municipal bonds, in which that firm had a large practice. My greatest problem was with bond buyers who urged me to give them a *favorable* opinion, without which their sale could not be completed. However, when war was declared in 1914 they feared its effect on the bond market. When I arrived at my office the following morning, there were about ten bond buyers outside my door, with bonds which they did not want, waiting to urge me to give an *unfavorable* opinion.

I was already building a small practice of my own. In one divorce case, my client was a man named Carl Ruby. The day before the trial the chief witness for his wife came to my office, told me she was angry with Mrs. Ruby, and wanted to testify for Mr. Ruby. I was amused and intrigued, but said that I could not use her as a witness. She then asked if she could answer the questions of Mrs. Ruby's lawyer by saying, "I do not know." I told her to try it. The following morning she was the first witness. She gave her name and address and thereafter answered every question, including the question, "Why don't you know?" with the answer, "I don't know." Opposing counsel, with mounting fury, asked the judge to fine her for contempt; but the judge refused, saying he was in no position to say what she did and did not know. Early in my practice I was also given a few criminal assignments. Another young lawyer and I were appointed to defend a circus performer accused of murdering a young woman. We prepared to defend our client on the ground of insanity. He proved the soundness of our defense by committing suicide in the jail just before trial. In another case my client was charged with first degree murder. The state's first witness was the defendant's girl friend, who was to tell of a confession. The prosecutor asked her to give her name and address. I then interrupted to ask to be allowed to examine her on her *voir dire,* to establish her qualifications as a witness.

"Sally, have you ever lived with John as man and wife?" I asked.

She was very smart and sensed that something not too good was coming, but she looked steadily at me and said, "Yes."

"Did you live with John as man and wife for several years?"

"Yes."

"Was this known to your friends and acquaintances?"

"Yes."

I then said: "Your Honor, this woman is the common-law wife of the defendant and she cannot testify against him."

The prosecutor had relied heavily on her testimony and was greatly distressed. When the judge said to him, "What do you have to say in answer to this?" he replied, "I would like to ask this woman some questions." He then said: "Sally, did you ever live with Henry Jones as man and wife?"

She hesitated but finally said, "Yes."

He continued this line of questioning which disclosed that she had shared her favors with many men. He then said: "She is not the common-law wife of the defendant—she is a common prostitute." The judge permitted her to testify; but I argued to the jury that the prosecutor had so damaged her reputation that nothing she said could be believed. The jury agreed and my client was acquitted.[5]

In the early years I also defended a man indicted for receiving stolen goods. His wife worked for a lawyer friend of mine, who asked that I handle the case. The district attorney was so certain he could win that he tried the case himself, which he did but rarely. He had the courtroom piled high with stolen articles from the defendant's home. My defense was that these articles had been stored for a friend. The courtroom was not so crowded but that I found room for the defendant's wife and two little babies. To the astonishment of almost everyone, my client was acquitted.

During my years at Oberlin, I met a Boston girl, Helen Mears. We had acted together in a student production of "The Taming of the Shrew." She played Katherine, the virago, to my Petruchio. Shortly after our college career ended we became engaged to be married. But there was no wedding. Just before Christmas in 1913 she became ill. Her brother telephoned me to say that her condition was desperate, and I took the next train to Boston. I was with her on Christmas Eve, at her home in Brookline, Massachusetts. She died that night. The snow was falling and the church chimes were playing "When He cometh, when He cometh to make up his jewels."

I returned to Cincinnati and my work, took up the cause of "proportional representation" in city government, and campaigned for a Home Rule Charter for Cincinnati. Although I was only twenty-seven, I was urged to be a candidate for Mayor. I decided to make the race, and in June, 1915, a Republican paper reported:

The Democrats have selected an attorney, Charles Sawyer, to lead them to victory this fall. He is an aggressive young man with some radical ideas. He knows the masses like to hear the cry, "the poor are growing poorer and the rich are growing richer." He is a fighter.[6]

During this campaign the Republicans again circulated the rumor, especially in the German Wards, that I was "dry." In an effort to dramatize the story, it was arranged to have a beer truck stop in front of my home in Madisonville. When the driver carried a case of beer to the front porch, my mother greeted him with horror. She and her family were being "insulted." "No one in this house has any use for it," she insisted. The driver could take his beer elsewhere. The episode was widely publicized, and in order to prove that I was not a teetotaler, I drank a large amount of beer at a big Democratic picnic. I handled many mugsful, but the effort went unrewarded. My platform had been based partly on regulating privately-owned utilities, and the campaign emphasized my youth. I was a young radical. I had been opposed by a conservative Republican, a substantial businessman who had been shrewd enough to let me alone. I ran almost four thousand votes ahead of my ticket, but I was beaten. My political career seemed to be at an end.[7]

Although my progress with Peck, Shaffer and Peck was rapid, I had not been offered a partnership. In 1915 I organized my own law firm with two close friends, Sanford A. Headley and Frank E. Wood. They were older than I, but congenial and hard-working lawyers. The first year I made $3,000, which at that time I thought to be a handsome income. My practice grew, but law practice, business, and politics were to be interrupted for two years.

3 Over There and Back

FEBRUARY 10, 1917—my birthday! I was thirty years old, enjoyed a growing law practice, had been deep in politics and would normally have been settled and satisfied. But war was on the horizon. I wished to be in it. In all candor my motives were mixed. I did not want to shirk my duty. But I was drawn to enlist by the excitement of the prospect. I still had the urge to do anything which I was afraid to do, and felt that if I were to go back into politics I would be greatly helped by having served my country in war. If I did not come back— "C'est la guerre." My law partners and I discussed the matter at length, and it was decided that the firm would sacrifice me to the cause.

My military career was not brilliant—I did not return a hero. But I tried. Although I had first thought of enlisting as a private, I finally decided to enter the Officers' Training School at Fort Benjamin Harrison, near Indianapolis. I was in good physical condition and overcame the handicap of taking an eye test without glasses by memorizing the eye chart while I waited for the examination. On the afternoon I received my orders to report to "Fort Ben" I was in Court. I left the court-

26

room, went home by streetcar, and packed what I thought I
would need. The next morning I took the train to
Indianapolis.

The Commander at Fort Ben was a Colonel John Glenn. He
may or may not have been a fine soldier. I do not know. He
was a big man and brown as a berry by constant exposure to
the sun. He had been with Pershing on the Mexican border
and was a great disciplinarian.[1] Twice a day he forced the
Ohio troops to march to the drill field, a mile and a half from
our wooden barracks. The Indiana troops, in brick buildings
next to the drill field, had only to fall in line. An Indianapolis
newspaperman by the name of Hector Fuller wrote glowing
reports about the Indiana troops, ignoring completely the
troops from Ohio. Our reaction was not friendly, and some
ribald Ohio soldier composed a parody on the song "Way
Down in Indiana," to be sung as we marched to the drill
field.

> We don't like your Indiana,
>   where it rains most everyday;
> And of Hector's bull we're surely full—
>   and the Indiana way.
> We don't like your old parade ground
>   and the chiggers in the grass;
> you can take the whole damned State of Indiana
>   and stick it up your goddam Hoosier ass.

We sang with vigor. Shortly thereafter an order came out that
Ohio troops were not to march to the parade ground singing
vulgar songs.

At Fort Ben we went through routine training with rifle and
bayonet, studied map making and other bits of martial lore. It
was not too interesting nor too educational. Yet we managed to
acquire the idea of discipline and complete obedience to authority. Before many days went by I was made a platoon
commander, supposedly an honor. We drank no liquor at the

fort, but consumed gallons of pink pop. We learned that we could dissolve the lead from our rifle barrels by soaking the cleaning cloths in the same soda. Apparently our stomachs were lined with sterner stuff. Social life at Fort Ben was limited. Occasionally Margaret Johnston, a girl from Glendale, Ohio, would drive over with friends to visit me. But I rarely went into Indianapolis, and passed what spare time I had keeping a diary. These were some of my observations:

Sunday, May 13th:

Cold—men in room speculating whether it's worse to be shot or freeze to death. By leaving on my heavy woolen socks and wrapping carefully in my two blankets I slept comfortably.

The room was aroused this morning by the announcement from one brisk humorist—"The salmon is ready, boys—What will you have?" This reference to the main article of yesterday's two meals set the room in an uproar.

Everybody now in khaki—a great leveler or equalizer—all individuality gone. As one talks with the individual, however, he finds the broken tendons of an abandoned business or profession hanging loose and a little bloody from the rupture of sudden leave taking.

Monday, May 28th:

Drilled for two hours on the parade ground. We did abominably—were sarcastically reprimanded by the captain. When the review came off, however, we surprised ourselves—it was quite inspiring, the band of course adding greatly to the effect. Napoleon knew what he was about when he gave his soldiers as many bands as possible.

Wednesday, June 6th:

Mayor Bell, in addressing the men of the camp this evening, said: "As I look out over your faces upturned before me I realize the nation's utter lack of preparedness!"—One man remarked "He said it in three seconds—and spent 103 trying to explain it." Another man explained to a lady onlooker—"It is a part of the hardening process."

Saturday, June 30th:
I have demonstrated my old capacity for sleeping under any circumstance by going to sleep on the ground within ten feet of the firing line while the pistols were popping in front of me. I woke up dreaming that I was stopping a team of horses.

Monday, July 2nd:
This evening in the mess hall we were assembled and asked individually if we felt that our serviceability to the government would be in any degree impaired by service with Negro troops; with but few exceptions the answer was "No." I, myself, am perfectly willing to take a Negro command if it be given me.

Thursday, August 9th:
Started out this morning on a maneuver—fifteen rounds of blank ammunition apiece. I was picked to act as Signal man for the Major. We marched out to our position and sat a short time in the rain when the news came to go back to the camp and answer to the roll call on commissions—excitement rampant!

Back in camp we were lined up in the company street while Captain Black read off the list of commissions which had been telegraphed from Washington, letting each man indicate whether or not he would accept. I was named as "Captain" and answered "yes." [2]

Governor James Cox had offered me a commission as a major in the Judge Advocate's Department of the Ohio National Guard, but this was not the way I wanted to go to war.[3] I turned down the Governor's offer and was ordered to Camp Sherman, Chillicothe, Ohio. Camp Sherman was to become a training center, but preparations had hardly begun. The barracks were not completed, the kitchens were unequipped, and rations had not yet arrived. I was assigned, by lot, to command the Twelfth Company of the Depot Brigade, and it was my chore to train draftees for three months before they were assigned to permanent units. I developed what was acknowledged to be the best company in the camp. I was a strict disciplinarian but did not undertake to direct the lives of my men when they were off duty. My soldiers were tough, clean, and good-humored. The winter of 1917–18 was the coldest ever known in that part of the country. One morning, with the temperature twenty-three degrees below zero, I marched my entire company five miles for rifle drill to the far side of the Scioto River, which was frozen solid. When we arrived, a second lieutenant drove up in a limousine and informed us that we need not drill that morning. He had been given the order the night before and had forgotten to deliver it. Needless to say, 150 men would gladly have murdered him on the spot. I told the men they could break ranks and walk back as carelessly as they chose, trying in the process to prevent their noses and hands from freezing. Every man wore two knitted helmets, and mustaches were frozen stiff with frost and ice. A division order required morning calisthenics every day. One morning at 6:00 A.M., as the men stumbled into ranks, frosty breath steaming from mouth and nostrils, Lerner Harrison, the battalion commander, shouted: "Come to attention, we are going to make you healthy if it kills you!"

After a few weeks I was made Provost Marshal for the camp, in addition to my regular duties. This provided me with plenty of ammunition for target practice, and I became an excellent pistol shot. I still kept my diary:

Thursday, September 6th:
    Our first quota of men will arive tomorrow. In my barracks at present the toilets are unfinished, no range or ice chest in the kitchen, no cots or lights—there is much to be done by tomorrow.

Tuesday, September 18th:
    It is rumored now that the Depot Regiments are to be split up into depot battalions and nobody knows where we may go. One story is that the 3rd Battalion, to which I belong, is to go with "The Rainbow Division" now ready, or preparing, for embarkation on Long Island. This is probably as fanciful as it is alluring.

Lecture this evening by Major Wood on British and French and German insignia and the various fine points of British military etiquette—must always carry cane and wear gloves, never carry a package, etc.

Sunday, September 23rd:
A sad and nasty experience tonight.
After a walk along the Scioto River with Captain Sahlin, I arrived in camp about 5:30. Passing regimental Hdqr. I saw a man sitting on a seat in front of the Sgt's office, rather slouchy in appearance, cap drawn over his face, and paying no attention to anything. He answered my questions sullenly; but finally said that he had been sent out of the 329th Reg't because they claimed he was a Negro and put with a few Negroes forming the skeleton of a prospective Negro regiment in Section N; that he was later sent from there to our regiment without papers, mess kit, or bedding. There being no one in the Adjt's office I arranged to have him eat his supper here and wait for me in front of the Hdqr. at 6:30. There I met him and talked with him until Colonel Wallace came. I took him over, got him a mess kit and two blankets and showed him his cot.

About 9:45 P. M. I heard Capt. Sharp yell "Get the Doctor" as he ran out of his room. I immediately followed him over to his barracks and upstairs where Lord, our stranger of the afternoon, was lying on the floor in a pool of blood with his throat cut. He had asked one of the Negroes to do it for him and then had done it himself.

Wednesday, December 19th:
A wonderful day of blunders—walked to the Rifle Range (five miles) only to find that the men wanted were four companies instead of four battalions which we sent out; back at noon in time for luncheon and a hurry call to take company to the Division theater, in order that our Hungarians, Rumanians, etc. might sing Christmas Carols which they don't believe in from printed words on the screen which they could not read. Back for a half hour and then to the same building for a lecture by Lt. Rossiter of the British Army; he had been captured by the

Germans and told of his experiences in the German prison camps. He was affected, unintelligent, a great bore.

Monday, December 31st:
The year is closing in a most unexciting and uninteresting manner.

A bulletin this afternoon stating that officers were needed for billeting duty in France; anyone interested might apply. I think I shall talk with the Brigade Adjutant tomorrow and find out what is wanted in this connection; I am firmly decided not to stay slowly whirling around in this Depot eddy, much longer.[4]

I remained at Camp Sherman until the summer of 1918. In June of that year Margaret Johnston and I were married. But we had only a few weeks together in Chillicothe before I was selected to attend the Army General Staff College at Langres, France. I was finally on my way overseas.

Before our ship left New York, I sat on the upper deck talking with Branch Rickey, later a great man of baseball— then a major in the Chemical Corps.[5] We noticed three coffins arranged on the foredeck and I said I hoped they would not be used. But soon after we put to sea, influenza broke out on board and within three days several men had died. The ship became a floating pest house. Men died by the hundreds, sometimes thirty and forty in a day. One entire deck had been turned into a hospital and men ordered to duty there would write farewell letters to their wives, sweethearts, or mothers, and dispose of all their belongings to friends onboard. Burial services were held every afternoon at three o'clock until the ship ran out of iron weights with which to make the bodies sink. Then the bodies were laid out on the top deck to await our landing. When we arrived at St. Nazaire there were so many bodies on the deck it was difficult to pick one's way across it.

Fortunately I was not sick during the fourteen-day trip. I had been assigned the job of supervising the "submarine watch" and spent most of my time out of doors. Major Rickey was found unconscious one afternoon with a temperature of 104 degrees. He would never have lived were it not for a little country doctor who had been looked down upon by the many other doctors on board at the beginning of the voyage. While the little country doctor heroically carried on, taking care of everyone, almost all the other doctors declared themselves "in quarters" during the last two-thirds of the trip. They stayed carefully away from the sick men. It was a cowardly and despicable exhibition. Several of us signed and forwarded a report, telling of what these doctors had done, or failed to do. What measures were ever taken I know not.

The night we disembarked at St. Nazaire I slept in a pup tent on the ground. The next day I received orders to move on to Langres, a fascinating old city encircled by walls that date back to pre-Roman times. The river Marne has its source just outside of Langres and from that spot one can look out over the battlefield where Caesar overcame the Nervii.[6] George Patton had been assigned to Langres in 1917. One of the unusual characteristics of this great soldier was his belief in reincarnation. He believed he had been in Langres before. "You don't need to show me this place," he said when he arrived, "I know it well." Of Langres, he wrote a charming verse, which ended:

> And now again I am here for war
> Where as Roman and knight I have been.
> Again I practice to fight the Hun
> And attack him by machine.
>
> So; the three old hags still play their game
> Still men the counters are;
> And many peg out in the game of peace;
> Pray God, my count shall be war.[7]

The work at the Staff College was interesting. In my class was Teddy Roosevelt, Jr., a manly person but not too bright, who frequently asked me the answers to questions.[8] Also in this class was my former Commander, Captain Black of Fort Ben experience, whose early training did not seem to have helped him too much. He, also, frequently asked me the answers. Times had changed. I worked hard and enjoyed what I was doing. Before many weeks went by, however, it became clear that the war would soon be over. Not all the members of this class graduated; but I made it. Needless to say, we all wondered what would be done with us now that the fighting had ended. I had been promoted to major and was first ordered to a place called Gondrecourt, to take charge of a reassignment center for soldiers coming from the front. After a few days I received orders to join the Eighty-ninth Division in Trier, Germany.

The trip to Trier was anything but pleasant. I traveled in a box car familiarly marked *"quarante hommes et huit chevaux"* and stood up all the way to Sedan. At Trier I reported to General Winn, commanding the Eighty-ninth Division. I was assigned as adjutant of the 178th Infantry Brigade with headquarters in a castle owned by a German named von Brock. There was really nothing to do. I took several trips to Coblenz with General Hahn, commander of the Seventh Army Corps, to which our Division and Brigade belonged. One day as we drove through the countryside he pointed out a small stone house nestled on the hillside across a little valley. It was his birthplace. He had returned there at the head of the conquering enemy army. There was plenty of drinking. One night General Hahn's chauffeur was too drunk to drive back from Coblenz, and his aide was in the same condition. So the general drove himself. He said: "If I had only been drunk enough to see two roads, I would have had an accident. As it was, I saw three and chose the middle one." There were many wine cellars in Trier where for hundreds of years champagne had been stored. On one occasion I visited a number of these cellars with some other officers, sampling champagne at each stop. The cellars were cool, and when we climbed back up into the hot air the effect was devastating. One historic monument at Trier was the Roman Black Gate or Porte Nigra; another was a Roman stone bridge across the Mosel, which had been used for two thousand years. One night a number of us rented a barouche with four horses and drove to the Roman bridge, at the center of which we solemnly saluted the full moon. While life was no hardship we were all anxious to go home. The role of an occupying army is not a pleasant one, although my own relations with the Germans were friendly. We saw but little of von Brock and his wife, who continued to live in a remote part of the castle. Frequently they would send me wine or flowers.

In Brigade headquarters was a Major Hugh Bates from Montana, a former cowboy who was not too modest about his pistol shooting. One day during luncheon my aide, Lieutenant Allen, bet a thousand marks that I could outshoot Major Bates. Bates and some of his friends accepted the wager. The following afternoon we set up the target in a little valley near the castle, and from a distance of twenty-five yards we proceeded to shoot it out with .45 automatics. For the first round of eight shots I had four bulls eyes and four near misses. Thereafter, I shot straight bulls eyes and won the thousand marks. News traveled fast in Trier. At the shoot we had a large German audience. How they had heard of it I never knew. The next day, as I walked along a street in Trier, the Germans would abandon the sidewalk, and give me a wide berth. My shooting had engendered respect.

After three months in Germany, I was ordered home. When our ship docked in New York my wife was there to meet me and I immediately approached General Shanks, the "debarkation officer," for leave to spend the night in New York. As I was about to enter his office, Captain Rogers, one of my officers, emerged, smiling broadly. Upon inquiry, he disclosed that he had just been discharged from the Army. As I stepped into the office, the general asked, "Major, what can I do for you?" Instead of asking for an overnight leave, I said, "Well General, I came in to see if I could get discharged." He immediately assumed a stern attitude and told me that nobody was discharged at that point. I told him politely that some people had indeed been discharged, and reminded him of Captain Rogers. While Rogers' rapid demobilization may have been due to his relationship with General Pershing and Senator Warren, I did not intimate any such thing.[9] The General gulped and said "Well, there were some special circumstances involved there." I told him that there were some special circumstances in my case. He then tried to be helpful and asked, "Such as death in the family, serious financial losses?" I said, "No, General, there is no death in the family, and I have had no financial losses because I have no finances; but I have a wife who hasn't seen me in a year; I am a lawyer who gave up his practice, who has nothing more to give to his country and would like very much to get out of the Army now." He laughed and said, "All right, if you can get your discharge papers signed by General Barnhart, you may go." I asked for the papers, knowing that General Barnhart, my commanding officer, was sitting in his limousine just outside the door. With the papers in my hand, I hurried up to him, saying, "General, before I say good-bye to you, I have one favor to ask." I had known Barnhart since Camp Sherman and we were good friends. "Will you please sign this paper?" He did not even ask what it was; within half an hour I was out of the Army.

I walked outside to find my wife and went with her to New York. The next day I came back to the wharf, trying to locate one missing piece of luggage. I called Camp Upton, asking for my aide, Lieutenant Allen. When he finally came to the telephone his first remark was, "Where the hell have you been?" I told him I had been enjoying myself in New York. He said, "You had better get out here in a hurry; almost everyone in the Army has been looking for you, including the Commanding General." I told him to please convey my compliments to the Commanding General and tell him to go to hell. He was a little startled at this comment, but steadied himself and asked me what was up. I told him that I was no longer in the Army. He then informed me that I was being sought because a telegram from Washington had ordered me to proceed to Camp Funston, Missouri, and take charge of the demobilization of the entire Eighty-ninth Division. If my discharge had been delayed even for one day, I would have spent another year at the least in Uncle Sam's Army.

4 Back to My Family, the Law, and Politics

MY WIFE and I left immediately for our home in Glendale, a pleasant little suburb of Cincinnati. There, for the next ten years, we lived quietly as I busied myself with a growing law practice and occasional business enterprises. There our five children were born—Anne in 1920, Charles in 1921, Jean in 1923, John in 1925, and Edward in 1929.[1] These were happy years and for the most part uneventful. Our home life was the normal one for a man and wife with a family of small children. My wife was devoted, self-sacrificing, and a wonderful mother. She was, however, not a silent type. She enjoyed, even craved, an argument. I had never been accustomed to family argument, and many times took refuge in silence. On one occasion, after a vigorous plea for some project, she sat and waited for my comment. When I did not reply, she said, "Well, I know what you would say if you would talk," and then proceeded to demolish her own case.

While I was overseas, my partners had separated; upon my return each of them asked me to join him. I joined neither. Instead, I became associated with Frank Dinsmore, a leading Cincinnati lawyer. When Judge Walter Shohl retired from the

Court of Appeals and returned to private practice, the firm
became Dinsmore, Shohl, and Sawyer. Many years later, I
severed my connection with this firm and joined my present
firm of Taft, Stettinius & Hollister with whom I continue to
enjoy a very fine relationship.[2]

William Cooper Procter, of Procter & Gamble, was one of
my clients. He had attended the officers' training camp at
Plattsburg, New York, organized by General Leonard Wood,
and came to have great admiration and respect for the general.
Early in 1920 Procter was visited by a group of prominent
Republicans from New York who urged him to become chairman of a committee to promote General Wood for the Republican presidential nomination. When he asked my opinion, I
said that he should not seek advice from a Democrat; but I
suspected that these men really wanted to make him the financial angel for their movement. He was sure this was not true
and would contribute no more than ten thousand dollars. He
agreed to head the Wood campaign and, in the early spring of
1920, set up headquarters in Chicago. He was a most extraordinary businessman but he now encountered problems which
had not confronted him in business. A prominent Chicagoan,
Colonel Albert A. Sprague, became the campaign treasurer.
Although General Wood's prospects were never very good,
they did not appear hopeless in the early days of the effort.
With Procter as head of the committee, politicians scented
money and many attached themselves to the Wood campaign.
Before long it was noised about that enormous sums were
being spent in Wood's behalf. Senator William E. Borah began
to investigate.[3] The publicity was disastrous for General
Wood. The New Yorkers who had pledged their undying support to him and to Mr. Procter lost their enthusiasm and their
nerve. The sources of funds dried up. The Wood Campaign
hobbled along with increasing difficulties and waning enthusiasm. It ended when a few men in "a smoke-filled room"
agreed to nominate Warren G. Harding.[4]

Meanwhile, the need for money had grown more urgent day by day. No one but Procter would put up any. Forgetting his initial commitment of only ten thousand dollars he gave money to the committee, guaranteed loans, and as chairman felt himself liable even for commitments made by others. By the time the campaign ended, these obligations had mounted to $800,000, all of which Procter paid personally.[5]

Shortly after it was organized, the Leonard Wood Campaign Committee had borrowed one hundred thousand dollars from the Merchants Loan and Trust Company of Chicago of which Sprague was a director. On the back of the note, below a stamped legend which read, "We, the undersigned, jointly and severally guarantee the payment of the within obligation," Procter and Sprague had signed their names. Procter's signature came first. Part of Procter's signature was written over the guarantee. This guarantee and the position of Procter's signature produced a bitter lawsuit. Soon after the convention, Procter received a demand from a Mr. Hulbert, president of the Merchants Loan and Trust Company, for payment of the hundred-thousand-dollar note. He replied that he would be happy to pay his half of the note and Colonel Sprague could make his own arrangements to pay the other half. Hulbert answered that Sprague was a valued director of his bank and he did not intend to look to him for any payment. He called upon Procter to pay the entire amount immediately, with interest, a total of $108,000. This Mr. Procter did.

Based on their joint guarantee, Procter, on my advice, then sued Sprague in the U.S. District Court in Chicago for his half of the obligation. The suit was filed in 1921 but every conceivable device was used to prevent it from coming to trial. Several times the trial date was set. On one occasion Procter and I went to Chicago on the assigned date to find in court with Colonel Sprague the Mayor of Chicago and other prominent citizens arguing to the judge that Sprague's presence at a hearing in Washington the next day was absolutely necessary.

The judge, over our objections, postponed the case. With such tactics, Sprague's lawyers managed to put off the trial until 1926. However, in that year we came before a judge from South Bend, Indiana, by the name of Slick. Neither his name nor his political background were too encouraging, but he proved to be honest, sensible, and unimpressed by Colonel Sprague and his Chicago friends. He ignored the pressures brought upon him to order a further postponement. After every other trick had been tried, the clerk of courts announced that he had no list from which a jury could be drawn. Judge Slick then ordered the United States Marshal to go downstairs to the post office, the drugstores across the street, and even out onto the sidewalk, and bring in enough people to fill the jury. This was done the jury was truly "taken off the streets." From this inauspicious beginning the trial proceeded.

The defense made two extraordinary claims: first, Mr. Procter had taken sole responsibility for the campaign when everyone else had left the sinking ship, and the Leonard Wood campaign had become his personal venture, he alone was therefore responsible on the note; second, the guarantee had been stamped on the back of the note after the signatures were there and Procter and Sprague were liable, not as co-guarantors, but as endorsers. Sprague, being the later endorser, was liable only to those who might have endorsed thereafter, but was not liable to Procter. We knew that this was not true. We claimed it was clear that some of the lines of Procter's signature were over some words of the guarantee, and not vice versa. This involved what handwriting experts call "the sequence of crossed lines." It might seem that the sequence would be evident, but it is sometimes exceedingly difficult to determine. Each side employed handwriting experts. During the trial I recognized at my opponent's table a handwriting expert whom we had employed several years earlier. I turned to a fellow counsel and asked about this man. My voice normally carries well, as it did in this case. The expert looked up,

turned white and immediately left the court room, never to
return. He had undoubtedly given the other side an opinion
contrary to the one he had given us. The defense witnesses
testified that the impact of the stamp resulted in a smoothed
surface wherever the lines of the stamp were impressed upon
the paper; if the signature were put on after the stamp the ink
would run along the lines of the stamp. Since the ink had not
followed the lines of the stamp the signature must have been
on the paper first. However, I produced an expert who had
photographed the back of the note and enlarged the photograph twenty-five times. From this picture it was clear that the
ink *had* run along the lines of the stamp, thus proving our
contention by the testimony of the defendant's own witnesses.
We also maintained that a reputable bank would never alter
the obligation of endorsers by placing a guarantee on the back
of the note after the endorsements. It is hard to believe, but the
defense was able to produce a witness who testified that this
was customary practice at the Merchants Loan and Trust
Company.

When Colonel Sprague took the stand he said that it had
been agreed by him and Mr. Procter that he was never to
become liable for his half of the hundred thousand dollars. He
had put his signature on the note because the bank wanted to
be sure it would be paid! I had obtained from the Senate files
a copy of the six-year-old testimony before the Borah Committee, but did not produce this document until the end of my
cross-examination. I then read to Sprague his sworn testimony
before the Senate committee that he was liable for one half of
this note and expected to pay his half if the campaign committee ran out of funds. I asked him: "You were under oath in
Washington when you testified in complete contradiction of
your sworn testimony of yesterday. Which time did you lie?"
The Colonel flushed and hesitated and after a long period of
silence said that he "told the truth yesterday." We learned
later that he had been warned that I might subject him to a

disturbing cross-examination and he must under no circumstances "lose his head." He was a man of violent temper, but
had told his counsel he would try to restrain himself. If he lost
his temper "it would be worth $62,000," the amount for which
we were suing him. After five days the case went to the jury. A
Cincinnati friend had told Procter that he would never win his
case in Chicago as "no outside lawyer had ever won a lawsuit
against local Chicagoans." The jury, however, brought in a
unanimous verdict in our favor. At the time of trial, Sprague
was a possible candidate for the U.S. Senate, but his candidacy faded soon after the verdict was announced. Arthur Sears
Henning, a columnist for the Chicago *Tribune*, said later that
Sprague would have given $25,000 to have avoided my cross
examination, as it ruined his chances for the nomination.[6]

During these earlier years I tried many other interesting
cases, in most of which, perhaps I am permitted to say, I was
gratifyingly successful.

We lived simply. I worked hard at the office but found time
for chores at home, such as cutting the grass. My wife urged
me to start playing golf and I finally yielded to her importuni-
ties. Once I began that fascinating and frustrating game, I
never again found time to mow the lawn. I took part in
amateur shows presented for the Glendale school fund or
merely for the enjoyment of the villagers. I remember one
rehearsal when I sang a song that went:

> I'd like to know where mosquitos go
> when the wintry breezes blow,
> What do they wear for underwear
> when they're under where I don't know;
> Do the young humdingers sharpen up their stingers
> in a warmer clime;
> I'd like to know where mosquitos go
> in the winter time.

and which I sang many times later for the amusement of my
young children. I had just left the stage when I was called to

the telephone and told that my wife was about to give birth to our second child. By the time I reached the hospital she was in extreme labor. Her doctor was a calm and conservative soul who believed expectant mothers couldn't be trusted to know when things were about to happen. The baby arrived before he did, and I handled the accouchement. I had been in the delivery room when our first child was born and knew something about the process. While I handled this delivery adequately, I left the arrival of our other infants to the doctors, although I was on hand for all of them.

As the father of five children and a former teacher, I was interested in education. For several years I was president of the Glendale Board of Education. At that time I was one of those innocents who felt that our boys and girls should enjoy the blessings of "progressive education." Shortly after my election as president I began the search for a suitably progressive educator. I interviewed many prospects and finally picked a glib and ambitious young man who immediately began experimenting with our school system. He inaugurated what was known as the "activities program." A boy was not taught how to spell "hammer" and "nails"; he was given a hammer and nails and told to do what came naturally. Spelling would follow; that was the theory. I learned that this did not happen automatically. The children survived this experience; but as the months went by I became disillusioned and finally suggested to this progressive docent that he move on. Meanwhile, he had been able to gather material for a book describing the success of progressive education in Glendale.[7]

During this time I received many tempting offers to leave the law. I was asked to take top positions with a firm of steel brokers and two banks. I bought the Ansonia Brass and Copper company but soon realized that the problems of that business were more than I could handle on a part time basis. After two years, I sold out at a profit. Meanwhile I bought a building supply company and two Pepsi Cola bottling plants. My interest and involvement in business carried over into my practice. I now appeared less frequently in court and became more active in corporate reorganizations, mergers, and stock issues.

Late one Saturday morning in 1922 E. W. Edwards, a leading Cincinnati businessman, telephoned to say that Powel Crosley, Jr., would be calling me. Crosley was one of the largest manufacturers of radio sets and owned the most powerful radio station in the world—WLW. He had been in New York and told Edwards on the train back that he wished to "talk immediately with a good lawyer." Edwards had recommended me. That afternoon Crosley called to ask if he might come to my office. He had been approached by several bankers who wished to buy his company and he had been negotiating a sale in New York for one million dollars. One million dollars was a large sum of money to him in those days and he had practically agreed to sell. But he had second thoughts and decided to try to get out of the deal. My job was to get him out. I left for New York the following day and accomplished what he wanted. Crosley's enterprises prospered, and long before he died he had drawn out of his business many times one million dollars. We became close personal friends and I continued to represent him for many years. I became a vice-president and general counsel of his company and participated in most of his business decisions.[8]

Powel Crosley, Reamy Field, a Cincinnati broker, and I had become interested in Amrad, one of the oldest radio companies in the country, which we later merged with Magnavox. Before the market collapse in 1929 Amrad stock had become very active on the Cincinnati Stock Exchange and I had gambled a large amount of money in it. This was the period when everybody was "in the market." I was also speculating in Crosley stock and many others. Late in the summer of 1929 I became concerned and asked myself what would happen if the bottom dropped out of the market. The answer was easy—I would be bankrupt. The next morning I began to sell, even though the experts insisted that we were on a "new price plateau." Day by day I sold securities until I had paid all of my debts, which had totalled about $400,000. And I continued to sell until I had accumulated a large surplus, half of which I invested in call loans and half of which I kept in cash. Then came the crash! On the 16 million-share day, November 3, 1929, I spent the morning at my brokers' offices, buying stocks. The next morning I called the broker from whom I had bought the call loans and said I would like to have my money. These loans carried the names of several leading Cincinnati businessmen and I had thought that they were as good as cash. I was told that the loans could not be paid. I threatened to sell the stocks I held as collateral and was told, "Go ahead and sell them." By that time the stocks were no longer worth the amount of the loans. Fortunately, I had enough cash to pay for the shares I had bought, and later, when things had quieted down, these call loans were paid.

While I had survived the crash comfortably, many of my friends had not. Among them was John J. (Jack) Pattison whose father had been governor of Ohio and president of the Union Central Life Insurance Company.[9] The Governor had left to Jack and his sisters a large block of stock in this important company which had enjoyed great prosperity for a number of years, mostly from heavy investments in farm mortgages which paid as high as eight and nine per cent interest. Following the market collapse, these mortgages began to go sour—the company was in peril. At this point Jack Pattison asked if I would represent him and his family and try to rescue their very substantial holdings in this enterprise. I said I would do my best. It was soon clear to me that only new management could save the company. This presented a serious problem; the stock was owned by three families and most of the shareholders were women. Once they had all been friends; now they scarcely spoke to each other at tea parties. I had to make these women agree and finally did persuade them all to join a voting trust of which I was chairman. To Howard Cox, who had been secretary of the company, I gave the title of Insurance Manager and put him in charge of the whole operation. Cox was able to raise 5 million dollars from the Metropolitan Life Insurance Company, but the condition of the Union Central was still critical. I then began to look for a new president. After a survey of several prospects, it seemed clear to me that the logical candidate was Cox himself. In January, 1932, he was made president. We arranged for a loan of 20 million dollars from the Reconstruction Finance Corporation, secured by thousands of farm mortgages. Cox cut both the dividend and official salaries, but was skillful enough to maintain good morale among the agencies. Due to his talents as an executive, we slowly worked out of our difficulties, although forced to foreclose on hundreds of farms. Years later, when these farms were sold, we were able to retain the mineral rights. When oil was found on some of them, we were partly compensated for our earlier losses.

The temporary crisis had passed, but the fundamental weakness remained. The voting trust would not last long and continued antagonism among the shareholders foreboded trouble. There was an obvious need to switch from a stock company to a mutual company. This took many years of litigation and a change in the Ohio Statutes. It was finally accomplished in 1954. The Union Central has remained one of the major insurance companies in the United States.

Meanwhile I had returned to politics in a small way, making a few speeches and working for Alfred E. Smith.[10] In 1930 I was urged to become a candidate for Congress. The district in which I lived had been Republican for many years and my opponent carried a popular name. My chances were not good, but I decided to try. My approach to public issues had changed. Now I said:

We have too much Government and particularly too much Government in Washington. This may be the statement of an old-fashioned theory, but many of the old-fashioned theories are as sound today as they were when first announced and the fundamental things in life do not change.

I had become conservative.

My most dramatic issue was to demand the repeal of the Eighteenth Amendment. My stand was noted throughout the state, and the Akron *Beacon Journal* gave me a leading editorial, headed: "CINCINNATI HAS A STATESMAN."

There's a Democratic candidate for Congress in the Cincinnati District who is no frightened rabbit. Charles Sawyer is his name. If Cincinnati is wise it will send this man to Congress. He has rediscovered the principles of Thomas Jefferson, and deserves to be given his chance to put them to work in the halls of Congress. We are glad to see him running upon a *Beacon Journal* platform, and hope he travels far.[11]

The voters, however, did not follow the *Beacon Journal*'s advice. Once again I was defeated, by 779 votes. I was urged to demand a recount and finally agreed. In some precincts as many as seventy-five votes were thrown out. The final count, however, showed a majority of 586 for my opponent. I decided that I had had enough of politics.[12]

But my decision was short-lived. In 1932 I was elected a delegate to the Democratic National Convention. The delegation was divided; some were for Al Smith—some for Governor Ritchie of Maryland. My initial efforts were for Newton Baker —I felt that he would be an ideal candidate. When I realized that Baker could not be nominated, I turned to Franklin Roosevelt. The convention opened with a bitter fight for the chairmanship between Jouett Shouse, the Smith candidate, and Senator Walsh, the Roosevelt candidate. Walsh won and started the Roosevelt band wagon on its way.[13]

The most tense and exciting moment came during a roll call of the New York delegation, when the name of mayor James J. Walker was reached. He had been engaged in a bitter feud

Charles Sawyer—"Yankee from Ohio" at three years of age.

Mr. Sawyer with his children when he was candidate for Governor of Ohio in 1934.

Mr. Sawyer at the time of his election to the city council of Cincinnati—"the youngest ever to occupy the seat."

Mr. Sawyer as a candidate for Congress, with James Farley, 1930

Dinner of the Democratic Committee, Columbus, Ohio, 1939. From left to right: Freer Bittinger, Democratic State Chairman; Senator Harry S Truman, then head of the Senate Preparedness Committee; Mr. Sawyer; Mildred Jaster, Democratic National Committeewoman.

with Governor Roosevelt. When the mayor did not answer, the chairman asked for his alternate. At that point the flamboyant Walker appeared in a dressing gown. It was 4:00 o'clock in the morning, but his voice was clear: "I hear that in my absence an alternate voted my name. May I ask the privilege of casting that vote myself? I ask that my vote be cast for Alfred E. Smith." Hour by hour the bitterness grew. As the convention neared its climax, the California delegation switched its votes, at the urging of William Randolph Hearst. He had worked out a deal to name Garner of Texas as Vice-President if Texas and California would go for Roosevelt. The California switch was announced by William Gibbs McAdoo. He was settling an old score. McAdoo had been a candidate for President in the Madison Square Garden Convention of 1924 where his nomination had been blocked by Smith. It now became McAdoo's privilege to announce California's vote for Roosevelt. That settled it and there began a new era in American politics.[14]

The Roosevelt forces had originally chosen as their theme song "Anchors Aweigh," in view of Roosevelt's previous navy association.[15] However, the first time the organist played "Happy Days Are Here Again," it took the convention by storm. It was promptly appropriated by the Roosevelt crowd to their great advantage.

This was perhaps my happiest convention experience. I had a choice seat at the greatest show on earth—and no responsibility. I had one vote, which I cast as my judgment dictated. But the planning, the maneuvering, and the conferring in which I later participated, did not burden me. I did make one contribution. I introduced into a meeting of the Ohio Caucus a resolution to repeal the Eighteenth Amendment. This was vigorously opposed by Senator Robert Bulkley, our Ohio member of the Resolutions Committee.[16] Although he had been elected to the Senate in 1930 as a "wet" candidate, Bulkley had been persuaded by some of his "dry" friends in the Senate to try to avoid a stand on this issue. He and I engaged in a heated argument. I said that if he refused to support and transmit our resolution, I would appear personally before the Committee and present it myself. He then backed down. The resolution was adopted by the committee and the convention, and the Eighteenth Amendment was repealed.

After a dramatic plane ride Roosevelt arrived at the convention to accept the nomination in person. His entrance was exciting, but disturbing. He hobbled to the microphones leaning on a cane with his son James helping to support him. Many, like myself, who had not up to that time seen him in person, wondered whether he could meet the terrific physical demands of the presidency. As I left the convention I sensed the historic importance of the result. The future of our country and the world depends upon the mental and physical health, the stamina, the courage, the imagination, the power of decision, the good judgment, even the whim of the single human being chosen at one of these party conventions. It was thrilling to have watched and participated in this event. Shortly thereafter I was invited to Hyde Park, where I met the candidate's family, including his mother. She was an impressive woman, proud of her only child, and contemptuous of the Theodore Roosevelt branch of the family.

Early that summer a friend wrote, urging me to become more involved in the "political battle." In reply I said:

You are very kind in your suggestion. I am frank to say that the political game attracts me considerably, but I am none too sure of my ability to make headway in it, and at present am so thoroughly occupied with business matters that I really have no right to think about it.[17]

But late in the summer of 1932, while I was on Long Island with my family, I received a telephone call. The Ohio State Democratic Committee was meeting and William Pickerel, our candidate for lieutenant governor, was withdrawing. Would I be willing to take his place? If so, would I leave at once and come to Columbus? After a long talk with my wife I decided to make the race. This was my fourth try for office and my first state-wide attempt; this time I won. I carried my own precinct and my own city by large majorities and Hamilton County by over twenty thousand votes.[18] My majority throughout the state was greater than that given to Franklin Roosevelt. My record of expenses for this campaign showed no contributions from anybody. Total expenditures were $1,452, which included a $500 contribution to the State Democratic Committee. It was a simple and inexpensive campaign, but I had been introduced to Ohio voters.

My term as lieutenant governor was not exciting. I presided over the Senate, which contained the same number of Republicans as Democrats. Occasionally, I cast the deciding vote. During the session a Republican senator introduced a resolution declaring that I was the best lieutenant governor the State of Ohio had ever had, but persuaded all the Republicans to vote against it. The Democrats all voted "aye." The design was to force me to cast the deciding vote. I voted against myself, with the Republicans. During that session a senator from Youngstown made an impassioned speech against a bill to increase the salaries of the senators themselves. He closed his speech with this intriguing peroration: "If this bill passes, many of the smiling faces which I now see around me will no longer warm these Senate chairs." Since I had sponsored the repeal resolution in the national convention, I was asked to help draft the so-called "Beer Bill," to regulate the sale of beer in Ohio. Finally, the entire committee, both Republicans and Democrats, called on me and asked me to rewrite the bill. As presented, it was almost wholly my handiwork. I was also instrumental in pushing through the resolution to repeal the Eighteenth Amendment. The sponsors were anxious that Ohio be the first state in the Union to ratify repeal. There was no important legislation during my term, except a bill creating an

Ohio sales tax. We had no sales tax, but Governor White thought one was necessary and drove it through in spite of bitter opposition.[19]

I learned something about lobbyists, their methods, their personalities and, perhaps, the need for them. For the most part their activities and their identities are known and they are a useful part of the legislative process. Lobbyists employ various methods, sometimes using attractive women. One afternoon in Columbus a certain Senator was enjoying a social occasion with friends, including a lobbyist, accompanied by a very attractive young woman. To the Senator's surprise, his wife came in, uninvited. In conversation with one of the men present the wife said: "I don't see why men want women like that around." The young woman overheard her and said, "If wives were like me we wouldn't be around."

I played no part in the dramatic events of Roosevelt's first administration. I did, however, offer the President one suggestion. During the bank holiday of 1933, I recommended that the government guarantee bank deposits. I contacted everyone I could think of who might further the plan, including Roosevelt's aide Raymond Moley and several influential newspapermen.[20] The administration sponsored the guarantee of bank deposits, but it would be difficult to determine the extent of my influence as others were advocating this idea at the same time.

5 More Politics, Business and Law

On MARCH 5, 1934, I received a letter from a Newark, Ohio, publisher saying that several veterans in his area were talking me up as a candidate for governor and saying, "I want a mat of your picture." I received many other letters suggesting that I run, and after strong urgings from county organizations and newspapers, I entered the campaign with the simple statement, "I am a candidate for Governor."[1] My six-word announcement was such a novelty that it attracted considerable attention. I was not to get the nomination by default. Two other candidates had entered the primary. One was William Pickerel, whom I had replaced on the Democratic ticket two years before. The second candidate was Martin Luther Davey, a former Congressman and tree surgeon from Kent.[2] He and I had been friends at Oberlin and I had supported his unsuccessful campaign for governor in 1928. In 1933, he had asked me to further his bid to become Secretary of Agriculture, and I wrote to President Roosevelt, "Davey is a man of great ability. He is dependable and possesses tireless energy."[3] My estimate was more friendly than frank; but he did not get the job.

Few people realize the exhausting effort that goes into a

53

state-wide political campaign. There is the publicity to be prepared, the endless plans and decisions to be made, the delicate matter of one's stand on controversial issues, the continual writing and rewriting of speeches, the adjusting of conflicts in schedules, and the vital matter of raising money— or trying to. Finally, there is the plain drudgery of traveling by day and by night from one end of the state to the other. In my case the effort was carved out of the time and energy demanded by my law practice.

As the campaign progressed, it was clear that the nomination lay between Davey and me. At a dinner at Mount Gilead, where each of us spoke, he said that he appreciated the type of campaign I had been waging. He remembered our college days together and promised never, at any time or under any circumstances, to say one derogatory thing about me. However, my chances appeared to be getting better and better. When Davey realized this, he decided to "take the low road." Three nights after the Mount Gilead meeting, he made a bitter attack upon me, saying that I respresented wealth and big business and was associated with the mammoth Union Central Life Insurance Company. I was handed a copy of his speech as I was campaigning in northern Ohio. I decided the best way to handle this attack was to ignore it.

Aid to parochial schools was even then a disputed and difficult issue. I did not believe in it. Davey had gone to Archbishop Schrembs in Cleveland and committed himself privately to aid for church schools. I myself called on the Archbishop and found him a very understanding and attractive person. But he was adamant on the subject nearest his heart. I told him I could not support it. He said he was sorry; he personally would like to see me nominated and elected, but Davey had given him his promise. I said, "Are you sure he will keep it?" "At least he has made the promise and you say you cannot," the Archbishop replied, "Under these circumstances I have no choice. I must support him." [4] I am certain that had

I enjoyed the strong support of the Catholic hierarchy I would have won the nomination and the election.

There was an interesting sidelight. Davey had always been close to the Ku Klux Klan, especially the Grand Dragon, Colescott. This had embarrassed him in his campaign for governor in 1928 when he was on the same ticket with Al Smith, a Catholic. In our campaign he was able to persuade Colescott to write and to sign a letter on a Klan letterhead, urging his followers in Ohio to support me. Thousands of copies of this letter were distributed on the Sunday before election—not to members of the Klan, but, as they left the church service, to the congregations of every Catholic church in the state.

I had been confident that I would win. I had lost some earlier contests, but had done very well in 1932. I was again to learn about politics; I lost the nomination. Davey called me immediately and undertook to bring me into his election campaign. He said I could have anything I wanted. I told him he had nothing I wanted. He replied that I was the only Democrat in Ohio of whom that was true. He won the election with no help from me.[5]

In spite of my preoccupation with politics my business involvements increased. In 1928, Cooper Procter had asked me to join him and his associate Harry Blair in their plan to buy weekly newspapers throughout Ohio. I said that I would be delighted. We were able to collect eighteen small papers, one of which was a daily. After several months, our company, Ohio News, Inc., was losing money at the rate of thirty thousand dollars per year. County newspapers could make money when they were run by a man and his wife, willing to operate a print shop and take part of advertising payment in trade; but the idea that we could effect large savings by the wholesale purchase of ink, paper, and labor proved illusory. Procter decided he had had enough and offered to transfer his stock to me for nothing if I would absorb future losses. I agreed.

Shortly thereafter, I bought two dailies in Washington Court House, Ohio, and merged them. However, as time went on, it became obvious that I would be forced to liquidate this venture. I sold all of the papers but one, including two semi-weeklies in Waverly, Ohio, which I bought back some twenty-five years later and believe it or not—later sold again. The one I did not sell was a small daily. In 1934, I had learned from a Columbus Scripps-Howard writer, Cal Lyon, that the *Lancaster Eagle*, the third oldest newspaper in Ohio, might be for sale.

I bought the *Eagle* and put Lyon in charge. Shortly after arriving in Lancaster, he opened fire on the opposition paper, the *Gazette*, financed by the principal officers of the Anchor Hocking Glass Company, Lancaster's big industry. Cal believed he could build up *Eagle* circulation by sensational attacks on Lancaster's leading businessmen. This they did not enjoy. They withdrew large amounts of advertising from the *Eagle* and supported a venomous circulation campaign by the *Gazette*. We were forced to match its offers. At one point we were giving a year's subscription for a hen and a dozen eggs. I finally decided to drop Lyon and to bring in one Kenneth Kerr, who had worked for Ohio News, Inc. I gave him the job of bringing about the consolidation of the *Eagle* and the *Gazette*. He was a joyous extrovert and was able to convince the businessmen of Lancaster that Lyon's attacks were not a reflection of Sawyer's philosophy. In 1936 the two papers were merged under the name of *The Lancaster Eagle-Gazette* of which I became the controlling stockholder.[6]

About this time it was suggested that I might bring a radio station into this small city and I made application to the Federal Communications Commission for a license. Meanwhile, Malcolm Forbes, whose father was the publisher of *Forbes Magazine*, started a weekly paper in Lancaster. He had just received a degree from Yale University and had written a thesis entitled "How to Run a County Weekly Newspaper." He was young and very sure of himself. He moved into Lancaster with confidence. I told Mr. Kerr that I wished him to be welcomed and well treated. Young Forbes, however, did not appreciate my attitude. He ran a flaming editorial, anent the prospective radio station, charging that "this man Sawyer" was trying to control all avenues of information in Lancaster. When I saw his article I wrote him a friendly and confidential letter saying that he would not make progress by the kind of journalism he had undertaken. He published my letter on the first page of his paper, with comments. I then decided there was no point in treating this young man generously. Within a year and a half I purchased the assets of his paper for $400. He left Lancaster and returned to *Forbes Magazine*, which he now heads.

My law practice was by this time almost exclusively concerned with business matters, although I did handle a criminal case for Procter & Gamble in Boston. Lever Brothers had been able to persuade the district attorney in Boston to bring an indictment against The Procter & Gamble Company, charging use of the mails to defraud. Some enterprising Procter & Gamble employees had managed to get hold of advance information about Lever's product, *Swan*, and had mailed the details back to the home office. One or two individuals paid small fines, but the Company was acquitted.

During the weeks through which I fought this extended litigation, I spent most of the late afternoons and evenings at the Union Club, the only place in the world where you can get a cocktail and a half—not for the price of one—but for the price of one and a half; and where you can sit in the secluded recesses at its rear and look over the sequestered and ancient cemetery where are buried James Otis, Daniel Webster, John Hancock, Samuel Adams, Josiah Franklin and his wife, the parents of Benjamin Franklin, Peter Faneuil, Paul Revere and other great Americans of our earlier history.

By this time I was handling many matters for Procter &

Gamble and represented that company before the Federal Trade Commission, defending its advertising of a dentifrice called Teel. In a hearing in New York I had severely cross-examined a dentist who had written a book entitled "The Use and Abuse of the Toothbrush." As he came from the stand he stopped to chat with me. In the course of a frank discussion he said, "I will make a confession, I myself never use a toothbrush." I replied, "I will make a confession too; I never use a dentifrice." The next morning Marshal Field's newspaper *P.M.* said, under an eight-column head, "What a bunch of crooks infest American business and the professions!—a dentist who never uses a toothbrush writes a book about the toothbrush and a Procter & Gamble lawyer defends the use of their dentifrice when he himself never uses a dentifrice." One of their reporters had overheard our conversation.

I became counsel for and involved in the affairs of the Paragon Refining Company through its President, E. W. Edwards. He had decided that Paragon should buy the Valvoline Oil Company, a very old company with a fine reputation. He was at his camp in New Hampshire; I was in New York. He sent me a blank contract, signed by him as president. I telephoned him that I appreciated his confidence but this nine-million-dollar contract must be approved by him in its entirety before I would close the deal. After the contract was drawn up in detail and then signed by him, the purchase was made.

In the early thirties things were not going well for Valvoline, nor for Paragon, and some of the stockholders insisted that the Valvoline stock be sold. When Edwards refused to do this, Cooper Procter, who was a director, resigned from the board. As things went from bad to worse, Edwards said he personally would purchase the Valvoline stock at the price paid for it by Paragon. However, he delayed doing so. I insisted that he go through with his purchase, even though I lost him temporarily as a client. I called a meeting of the directors in my law office. All of the directors, including Ed-

wards, attended, and Edwards agreed in writing to buy the
Valvoline stock immediately.

Shortly thereafter I was told that a United States marshal
was outside and wished to speak to me. As I greeted him, I
was served with summons in a damage suit for six million
dollars against me and the other Paragon directors, who were
charged by certain shareholders in Cleveland with neglect and
malfeasance for not having forced Edwards to buy the Valvoline stock. Within two days Edwards had raised the necessary
money in New York and had bought the stock from Paragon.
The suit was continued, however, solely for the purpose of
collecting attorneys' fees, amounting to one hundred twenty-
five thousand dollars. The case went to trial in Cleveland. The
important point was the exact time Edwards had signed the
agreement to buy. Was this done before we knew we were
being sued? During the trial the plaintiffs suggested a settlement. The other defendant directors were busy men, did not
like the unpleasant atmosphere of the trial, and welcomed the
chance to end it. Edwards' counsel found that the case could
be settled for fifty thousand dollars; and everyone but me was
willing to pay—I refused. I had done nothing wrong. I did not
propose to pay fifty thousand or five dollars and thus admit
that I had not fully performed my duty. In view of my refusal,
the case went on—and ended happily for all the defendants.
The decision was affirmed in the Court of Appeals and the
plaintiffs collected nothing.[7]

Reamy Field and Powel Crosley and I had joined in several
business ventures; we now undertook to engage in sports.
Crosley was very rich, but was involved in no Cincinnati
enterprise other than his radio business. Field suggested that
the three of us buy the Cincinnati Reds, which had been taken
over by the banks. The deal was made. Crosley immediately
became fascinated but wished to have control. Field and I and
Leland Stanford (Larry) MacPhail, our manager, turned all
our common stock over to him. In time the Reds became

Crosley's major interest and proved to be a very profitable investment. Part of the success we enjoyed was undoubtedly due to the energy, the imagination, and the drive of MacPhail. Larry McPhail was and is a colorful character. As World War I came to an end, the Kaiser was at Amerongen in Holland. MacPhail and Luke Lea, one-time Senator from Tennessee, sitting in their camp in France with nothing to do, cooked up a plan to kidnap the Kaiser and use him as a hostage for peace negotiations.[8] Their maneuver succeeded until they had penetrated into the castle and into the room adjoining the one where the Kaiser was asleep. At that point some shrewd German guard became suspicious of this "peace mission" and the attempt aborted; not, however, before MacPhail was able to pick up a fancy ashtray which he has kept as a souvenir.

MacPhail had been manager of a Columbus team in a minor league and had there introduced night baseball. When we bought the Reds there was no night baseball in either major league and opposition was vigorous. Players said that they would not be able to see the ball. Managers were afraid of change. However, MacPhail was certain that night games would greatly increase our attendance and we told him to go ahead. Our first night game was spectacular. As dusk settled over the ball park and the darkness deepened, the overflow crowd of spectators sat quietly, waiting. I had prevailed upon President Roosevelt to push a remotely controlled button in the White House. Suddenly, at eight-o'clock, the button in the White House was pushed and the entire field and stands were bathed in brilliant light. A sigh, and then terrific applause, burst into the night air.[9] At first we played only one night game a season with each club in the League. When the players found that they could see the ball, and when fans who could not get to a ball game in the daytime crowded the night games, night baseball became fashionable. Night games have since greatly overshadowed (if I may use that metaphor) day games.

My involvement in both baseball and politics imposed some problems in 1940, when the Reds were in the World Series. Almost every Democrat in the country was sure I could find him a seat. In preparation for this demand, I bought seven thousand dollars worth of tickets; most of which, in all fairness, was paid back to me. Not only politicians wanted tickets. The late Monsignor Quinn wished two tickets for himself and a friend from out of town. Both of them were very fond of baseball but preferred not to be conspicuous in their clerical garb. I furnished the tickets and, dressed as laymen, the two of them saw the entire series. The Monsignor's visiting companion, who went unrecognized, was a very important prelate —in fact, later a Cardinal.[10]

My time was not spent entirely on business, politics, or my law practice. I bought a farm near Wilmington where I began breeding saddle horses. Once I owned twenty-three brood mares and considered myself something of an expert in tracing the Rex Peavine lines. The farmhouse had originally been a school and had a huge fireplace in its very center. I used it as a resting place during my travels across the state and a place of entertainment for large groups of politicians.

I hunted frequently, often in Tennessee. There one afternoon I was walking alone while my dogs were working in the distance. At the edge of a field I came to a smoothly flowing creek about eight feet wide. In front of me was a sycamore root, on the other side a beautiful piece of flat white sand. I hesitated for a moment, put my foot on the root and jumped. I landed on both feet—and began to go down. I was in quicksand! I said to myself, "This is it," but instinctively I flattened out and started to crawl, holding my gun flat to keep from sinking. I finally came to the far edge of the sand, twenty feet away, where I lay exhausted and breathless. Back at the clubhouse, I was told that this was a well-known spot. Three months before a mule had gone into it and was never seen again.

6 *Politics*

SHORTLY AFTER Davey had been elected governor, we began to hear rumors of payoffs from contractors and liquor permit holders. As Davey's term was ending, the rumors became more frequent and specific. My supporters in growing numbers kept urging me to run again. I finally announced that I was prepared to run, but I learned soon after that my wife was fatally ill. She had been stricken with cancer in 1932. A prompt operation had seemed successful, but the cancer returned. I withdrew from the race. After suffering bravely and quietly, she died in 1937.[1]

Although I had decided not to run for governor, I did attend the 1936 convention and was chosen national committeeman from Ohio. I was not so deeply touched by the honor that I failed to recognize the unrewarding task I had assumed, but I immediately went to work. Normally the campaign in Ohio would have been directed by Francis Poulson, chairman of the executive committee, appointed by the Governor. However, a feud was going on between Davey and Harry Hopkins, Roosevelt's right-hand man, resulting in a wide breach between the national and the state administrations. James Farley was certain that if the Ohio campaign were run by Poulson, all the effort and money would be used to elect Davey.[2] Furthermore, there was strong feeling that Davey would be defeated by John Bricker. To put the campaign under Davey's leadership would be the kiss of death for Roosevelt. I decided to set up a separate Roosevelt headquarters, and was immediately in the thick of the campaign. Farley's advisors were by no means optimistic about Ohio. Congressman Lemke, running for President on a separate ticket, seemed certain to get many Catholic votes.[3] I made strenuous efforts to see that this did not happen. The result was gratifying and astounding—Roosevelt carried the state by 620,000. This great victory, however, had one unfortunate side effect. Although Davey ran 500,000 behind the President, he was carried in by the landslide.[4]

Throughout the campaign I was continually bedeviled to raise money for the National Committee and did raise substantial amounts. However, Forbes Morgan, treasurer of the Democratic National Committee, without consulting me, had approved a *Democratic Handbook* circulated by a private company. Many business concerns were induced to pay large sums of money for "advertisements." I was irritated at this effort and aghast at its success. I called Morgan and asked him to send me a list of the handbook advertisers in Ohio. I then learned that businessmen had been threatened with everything the federal government could do to them and promised everything which the federal government could do for them. From terror or avarice they had responded generously.

Following the 1936 election rumors came from Washington that I was to receive a Cabinet job. An "unnamed high source" in government was quoted:

Sawyer's political sagacity, as demonstrated in the Ohio campaign, may result in his selection to replace Postmaster General Jim Farley at the head of the government's patronage machine, if it proves that the time is now ripe for Farley to step aside.

A possible alternative is the use of Sawyer's wide business experience in the job of Secretary of Commerce.

President Roosevelt is understood to feel that this position requires the energy and initiative of a younger executive than the incumbent, Daniel C. Roper, as well as a man whose sympathies dovetail somewhat more closely with New Deal industrial ideas.

The dispatch listed other "possible niches" for Sawyer, as in the Department of the Interior.

Of these two the former would seem to be the best bet, since Secretary Ickes' grip on the Interior secretaryship seems to have been tightened by his hammer-and-tongs campaigning during the last month before election.

Sawyer's appointment somewhere in the new Cabinet is now regarded as virtually assured.

I, myself, however, was skeptical, suspecting that this release had been planted—and not by a friend. The procedure is an old one, which appears to boost a man while really hurting him. The story obviously would alienate Farley, Roper, the Attorney General, and the Secretary of the Interior, when it was suggested that I might succeed any one of them. It was nonsensical to say that I might succeed Farley.[5]

The Davey-Sawyer feud simmered during the political off-year but flared in 1938. The big political event of the winter was the Jackson Day dinner, to be held in Columbus on January 8. It was organized by Poulson, who had somehow neglected to invite the National Committeeman—me. I announced that, even if uninvited, I would attend and make a speech. If necessary, I would make it from the balcony of the Neil House, where the dinner was to be held. The balcony was a perfect spot from which to address a very large crowd below. By the day of the dinner interest had mounted to fever heat. Poulson, under tremendous pressure, caved in. At the last moment he called me on the telephone, asked me to attend the dinner, and said he had reserved a place for me at the head table, next to Secretary of Commerce Roper, the guest of honor.

At the dinner excitement and suspense grew apace. I had

not released my speech in advance. As I rose to my feet one could have heard a ballot drop. This is part of what I said:

The Democratic Party in Ohio has a proud history. From the beginning it has been the party of liberalism and idealism. It has also been the party which typified the common virtues including, among others, common honesty.

In 1936 a great Democratic President, Franklin Delano Roosevelt, secured the largest popular vote ever given a Democratic candidate for President in Ohio. At that time party success seemed assured forever.

But tonight we are in danger. No party can take forever the punishment which the party is now getting in Ohio; not from without—from Republicans, but from within—from Democrats. Hatred and suspicion are fomented, jealousy is rife, public officials who should cooperate are at war with each other. Charges of corruption and graft are rampant. Men in high position in the party have become mysteriously rich; state employees are nervous, unsettled, and apprehensive of the future. Those who seek office this year are worried about the prospects. Either this situation must end or we will be in danger in November.[6]

I had thrown down the gauntlet; I would go after Davey in the primary. This decision was not made lightly. Many governors had been defeated in an election; no incumbent governor had ever been defeated in a primary. With Davey's control of the most effective and disciplined political organization ever seen in Ohio, there was a likelihood that I would not win. But I intended to win.

On one day I made a 140-mile swing through southern Ohio, speaking at Batavia, Clermont County, at 11:00 A.M.; Fayetteville, Brown County, at 12:30 P.M.; Hillsboro, Highland County, at 1:30 P.M.; Washington Court House, Fayette County, at 2:30 P.M.; Greenfield, Highland County, at 3:30 P.M.; Waverly, Pike County, at 4:30 P.M.; Peebles, Adams County, at 6:00 P.M.; West Union, Adams County, at 6:45 P.M.; Georgetown, Brown County, at 8:00 P.M. And every day was the same. I received heartening endorsements from newspapers throughout Ohio—not only big city papers, but country papers. I was backed by farm organizations, labor unions, veterans' groups, and teachers' groups. Newton Baker, Senator Atlee Pomerene, and James M. Cox, the former Governor and 1920 candidate for President, all spoke out for me.[7] However, the going was not as good as it looked. Davey was a skilled and energetic campaigner and had the support of the party organizations of Franklin (Columbus) and Cuyahoga (Cleveland) counties. It was the bitterest campaign ever waged in Ohio. Buttressed by enormous contributions from those he had favored, Davey worked feverishly. He spent almost 1.5 million dollars. I also spent a large sum of money, most of which came out of my own pocket. The campaign revealed again how promises of money and help evaporate in the heat of battle.

Every man in politics makes mistakes. A man can survive almost any mistake if he keeps on going; the fatal mistake is to conclude that one mistake has been fatal. My most stupid and inexcusable mistake occurred during this campaign. I had been accusing Davey of corruption and had the support of thousands of people who felt that my charges were true. One night, by accident, or perhaps not by accident, he and I were at the same dinner. As the program was about to end Mayor Russell Wilson of Cincinnati, who had arranged the dinner, brought Governor Davey to my side and said, "Why not put your arms around each other and smile." Davey put his arm around my shoulders. My instinct was to refuse, but this might indicate that I was a "poor sport." I had but a second to decide; I put my arm around him. The following day there was a picture of this happy event in every paper in Ohio and in many throughout the country. Some smart reporter made the act more colorful by saying that we were singing "Let Me Call You Sweetheart." On my way home that night I realized my blunder. If my statements about Davey had been true I could not possibly have appeared that friendly. I feared that I was finished. When I saw the newspaper the following morning, I was certain of it. However, I did not stop fighting; when the votes were counted I had won.[8]

The President immediately asked me to come to Hyde Park, where I was received with open arms and many compliments. Early in this campaign Roosevelt, always the politician, had tried to avoid a primary fight between Davey and me, by securing my withdrawal. Charles West, a friend of the President, was eager to be a candidate for Governor. Roosevelt asked Senator Bulkley to persuade me to withdraw in West's favor. Davey would then do the same. Bulkley had consulted John Owens, secretary of the United Mine Workers, a powerful figure among labor and one of my ardent supporters. He took Owens to the White House to talk things over. Owens said he would not switch from Sawyer to West. Roosevelt asked Owens if a Cabinet post would persuade me to withdraw. Owens doubted that I would withdraw even if I were offered a Cabinet post. Later Owens told me that it was to be the War Department, as it was then called. Roosevelt asked Bulkley to contact me. As soon as he left the White House, Owens rushed to a telephone and alerted me to Bulkley's call. When Bulkley did call, I said that I appreciated the President's offer to put me in his cabinet, but I would not withdraw.[9]

Davey was extremely bitter over his loss. He went into seclusion for two or three weeks amid rumors that he would fire any state employee who supported my candidacy. The story was that Davey had made a deal to support John Bricker, the Republican candidate, who had promised to give Davey thirty per cent of the state patronage. During the campaign I charged Bricker with this deal. He made no comment until we spoke together at Ironton. Bricker and I were good friends and still are. At each of our joint appearances I had given to him the choice of speaking first or last. That night at Ironton, he said, "If it makes no difference to you, I would like to speak last." I said, "No, John, this time I wish to speak last." I had been told that this was the night he would deny my charges.

We flipped a coin and I won. Bricker spoke first. He denied the charges and dared me to prove them. In reply I said, "Bricker has dared me to prove my charges; I will now do so." I then drew from my pocket a dozen affidavits from Democratic employees in the highway department, liquor department, and other state offices, each of whom swore under oath that he had been promised by Davey, or his representatives, that if he worked for Bricker he would keep his job; if he worked for Sawyer, he would lose it. Some months later Davey's secretary referred to Bricker as that "double-crossing s.o.b." Her theory was that Bricker had double-crossed Davey by not going through with the deal by which Davey attempted to double-cross me. My revelations might have hurt Davey, but they didn't damage Bricker, at least not enough, for I lost the election.[10]

I have said that politics is a disease. Over the years, as I ran for office, sometimes defeated and sometimes elected, this sickness had taken a heavy toll of time and energy and money; but this final campaign accomplished a cure. I was relieved and happy. I had made my last run for office. However, I was still the National Committeeman from Ohio and enjoyed, or at least engaged in, one last political experience in 1940.

Davey's defeat in 1938 did not keep him from trying again in 1940. Former Governor White also was anxious to run. But no candidate spoke out until I said publicly that I would not run. Davey announced at once, White followed, as did several others who thought my victory over Davey showed that he would be easy to beat. Davey won the nomination handily.

I was not a candidate but was responsible as committeeman for selecting our delegation to the national convention. My first move was to call a meeting of the state and executive committees. I wrote to the members:

There will be two major questions—who will the delegates be? and what will they do when they get there?

I'm in favor of setting up a delegation-at-large which represents all groups, and all sections. Specifically, I favor including on the delegation-at-large Senator Donahey, former Senator Bulkley, former Governors James M. Cox, George White, and Martin L. Davey, and certain others who have been similarly honored by the Democratic Party.

I favor a clear-cut statement on the third term. There are those who think we can pussyfoot on this issue. My position is well known – if Mr. Roosevelt should be a candidate, I'm for him. If he isn't a candidate we can be for a favorite son or for anyone of a number of good Democrats of national prominence who are now mentioned.[11]

I had asked Senator Donahey to be the favorite son candidate and he was considering the matter.[12] Suddenly, Art Limbach, chairman of the Executive Committee, gave out a statement, without consulting me, that Donahey was to be the "stalking horse" for Roosevelt. Donahey was not for Roosevelt and promptly stated that he would not be a "stalking horse" for anybody. As a result I was named the "favorite son" candidate. The Committees met in Columbus and after some minor opposition by James Huffman, Donahey's son-in-law, the program which I had recommended was adopted. I then went off for a ten-day fishing jaunt with my own favorite sons. Following that I flew to Chicago. I was not only the "favorite son" candidate, but also chairman of the delegation.

It was clear from the beginning that Roosevelt would be nominated. Farley, Paul McNutt, and others undertook to block his renomination, but they were ineffective.[13] As usual, Roosevelt was able to do the timely and dramatic thing; at the right moment Eleanor Roosevelt appeared on the platform. In her quiet, completely poised and gracious manner, with her nasal, monotonous, but appealing voice, she made a tremendous impression upon the convention. Following Roosevelt's nomination, precedent required that a committee officially notify him. I was one of the three members of that committee. James Byrnes was the chairman. The actual notification was made from a small telephone booth in the lobby of the Convention Hall.[14]

The only real interest centered upon the Vice-Presidential candidate. In view of our large block of votes I was approached by several of those who wished the nomination. Members of my own delegation began a vigorous campaign to promote me. I took the suggestion lightly but did not discourage it. My old friend and predecessor as National Committeeman, W. A. Julian, Treasurer of the United States, took the lead in calling a caucus of our delegation to discuss the matter. Following this caucus he sent the following telegram to Roosevelt:

Ohio is a pivotal state. In fifty years no candidate for President has been elected without the vote of Ohio. The Ohio delegation unanimously request me to urge you to consider favorably the selection of Charles Sawyer for Vice-President.

While Roosevelt had withheld any statement of his preference, it was clear shortly after his nomination that he wanted Henry Wallace.[15] A majority of the convention and many Ohio delegates were opposed to Wallace. One of our delegates, Francis Durbin from Lima, became greatly incensed. Late in the afternoon, while downing quantities of alcohol with a group of newspapermen, he was egged on by them to make a speech nominating for Vice-President one of their number, Bascom Timmons, from Texas. In the evening when Durbin came to the convention floor, he told me with gusto what he was planning to do. I immediately went to the rostrum and told Alben Barkley, the chairman, what Durbin had in mind and asked him to recognize no one but me to speak for Ohio.[16] Barkley said he would do just that—I had nothing to worry about. As the proceedings moved toward the nomination of a candidate for Vice-President, Durbin suddenly rose in the Ohio delegation, reached for a portable microphone, and said he wished to address the convention. Barkley, to my consternation, said, "Any delegate has the right to address the convention. The Chairman is happy to recognize Francis Durbin of Ohio." The throng sensed that something unusual was about to happen. Durbin, obviously drunk, worked his way through the crowded aisles to the platform. Several people tried to stop him, but he kept on and was finally escorted by police. The delegates and the galleries were applauding in a frenzy of fun and excitement. Durbin walked unsteadily to the front of the platform, bowed low to Barkley, took off his coat, and with a grand gesture put it in Barkley's hand. The delegates were rocking with laughter. Stepping to the microphone, his shirt wet with sweat, he began his speech. He was against nominating "that Republican, Henry Wallace." He wished to place before the Convention the name of a great Democrat. He hesitated, seemed bewildered, and then came out with the name "Bascom Timmons," of whom the delegates had never heard. This brought tremendous applause. Pleased and apparently surprised—if the delegates felt that enthusiastic about this suggestion why not make another one?—he next nominated Jim Farley. That brought greater applause—Well!—this was going beautifully!—Why not a third candidate? He then nominated "a great Democrat from Ohio, Charles Sawyer."

By this time the convention was in an uproar. I sat in my seat, wondering what to do. I was chairman of the delegation. Durbin had not only made a fool of himself, but had not helped me by including my name in his group of nominees. Should I sit there and do nothing? Should I go to the platform? I decided on the latter. But what would I say? I addressed the chair, asked to be heard, and made my way to the platform. The delegates were enjoying my dilemma. When I arrived at the microphone I voiced

the hope that the delegates appreciate the tremendous contribution of entertainment which Ohio has made to this somewhat uneventful and unexciting convention. This may be the proper time to announce that Ohio will follow the wishes of Roosevelt and vote for Henry Wallace.

I received an ovation and was later accused of having arranged the whole performance in advance.

In connection with the Wallace nomination I received a post convention letter from Claude R. Wickard, Undersecretary of Agriculture, who had acted as Wallace's manager.

I wish to thank you for the very generous aid and support which you gave Mr. Wallace during the Democratic Convention in Chicago. It seemed to me that the Ohio vote was the turning point on Thursday night.[17]

My help for Wallace in that convention was interesting to recall at a later time when he and I had a "knock-down drag-out" argument in Washington in 1948.

I ran the 1940 Ohio campaign for Roosevelt, operating under a considerable handicap because Ed Flynn, the new chairman of the Democratic National Committee, was somewhat naive and completely uninformed about the Ohio situation. At one point I wrote to him:

With reference to the complaints which you say have reached you, in view of the fact that you wish to keep them anonymous and in view of the fact that they are not specific, don't you think we might forget them? I will continue to try to carry Ohio for Roosevelt as I have in the past.

Roosevelt won in Ohio by 146,366 votes, while Bricker defeated Davey by 346,467.[18] Immediately after the election, Flynn stated publicly that as far as Ohio was concerned he was "going to knock heads together." This created ill will, jealousy, and frustration. In an effort to placate Davey's followers, he leaked the story that I was not to be in charge of patronage. Since we got no patronage, the statement was ironic. After a personal meeting I sent him a letter, ending as follows:

May I suggest this final thought? Concern over patronage should not be permitted to develop out of proportion to its importance. We cannot afford to let the public feel that our only concern is a scramble for jobs. Ohio is a Republican state. We cannot elect anybody without the independent vote. My effort during both Roosevelt campaigns, and particularly the last one, was to secure this vote. The result speaks for itself. The independent voter cares nothing about patronage. Let us not disgust and alienate him by airing this matter.[19]

I remained national committeeman until 1944, but was no longer involved in Ohio politics. My growing law practice and numerous business affairs were enough to occupy my time completely.

However, my time and energy and money had not been wasted. My years of political activity had been interesting, exciting, and educational. I had been taught some things about elections. They are mostly won or lost by the candidate. And one quality is important—his judgment in deciding when to run. There are persuasive examples of the theory that an ambitious office-seeker should continue to run time after time until he wins. However, there are times when it is just as well to stay out of the race. Once in the contest the result depends largely upon the candidate himself. The attractiveness of his personality, his sense of timing, the impression of candor and honesty which he creates, the things which he promises or refrains from promising, the judgment he shows in emphasizing or avoiding issues, the vigor with which he attacks or the politeness with which he treats his opponent, the abundant energy with which he pursues the campaign—these are the things which enable a candidate to win. There is also luck, plain luck: an illness of the candidate or his opponent; a stupid statement by his manager; some casual remark supposed to be confidential which becomes public; a supporter's ill-advised attack on one's opponent which reacts in his favor —these can play a great part and the candidate himself cannot control them.

Political activity, however, involves more than elections. It involves planning; day-by-day and month-by-month activity; contacts, both high and low—by what is known as "the organization." Behind the scenes are thousands of "workers" who make up the body of the party. They give their time, their thoughts, their energy, and in some cases their devotion, working to elect able and high-minded candidates to office. The candidates are not always able and high-minded—nor are the workers. There are thousands of party workers who are unselfish and dedicated; but the vast majority, many thousands more, are interested in money or jobs. Above this hoard of "foot soldiers" are the "bosses," and at the top is the National Committee.

Of what value is this hierarchy of organization? Truthfully, very little. It collects money avariciously and spends it, for the most part, foolishly. Its greatest contribution can be the selection of a good candidate, although even here it plays a minor role. Candidates do their own maneuvering and as elsewhere the rich ones have a big advantage. Money is of increasing importance. Years ago idealists thought up the direct primary to enable voters to exercise their own free choice, untroubled by the bosses. As with some other theoretical concepts, it has not produced the anticipated result. Power has passed to the rich. Need I do more than mention the names of Rockefeller and Kennedy? Those who may not be rich must be able to collect vast sums of money. Aside from the candidate's own money and that of relatives and friends, only a small part of what he collects comes from idealists. Money comes from those who expect to benefit. Many times the same man contributes to both parties. He is planning to ask a favor or to defend himself against attack.

But what about the foot soldiers—especially those who want jobs? Many are disappointed, but some do land—with what result? None, except to burden the taxpayer. It was argued against Roosevelt's third term effort that if re-elected he would, through patronage, be in office for life. This was an illusory concept. Patronage is a source of problems, not a source of power. In a small community it may be helpful. Federal employees, however, soon acquire civil service status and lose their interest in the party, along with their political

usefulness. Those who write about the power of patronage
forget the statement of Senator Boies Penrose, "If there are
seven applicants for a job, the man who makes the appointment has six enemies and one ingrate." [20] As for Roosevelt, he
paid no attention to patronage or, for that matter, to the
Democratic party organization. Farley once told me that he
himself was unable to get any close friend appointed to a
federal job.

People think that politicians are crooked and selfish. This is
only half true. They are rarely crooked; but they are selfish—
as are other men. They wish and try to be elected, although on
occasion public officials rise above selfish considerations. A
notable example resulted from Roosevelt's effort to pack the
Supreme Court. A number of senators who were deeply offended by this maneuver risked their political lives to oppose
it.

What of those whom we elect to office—including Presidents? They are just like the rest of us; no better—no worse.
Occasionally a great one makes it—but not often. When one is
asked—is this man big enough to be President? the truthful
answer is always "No." No man is big enough to be President.
We must choose between two fallible human beings. Having
elected one of them, we can only cross our fingers and hope
that he will have the physical energy to last out his term and
the good judgment to make the right decisions most of the
time, as he faces and deals with the monumental problems
which will confront him.

Campaigning is enjoyable but has its unattractive side.
When you have traveled with another candidate and have
heard his speech repeated until you can give it word for word;
when you have eaten potato salad and meatloaf night after
night, when you are honored continually by being chosen the
last speaker on a long evening program, you begin to doubt
that the office is worth it. At a dinner in Youngstown I was the
seventeenth speaker. Strangely enough the audience did not

drop dead, but stayed until the end. One summer night a dinner was given for me at Newark. It was insufferably hot, and fifteen hundred people were crushed into a room designed for five hundred. As the dinner drew to a close, Governor White asked if he might say a few words and leave—he had "important business at Columbus." His only business was to get out of that stifling room. Congressman Andrew May of Kentucky was also a speaker. He, like Governor White, wished to get out of the oven. He asked if he might speak ahead of me. As the guest of honor I had been given the choice to speak first or last; but I yielded to May's request. He was introduced by Ohio Congressman Charles West. It took West twenty minutes to introduce May, and it took May thirty minutes to convey his message. As he concluded his talk, he said in his Kentucky drawl:

Brethren and sisters, I wish I could stand at the door as you leave this room and shake the hand of each one of you. That, however, will be impossible. I must hurry out to make my train to Washington. All I can say is God bless you and goodnight.[21]

At that the exodus began. Before the chairman could even make himself heard there were only 150 people left in the hall. He begged them to be seated and give ear to the guest of honor. I looked at the loyal souls who remained and said it was not fair to make them stay while the others were enjoying the cooler air outside—I would make no speech, only thank them for their courtesy in remaining to hear me. This seemed to make a hit.

7 *Business and Family*

EARLY IN 1939 a client walked into my law office to ask if I would be interested in buying a radio station in Dayton, Ohio. For many years I had been vice-president of the Crosley Corporation and had become familiar with radio. I said I would look into it. The owner of the station, WSMK, was Stanley M. Krohn, an early radio ham, who had received one of the first licenses granted by the federal government. He knew much about radio, but not too much about business. Advertisers were leaving and he was on the verge of bankruptcy. He had been negotiating with a group in Dayton, who knew of his desperate situation and were trying to get a bargain. They had offered him ninety thousand dollars; I offered him one hundred twenty-five thousand and made a deal. After my first year of operation the station was making a profit. Shortly after buying WSMK, changed by me to WING, I purchased a controlling interest in a Springfield, Ohio, station, WIZE. Later I bought WKLO in Louisville, Kentucky. From time to time I was offered other radio stations and did purchase additional ones in Columbus (WCOL), Boston (WEZE), and Milwaukee (WRIT). Here, as elsewhere, I learned the importance of management.

77

Theorists work with graphs and charts. They rarely give adequate consideration to the human element. The difference between the company which fails and the company which succeeds lies in the character, the imagination, the hard work, and, in particular, the good judgment of the man or men at the top.

Not all of my business ventures turned out well. At one time I purchased stock in a margarine company, producing Churngold. I did not carefully investigate the management. Soon I discovered my mistake. A directors' meeting was called to discuss reducing the "goodwill" item in our financial statement from one million to one dollar. This seemed to me a relatively unimportant matter; what appeared important was our commitment to buy one million dollars-worth of soybean oil at thirty-eight cents, its highest price in several years. I recommended that we immediately work out of it. Our president was a chemistry professor who knew quite a bit about oils and chemistry. He and the chairman of the board, who had wanted to discuss the goodwill item, were certain that the price would not go down. They prevailed and I backed down. Within sixty days the price had gone from thirty-eight cents to thirteen cents. Churngold lost over five hundred thousand dollars. I decided to get out—and did. And this wasn't my only lesson in management. "Tectum" was shredded wood treated chemically and compressed so that it could be sawed into boards. These boards would hold nails, were termite-proof and fire-proof and were lighter than the equivalent amount of wood itself. Tectum was cheap, as it could be made from the scrubbiest trees obtainable. The chemists who had invented this process had no money, but they had interested a friend of mine, Darrell Jones, of Newark, Ohio. Jones in turn persuaded me to go into the venture. Shortly after we began manufacture, the two chemists encountered and created one difficulty after another. Within a short time I was asked to put in more money. With the third request for funds, I decided to give up.

I also had a family. I was a widower with five children, each of whom deserved attention. At the time of their mother's death, Anne was at Vassar, Charles at Choate, Jean at Dobbs, John at Lawrenceville, and Edward at home. Like many another busy father I probably did not give them the time and attention I should have given—but they have grown up and have had children of their own (now nineteen of them) — and have been a credit to their mother and to me. Charles was a somewhat venturesome youth and when he left Choate in 1940 he took a cruise around the world on the schooner *Yankee*. He had been gone for about one year when I decided to travel to Latin America and catch up with him. This was a fascinating trip. I flew in a DC-3 over the Amazon and vast trackless forests and landed on top of a mountain at Berreiras, to which gasoline was carried by men on foot. From there I flew into Rio, past the famous statue of Christ, circled the Sugarloaf Mountain, and landed on a grass field. But I had failed to secure a visa to visit Brazil. As I went through customs at the Rio airport I was told that I could not stay. When I asked what would be done, they said, "You will be sent home on the next plane." I turned to the young but very alert Pan-American representative standing by my side and asked when a seat on the next plane would be available. He replied, "In two weeks." It was the plane I had planned to take back. I was then finger-printed and told that I must spend the intervening time in jail. When I asked if I might have a choice of jails, the customs officer, who had a sense of humor, said he thought it could be arranged. I told him that I would like to be jailed in the Copa Cabana Hotel. This he agreed to. I was never legally in Brazil until the day I left.

I flew from Brazil to Trinidad. My plan was to fly from Port of Spain the next day and surprise Charles at Georgetown, British Guiana. It suddenly occurred to me that I might get to Georgetown sooner and be certain to arrive before the *Yankee* left if I were able to travel by boat that night. I made several contacts in an effort to secure passage on one of the British ore

boats then in the harbor loading bauxite. The Germans had
many submarines in the Caribbean and I was informed that
these boats were taking on no passengers. I called at the
American consulate about every hour. On one of these visits
the Consul told me that the finest ore boat ever to come into
port was just arriving, the *Pathfinder* owned by Alcoa.

I have referred earlier to the famous Charles Hall gift to
Oberlin. Charles Hall, in his senior year at Oberlin, discovered
the process for making commercial aluminum. After repeated
efforts to interest bankers and businessmen, he was finally able
to secure help from a group in Pittsburgh. Then was formed
the Aluminum Company of America. When Charles Hall died,
still a young man and a bachelor, he left a large part of his
Alcoa stock to Oberlin College.

The *Pathfinder* was to leave almost immediately. I hurried
down to the docks and spoke to the Alcoa manager. I told him
of my desire to get to Georgetown in time to catch up with my
son, whom I had not seen for many months. He remained
unimpressed. I then said, "Would it mean anything to you if I
were to say that I am one of the largest holders of Alcoa
stock?" He said, "It certainly would." I then said: "I am a
trustee of Oberlin College, which is a big holder of Aluminum
Company stock. I think it is time a trustee looked over some of
the college properties." He replied, "So do I," and gave me the
finest stateroom they had. There were two other passengers, a
British scientist and a scrap buyer. We left late in the afternoon and arrived in Georgetown about four o'clock in the
morning. On the way, I saw over the Orinoco River the most
beautiful sunset I ever witnessed, a flaming, throbbing, orange
ball of fire against a background of changing color; huge,
overwhelming—then slowly sinking into dusky night.

I had slept fitfully, as I was extremely eager to see Charles.
In the early morning, perhaps five or five-thirty, I dressed, left
my stateroom, looked across the harbor through the mist and
could see in the distance the schooner *Yankee*. I walked unmo-

Celebrities Golf Tournament, October 2, 1951. Mr. Sawyer with Michael DiSalle, then Director of Price Stabilization, later Governor of Ohio, and Dizzy Dean.

Mr. Sawyer with Bob Feller (left) and Johnny Vandermeer (right) at the All-Star game, July 6, 1938.

Photograph taken on the occasion of President Franklin D. Roosevelt's visit to Cleveland in 1934. Left to right: U.S. Senator from Ohio Robert J. Bulkley; Mr. Sawyer (then Lieutenant-Governor of Ohio); and President Roosevelt.

President Roosevelt's visit to Cincinnati in 1936. Left to right: Mr.
Sawyer (then Democratic National Committeeman); Senator Robert J.
Bulkley; President Roosevelt.

The *Island Queen* destroyed by a freak explosion at Pittsburgh.

lested over the docks and climbed aboard the *Yankee* before anyone was up. The Captain, Irving Johnson, came on deck. I asked for Charles and was told that he was not on board but was up the Amazon River, panning gold with an aviator named Williams. He would, however, be back that night. I then went to the Tower Hotel where my fellow passenger, the scrap buyer, had said that he could easily secure accommodations. Neither of us could get a room. Leaving the scrap buyer sitting with his bags and mine in the hotel lobby, I went to the British authority, Colonel Steele, to request a permit to board the *Yankee*. He said no permits were being issued. When told that I had already been on the *Yankee* he was disbelieving and asked how I had accomplished it. I said that I had walked on. Having been refused a pass, I asked the Colonel if by any chance he could find me a place to sleep. He said he was sorry but could not help. While I was in conversation with the Colonel, a big British sergeant was standing by. That evening, while we were in the lobby of the Tower Hotel, the sergeant came up and asked if I would be willing to sleep in a nightclub. I asked if the sheets would be clean. He said they would. The nightclub was known as the Belle Reve. I asked if I might take my friend and was told that the Belle Reve could accommodate both of us. Meanwhile I had invited my son Charles and others of the crew to have dinner with me at the Tower Hotel. When the dinner party broke up I invited Charles to come with us to the Belle Reve. It was a typical nightclub — dark and unattractive. After about an hour, my son went back to the *Yankee*, and the scrap buyer and I went upstairs to bed. As we tried to sleep we were harassed by the trade winds, which were blowing right through our bedroom, practically ripping off the sheets. We were also kept awake by the small orchestra downstairs. Finally the orchestra music stopped; I breathed a sigh of relief, thinking I had only the trade winds to contend with. Soon, however, a phonograph started up and continued for about two hours. When I met my son for breakfast, he asked how I had slept. I said, "Not too well," and gave him the explanation. When I asked him how he had slept, he said he got to bed late. When he had returned to the ship, the rest of the crew asked him to show them the town. The only place he knew was the Belle Reve. They had been the ones who had played the phonograph.

When Charles returned home in 1941 he tried to enter our Air Force. He took two examinations, but there were so many delays he grew impatient. He went to Canada and enlisted in the Canadian Air Force. After a few months training he went to England as the pilot of a Lancaster bomber and completed his limit of thirty-one bombing missions over Germany. He left Europe to return to the United States without knowing that I had been appointed Ambassador to Belgium. His plane and mine crossed the Atlantic at the same time going in opposite directions. By that time I had remarried. My second wife, Elizabeth de Veyrac, was a former Glendale girl whom I had known when she was a child. Attractive and bright, she had lived in Europe for many years and spoke several languages. Needless to say, she was well suited for the life we were to lead when I was appointed to the Brussels post.

8 Ambassador and Minister

I HAD neither sought nor expected any reward for my political activities. Nevertheless, two of my most rewarding experiences unquestionably resulted from my years of political service. The first was my appointment as Ambassador to Belgium and Minister to Luxembourg. Shortly after the 1944 convention I was approached by a member of the President's staff who asked if I would like to become an ambassador. Yugoslavia was the first post mentioned; I was not interested. Would I like to be Minister to Norway? While slightly tempted, I again declined. Finally, Roosevelt himself suggested "Ambassador to Belgium and Minister to Luxembourg." He dwelt on the fine record Brand Whitlock had made there during World War I and stressed the importance of a post at the crossroads of Europe.[1] He said he hoped very much that I would accept. I did. This was a different kind of offer. Brussels had just been liberated and I would be arriving close on the heels of a retreating enemy.

On October 25, 1944, after arranging my personal affairs and spending a short time in Washington, I took off with my wife from New York.[2] We landed first at Bermuda, where we were guests at Government House. Although we had intended to leave Bermuda immediately, we were delayed by poor weather. Lord Burghley, the great hurdler, was then governor-general. He was a most gracious host and escorted me on a tour of the island. I was fascinated by his frank discussion of British personalities. I was to work closely with the British during the next two years and this first contact with official England was interesting and encouraging.

The weather improved the third day and we left at two in the afternoon, expecting to land at Horta in the Azores early the following morning. I slept well that night and when I awoke, went forward to chat with the captain. When I asked if we would soon reach the Azores, he replied that we had already passed them. He had been unable to land the amphibian plane because of heavy seas, "the swells of Horta." Head winds were slowing our progress and a gauge in front of the captain's seat showed that we were consuming more than the normal amount of gasoline. As the hours wore on it was doubtful that our fuel would last. There was just about enough gas left to fill a teacup when we finally landed in Lisbon at five that afternoon. Four hours later, we took off for Ireland. Our plane developed a serious oil leak when it was only a few minutes off the ground. We turned back and landed as quickly as possible to avoid a fire. Our second take-off in another plane was delayed until two o'clock in the morning. This plane had no heating arrangements; I was never so cold in my life. We landed in Ireland about six o'clock and went from the airport at Foynes to a hotel in Limerick. This was my first visit to Ireland. I was eager to see even a small part of it. We drove for several hours through the countryside. It was much as I had expected—indications of poverty, many small and ancient dwellings, barns which were simple but well-kept, and thousands of hogs!

It had been cold in the plane, it was also cold in Ireland. That night we were still shivering and an effort was made to alleviate our chill by placing several large hot bricks in our bed. When the maid informed us that the room had been occupied the previous night by a daughter of De Valera, then Prime Minister of Ireland, my wife replied that she must have been a "pretty cold number" as the bed was the coldest we had ever occupied.[3]

The following morning we flew to Croydon Airport near London. During three days in London I had extended talks with Arthur Schoenfeldt, the very able chargé d'affaires, who spent many hours briefing me on the situation in Belgium and Luxembourg. He had maintained contact with the Belgian government while it was operating from London. As the Germans moved into Belgium in 1940 Hubert Pierlot, the Prime Minister, and Paul Henri Spaak, the Foreign Minister, together with other Belgian officials, had escaped across France to Spain and from there to London, where they performed as best they could the job of representing their country. King Leopold, whose army had surrendered to the Germans, was kept prisoner in the Laecken Palace in Brussels. When the situation was reversed and the Allies pressed across Europe the Germans moved Leopold to Austria. The government's sojourn in London and the King's imprisonment in Austria both had repercussions for me. Although Leopold had been captured by the Germans, Charlotte, Grand Duchess of Luxembourg, had managed to reach England. She was still in London, and on the second day of our stay I called upon her to present my credentials. I was much impressed by her appearance, her manner, and her wide range of information.

At this time only military planes flew to Belgium. The Germans were still bombing England and our departure was delayed. We went twice to an airport outside London for the take-off; but each time returned. On the third day, in mid-afternoon, we made it. After we were airborne I learned that our pilot had never flown into Belgium and was not too sure how to get there. As we crossed the English Channel, sudden explosions rocked the plane. The Germans in Dunkirk were firing at

us. The captain, who had not known the Germans still occupied Dunkirk, veered rapidly away from this interruption and
we went merrily on our way to Brussels—or so we thought.
Accompanying us was the United States chargé d'affaires in
Luxembourg, George Waller. He had for many years been
almost a fixture in the duchy, where he was highly regarded by
both the people and the Grand Duchess. He had been with me
when I called on her in London. A few minutes after the
Dunkirk episode Waller came back to where I was sitting. He
was almost ashen and asked if I knew where we were. I had
not the slightest idea. He informed me that we were only five
miles from the German lines. I rushed to the front of the plane
to give this information to the captain, who turned abruptly
once again. For another hour we flew over Belgium, trying to
locate an airport near Brussels and finally landed—at the
wrong one. After a short wait Julian Harrington, later Ambassador to Panama but then counselor at Brussels, showed up
and escorted Mrs. Sawyer and me to the American Embassy.

It was a dreary and foggy late afternoon and fast becoming
dark. We drove to the embassy over cobbled streets and past
old buildings. We sensed a contact with history, with events of
long ago. In those days the State Department did not believe in
spending money on homes for our ambassadors. In many cities
we did not own our embassy. In Brussels we had paid in rent
far more than it would have cost us if we had bought the
property outright. This policy has since been changed, and the
present American embassy in Brussels is owned by us. It is
better located and larger than was our embassy in 1944. It
does, however, lack the charm of the old Palais d'Assche.

It was indeed a palace we then occupied, opposite a little
park known as Freres Orban. The palace was owned by the
Marquis d'Assche. King Albert had lived there when he was
still a prince. There were beautiful stairways to the second and
third floors, with low risers which twined about a small "lift"
for those who did not care to climb. The bedroom in which we

slept had been used for accouchement by Queen Elizabeth; both King Leopold and his brother Charles were born in that room. Outside, the enormous arched entrance to the building had a solid iron gate which was rolled down at night, usually with a great thud. When the German v-bombs were hitting around us and my wife was nervous, I would tell her that the front gate was being lowered. Inside was a spacious garden and grounds and what remained of the old stables.

The building was reasonably well-arranged for our purposes. At first I used the second-floor library as my office. From there I hoped I could watch the course of V-1 missiles as they streamed over Brussels, headed for Antwerp. I was severely and repeatedly criticized by my wife for standing before the window. Although the chances of being hit were small, the concussion could break glass for quite a distance. During a bombing attack we were supposed to go to the lower part of the building. We did this once or twice and then, as did most people in Brussels and in London, paid little attention to safety measures. If we were to be hit, we would be hit. Although I heard many bombs go over, I did not see one for several weeks.

My first official act was to present my credentials to the chief of state. This I did the second day after my arrival. First I addressed a letter to Paul Henri Spaak, Minister for Foreign Affairs.

Brussels, November 3, 1944

Excellency:

I have the honor to inform Your Excellency that I have been appointed by the President of the United States as Ambassador Extraordinary and Plenipotentiary near the Government of His Royal Highness the Prince Regent of Belgium, to succeed the Honorable Anthony J. Drexel Biddle, Jr.

I should be extremely grateful if Your Excellency would be good enough to indicate the day and hour when His Royal Highness may be pleased to receive me in audience, in order that I may, in obedience to the instructions of the President of the United States, place in His Royal Highness's hands my letter of credence, as well as the letter of recall of my predecessor, Mr. Anthony J. Drexel Biddle, Jr.

I have the honor to enclose herewith copies of my letter of credence and of Mr. Biddle's letter of recall, and am happy to avail myself of this occasion to assure Your Excellency of my highest and most distinguished consideration.[4]

As regent, the Prince was the head of state in the absence of his brother King Leopold. My first contact with Prince Charles was impressive. I was welcomed with ceremony in an enormous room. As I entered, he was standing to greet me. I presented my letter from President Roosevelt.

Great and Good Friend:

I have made choice of Charles Sawyer, a distinguished citizen of the United States, to reside near the Government of Your Highness in the quality of Ambassador Extraordinary and Plenipotentiary of the United States of America. He is well informed of the relative interests of the two countries and of the sincere desire of this Government to cultivate to the fullest extent the friendship which has so long subsisted between them. My knowledge of his high character and ability gives me entire confidence that he will constantly endeavor to advance the interests and prosperity of both Governments and so render himself acceptable to Your Highness.

I therefore request Your Highness to receive him favorably and to give full credence to what he shall say on the part of the United States and to the assurances which I have charged him to convey to you of the best wishes of this Government for the prosperity of Belgium.

May God have Your Highness in His wise keeping.

Your Good Friend
FRANKLIN D. ROOSEVELT [5]

I found the Prince Regent quiet, shrewd, friendly, and anxious to learn about conditions and attitudes in America. He chatted in perfect English. The re-election of Roosevelt seemed to

please him. He asked about my son Charles in the Canadian
Air Force and about Cincinnati. Obviously he had done his
homework. Prince Charles was tall, sandy haired, calm, and
soft voiced, but a man of great stamina. He said to me later
that he had an advantage over other people: they could not sit
down while he stood and he could, without tiring, stand longer
than any of them. He had a keen mind and a sense of humor.
He never exhibited emotion. As time went on, I acquired great
respect and liking for him. During the war he had joined the
underground organization, the Maquis, and had endeared himself to the Belgian people by his courage. Although a member
of the royal family, he participated in the dangerous activities
of those patriots who harassed and attacked the Germans.
Before the war he had traveled incognito in the United States.
He still corresponded with people whom he had met then, who
did no know that he was other than an ordinary Belgian
citizen. They addressed their letters with his assumed name
and sent them to an address in England.

As I was about to leave, I said that I would like very much
to send him some coffee and cigarettes. After a moment of
hesitation he said he would be glad to accept them, as "the
ravitaillement" was not too good. That afternoon I sent him
six pounds of coffee, some cigarettes and some cocoa, with a
note addressed to his aide, Baron Goffinet. Within a short time
Goffinet came in person to say that the Prince was greatly
pleased and touched and wished immediately to express his
thanks for my kindness. Later, when General Eisenhower
lunched with him and complimented him on his coffee and a
chocolate souffle which he served, Prince Charles replied that
Eisenhower had the American Ambassador to thank.[6] I saw
quite a bit of the Prince during my term of service and he
became our frequent host. Occasionally he would drop in at
the embassy unannounced and play ping-pong, which he did
very well.

Shortly after my arrival I began my series of calls upon the other ambassadors. The ambassador first in a country is the Doyen, the dean, of the diplomatic corps, and whenever precedence is involved he leads the procession. The other ambassadors follow him in the order of their arrival. The experienced nations maneuver their ambassadors into position as quickly as possible. The Papal Nuncio and the Chinese and British Ambassadors had preceded me. At an early date I called on the British Ambassador, Sir Hughe Knatchbull-Hugessen.[7] He was a man of great charm and had come to Brussels from Ankara. There he had been the victim of his valet, a German spy, who had stolen the keys to the safe while the Ambassador was playing the piano, which he did for hours at a time, and managed to remove many secret documents; but this was not known even to Sir Hughe at the time we were in Brussels. It seemed clear from the beginning that there would be advantages in establishing a cordial relationship with the British Ambassador. As time went on we shared confidences, although at all times each knew where to draw the line. He often gave me advance information about the actions of my own State Department, of which I sometimes learned much later and occasionally not at all. My early success with Sir Hughe was due in part to my ability to supply him with what he called the "sinews of diplomacy," whisky and wines, which strangely enough he then found difficult to obtain. I had inherited a small supply of liqueurs and wines left behind by one of my predecessors, John Cudahy, when he fled Brussels in 1940. The Germans apparently did respect diplomatic immunity. Nothing which had been left in storage by Ambassador Cudahy had been touched, including his wines, liqueurs, and his clothing. He had left a heavy fur-lined coat which I appropriated, as I had no garment heavy enough to withstand the penetrating damp and cold of Brussels.

The Papal Nuncio, Msgr. Micara, was *sui generis*. Shrewd, wordly-wise, an understanding and skilled diplomat, he had been in capitals all over the world. We became very friendly.

He was fond of good food and good wine and frequently came to luncheon at the embassy. In turn, he was insistent on my visiting him. Later, he became a cardinal and a member of the Curia.[8]

My relations with my fellow diplomats were excellent. I was on close terms with the Norwegian Ambassador and the Swiss Minister. My dealings with the Russian Ambassador, Mikhail Sergeev, were surprisingly pleasant.[9] He was a solemn person, but not without humor. His friendliness was encouraged by an incident which occurred shortly after his arrival. A cable addressed to him was delivered by mistake to my embassy. I promptly contacted him and sent on the document, unopened. He was very grateful. A few days later I received a hurried call, asking if he might come to my embassy immediately. Within ten minutes he showed up and told me that one of his secretaries had been held up by American soldiers and relieved of his purse. Sergeev looked at me steadily, expecting some expression of dismay or apology. Instead I smiled and said he would be interested to know that one of *my* secretaries had been held up by American soldiers who had taken not only his purse, but also his automobile. The Ambassador saw the humor of my story and the point. I said that if Russian soldiers had occupied Belgium their misconduct would probably have been just as great. What Sergeev had foreseen as a diplomatic crisis turned into a gossipy session about how "soldiers will be soldiers." While I was in Brussels, several strange visitors arrived at the Russian embassy. One dark young military man, with watchful eyes, whose probable assignment was to spy on Sergeev as well as the rest of us, came to our embassy a number of times to play ping-pong with my wife. Stefan Glaser, the Polish Ambassador, was a sad figure, a sensitive individual who suffered along with his people. He had been a teacher with a fine scholastic record. Both he and his wife mourned, with good reason, the fate of their country. While they were in Brussels, the Polish oil fields in Galicia were seized by Russia. They were an intelligent couple and saw, all too clearly, what lay ahead. I frequently saw the French Ambassador, Monsieur Raymond Brougere, a friendly, talkative, and impatient person who did not hesitate to criticize his nation's allies. He had a low opinion of Marshal Pétain and said that Admiral Leahy was not aware of what was going on.[10] Brougere stirred up quite a mess by advocating that the Walloons break off from Belgium and join France.

The differences between the Flemish and the Walloons is one of Belgium's problems. Flemish is spoken in the north, around Antwerp and Ghent, French in the south near Liege. Every government document is printed in both languages, and most government officials speak both. There is, however, more than language which distinguishes the two parts of Belgium. The Flemish are devout Catholics and conservative; the Walloons are less religious and liberal.[11]

The language difference presented some difficulty for my wife and me. She spoke French fluently, and I could speak and understand it reasonably well. Flemish, however, was another matter. Once I made a short speech in Flemish at Antwerp, which seemed to make quite a hit.

Although I had been to Europe several times, I had never been there during the winter. I was unprepared for the Belgian weather, which is even more unpleasant than the English weather. The winter of 1944 was the worst in years. The ground was covered with snow and ice and the air was thick with heavy fog. Since we were within easy range of German bombers, there was a strict blackout and we almost never drove at night. With the amount of military traffic in the city, it was difficult to drive even during the day. So we walked— through the damp and the cold. One afternoon my wife and I were caught in a heavy downpour of sleet and rain. When we arrived home, her shoes, which were made of paper, had disintegrated.

It was a hard winter for the Belgians also. They were not

well-clothed and not too well-fed. Unless they were rich, the women wore no stockings and their legs were often blue with cold. But there were few complaints. Food prices were very high; eggs cost one dollar each. We at the embassy did not suffer for we received most of our supplies from the Army. Later, in February of 1946, the Army charged the embassy fifteen thousand dollars for food furnished from December 1, 1944, through August 1, 1945. It was pointed out to the Quartermaster General that repeated attempts had been made to pay for our food when we received it, but we had then been told that the Army had no means of collecting. The matter was dropped, except for the effort to collect seventy-five cents a day from those who were still in Brussels.

The Belgians were calm and able to joke about themselves, their problems, and their disasters. They were friendly toward Americans, respectful toward the British, suspicious of the French, and full of hatred for the Germans. An austerity program was inaugurated by Camille Gutt, the finance minister, to tax "war profits," which greatly distressed wealthy Belgians. But Gutt's program was designed to put Belgium on her feet economically and it was highly successful. He was a man of great ability and drove his program through, in spite of bitter opposition. The rich reviled him; the others said, *"Gutt mit uns."* He was soft-spoken, diminutive in figure, but not in character or intellect. He was a Belgian who had in no way collaborated with the Germans.

One major problem confronting the Belgian Government at this time concerned "collaborators." What should be done with them? During the occupation, while the Resistance groups were risking their lives to fight the invaders, others were getting along with the Germans, even working with them. When the Germans had been driven out, the patriots wanted revenge against collaborators. It was not, however, easy to separate "the sheep from the goats." Most patriots were inclined to the view that businessmen who had operated their

factories during the occupation were collaborators. Businessmen disputed this. One of them told me there was a clear test:
if a factory produced more than it had previously, the owner
collaborated. If the owner continued to run his factory but
produced less, he was a patriot. Many collaborators tried
desperately to get back into the good graces of the government. Some hoped to clear their names with our help. King
Leopold's sister had married an Italian prince, and she was
charged with arranging meetings between Leopold and Hitler.
Shortly after my arrival, she tried unsuccessfully to arrange a
meeting with me. I had been warned that she was suspect and I
avoided receiving her. On a few occasions Mrs. Sawyer and I
attended social gatherings where the atmosphere was definitely
"collaborationist." On one occasion this was so obvious that
we left promptly. The charge of collaborating reached everywhere, even into the household of Queen Elizabeth. Willy de
Gruyn, her chef de cabinet, was a chief target of the critics.[12]

I recall also a diplomat named Baron de Bassompierre. He
had been long in the foreign service and in Tokyo, where he
was the Belgian Ambassador, he had been very friendly with
our Ambassador Joseph C. Grew. He and Grew spent much
time playing tennis. Shortly after my arrival in Brussels I
received a package of tennis balls from Grew, then Undersecretary of State, for delivery to Bassompierre. Bassompierre,
whose wartime record was questionable, was trying to establish the fact that he was highly regarded by the United States.
He missed no opportunity to come to the embassy on social
occasions, sometimes uninvited. I felt that he would capitalize
on the gift and wrote to Grew, explaining the situation. He
wrote back, thanking me and asking that I not deliver the
gift.[13]

There were two governments in Brussels at that time, and
their views were occasionally divergent. The Belgian officials
who were able to escape through France and Spain had for
four years been functioning in London; when the Germans

retreated from Belgium these officials moved back to Brussels. Hubert Pierlot, the Prime Minister, was a stolid, honest, unimaginative lawyer. He was not an effective administrator and was tremendously impressed by the British, with whom he had lived and worked. The dominant figure in the Belgian government was Paul Henri Spaak, the Foreign Minister. Spaak was a magnificent orator and a man of outstanding ability.[14] Throughout the post-war years his stature has grown. Pierlot's government included a few other men of real ability, but for the most part they were nondescript. Incidentally, I would put the three Communist ministers, Marteau, Demary and Dispy, in the first group.

The second government in Brussels was the military, representing SHAEF, Supreme Headquarters Allied Expeditionary Forces. With much of Belgium occupied by Allied forces, it was necessary to have there a branch of SHAEF, which was represented by General Robert ("Bobbie") Erskine for the British and Colonel John Sherman for the Americans. This was a typical arrangement—the British always had a general, we always had a colonel. These two, with a fairly large staff, handled Allied military matters and dealt continually with the Belgian government.

The civilian government had difficulty controlling the resistance groups, who still held a large number of weapons. The government desired that all arms be turned in and issued an order to this effect. The Communists immediately gave out violent and inflammatory statements against the order and urged its disobedience. The Communist members of the Cabinet resigned. Crowds marched on the government buildings and the government had no adequate force with which to handle them. The Allies were faced with the problem of how to treat these demonstrations and those who incited them. It was clear to Erskine, Sherman, and to me that we should not enforce Pierlot's order with Allied military forces, much as Pierlot wished this to be done. The issue was developing great bitterness and promised serious consequences for the government and for the military effort.

Pierlot had forbidden meetings. General Erskine, Colonel Sherman, Sir Hughe, and I met frequently to discuss this move. It was my view that public meetings should not be prohibited nor free speech prevented, and the others agreed. A mass demonstration was called for November 16, and thousands gathered. I was calling on Pierlot that afternoon. As I stood in his office, looking out the window, enormous crowds outside were shouting for his resignation—*"Demission."* They were not, however, disorderly. Many women and girls were among the demonstrators. After watching the spectacle for a short time I suggested that the Prime Minister had many pressing matters to attend to and it would be well for me to let him get back to them. Several of his assistants rushed up and suggested that I leave by a back door. I really wanted to mingle with the crowds, but rather than appear stubborn or ungrateful I left by the rear door, where my car had been sent to meet me.

General Erskine was not only a very likeable character; he was also adroit. Just when all hell seemed about to break loose, he met with some of the resistance leaders and made the happy suggestion that they turn in their arms, not to the government but to him. Since he was greatly respected by the resistance leaders, they agreed to his request.[15] Erskine had been chief of staff of the British division in Africa known as the Desert Rats. He was a big ruddy-faced Scot with a keen sense of humor and great charm. He was earthy and gay, but capable of deep emotion. Somewhat later, in a reception for Churchill at the Grande Place, when a group of Belgian girls sang "My Heart is in the Highlands," he unashamedly burst into tears.

From the time I arrived in Belgium I heard stories of the infamous internment camp of Breendonck. I talked with some who had been imprisoned there and I wanted to see it. Toward the end of November my wife and I were taken there by a

British officer—Captain Deacon. We drove fifteen miles out of
Brussels, turned off on a side road and crossed a drawbridge
into the citadel. While we were inside, inspecting various
gruesome sights, a buzz bomb went off about a mile away. The
guide said we were lucky to be in such a safe place. On the
way back we saw the crater which the bomb had left. This is
what I said when we returned:

I have seen Breendonck. On a cold gray afternoon I walked
across the bridge over the moat and into that sinister pile of brick
and concrete where so many brave Belgians entered, never to
return.

It is impossible to describe the atmosphere of this prison. I saw
the courtyard where prisoners were made to stand without food
and drink for forty-eight hours with their faces against the wall
and where any movement resulted in unbelievable beating and
stabbing with bayonets. I saw the gas chamber where men were
partially gassed and then permitted to revive long enough to be
abused verbally by a guard safely outside the danger zone. I saw
the torture chambers where the victims were hung and burned and
beaten. I saw the silent row of posts against which were tied those
who were condemned to be shot. I saw the scaffold from which,
when the trap was sprung, men were hung three at a time. I saw
the little brick cells where prisoners were forced to stand without
speaking hour after hour and day after day in complete darkness.
I saw on those brick walls the messages of despair, of religious
hope, and unbelievably pathetic outpourings of affection for their
families, which were scratched by the fingernails of the victims.
On these same walls I saw rows upon rows of marks by which they
checked the number of days of their imprisonment.[16]

Early in November I attended a meeting with General Ei-
senhower and his staff. I was the only civilian in the group.
With Eisenhower were Air Marshal Arthur William Tedder,
Rear Admiral Bertram Ramsay, Generals Omar Bradley and
Walter Bedell Smith, and a number of other distinguished
figures. Eisenhower said that the last time he had been in
Cincinnati, he had seen the White Sox, referring to them as the

"Black Sox," sell out to the Cincinnati Reds.[17] That afternoon I attended a session of the Chamber of Deputies and heard him address that body. All the other speeches were read, but he spoke without notes, clearly and logically. During the remainder of my stay in Belgium, I had occasion to see Eisenhower many times. He was always unassuming, frank, and considerate. He was as popular in Europe as he was later in the United States. His chief of staff, General Walter Bedell Smith, was somewhat of a martinet, but a lovable and understanding person underneath.[18] I came to have a very high regard for both of these men.

I was not only Ambassador to Belgium; I was also Minister to Luxembourg. During the first few days in Brussels I was so busy with Belgian affairs that I had no time to make the trip to Luxembourg. Winthrop Greene, who had been chargé d'affaires at Luxembourg while Waller was away, suggested that I come there before he left. He said I would need a military pass and a letter, fixing my rank equivalent to that of a general. This would insure proper treatment in case of my capture by the Germans. I left on the morning of November 10. The trip began in a driving rain which grew steadily worse and finally turned to snow as we went through the Ardennes. We arrived in Luxembourg in mid-afternoon. Fortunately my hotel had a warm room and hot water. When I complimented the clerk the next morning he said I was lucky; there was hot water and heat only two days a week and I happened to be there on one of those days.

I was fascinated by my first view of Luxembourg. It is, of course, very small, but like some other tiny things, it is very impressive, a jewel of a city, surrounded by a series of walls and battlements which over the centuries, at one period or another, have been used to resist sieges from without. The picturesque entrance to the city overlooks a little valley which Goethe described as the most beautiful spot in the world. The city is steeped in history. Charlemagne, Napoleon, and many other great figures spent time there, usually while at war. I was favorably impressed by Luxembourg's people and was particularly taken by Foreign Minister Charles Bech, whom I met that first day and for whom I later came to have great regard and affection. Dupong, the Prime Minister, was a slow-spoken but clear-headed individual who was at all times sensible and realistic. On this visit I called again upon the Grand Duchess, in a less formal atmosphere. I was impressed not only by her appearance and manner and her wide range of information but also by her obvious common sense and shrewd approach to affairs of government. I left after one day, greatly cheered by my visit to that little country.[19] Frequent later visits strengthened my favorable opinion. I have said many times that if I were to spend my remaining years outside the United States I would prefer Luxembourg to any other country I have ever seen.

In Brussels, much of my time was taken by the many visitors who came to the embassy. Aveling, counselor of the British embassy, dropped in frequently. He was a tall, gaunt character, with long experience in the foreign service. His manners and conversation were impeccable, but bland. Rain or shine, he always carried an umbrella. On one occasion he left it in the downstairs office in such an inviting way that some evil-minded joker dropped a lighted cigarette into it. The umbrella was soon afire. The alarm was spread, but the only loss was Aveling's umbrella. He was concerned and considerate about our attendance at church services. Shortly after my arrival he reported his embarrassment that "no pew in Christ Church had been reserved for the American Ambassador." I said that if one were reserved I would use it when I attended church but would feel in no way slighted if it were not. If no pew were assigned, my absence would not be noticed; and this absence would certainly occur if it continued to be as cold in the church as it had been on the previous Sunday.

There were, of course, many Belgians who came, usually to

ask a favor, but occasionally to do one. Among the most charming was a former Belgian ambassador to the United States, M. Thuenis.[20] My wife and I saw him and Madame Thuenis frequently, both at the embassy and at their home. He called one day with a Major Hoffman to ask that I become the Honorary Chairman of Belgian War Relief. Other American ambassadors had acted in that capacity, and I agreed to continue the tradition. Both of my visitors, in reminiscing about life in Brussels, were exceedingly frank and amusing. The major gave a vivid and not too complimentary picture of Brand Whitlock. Whitlock had been indisposed almost all of the time he had been in Belgium and never arose before eleven or twelve o'clock. When President Wilson was about to arrive for a visit, Whitlock had asked Hoffman and Norman Armour to take charge of all the arrangements.

As might be imagined, representatives of the leading news services and broadcasting networks were in and out continually. One of my early callers was Walter Cronkite, later a broadcaster in Washington and New York. He had just come from the front in a glider, with nothing but the clothes he had on.

There were also visitors who had worked with the underground. Shortly after my arrival I met Olga Jackson, who had parachuted into Belgium. She was a good-looking English girl in her twenties who confessed that she was bored with her present job. It was "now necessary to make so many reports." She missed the excitement and the danger of her previous assignment. She was quite willing to talk about the things she had done and those with whom she had worked. She told of a Belgian girl, named Andre, who had taken to Spain the Germans' first liquid air bomb, which she had picked up in Belgium. She had made her way as far as Paris when the Gestapo came through the train to inspect baggage. Her bag was on the rack over her head and she was carrying the bomb wrapped in heavy paper. When the German asked to look at her suitcase she said, "Would you mind holding my package while I get it down?" He agreed and held the package while she produced the suitcase, which he examined. He returned the package to her without glancing at it. This superb audacity and presence of mind was shown by a girl nineteen years old. She was arrested shortly thereafter and shot.[21]

We heard other stories of bravery. Late one afternoon a lone Belgian aviator had flown in from London, zoomed over Brussels at treetop level and machine-gunned the headquarters of the Gestapo. The Germans swarmed out of the building in a frenzy and began to arrest people indiscriminately. When Prince de Ligne, who happened to be there and later told me the story, asked a German officer why those people were being arrested, he was told that they "seemed too happy." It was learned later that a British secret agent who had penetrated the heart of German espionage had been killed in this raid.

I was always glad to see Paul Henri Spaak and Camille Gutt. In a conversation with these two, Spaak told of going to Paris with Gutt to interview De Gaulle. On the way their car was stopped by an American soldier. Spaak said to the soldier, "We are the Belgian Government." The soldier replied, "I am the American Government." Spaak said, "I am the Foreign Minister of Belgium," whereupon the soldier put out his hand, said "Put her there!" and told them to drive on.[22]

Queen Mother Elizabeth, the widow of King Albert, lived at the Laecken Palace, and shortly after our arrival Mrs. Sawyer and I called upon her. We found her to be a most interesting personality—small, almost sparrow-like in appearnce, but gifted with tremendous energy. She was extremely pleasant and talked freely about the war. She told of being bombed first by the Germans, then by the British, and finally by the Americans, pointing to the craters in the palace gardens caused by the American bombs. Of sixty-five, nineteen had not gone off. When I showed concern over this, she asked with a little smile if I regretted the fact that they had not exploded. I replied that for her sake I was happy, but hoped that the average of our "duds" did not run so high. While she was small and not robust in appearance, she was completely fearless. At her request Colonel Sherman once took her for a ride in a jeep and he permitted her to take the wheel; whereupon she terrified him by driving over seventy miles an hour. Her varied attitude toward her two sons was a matter of common gossip. Leopold, the King, was her idol, but she apparently cared little for Prince Charles, although he looked very much like her. Her likes and dislikes were freely revealed—which was also a characteristic of the Belgian people who had been governed by her two sons. She came from a long line of German royalty and was well aware of her sovereign background.

One of the important men in Belgium at that time was Cardinal Van Roey. He was stoilid, slow-spoken, but very intelligent. He was apparently quite a different person from the famous Cardinal Mercier of World War i. General Alexander Von Falkenhausen, head of the occupying army, said that Cardinal Mercier barked a lot, but Cardinal Van Roey would bite.[23] I wished to call upon him at Malines as soon as possible and in late November did so. As we approached Malines we heard the sirens of an "alert" and knew that a bomb had hit somewhere near. When we arrived at the cathedral, the evidence of bomb damage was massive. The bomb had struck less than one hundred yards away, hitting a clinic filled with nurses and patients, many of whom had been killed. As we mounted the stairs to the room where the cardinal was to greet us, we were forced to step on piles of broken stained glass. The head of Christ had been blown out of one large window. Even in the room where we met the cardinal the rugs were covered with glass. Van Roey was completely calm after the bombing and referred to it without emotion. He was Flemish yet spoke in French and slowly enough that I understood everything he said. He was most objective about the proper treatment of Germany after the war; there was no hatred. I was very favorably impressed. Upon leaving we went to the scene of the bombing—one of indescribable confusion and horror. Dead and wounded were being carried out on litters; the streets were packed with weeping women and men; nurses were working frantically in blood-stained uniforms. I walked among the crowds for a few minutes and then climbed back in my car and left for Brussels.[24]

9 Battle of the Bulge

ALTHOUGH MANY diplomats have little affection for congressional junkets, I approve of them. I believe there is definite benefit in having congressmen see for themselves what the United States is doing and attempting to do in other countries. The money spent is infinitesimal compared to the amount which we distribute so gaily and lavishly throughout the world. While a few misbehave, the great majority of legislators honestly try to learn what is going on. Even in the early days of my service, we were receiving visits from congressional groups. At one luncheon the chairman of the delegation sitting next to my wife remarked that it must be pleasant to be an ambassador. He was referring to the excellent luncheon. She asked if he thought that the United States was paying for it— he replied that he did. She then told him that this luncheon was costing me personally over two hundred dollars.

How does an ambassador with but little or no private means meet the social obligations of his office? He has only his salary and an insignificant "representation allowance" to use for entertainment. While I am not as outraged as some by the pay given our ambassadors, I feel strongly that our allowances are niggardly, especially when compared with the amounts given by other countries to their ambassadors.

While Congress is miserly in this regard it is lavish with manpower. One of my most annoying and persistent problems resulted from the number of new agency employees spawned from Washington. Among these new agencies, the most troublesome was F.E.A., the Foreign Economic Administration. It was created, as were many others, on the theory that every new problem can and should be solved by a new agency. As early as November 14 I cabled the State Department that I would appreciate being consulted before Washington sent any more representatives of F.E.A.[1] Not that everyone in the F.E.A. was incompetent, although many were. A particular exception was Philip Reed, who came to Brussels from London. He did not believe, as many agency heads do, that there was something sacrosanct about his mission. He showed a sense of realism and a sense of humor, and his approach to our practical problems was refreshing. He appreciated my difficulty in running an embassy with so many outsiders milling around, flaunting their authority. He agreed that, as chief of mission, I faced an intolerable situation when I was forced to accept and put up with dozens of men, appointed without my knowledge and consent, who regarded themselves highly and in many cases felt that they could act independently of my wishes and my program.

Watching the stupid proliferation of United States agencies abroad, my respect for the British and their management of foreign affairs grew apace as the weeks went by. This respect was tempered by a growing realization that official Belgium felt an especial attachment to Britain. The situation was aggravated by the eagerness of John Winant, our ambassador in London, to attend to my business. At his embassy in London he would receive and confer with high officials of the Belgian government. My staff became incensed and urged me to protest to the State Department. I suggested that we wait a while.

Shortly thereafter, when I learned of a particularly offensive intrusion, I contacted Winant directly. I said that I had read in the Belgian papers of his interview with the Belgian Prime Minister; as the American Ambassador to Belgium, I was interested in what had been said and asked what he had learned which might be of help to me. This approach was not so subtle that he missed the point. He was greatly embarrassed and said their conversation had been entirely personal. This I knew was not true. My call had the desired effect; from then on he ceased to act as if Belgian affairs were his responsibility.

The British had many advantages in dealing with the Belgians. Belgium was the child of England; her relations with England had always been close. The Belgian Government had escaped to London, and when these officials returned to Brussels, it was natural for them to continue looking to London for help. At an early date I expressed to the British Ambassador my feeling that the Pierlot Government was completely indifferent toward America and Americans, and knew of our existence only as a Santa Claus. Sir Hughe agreed with me. As the Allies, led by the Poles, moved rapidly across Europe, the British Twenty-first Army under Montgomery set up headquarters in Brussels. The Americans were further south, though certain units had moved ahead and were close to the Rhine. The presence of the British Command in Brussels increased the normal tendency of the Belgians to seek guidance from England. The British were well aware of this attitude and strove in many ways to prove to Belgium that England was her real benefactor. During the blitz, the United States had given Britain a number of ambulances. The British later gave them to Belgium, described as "Queen's messengers." Few Belgians had any idea that they had originally come from the United States.

Shortly after my arrival, I began an effort to assist with Belgium's supply problems. Rarely did I receive any thanks. I kept silent until Pierlot, during a visit in his study, said he wanted to tell me frankly about the Belgian situation—their needs. I said that I would be equally frank: since November 16 when he and I had looked out of his window at the crowd below, he had brought none of his problems directly to my attention, although I knew that he had conferred with the British Ambassador in Brussels, with many British officials in London, and even with the American Ambassador in London. I told him of things I had done. The Belgians had been milling around and getting nowhere with their supply problems, when I urged the appointment of an able businessman, named Kronacher, as the Belgian supply emissary to the United States. I reminded Pierlot that before Kronacher left for the United States he had called on me for advice and suggestions. His trip had been most successful. Yet when he returned to Brussels, he had not contacted me nor sent me any word at all. My comments were harsh. Pierlot was greatly shaken and asked me to return in the afternoon, which I did. During the second interview he was contrite and apologetic.[2]

Yet in spite of this, only a week later I learned, not from the Belgians, but from the British Ambassador, that Spaak was planning to go to London and ask Churchill to order General Erskine to take over the management of Belgium. I had been told nothing of this plan, which from every standpoint, as I saw it, was a mistake. I made it clear to Sir Hughe that I regarded this suggestion as wholly unacceptable to us and if it were carried out, Great Britain would have this baby in its lap with no help from the United States. The Belgians never discussed this with me but Spaak did not go. I did not confine my criticism to Pierlot. I made a studied effort to make clear to all Belgian officials my resentment of the preference they gave the British. This finally bore fruit. At a dinner at our embassy on January 23, Pierlot's chef de cabinet, de Staercke, said that they all now realized their mistake. He agreed that their contacting of Ambassador Winant was a stupid error, and said that he hoped I would now look to the future. Subsequently, I was able to talk at length with the Prince Regent. I said that I resented the effort of Belgian officials to curry favor with the British and their habit of discussing Belgian affairs in London.[3] From that time on I was closer to the activities and the thinking of the Belgian Government than any other ambassador.

The discrimination against America and Americans was evident in other ways. With the British Twenty-first Army making its headquarters in Brussels, there were thousands of British and Canadian soldiers in and around that city, and it was necessary to find accommodations for them. However, as the battle line moved east more Americans came into the area. The problem of finding accommodations was pressing. British and Canadian clubs had refused admittance to any American soldiers. The Hotel Metropole was ordered by the British to admit no Americans. Happily, a British major in charge possessed common sense. Within two hours after arriving in Brussels from Paris he was confronted by one hundred American soldiers sent there to spend the night. He refused to leave these men in the streets when beds were available. To solve the problem an effort was made to open a so-called "A.E.F. Club" for both Americans and British, under the sponsorship of a committee headed by Lady Tedder. Lady Tedder, like some other women who were then very busy in Europe, was not too effective. It was common for women of no experience or competence to flaunt their uniforms and positions and be insufferably snobbish. Nor was this confined to the British. A Miss Moran of the International Red Cross, coming from Paris on a "tour of inspection," was so supercilious that she made that great organization look ridiculous. These women furnished a marked contrast to the brave and conscientious girls who were nursing British and American soldiers at the front. In an effort to remedy the housing situation, Mrs. Sawyer and I examined a number of possibilities. We were amused when examining one large residence which had belonged to Krueger, the match king, to find fairly patent evidence of its use by the Germans. On the second and third floor over the door of each room was the name of a Fraulein—Katrina, Lillian, etc. Whether these young women had been Belgian or German was not ascertainable.

Early in December I had undertaken to make contact with American commanders at the front. Arrangements were made for me to lunch with General Hodges at First Army headquarters, then at Spa. Colonel Sherman was to accompany me and came to the embassy for breakfast. In Sherman's Chevrolet we left the embassy about quarter of nine on December 14. A thick fog had settled over the countryside and the driving was not good. We had just left Louvain and were passing a long line of British lorries moving in the opposite direction. Suddenly a truck loomed up dimly in front of us and hit us head-on. The impact was terrific. I may have lost consciousness briefly, but I saw our driver mashed against the wheel and windshield and Colonel Sherman lying across the back of the front seat. I was able to climb out of the car but after a minute or two began to feel faint and slid back in. Meanwhile, Colonel Sherman came to, climbed out of the car dazed and groping, and came around to my side to ask if I were hurt. I said I thought not. I must have been thrown over the front seat as I found my glasses, intact, under the foot pedal. How they got there without breaking was a mystery. Fortunately, I had been wearing the large fur coat of Ambassador Cudahy, which perhaps saved me from serious injury. A large crowd gathered immediately, including both English and American soldiers. As our driver's teeth had been knocked out and his chest crushed, some of the English volunteered to take him to a hospital at Tirlemont. An American major from Spa was kind enough to pick up the Colonel and me. Before leaving I rescued the small American flag from the front of our car and turned out our lights. The major's car broke down before we made it to Tirlemont and we walked a short distance to the officers' school there. From that point we were driven to a hospital at Liege. I had a severe pain in my left leg near the hip, some nausea and dizziness. Colonel Sherman had two bumps, one the shape of an egg, at the top of the forehead. Later General Erskine in a jocular mood referred to this bump and said that with egg prices so high Sherman had done very well. Arriving at Liege, we phoned First Army Headquarters that we would not be able to make the luncheon and then went to a hospital, which turned out to be the Cincinnati unit. I knew several of the doctors and one nurse who lived only a short distance from my home village of Glendale. Major Stephenson, a doctor from Glendale, did not seem worried about my thigh but gave special attention to my ankle, although I told him there was nothing wrong with it. He was right, however, for it began to swell soon after. One of the doctors said that the British driver, when he ran into thick fog, probably thought he was back home in London where it was proper to drive on the left side of the road. In Germany almost one year later General George Patton, starting out for a day of pheasant hunting, suffered an identical accident. His car was hit by a truck coming in the opposite direction, his spine was shattered and he died nine days later. I was very lucky.[4]

Most people in Belgium assumed that the war had moved out for good. Collaborators were being prosecuted; former members of the Maquis were out in the open, telling their stories. Peace had arrived, or so they thought. They were to be disillusioned. I was walking on crutches as a result of my accident, but on December 18 I visited a Polish division, then at Eindhoven in Holland. The Poles were by common agreement the bravest soldiers in the Allied armies, and I was greatly interested in seeing some of them. The Polish marshal was kind enough to bring out his entire division, or what part of it could be spared, to be reviewed by me. This was no "spit and polish" group—but they looked as though they could fight. When I asked how many of these soldiers had been recaptured from the Germans, he asked that any man who had been a German prisoner hold up his hand. Half of them put their hands up. At luncheon with the marshal, I noted that he was receiving frequent and apparently startling messages. He finally told me that German paratroopers were being dropped behind the American lines in the Ardennes. This was my first information that war was coming back to Belgium. Its significance was unknown at that time but we knew it soon thereafter. This was the Battle of the Bulge.

A few days later the magnitude of the attack was revealed. Seventeen German divisions had attacked in the Ardennes forest and broken through the Allied lines. The threat to Brussels and Antwerp became appallingly real. On the twenty-first of December I was planning to leave for Paris early in the morning to attend a SHAEF meeting. At the last minute I decided that my trip would be a mistake. The Germans had kept an extensive spy system in Brussels and my departure would immediately be known to them. A report that the American Ambassador was fleeing from Brussels would not help our cause. The following day Consul General Keeley came in from Antwerp to report that 150 German paratroopers had been dropped between Brussels and Antwerp with orders to wreck the docks at Antwerp and to assassinate American officials, including me. Three had already been captured, dressed as American officers. When Keeley had asked what would be done with the prisoners, he was told that was no problem—they had already been shot. This was not the fate of German soldiers who were captured in their own uniforms. They were treated as prisoners of war. One arrogant German made a great fuss in the prison camp demanding to see the commandant. He complained that his money had been taken from him. The commandant asked, "Were you not given a receipt?" Whereupon the German said, "Yes," and produced a slip of paper that said, "The bastard had 11,000 guilders which he doesn't now have."

On December 23 I received a cable from the State Department authorizing me to leave Brussels. I immediately drafted a
memorandum with transportation assignments for each one of
us, including all of my staff. The Von Runstedt attack had
been timed on the basis of German weather predictions, which
proved to be accurate. It had been practically impossible for
our planes to fly, and at first the German tanks and troops
moved swiftly toward the Meuse River, with scarcely any
harassment from the air. However, the weather suddenly
changed. On the very day I received permission from the State
Department to leave, the sky was blue and cloudless. Beginning early that morning and throughout the day, we could see
hundreds of white streaks trailing from our bombers and fight-
ers as they went over for the counterattack. I decided not to
leave.[5]

The battle was approaching a climax, and Brussels was a
tense and terrified city. On Christmas Eve, Mrs. Sawyer gave a
large party at the embassy attended by hundreds of Americans
and by many Belgians. We hoped to give the impression that
we were not panicky. Most Belgians and many Americans
believed that we knew everything that was going on. My wife
was besieged by women, some in tears, who asked what they
and their families should do. She told them that there was
nothing to worry about—to be calm and sit tight. She herself
was not at all sure about her advice, but she proved to be right.

By December 26, the German advance had been stopped
short of the Meuse. Still, the battle continued well into January, as the Germans fought bitterly to hold their gains and
straighten their lines.[6] We in Brussels were not immediately
aware that the threat had ended, for enemy planes and bombs
were now striking desperately at Antwerp and at Brussels. At a
luncheon on December 27 we were told that the night before
the Twenty-first Army Headquarters had spotted a German
Messerschmidt swooping down and machine-gunning a tram
car in Brussels. This report was correct and the realities of war
came close to me personally four days later.

Ambassador and Mrs. Sawyer in the library of the U.S. Embassy, Brussels, November 1944.

Ambassador Sawyer (wearing the coat which probably saved his life) with the Ninth TAC Dive Bomber Squadron, January 31, 1945.

Mr. Rizzardi, of the Brussels newspaper *La Meuse*, interviewing Ambassador Sawyer, April 12, 1945.

Ambassador Sawyer at the Inauguration of Franklin Roosevelt Avenue,
Brussels, July 4, 1945.

May 5, 1945, Belgian Government officials and Ambassador Sawyer at the Decoration of Resistance Leaders. Left to right: L. Mundeleer; R. Gillon, President of the Belgian Senate; F. Van Cauwelaert, Speaker of the Belgian House of Representatives; Prime Minister Van Acker; Ambassador Sawyer.

At Decoration of Resistance Leaders, Grand Place, Brussels, Ambassador Sawyer with Prime Minister Van Acker and Colonel John Sherman.

My wife and I were planning to dine on New Year's Eve at the chateau of the Baroness de Selys near Genappe. This was our first evening out of Brussels since our arrival in Belgium and I thought it well to take an MP, in addition to the chauffeur. It was a clear night and quite cold. In fact, when we arrived at the chateau the ground was glazed with ice and Mrs. Sawyer slipped and fell flat as she stepped from the car. When we entered the house we found no heat. However, this problem was partially solved, for our charming young hostess had underestimated the number of her guests. As a result, we sat very close together at the dinner table. We left about 11:30 P.M. and started back to Brussels to attend General Erskine's New Year's Eve party. The countryside was bathed in moonlight. As we were passing the "Lion of Waterloo," the statue marking the spot where Wellington sat on his horse and watched the battle, I remarked to my wife, "It seems that every European war ends with a battle on the soil of Belgium; we are now only forty minutes away from the battle front. But you would never know it with this perfect moonlight, not a sound, and a blanket of snow over everything."

I had scarcely uttered the words when there was a thunderous blast, and flames shot up in front of the car. Benoit, the chauffeur, stepped on the brakes, turned off his lights, swerved the car to the right and stopped. At first I thought a bomb had struck, but then realized that we had been strafed from the air. In a moment I realized that we were all unharmed. We scrambled out of the car and stood shivering next to a brick wall while the plane came back and circled overhead. Strangely enough we could not see the plane, even in the bright moonlight. We stood there for some minutes until our German friend finally left. We then went on into Brussels, this time with our lights *off*. It was New Year's morning 1945. We attended the party at General Erskine's mess, where we stayed but a short time.[7]

The New Year's Eve experience was exciting and a little wearing, but I slept soundly through the rest of the night. My wife did not sleep. About eight o'clock on New Year's morning we heard the roar of low-flying planes. Looking out the window, we saw many of them coming over the housetops from the east. My wife said she was sure they were German planes —she could see the faces of the pilots. Then we heard firing. She was right; the enemy was back again in Brussels. The planes were attacking the Evere Airport about two miles away. I stood at the window, watching them dive and circle and fly back and forth at high speed. The British and Canadian air group at Evere was caught flat-footed. Later we learned that the officer in charge of the airport had given himself a leave to spend New Year's Eve in London. Sixty-eight British planes were destroyed. Only one Canadian plane got into the air, its courageous pilot apparently being the only one not nursing a hangover from the night before. He climbed only a short distance before he was shot down. The story put out by SHAEF was that little damage had been done. Unfortunately, this was far from true.

The next day Benoit asked me to look at the Cadillac. There were several dents and a small hole at head-level, opposite the driver's seat. Apparently many bullets ricocheted, but the German had not given us the spray of direct shots which would have finished us off. Later, toward the end of the month, as I set out to investigate an airport at Nivelle, Benoit said he would like to show me the place where we had been machine-gunned. I immediately recognized the spot. On a brick wall beside the road there were at least twenty bullet marks, some quite large. Benoit, who had seen the cobblestone road when the snow had melted, said there were many more marks there. Many years later, on a trip to Belgium, my daughter Anne and I drove to this spot. It was still possible to see where the bullets had struck the brick wall. Even more recently, while in Belgium, I again happened to drive by this spot and saw the bullet marks.

On New Year's Day I went, according to custom, to "sign

the book" of the Prince Regent and the Queen Mother. Shortly after my return to the embassy, Sir Hughe came in. We discussed the critical situation at Antwerp, where bombing was continuous and intense. I had suggested to Keeley, our Consul General there, that all of the staff be allowed to sleep outside of Antwerp and take turns at the office. This program was agreeable to all except one man, Edward Anderson, who refused to leave. He felt this would let down the soldiers and sailors who were unable to leave. Anderson was one of the finest and most courageous public servants I ever met, the type of Foreign Service officer who should be encouraged and promoted. He later left the service and decided to live in Belgium.

On January 2 I learned that the British and Canadian air losses at Brussels had been balanced by the American Tactical Air Force. One squadron alone had shot down thirty-three attacking German planes. This group had not been on leave, celebrating New Year's Eve.

Mail was irregular and arrived in batches. On the morning of January 5, I received forty-one letters, the first for many days. A month and a half later, a load of boxes, which had been on the way for weeks, finally reached us. There were 177 boxes of food alone—it was a problem to find places to store them.

Early in 1945 I began to have serious doubts about UNRRA, the United Nations Relief and Rehabilitation Administration. As time went on these doubts changed to a conviction that its operation resulted in a useless, stupid, and occasionally harmful expenditure of money. In the spring I had a frank talk with the British Ambassador. He agreed that UNRRA created great dissatisfaction, but said Churchill had issued instructions to the British Foreign Office to say that UNRRA was a good thing. In spite of Churchill, whose attitude was understandable, UNRRA grew more unpopular day by day. I talked about it with many people. Senators Russell and Maybank, when they came through Brussels, agreed that we should end our policy of wasteful generosity and particularly our sponsorship of UNRRA.[8] One of the efforts which aroused my antipathy was the UNRRA recruitment program for Germany. Although the Belgian Government had refused to recognize UNRRA, its staff was recruiting Belgian doctors and nurses to work in Germany. Belgian doctors were getting forty-three thousand francs a year, but UNRRA was offering them between one hundred five thousand and two hundred twenty-eight thousand francs. Belgian nurses were getting twenty-two thousand to thirty-nine thousand francs but were offered from forty-four thousand to eighty-eight thousand francs by UNRRA, with many additional privileges. By early summer seventy doctors, over one hundred trained Belgian nurses, plus nine hundred other Belgians had been recruited by UNRRA. The Belgians were not only resentful of the great harm done to Belgian hospitals and medical services by this outrageous program, but felt that money was thrown away by compensating these employees out of all proportion to their abilities. I was also angered and shamed by the action of UNRRA when Von Runstedt attacked. UNRRA representatives had been swarming all over Luxembourg. When the first shot was fired in the Battle of the Bulge, they got from Luxembourg to London with unparalleled speed. UNRRA activities and our generosity in other fields fed our reputation as an easy touch. When the chargé d'affaires of the Italian embassy reported for duty, Uncle Sam paid his way—we were putting out large sums of money to enable our recent enemy to function. I was asked to check up on Italian expenditures in Belgium. My investigation disclosed that the Italian chargé d'affaires was spending three times as much American money as was the American Ambassador.[9]

My ankle had continued to bother me. On January 8 I went to a British hospital in Brussels for an x-ray. When the doctor came out with the x-ray, he asked if I had suffered any pain. I replied that I certainly had. He said, "Well, you've been walking around on a broken ankle."

At this time the most important city in Europe was Antwerp. It was the funnel through which a great part of allied armament and supplies was channeled. It was the prime target for the Germans. They had been hitting the port with V-1's and V-2's for some time, but they now launched a much heavier attack. Among the untold stories of American effectiveness was the defense of Antwerp by Colonel John Armstrong. I visited Armstrong's headquarters, sat in his board room, and watched the indicators on the screen showing the bombs coming over the target area, moving toward Antwerp and dropping out of sight as our anti-aircraft guns knocked them down. As many as a dozen bombs would be in the air at the same time; thirty-seven had been launched against Antwerp that morning before I arrived. In spite of the constant bombing, supplies continued to move. In February, on another trip to Antwerp, I learned from Armstrong that Antwerp was handling more goods than the port of New York; in one day they were unloading as many tanks as were lost in the entire battle of the Ardennes. Not all the consular staff in Antwerp were like Anderson, whose service was heroic. Another man asked to be relieved of service there. He told me how beautifully he had been situated in New Brunswick with riding horses, sail boats, and so forth. He hinted several times at the possibility of a Congressional investigation of the employment of State Department people in a zone of such military danger.

Napoleon said that an army moves on its belly. A nation does not move on its belly, but it must have something to put into it. At the turn of the year, Belgium was facing famine. From the time of my arrival in Brussels I had tried to acquaint Washington with the critical food shortage. As early as December 13 I had cabled:

Discussions with authorities here including SHAEF indicate critical shipping problem may lead Allied authorities in Paris or Washington to cut down food shipments into Belgium. For the next few weeks army has undertaken to supply 2000 calories per day. In my judgment it is essential from every standpoint that this commitment be met. I cannot too strongly urge desirability of utilizing part of either British or American army stores which are at least, if not more than, adequate and in addition or in lieu thereof part of accumulated stocks for Holland which cannot now and may not for several months be used, due to flooding of Holland by Germans.

A temporary investment of food supplies and shipping will in my judgment bring tremendous dividends both in the military field and in the avoidance of irritating and perhaps tragic civilian problems in this country. Belgians are critical of food and cigarettes being given German prisoners while they themselves are on the verge of starvation.

Political situation at the moment quiet, but if food problem is not adequately met I predict serious trouble. The requirement of food and shipping to solve Belgian problem is so small and the benefits from furnishing them are so large I hope this matter will be given most serious and immediate attention by the highest authorities.

The British Ambassador is making a similar representation to his Government today.[10]

I referred to supplies of food in England where millions of tons were stored. From that time on I stressed to Washington and to Eisenhower that at least a part of these supplies should be made available to Belgium. I cabled the Department again when I learned that the two thousand calories commitment was to be abandoned because the same ration could not be given to the Dutch.

It would be impossible to explain satisfactorily the failure to meet it on any such basis. Certainly the fact that the Dutch cannot be fed properly is no reason for not feeding the Belgians, if it is possible to do so. Furthermore, I might point out that the Belgians today are making a very substantial contribution to the war effort not merely in the use of their mines, ports, roads, canals, railroads, and some factories, but that the occupying armies are purchasing and consuming large quantities of vegetables.

On January 17 I referred again to the delicate question of the "stocks in England."

From my analysis the problem appears to involve only the transfer of stocks now in England by means of transportation now in England or under the control of the British, and which transportation I am informed is now available.

On February 2 I cabled:

No lard or fat meat is available. Milk is unavailable except to children or expectant mothers. Old people get none. Black market price of butter is $5.00 a pound.[11]

The British had earlier opposed my plan to fly vital supplies into Belgium by ATC (Air Transport Command). I reported to Washington:

It has been said that the British wish to prevent or postpone an operation which may be of benefit to American aviation in the post-war period.

The Belgians, under pressure from the British, did not encourage the use of ATC transport. But I predicted:

If we offer to bring in food supplies by ATC it will be extremely difficult for the Belgian authorities to do anything but help us bring them in. They probably would wish to support the British attitude in case of conflict with us but neither they nor the British can risk refusing our offer to bring in food and supplies for the benefit of the Belgian people.[12]

My suggestion was not followed. I was full of admiration for the success of the British in looking out for themselves; I was concerned that we were not doing the same.

Late in January it was evident that the Pierlot Government was in trouble; but no ambitious man outside the government wished to come to power at that time. As de Staercke put it, "The old carcasses have floated to the top of the pond, but the live young fish are swimming far below the surface where they cannot be seen." On February 2 the government fell. De Staercke gave me a complete account of the day's activities.[13] The Socialists had resigned from the government and demanded a full Parliamentary debate. Pierlot attacked the illegality and impropriety of the Socialists' resignation until after interrogation in Parliament. As usual, he was being legalistic. On February 3 I cabled the Department:

It is impossible to say who will furnish the necessary administrative talent but . . . the man whose stature seems to grow is Van Acker. He is willing to form a Cabinet if given complete powers. The fact that he is willing to run the risks of government under these conditions is hopeful; it shows that he has courage and determination.

I had a long talk with Van Acker yesterday. He spoke with assurance of what he would do if he were made Prime Minister. All that he asks is—first, a guarantee that after the Belgians have produced enough coal for the military effort they will be permitted to distribute the balance among themselves as they see fit; second, that a definite importation of supplies be guaranteed by the Allies and carried out. If these things are done, he is willing to undertake to govern.

Van Acker is Flemish, a solid but not a brilliant man who seems to have the support of a wide range of political elements. He has one distinct advantage over most of the members of the present Government; he was here in Belgium during the occupation.[14]

Achille Van Acker became the new Prime Minister. The food problem remained, but a new captain was at the helm. As time went on Van Acker and I developed a close friendship. When he would come straight to the American embassy after visiting the King, Spaak, with a grin, would say he was getting jealous, because Van Acker was reporting to me first.

By February 5 there was a threat of real famine and the British Twenty-first Army Group agreed to advance supplies. On February 12 I cabled:

I am informed Kronacher has purchased food in America and is ready to ship it. It is incomprehensible to me that he has not been

permitted to do so . . . Belgium is literally living from day to day
and the situation is so critical that I cannot comprehend any
action in Washington which prevents the shipment of food actually purchased there.[15]

Many years later, rummaging through files in the State
Department, I found a memorandum which indicated that
someone had been reading my cables.

March 2, 1945. Ref. my letter February 1, 1945.
I think you will find the attached dispatches worth glancing at.
They are pure Sawyer and reflect the Ambassador's intense personal concentration on his job which, as he conceives it, is to do
right by Belgium to the credit of his mission and the United
States. His determined efforts to move discussion of Belgian problem to Brussels and away from London and Versailles apparently
has had a good practical effect and may have improved Belgian
morale.

From the beginning I had difficulty in persuading our State
Department to permit discussions of Belgian affairs to take
place in Brussels. On one occasion I was asked by the British
ambassador if I would go to London to discuss the Belgian
food situation. I refused to go; the place to talk about this
subject was Brussels. I then received a cable from the State
Department in Washington, asking me to go to London. I told
them also that I would not go. Next, I was asked to go to Paris.
This also I refused to do, realizing full well that I might be
replaced for my intransigence. However, I was finally able to
report that everyone had come to agree with me and Generals
Bedell Smith and Grasset would come to Brussels.

On the morning of Friday, February 13, General Smith and
his staff came in from Paris. We met with General Erskine and
the British Ambassador. The meeting began with a speech by
Smith, who monopolized the conversation and indicated that
everything was settled. I remained silent during this mono-
logue. After it ended I began to ask questions. The atmosphere
changed rapidly, and before the conference was over Smith
was listening attentively to what I had to say. It became clear

that Eisenhower and Smith had not been correctly informed about the supply situation in Belgium. They had agreed to ship twenty-five thousand tons of food, but they did not know that only ten thousand tons had been sent. The next day General Smith met with Prime Minister Van Acker and repeated almost word for word much of what I had said the previous afternoon. Van Acker, instead of asking for things he wanted from the Allies, told what he proposed to do. He would be responsible for everything but food. If the Allies brought in food he would see that the other problems were solved. He had been Minister of Labor, but he would not tolerate strikes. If black-market operators did not obey the law he would take over their businesses. This was a refreshing and new approach. Van Acker made a great impression on Smith, who promised him that the Allied commitments would be met. When General Smith left, his attitude had changed; he was most cordial, urged me to come to Paris to see him and said he would send a plane for me.[16]

At my urging, Eisenhower sent a cable to General Marshall, parts of which read as follows:

The new Prime Minister gives the impression of being a strong man, and he has informed my representatives that he intends to take what I consider a very courageous line of action to insure continued production of coal and operation of the docks and railways. The best, and in fact, the only support we can give this new government is to meet our food commitments on schedule.

It is urgently requested that 100,000 tons of food from the United Kingdom stocks be made available immediately to 21st Army Group to arrive in March to offset lag in shipping. United States shipments for March consumption can *NOT* arrive in time. To expedite action I am notifying War Office of items and quantities included in the 100,000 tons. . . .

I regard the situation produced in Belgium and Holland by the lag in the arrival of Civil Affairs ships as being sufficiently serious to warrant civil affairs requirements being treated as a matter of operational urgency.[17]

On February 14 I cabled:

In my judgment the solution to the immediate problem is a
diversion of a very small part of the very large "catastrophe" or
"collapse" stores now held in England. I am told these stocks
amount to approximately seven million tons. I am also told that it
is possible they are being kept in storage so long that some of
them will be worthless if they are not soon used. . . . This is the
real and simple and perhaps the only solution to the immediate
Belgian supply problem and *it can be settled only at the highest
level.*

On February 22 I cabled:

The British Ambassador told me yesterday evening that a Cabinet meeting had been hurriedly called by Mr. Churchill and an
agreement had been reached to divert to Belgium 100,000 tons of
"catastrophe stocks" now stored in England. I am greatly pleased
and relieved at this action.

The British, however, did not deliver, and were apparently
expecting part of their commitment to come from America. On
February 26 I cabled:

No one here wants to be unfair to the British but there is a
suspicion which is growing that they are holding large stocks of
food in England which are not necessary for their use and will not
be necessary on any emergency basis, while the emergency in
Belgium is critical. If this is true, can we not produce action on
their part by disclosure of the real figures?

If the real figures show they are retaining supplies far in excess
of their needs they cannot complain if this is made public. It
might be well also to add to these figures the amounts actually
delivered to Belgium by England and the U.S. respectively. If the
British object to making public these figures on the basis of
military necessity, there can be no such objection to making them
available to the Belgian Government.

In an effort to force action I sent repeated nagging cables,
asking for specific information. A sample, on March 15, read:

How many ships from North America are now loaded for Belgian National Program and how many will have left from beginning to end of March? [18]

I was also urging that some supplies for Belgium be obtained from Germany. Every civilian, British or American, with whom I talked approved this suggestion. Clement Attlee, with whom I discussed the matter, said he was in complete accord. But the British and American military authorities objected. They were anxious to save themselves trouble and problems during the contemplated occupation by keeping ample supplies in Germany.

John Ernest Solvay, head of the vast Belgian Solvay empire, called on me. He had just come from England. His English friends assumed that the British must do something to keep the Germans from starving and he remarked that both America and Britain had a childlike sentimentality toward their enemies. Incidentally, he also held strongly the opinion that we should not share the secret of the atom bomb. He had little faith in the future. The French were helpless. Neither the British nor the Americans had a policy; but the Russians did. "When one of three men knows exactly what he wants, and the other two have no idea what they want, the first man will have his way." [19]

As a sidelight on the supply situation, I personally discovered in an unused subway tremendous stores of clothing, soap, and other articles which had originally come from the United States, had been lying in England for two years, and had been recently sent by the British to Belgium. From this underground cache tons of clothing were being distributed, with no supervision. Fifteen thousand men's suits and thirty-six thousand pairs of women's stockings had been sent to Houffalize on February 16, although there was nothing like that number of people, men or women, in Houffalize. It is probable that much of this material reached the black market.

10 *Peace*

THE BATTLE of the Bulge had come and gone. The enemy's frenzied and final effort had reached a climax at Bastogne where General Anthony C. McAuliffe had answered the German demand for surrender with the classic reply of "Nuts!" On February 9 I set out for Luxembourg. As we passed through the scenes of the fighting, the roads became impassable and my Cadillac ended its trip at Bastogne. Colonel Warden, the commander there, showed us what was left of the ruined town, and I met many who had survived the attack, including a group of nurses. I reached Luxembourg by jeep after dark.

The next day (my birthday) was a busy one. I heard many stories about parachutists who had been dropped behind our lines. Of the first wave, twenty-eight were picked up—all wearing American uniforms, all speaking good English and all immediately shot. Before they were captured they had murdered a number of Luxembourg citizens. They had also wantonly killed cattle, hogs, and horses. Following breakfast I made an early call on General Patton, whose headquarters were then in Luxembourg. This was my first meeting with the famous general. When I entered his headquarters that morn-

125

ing, Patton was seated on a platform raised a foot above the floor. There was a large white bulldog by his side. His holster held an ivory-handled revolver. He was a big man, and furnished a marked contrast to Field Marshal Montgomery whom I had found even smaller than I had expected.

That same day I met Prince Felix for the first time. He was fine looking, strongly built and erect, and seemed much younger than his fifty-one years. An intelligent and agreeable person, he had a keen sense of humor. In my presence, he engaged Foreign Minister Bech in a most frank discussion about recognizing the Polish government in Lublin. They were greatly concerned about Russia. Before leaving I invited Prince Felix to dine with me in Brussels the following Sunday. He said he would be happy to do so.[1]

The road back was worse than it had been the night before. It was a sea of mud, rocks, and holes. From Bastogne I went to Houffalize, where the destruction was far greater. Tanks, trucks, wrecked planes, dead horses, and cows were everywhere. Although people had smiled in every town through which we had passed, no one smiled in Houffalize. We passed through another scene of desolation in Marche and drove on to Brussels, arriving at the embassy late in the wintry afternoon.

When Prince Felix came to dinner, he talked freely. He was suspicious of the Belgians and told a most amusing story of how Camille Gutt planned to meet Du Pong, the Luxembourg Prime Minister. The interview was postponed because of the German panzer attack. Later a Luxembourg representative in Brussels asked to see the portfolio of the subject to be discussed and was amazed to find in it a complete report, including questions and answers, on the interview between Gutt and Du Pong, which had not taken place.

As time went on, I came to have a growing admiration, and even affection, for Paul Henri Spaak. He was witty, gay, and emotional, a charming companion with a "face like Churchill and a voice like Charles Boyer." He is, with the exception of Newton D. Baker, the most moving orator I have ever heard.

He is a Socialist; but at no time did I have any feeling that this ideology was important—his only concern was the welfare of Belgium. As my admiration grew, it occurred to me that Spaak would be a great addition to the conference about to take place in San Francisco. Late in February I suggested to the State Department that he be invited to attend. Shortly thereafter I received word that he would be a delegate. At the time he was in Paris talking with de Gaulle, but upon his return I told him what I had recommended. He was greatly pleased at the possibility that he might be invited. I could not tell him that the invitation was on its way. A few days later I presented it, and he immediately asked many questions—How many persons would be in the delegation? How would they travel to the United States? What was the weather like in San Francisco? I told him the weather in San Francisco would be a great improvement on the weather in Belgium. I said that I knew he was thrilled over the invitation but would have some headaches. His first problem would be to select the delegation, for many would want to go.[2] Soon after this I had occasion to talk with Sir Hughe. He was surprised that he had not been given advance notice of the Spaak invitation. I said I had been under a pledge of secrecy and had assumed that his own Foreign Office would let him know. It was comforting to discover that even the well-run British Foreign Office was not perfect.

As the Germans were driven further back across Western Europe, both the Belgians and Luxembourgers began to talk about what they would like in the way of reparations. Belgium wanted a small land addition, including Aix-la-Chapelle, which would enable them to annex a power dam built by the Germans. Spaak said he thought this was a modest amount to ask for all the damage done to Belgium by the Germans. I agreed. The Belgians and Luxembourgers each wanted a dam—the Belgians wanted a dam already built; the Luxembourgers wanted one to be built for them.

On March 12 Harrington and I went with Commodore John

Hutton to downtown Brussels to see a captured German one-man submarine. It carried two torpedoes and had an operating distance of one hundred miles. The Commodore said they had destroyed five of them between 5:00 A.M. and 1:00 P.M. that day and had been destroying them continuously during the preceding few weeks. An interesting sidelight on this exhibit was the crowd of Belgians who gathered to look at my parked Cadillac, completely ignoring the submarine. The submarine was a minor incident of a war already too long drawn out; the Cadillac was something new.

On March 14, I drove to Louvain. The weather was the finest since we had arrived in Brussels. I spent two hours looking over the ruins of the university—what the Germans had done in 1940, what the British and Americans had done in 1944, and what German buzz bombs had done recently. The most poignant spectacle was the destroyed library, rebuilt after the last war with contributions from school children in America. This beautiful structure, designed by Whitney Warren, had held 900,000 volumes. The Germans bombed and fired the library and would not let Monsignor Waeyenbergh go in to remove any of the precious documents, even when the damage was complete. He showed me, however, a secret compartment where they had managed to save some of the most precious manuscripts and about fifteen hundred volumes of valuable books.[3]

During these weeks there was a continual parade of important figures, most of them from England. There were of course many Americans, the most prominent of them being General Patton. Patton was idolized by the Belgians. He was invited by the Prince Regent to come to Brussels to be decorated. After the ceremony, as he drove from the palace to the embassy, enormous crowds gathered to cheer him. Upon his arrival, he was mobbed by the press. After giving a brief statement he asked me what I thought of it. When I said I thought it was fine, he said, "I must be very careful; I have got myself into lots of trouble lately by not keeping my Goddamn mouth shut." Shortly before that he had given a statement that the Nazis were like the Republicans or the Democrats in the United States. His conversation was extremely forthright and interesting, although vulgar. He was not modest; but he had a sense of humor. Having been ordered by Eisenhower to cover Von Runstedt's flank, he spent the first night in the field with no one but his sergeant. The next day his sergeant asked, "Why do you keep all those officers around, we can run this campaign all by ourselves." In commenting upon his Sicilian campaign, I said that he had traveled four times as fast as Montgomery; he commented "Four times? Hell, I traveled ten times as fast as Montgomery!" We saw him later that night at a reception given by the Russian Ambassador. This affair exhibited no evidence of simplicity. The Ambassador wore an elaborate uniform, his wife was exceedingly well dressed, the house was beautifully furnished and the entertainment elaborate. There was an interesting story circulated even at the reception that the Ambassador's wife was not his wife, but a spy planted by the Russian secret service to keep an eye on him. Patton seemed to be enjoying himself. In our earlier conversation he asked whether or not he should go; I said I thought he should. He replied that he would not stay long as "You know they don't like me." Yet he was still there when my wife and I left.[4]

Among the interesting visitors from England was Clement Attlee. Attlee was a diminutive figure who smoked a pipe incessantly. He was quiet, but clear and forceful.[5] When I voiced my admiration for Churchill as an orator, he asked if I had ever heard Lloyd George. Attlee said that in his prime Lloyd George presented a magnificent spectacle as he addressed the Commons. He told an amusing story of a conspiracy of silence against Churchill, when he was about to attack Attlee's Labor Party. Attlee suggested to his group that, instead of replying, they say nothing. Churchill rose and began with some bitter and insulting statements; he then paused and looked around, waiting for someone to interrupt. There was complete silence. When this had happened three or four times, he ran out of steam and sat down.

Since the British Twenty-first Army had its headquarters in Brussels, I met Montgomery from time to time. Like General Patton, he was always putting on an act. Patton had his white bulldog, Monty had his cat. He was small, dried-up, and unimpressive, but possessed a sense of humor and a keen mind. He enjoyed reminiscing. He had an extremely high regard for General Marshall and his handling of the whole United States military effort. He spoke amusingly of the problem of picking generals in wartime. He suspected the best method was that of the Russians; before any big war they poison the older generals because the unfit rise during peacetime. They then promote the younger group to make war.

One day I was handed a cable, drafted by me, in which I noted changes. An embassy secretary explained that the department had ordered us to save money wherever possible and this included cutting the ambassador's cables. I ordered the cable sent exactly as I had worded it. I then addressed the department, indicating my enthusiasm for saving money but telling how money could really be saved. I sent a letter and *not* a cable, saying that large sums could be saved by using cables *only* when a letter would not suffice. I cited a specific instance. We had been ordered by the department to *cable daily* extended quotations from the Belgian press. I pointed out that no information disclosed by this vast expenditure called for any peremptory action. Information furnished by mail, instead of cable, would be adequate. Furthermore, quotations from the press, unexplained, gave a completely erroneous impression of Belgian opinion. There were two Flemish and ten Walloon newspapers, but the population was divided almost equally, as was public opinion. Also, I doubted that these cables were read with the care which would justify this outlay of money—if they were read at all—or that any action was ever taken based upon what they contained. I concluded that "if the Department really wants to know the state of opinion in Belgium, ask the ambassador." I repeated this suggestion personally upon my return to Washington later in the year.

While the shortage of food had been acute in the early part of the year, the Belgian food problem had vanished by spring. However, egged on by UNRRA, our State Department began to work itself into an agony of concern about the starving people of Western Europe, including the Germans. Toward the latter part of April, I received a complicated and unintelligible cable announcing a program. I replied on April 28:

I am told that it is planned to import 300,000 tons of wheat per month beginning with June, some of which is to be used for Germany. Entirely aside from the question of our obligation to feed Germany there is the question of our ability to store and mill this quantity of wheat. The storage capacity of mills in Belgium and Northern France is 110,000 tons and the milling capacity is 126,000 tons per month. If wheat is brought into Antwerp in any such quantity as is contemplated, it will spoil.[6]

On May 4 I cabled the department:

I see signs of our usual aptitude for generosity. . . . The food situation in Europe is not as acute as has been alleged. We should not relax our efforts to help our Allies, but we should not allow ourselves to become hysterical. Supplies of all kinds are piling up at Antwerp. During April the American civil affairs program imported 112,000 tons of food, 45,000 tons of which have been moved to Lille, Liege, Charleroi, and Verdun; 67,000 tons remain undistributed.

In the matter of food I strongly urge that we perform promptly and fully for Belgium and our other Allies. This will not, however, call for "the severe cuts that must consequently be taken in the United States consumption" referred to in your telegram.

What I fear and what others fear is that this belt tightening is to be for the benefit of Germany; or will work out that way. Recently in a military hospital here I visited American soldiers who had been released from German prison camps. The stories of their sufferings confirm the reports which have been coming through every channel with reference to the treatment of prisoners by the Germans. Our soldiers who have been prisoners of war would have starved to death if it had not been for Red Cross supplies. While we were observing strictly the Geneva Convention and giving German prisoners much better food than that being received by the Belgians our soldiers were being marched hundreds of miles across Germany and were given either nothing at all or one loaf of bread per day for nine men, two small potatoes, and occasionally a cup of ersatz coffee.

The Belgians discuss our probable attitude when hostilities cease. When told that we cannot let the Germans starve, the answer is, Why Not? If we have any obligation to keep them from starving, upon what is it based?

Furthermore, the Germans will not starve. If put to it they will take care of themselves. I served with the Army of Occupation in Germany after the last war and saw with my own eyes the adequate supplies of food which the German citizens had stored in their cellars at a time when certain Generals were wiring to England that the Germans were starving. The same pleas will be made again. The American citizen and the American housewife should be willing to make sacrifices to aid those of our Allies who are in need. They should not be asked to make any sacrifices to help our recent enemies.

One further thought—we have been considering the American housewife. Is it too early to think of the American taxpayer? [7]

Archibald MacLeish, Assistant Secretary for Public and Cultural Relations, and Willard Thorpe, Assistant Secretary, had done several broadcasts telling of the great need to help Western Europe. I wrote to MacLeish:

I suggested several months ago that you come over here to visit us, and I would be delighted if you could now find occasion to do so. I think you would find that there is no great cause for alarm with reference to food and clothing. I personally have no sympathy whatever with the view that we need to make sacrifices for

Germany or Italy. The Germans will not starve. I have been in Germany myself and my observation is confirmed by almost everyone coming from there: the Germans are in excellent health, the food is good, and while their ration is being reduced and may be reduced further, they will be no worse off than were the Belgians under the German occupation. I am convinced that the United States is regarded in Germany as a nation of "suckers" to be taken advantage of as long as our naïvete persists.[8]

Late in March my military aide, Colonel Dunn, informed me that his daughter had met a young American pilot while coming over on the *Queen Elizabeth*. The pilot's name was John Sawyer. When asked what he looked like, the girl seemed to have no clear picture, except that he was very young to be a pilot. It was my son John. Since he was then only nineteen, her impression was understandable.

Late one afternoon the Archduke Otto of Austria dropped in. He recalled meeting me the previous year in Palm Beach. He was in Brussels to avoid being in Paris, where he was being sought by a Gestapo agent—the Czech who rescued Mussolini from the Allies. When I asked him why a Czech should be operating on the side of the German Gestapo, the Duke launched into a discussion of the Czechs. Otto admired the Czechs—they were the only nation able to be on both sides of a war. At home they collaborated fully with the Germans while Beneš was creating the impression in London that they were doing the opposite. Otto referred to a night in New York when the son of Masaryk, inebriated, had boasted that ever since 1508 the Czechs had managed to keep on both sides of every war. Otto spoke feelingly of the Poles as a nation with great ideals and willing, if necessary, to die for them. He also spoke amusingly of the food shortage in Paris; he felt certain some Parisian housewife would before long murder the French Food Commissioner because he was so unbelievably inefficient.[9]

During this period I was becoming incensed at the timid and unrealistic attitude of our State Department. I was particularly irritated by their approach to our "Prisoners of War" problem. In this they were supported by the legalistic attitude of the Judge Advocate General. On March 20 I cabled:

In the Ardennes the Germans planted thousands of mines. Before the people of that area can cultivate their fields and use their premises these mines must be removed. It is felt that because of Article 23 of the Geneva Convention, German prisoners now working in the Ardennes cannot be used for removing the mines which they themselves put there. As a result Belgian citizens risk their own lives while Germans sit by in safety, and while the Belgian's stomach is empty of food he sees the German prisoners sit by the roadside contemptuously and eat food which is in quantity and quality better than anything he has seen for many years. It is difficult to describe the depth of fury which this creates in the Belgian breast.

The general purposes of the prisoners-of-war convention are clear and commendable. It is obvious, however, that the framers did not visualize some of the fantastic results which have occurred. Every document couched in general terms must, of course, be interpreted. Other agreements have been liberally or at least reasonably interpreted to make them applicable to present-day conditions. There would seem to be no reason why this cannot be done with the prisoners-of-war section of the Geneva Convention. For instance, some authority has interpreted the Geneva Convention to prevent the employment of German prisoners in coal mines. Although thousands of miners in Belgium and in the United States are engaged in mining for the benefit of the war effort and as a part of our normal economy, we cannot put German prisoners to work. The military authorities say their hands are tied. Can't they be untied or at least loosened a bit? Why not let the provisions of the Geneva Convention be interpreted by General Officers on the ground dealing with the specific problem? This will in no way involve an official relaxation of the provisions of the Convention but will permit a practical solution of a problem which at the moment, in this area at least, is creating difficulties among our Allies.[10]

My suggestion was followed.

The Allied armies were now well into Germany and I de-

cided to visit our commanders at the front. On March 24 I
went with Major Browning, a former governor of Tennessee,
to Ninth Army Headquarters. We had breakfast at 5:45. The
sun came up about 7:15 as we drove through Louvain. In
Germany my first impression was that there was little difference between Germany and Holland. This impression soon
vanished. No Allied soldiers were seen speaking to or noticing
any of the civilians, even children. They were under orders not
to fraternize. This, I might add, did not last long.[11]

On the way to Gladbach we stopped off at the Nineteenth
Tactical Air Force Headquarters, where for an hour and a half
I stood in the control room and heard the conversations between the control room and the pilots, as the latter were
making their attacks. "Here we go!—an engine and twenty
loaded freightcars ahead of us"; then the rattle of gun fire—
"we got him!"

German cities had taken terrific punishment—Aachen, Dort-
mund, Cologne, Krefeld, and others. However, the Germans
did not seem downcast. They eyed us, with no particular
interest. We noticed many farmers working in the rich fields.
Their stock seemed to be in good condition. We arrived at
General William H. Simpson's headquarters at 10:45, but the
general was away, on the attack. While we had seen nothing
moving on the road I had known that the Ninth Army was to
begin its attack that day. The general's headquarters, situated
in an old courthouse, was one of the few buildings in Gladbach
not completely destroyed.

There was some evidence of friction between the Americans
and the British. The crossing of the Rhine was on schedule,
except at Wesel, where the British had asked the Americans to
put a bridge. The Americans said they would do so if the
British would clear the other side of the river. The British had
landed two commando brigades and it was assumed that they
would get the enemy off the opposite bank. This had still not
been accomplished when I left the following morning.

While waiting for General Simpson to return, I motored through the country and visited a camp for displaced persons. There were 3,600 of them, representing twenty-two nationalities. The camp did not smell too sweet, although large amounts of disinfectant had been used. The colonel who was our guide said that he had entered immediately after the Germans left. There was a foot of filth and excrement on the floor and the stench was so foul he could not go in. Eight people died before they could be taken to a hospital.

The discipline was good and there was an attitude of friendliness. Most of the DP's at this camp were Russian and I found one group of twenty-five Russian women, peeling potatoes and singing at the top of their voices. The DP's I saw looked well and well-fed. A loudspeaker on a truck went through the camp, telling the inmates in each of their twenty-two languages what they were supposed to do.

I went to Krefeld with General Galleen and on to Erdingen to see a part of the Krupp works. This building was being shelled intermittently, but we went in anyway. It was not the main Krupp plant, but it was immense. There were about seven hundred fifty thousand tons of steel in various stages of fabrication. As we entered the enormous structure water was spouting into the air from a steel pipe. A shell had come over a short time before and broken the pipe.

As we were about to leave I was asked if I would like to see an observation post on the front line. I said that I would. We went through winding roads into what was apparently another part of the Krupp plant and came to some sheds, where we found a company of American soldiers. We went up two flights of stairs and into a little room at the top. There a soldier with field glasses stood near two small windows. I looked out and found that we were on the very edge of the Rhine. The Rhine was not as wide as I had expected and the banks were not steep. I could see nothing except clouds of dust where our shells were crashing into the town on the other side of the

river. One German shell came our way but I never knew where
it hit.

We arrived back at Simpson's headquarters at 6:00 P.M.
When we had washed and come downstairs, General Simpson
came in. He was extremely friendly and impressive—tall, bald,
and rugged. The attack was going well. During dinner he
speculated as to whether he or "George," as he called General
Patton, would get to Berlin first. He and Patton had been in
the same class at West Point. He also spoke of meeting
Churchill and Montgomery on Sunday morning. Churchill was
most anxious to cross the Rhine with Monty—first! The general chatted with us until 9:30, when he excused himself,
saying he was forced to leave "by reason of a little business."
In view of the fact he was directing a major part of the final
battle of the war, this was a slight understatement.

Our next stop was to be First Army Headquarters, to see
General Courtney Hicks Hodges. We bumped through the
ruins of Cologne in a jeep sent by him. Cologne had been so
bombed that it seemed as if a strong wind would blow down
the entire city. The head of civilian government in Cologne
told us of finding sixty decapitated bodies when he moved into
the city. These people had been executed just before his arrival and the heads removed to prevent identification. We were
advised against going into the cathedral; it was an American
Army observation post and under heavy fire. We did not enter
it but did climb six stories in an adjacent building which was
littered with debris. It seemed as if it might collapse at any
moment and bury us under the rubble. From the top of this
building we viewed a scene of utter destruction. After a few
minutes, we slid down and went on. Everywhere were signs of
violent fighting; overturned tanks, burned-out shells, broken-
down trucks, and so forth. As we arrived at General Hodges'
headquarters, he was receiving reports of the battle. The attack was going beautifully at all points but one. His plan was
to encircle Coblenz and meet up with General Patton further

east. I was impressed by Hodges as I had been by Simpson, although he was a wholly different type. His staff was competent, alert, tough, and on the job.

The next day after luncheon I went with a Colonel Lewis from Cincinnati to visit another DP camp. On the way Lewis told of a German "gentleman farmer" who had been employing Russian slave laborers. He had thirty-eight persons working seven days a week, twelve hours a day. This had gone on for three years. At first he refused to talk with Colonel Lewis, sending out word that he was sleeping. When the Colonel sent in a peremptory demand, the German came out dressed in plus fours, immaculately groomed. The colonel indicated that reforms were in order. The farmer agreed to increase the wages of his laborers 100 per cent, cut down the hours to ten a day and the days to six a week. Lewis then told the "laborers" that they were free to leave. Strangely enough, they chose to remain. They suspected that the offer of liberation might not be real and were not sure what would await them at home.

That afternoon on our way back we came through several badly damaged cities. The worst bombed was Duren. The odor of dead bodies filled the air. No one was on the streets except a few American soldiers. Allied authorities estimated that sixteen-thousand dead Germans lay buried under the ruins of that city. At Aachen we found only a few buildings which had withstood the bombings. These had been built for the Gestapo. They had walls six to eight feet thick with a complete heating, cooling, and ventilating system. They were designed to withstand anything and they had. Interestingly enough, every one of them had a large red cross painted on top of it.

I was in Brussels on April 14 when I learned of the death of President Roosevelt. I promptly sent the following cable to Truman:

Personal for the President:

We are thinking today of ROOSEVELT. We are also thinking of you. Over here we will do everything we can to assist you.

On April 18, in accordance with custom, I sent the following letter:

My dear Mr. President:

In order that you may be quite free to make any replacements or changes among your chiefs of missions, including this one, I am hereby respectfully submitting my formal resignation as Ambassador to Belgium and Minister to Luxembourg.[12]

Our Memorial Service for Roosevelt was impressive. Queen Elizabeth was there and all the members of the diplomatic corps. I walked with the Queen to her car and chatted with her for a minute or two before she left.

While my association with Roosevelt had not been intimate, I had seen him many times in Washington, Hyde Park, and on campaign trains. I soon learned of his ability to keep visitors from getting their messages across, especially when he sensed that the message was one he did not want to hear. He would begin the conversation and carry on entertainingly and uninterruptedly until it was time for the visitor to leave. On occasion, however, he talked with me frankly; and really listened. I recall one conversation during his third campaign, when I said that his only handicap was the normal tendency of people to tire, quoting the story of Aristides, put to death by the Athenians because they were tired of hearing him called "The Just." Roosevelt then made an interesting comment upon Republican strategy. They had charged "Regimentation." "They will get nowhere talking about 'regimentation.' The public does not give a damn about it. They should talk about my weakness in administration. There I am really open to attack." Roosevelt was a charming man, especially after one or two drinks. Yet few of his actions were governed by emotion. He was a calculating individual and prided himself upon his objectivity and political skill. Roosevelt was sometimes charged with not keeping his promises. I was not bothered by this characteristic. If possible, every man should keep his promises. But when a man becomes President of the United States his decisions and actions should be governed solely by the country's needs, as he sees them, at that time. Roosevelt was keenly aware of the dramatic effect of the things he did. His physical courage was amazing. Crippled as he was, he never gave in. I recall a summer night in Cleveland when he spoke to an enormous throng. He was obviously in pain. He gripped the stand in front of him with both hands, steadying himself, sweat pouring down his face; but he was as gay and outgoing as if nothing was wrong.

The end of the war was in sight when I flew to Rheims on April 20 to lunch with General Bedell Smith. I had a most interesting two hours.[13] He told of examining certain documents which described events before the Belgian Government went to London. They appeared unfavorable to King Leopold. He also told of a dinner in Brussels where the King of England at the close of his speech referred to "those Americans who are over here trying to run everything." The following day his American aide, whose presence had been overlooked, told the King what he thought of his statement. The King was very apologetic and said he had drunk too much and did not mean what he said. Smith spoke of treasures we had captured in a salt mine, including great baskets of gold-fillings and plates from the mouths of persons whom the Germans had liquidated. He also said that any time I wished to travel across Germany he would furnish the transportation. He more than made good on this promise. During the conversation I mentioned that my son John was in the Air Force. Smith said it would be no trouble to have John visit me in Brussels. I said I would not wish to embarrass the boy in any way. He said that I need not worry; John would not be embarrassed. Three days after I had lunched with Smith, John showed up in the early evening at the Embassy. He had received orders "to report to Brussels to follow orders of the Commanding General," had hitchhiked his way to Paris by plane, by another plane to an airport near

Brussels and by jeep to the Embassy. He and I talked until
2:00 A.M. The following morning I took him with me on a trip
to Antwerp. The bombing there had stopped. John went with
me that night to a showing of "Gone With The Wind." After
the showing, which lasted four hours, the entire staff came to
the Embassy for a buffet supper. The following day I was too
busy to have much time with John, though I did drive him to
the Ravenstein Golf Club. He left about 5:00 P.M., feeling that
he would not be back again. He expected to be ordered to the
Pacific.

Many of us who respected and admired the Prince Regent
felt that he deserved some decoration from our Government. I
had discussed this with Bedell Smith and others, and it was
decided to give him the Chief Commander Degree of the
Legion of Merit, the highest decoration which the United
States Government could give to a non-military figure. It was
desirable, in view of the possibility of King Leopold's early
return, that this be done immediately. The ceremony was
carried out in the same palace room where I had presented my
credentials. I read the citation. The Prince was deeply
moved.[14]

On May 7 I left Brussels early in the morning for Bruges, to
watch the Procession of the Holy Blood. This ceremony is
centuries old but had been discontinued since 1939. It was one
of the most picturesque, fascinating, and beautiful things I
ever watched. We were transported back into the Middle Ages.
The monks and their robes and many spectacles out of the past
were in striking contrast to a motorcycle which was trying as
best it could to meander through the procession and the accompanying throng. The blue sky above and the white swans
on the canals added to the colorful scene.

As we were returning, I saw flags flying, banners waving
from windows, and trucks covered with flowers and trees.
Crowds of people jammed the streets. I turned on the radio
and found that the war was to be over the following day. After

arriving in Brussels we heard and saw more of the celebration. In fact, it lasted all night. The next day I received the following message from General Eisenhower:

A representative of the German High Command signed the unconditional surrender of all German Land, Sea and Air Forces in Europe to the Allied Expeditionary Force and simultaneously to the Soviet High Command at 0141 Hours Central European Time, Seven May under which all forces will cease active operations at 00012 Hours Nine May.

Effective immediately all offensive operations by Allied Expeditionary Force will cease and troops will remain in present positions.[15]

Suddenly, my problems as ambassador had changed.

11 Belgium and Her King

THERE ARE but few kings left in this world. Many Communist leaders are as despotic as any monarch who ever lived; but the old king racket, as history has known it, seems to be petering out. This is well. That a man without brains or ability or even sanity should control the lives of his fellows and enjoy the prestige and the vast privileges of a monarch merely because he is the son of his father certainly makes no sense. However, in certain countries a king seems to furnish some mysteriously vital element of government. This is true in England; and in Belgium.

During my early days in Brussels, the King had been a distant and relatively unimportant figure. There had, of course, been discussions about King Leopold and his future.[1] There was a wide divergence in Belgian opinion about the King's conduct before and after his surrender. The government of Belgium was socialist. The socialists and the French, or Walloon, sections were bitterly anti-German and, to a lesser extent anti-Leopold. On the other hand, the Flemish sections of Belgium and the strong Catholic party were pro-Leopold. In January I had been approached by Louis Frédéricq, who had

143

been Leopold's chef de cabinet. He gave me a fascinating account of the King's capture and his conduct from that time on until Frédéricq saw him taken away by the Germans on June 6 or 7, 1944. Frédéricq was anxious to persuade me that the King was like any other prisoner captured with his troops and had not negotiated nor cooperated with the Germans.

Frédéricq said he had known nothing of the King's second marriage until he heard about a comment from a doorman at the Laecken Palace, who had learned of it from a postman, who had opened a letter sent by the Cardinal and discovered that His Eminence had performed the marriage ceremony between the King and Liliane Baels. The King had been imprisoned by the Germans in the Laecken Palace. At some point during his imprisonment, Liliane Baels, later known as the Princess de Réthy, daughter of the governor of the province of Hainaut, came to the palace to live. After some months she and the King were married. It was said that Cardinal Van Roey had urged the marriage. This was the King's second marriage. Queen Astrid, his first wife, had died in an automobile accident in Switzerland.[2] Leopold himself was driving the car in which she was killed. At the time of my service, Astrid was a saint in the eyes of the Belgian people. Her picture decorated windows in every part of the country. Her simplicity, kindness, and devotion to her children and to her husband were praised by everyone. Belgians were shocked to learn that their King, blessed by his marriage to Astrid, had married a commoner. The nobility regarded this action with scorn and others were hardly more enthusiastic. As one businessman put it to me, "My daughter is as good looking and attractive and competent as the girl he married. I don't know why he could not have picked her."

As spring approached, no one knew where the King was or that he was still alive. He was supposedly held by the Germans; but no one was certain. Late in March, as the end of the war approached, the fate of the King became a constant topic

Elizabeth, former Queen of the Belgians, with Ambassador Sawyer leaving the church at Brussels following the memorial service for Franklin D. Roosevelt, April 16, 1945.

At Ambassador Sawyer's request President Truman came out of his plane to meet Prime Minister Van Acker just before leaving Brussels for the Potsdam conference with Churchill and Stalin.

Ambassador Sawyer with General Eisenhower and General Jacobs, May 30, 1945.

Memorial Day, 1945, at Henri-Chapelle Cemetery, near Liege. Left to right: General Jacobs, General Eisenhower, Ambassador Sawyer.

On the cruiser *Augusta* at Antwerp, July 15, 1945, as President Truman was on his way to Potsdam. Left to right: Admiral Leahy, Admiral Stark, Secretary of State James Byrnes, Ambassador Sawyer, President Truman, General Eisenhower.

Ambassador Sawyer with General Eisenhower and Admiral Stark boarding the *Augusta*, July 15, 1945.

of conversation. Spaak talked with me at length; he felt that the Germans would hold the King for ransom. Should Leopold return it would present a most difficult political situation. The King was unlike the Prince Regent; he was fixed in his ideas and difficult to handle. The Flemish would be happy to see him back, the Walloons would be very sorry. De Staercke, now chef de cabinet to Prince Charles, confided in me his concern about relations between the Queen Mother and her younger son. However, the Queen Mother and her son Charles were agreed on one thing—they wanted the King's return. Charles wished the King back so that he could resign. The Queen's household wished to be first to see the King when he was freed, but de Staercke suggested that the King be taken to Switzerland, and Van Acker, the Prince Regent, the British Ambassador, and I be the first to see him. I did not tell him at that time that I was determined to keep out of this affair. De Staercke said there was one thing upon which everyone agreed; the future of Belgium would depend upon the manner in which the King returned. If he should come back suddenly a revolution was possible. On April 3 Van Acker, Spaak, Erskine, Sir Hughe, and I held a meeting about the King. Spaak requested that the King be asked to remain out of the country until a government group could call on him, this group to consist of the Prince Regent, the Prime Minister, the Foreign Minister, and Baron Holvoet. I asked that this be put in writing. Sir Hughe objected, but Spaak readily agreed.[6]

Within a few days Franz Van Cauwelaert leader in the House of Representatives, came to call. He echoed de Staercke, saying everything depended upon the manner of the King's return. If the King were to permit the government to carry on, acting within its constitutional rights, things could go well. If the King attempted to restrict the rights of Parliament in the slightest degree, serious trouble would follow. The majority of the people, in his opinion, were not in favor of the King's return. He was concerned about Leopold's authoritarian ideas, which had been apparent even before the war. That same day I saw the Prince Regent. He was disturbed by the possibility that the King might refuse to talk with the visiting group if his wife were not allowed to take part. If that were the King's attitude, he, the Prince, would refuse to talk. He hoped that it might be arranged for the King, his wife, and children to come back separately. He intimated what had been said by others—if the King returned with his wife it would emphasize his unpopular marriage.[4]

This was the situation on May 7, when I learned that the war in Europe had ended. The next day came the news that the King had been rescued by American soldiers in a castle at Strobl, near Salzburg, in Austria. The King problem was no longer academic—it was real. I cabled the State Department:

Official word received today via army of the liberation of King Leopold at Strobl, Austria. He, his wife, and children are well. Delegation heretofore discussed will leave Brussels at six tomorrow morning. As previously reported situation is explosive. Much will depend upon the results of the first conference with the King and his statements and actions thereafter. The prospects for a tranquil return are not good.[5]

I telephoned the Queen Mother as soon as I received word of the King's rescue. She said she would never forget my kindness.

That day Van Acker came to the embassy to talk about his trip to Salzburg the following morning. The first delegation was to include the Prince Regent, the Prime Minister, several members of the cabinet, and de Staercke. In an effort to be fair to the Leopold group, he would also take M. Frédéricq. Van Acker fully realized the importance of this meeting for Belgium and for Europe. We talked at length about the role of the King. I said the monarchy was an "amalgam." He said this was exactly the word—the country could not stick together under any other system.[6]

The delegation returned from Salzburg with nothing settled. Each of the principal participants reported to me his version of the meeting. Monsieur Frédéricq said the King and his family had been in hourly fear of being killed and that the ss guards would indeed have killed them if American troops had not moved in quickly. It seemed clear from Frédéricq's conversation that he was certain the King would come back. Spaak was worried about the King's plans to return. He said Leopold had changed in appearance, but not in outlook—"he is still a fascist." An immediate decision was necessary; the country could not stand such a state of confusion. He had tears in his eyes when he talked about Belgium and her present situation. The only happy note was his reference to the beauty of the King's wife. Spaak had just come home from San Francisco. When I asked him about returning, he shrugged his shoulders—he could not tell what would happen.[7]

The next day I talked with de Staercke. As we discussed the interferences, the petty jealousies, the indecisions, the various influences upon the King, his imprisonment, and his rescue by the Americans, de Staercke remarked that the whole thing was Shakespearean. The unforgettable beauty of the Austrian mountains, the picturesque White Horse Inn, the almost unreal quality of the setting contrasted so dramatically with the realities which awaited the King's word. The only person who influenced the King was his wife. The country's future depended upon his decision, and his decision depended upon his wife. "Cherchez la femme."[8]

An amusing sidelight was the attitude of Colonel Wilson, who had rescued the King from the Germans and saw himself in the role of the King's advisor. A confidential report to me stated: "Wilson is infatuated with the fact that he has found a real King and with the beauty and charm of the King's wife." It was not long before the Queen Mother said she would like to see the King, which I arranged. During the ensuing weeks, Van Acker made repeated trips, urging the King to abdicate.

On several occasions it was suggested that the British Ambassador and I go to see the King. I declined; the problem was Belgian.

In a lengthy conversation with the Prince Regent it appeared clear that he was in no way trying to maneuver his brother into a bad position. He said it was necessary to remain calm. In an amused and touching way he said that some thought him lacking in political "sagesse." I commented that he had done very well politically—he was easily the most popular man in Belgium.

Immediately after the American army had the King in charge, we assumed our usual generous role. We put air transportation at the disposal of the Belgian government and the King's friends, and began what I called "the milk run" between Brussels and Salzburg. On June 16 Van Acker reported to me that the King was returning, and had prepared the speech he would deliver to Parliament. But the King's views and plans changed from day to day, and seemed to depend upon whom he saw last. The British were disgusted by the impasse and suggested that the King be ordered out of the territory controlled by the Allied Armies. I opposed this as unwise. Van Cauwelaert, leader of the house, and Robert Gillon, president of the senate, also visited the King. On June 24 Van Cauwelaert lunched with me. He showed me a letter from the King in which Leopold suggested that he was looking forward to cooperating with Parliament; they all had but one interest, the country. He also showed me a typed copy of the Parliament's reply. The exchange of these amenities settled nothing, they seemed to indicate that the King was trying to strengthen his position preparatory to returning, although some suggested that these gestures were a way of saving face before he abdicated.[9] At a luncheon given by Baron Deschamp, the Baroness d'Alard said she would give me two hundred thousand francs if I would tell her why Van Cauwelaert came to see me immediately after returning from his visit with the King. I said that her bureau of information was working very well. She said everyone was interested in the way high officials in the Government seemed to be continually consulting with the American Ambassador. Things had changed since December.

There were as many plans as there were problems. An election was suggested by the British Ambassador. Since the registration lists were very old and many men were out of the country, this idea was quickly abandoned. Van Acker and his cabinet threatened to resign, suggesting that the King form his cabinet before his return. This was made public.

One of the minor problems involved transportation for the King's return. It was seriously considered by SHAEF and our State Department that Eisenhower should refuse to furnish a plane. I was strongly opposed. I cabled:

The Allies have repatriated over 230,000 other prisoners of war. They have furnished transportation for the Prince Regent, Prime Minister, and members of Leopold's household to go back and forth from Salzburg to Brussels. It will be difficult to refuse the same service to the King himself. If a plane is not furnished the King will probably ask for an automobile, and even if he is able to obtain an automobile from others, he must ask for gasoline from the military authorities. If they refuse to furnish the plane, they should refuse to furnish the car or gasoline. As a result the King will be a prisoner; having been a prisoner of Germany for one year he will now be a prisoner of the Allies.[19]

The move was abandoned.

Toward the latter part of June, someone discovered that two men named Meissner and Schmidt had retained notes from a meeting between Leopold and Hitler. These notes indicated that the King had agreed to Hitler's control over Belgium, and had discussed certain non-Belgian problems, dealing with the disposition of parts of the British Empire and parts of France. When Spaak and Van Acker saw these notes their determination to prevent the King's return became adamant. About this time I myself was shown original notes of the King's close advisor indicating that Leopold had arranged his own departure from Belgium. In my cable of July 9, I stated:

I personally saw these notes and they are in amazing revelation of the state of mind of the King last summer. His chief reason for wishing to be deported seems to have been to avoid the embarrassing but inevitable task of prosecuting collaborators who had been friendly to him.[11]

As time went on the King suggested a program by which he could stay away but not give up his throne. When no one would form a government for him, he told General Ganshoff that he had three alternatives: (1) to stay in Wolfgang and do nothing; (2) to return and not undertake to form a government; (3) to announce that he was not abdicating but was not coming back and the government could operate as it saw fit.

By this time people were becoming weary of the stalemate. I myself felt we should get out of the transportation business. I recommended that we inform the King that no transportation would be furnished after a certain date. On July 15, when Truman and Byrnes were in Belgium, I brought the matter up. In my cable of that day I stated:

I discussed this matter today with President Truman, Secretary Byrnes, and General Eisenhower. All are in agreement. Eisenhower requests that his military superiors in Washington give him instructions. For eight weeks the King has had at his disposal every facility American military forces can make available. In my judgment the situation is becoming ridiculous. The United States and Belgium have everything to gain and nothing to lose by a clear-cut proposal to the King.

The following day I cabled Byrnes:

Meanwhile I would furnish no more transportation for visitors to King. Furthermore I would tell him that if he refuses or neglects to avail himself of this offer by the end of the period in question we will no longer furnish him with rations and he will be completely on his own to deal freely of course with the Belgian authorities or others, but with no responsibility of any kind whatsoever on us.[12]

Although Byrnes had personally agreed, his subordinates in the State Department urged that we not be "precipitate." My suggestion was not followed.

On the morning of July 21, 1 went to the Saint Gudule Cathedral to attend the Mass celebrating Belgium's Independence Day. The "King question" was still acute; feelings were running high. All meetings had been prohibited and there was some question about holding this Mass. However, it had not been called off. The cathedral was packed. As the Mass began, suddenly shrill shouts of "Vive le Roi" echoed throughout the cathedral. From outside, we could hear similar shouts. The church immediately became a mass of sounds. Bedlam reigned. Numerous young men were thrown out by gendarmes and the mass continued for about twenty minutes. Then it ended abruptly. The Queen Mother left to the accompaniment of renewed and growing shouts of "Leopold" and "Vive le Roi." Then there was silence. The diplomatic corps, moving in order, with Nuncio Micara at the head, started for the door. As the corps approached the door it was slammed and held shut. I walked out of line up ahead of the British Ambassador, Monsignor Micara, and the Chinese Ambassador, and asked why the door was shut. I was told that the crowd of five thousand outside was vicious and unmannerly and it was thought unwise to risk embarrassment or injury to any of the ambassadors. I said that I saw no reason to stay inside and await developments. I, at least, intended to go out—and I did, against the protest of the men at the door. I walked to the curb where the crowd was yelling "Vive le Roi!" and stood alone looking for my car, when suddenly I heard a noise and hurried footsteps behind me. Turning, I saw Spaak. He rushed to my side and gave forth a spectacular tirade against the demonstrators. He demanded they break up so that my car could take me away.

This crowd was violently anti-Spaak; he was doing an extremely courageous thing. However, his courage and authority were so impressive that the crowd gave way and I was able to leave. By that time the others had come out of the Cathedral and were driven away. Later, Spaak said he was grateful that one member of the diplomatic corps had refused to be locked inside the Cathedral.[13]

Parliament in July passed a bill continuing the Regency. Gradually things quieted down. On August 11, I cabled:

Situation with reference to King Leopold is now quiet. The King is reported to be moving to Switzerland. Van Acker left today on vacation.[14]

During the remainder of my term as ambassador the King matter remained unchanged. Leopold did not return to Belgium but refused to abdicate. He spent most of his time in Switzerland. In March of 1950, a referendum was held, at his request, which favored his return by a narrow margin—57 per cent.[15] The King finally did return, amid scenes of violence. The Prince Regent was excluded from the Palace; fighting broke out in the streets, speeches of great violence were made; Spaak himself led demonstrations.

The solution of this explosive problem was eventually furnished by Prince Baudouin, a son of Astrid, who was devoted to his country, to his father and, interestingly enough, liked his stepmother. He was also the idol of his grandmother, Queen Elizabeth. Young as he was, Baudouin showed admirable character and the country united in supporting him. Leopold abdicated and Baudouin became King on his twenty-first birthday.

12 Adieu La Belgique

WHILE THE future of King Leopold was my main concern during the spring and early summer of 1945, I had plenty of routine chores as well. Some were trivial. Toward the end on June, I received notice that a number of movie magnates were coming to Europe and arrangements had been made for me to give them a reception "at 18:30 hours on June 29." This was done without contacting or consulting with me. However, I gave the party. The moguls came, the top men in the motion picture industry. Their chief interest was getting films into Belgium, which effort they claimed was being thwarted by the British. This probably was true. After they left, Alphonse, one of my butlers, was dismayed to find all of our match boxes gone, including a very fine one in green leather. Other odds and ends were also missing.[1]

I had been intrigued by the possibility of using Radio Luxembourg, the most powerful station in Europe, as a "voice of America" and suggested this to the State Department. The station had operated before the war through the BBC network; it had been used to good effect by the enemy. General Patton's troops ran over Luxembourg so fast that the Germans had no time to destroy it. It was sadly neglected, but offered great possibilities. After the Battle of the Bulge I began negotiating with the manager, a Mr. Poulvey, for a contract by which the United States Government could operate the station. Waller, our chargé d'affaires at Luxembourg, discussed the matter with Luxembourg authorities. They said they would be happy to deal with our government. They pointed out, however, that the French ownership amounted to almost 40 per cent and the Luxembourgers could hardly ignore them. I then arranged a contact with Havas, the French owner. Their representative came to Brussels. I also began discussions with the British.

While I was contacting the proper parties to arrange for us to take over, I received from Acting Secretary of State Grew a request that I do what I could to assist negotiations which would permit the Office of War Information (owi) to control the Luxembourg station for an indefinite period. I soon learned, to my chagrin, that negotiations had been going on all over the place. I addressed a cable to Grew:

I gather from recent messages that it will not be necessary for me to do anything with reference to this matter unless the efforts of others are unsuccessful. When a matter of major importance for the United States and Luxembourg has been discussed and advanced to final stages without consultation with me, when approval by the State Department goes to the Embassy at London and not to Brussels, when I am not favored with copies of telegrams or dispatches, nor consulted in any way, with reference to the matter in question, it would seem that a review of the status and functions of the Minister to Luxembourg would be in order.

I also dictated a letter, pointing out that even before I left the United States I had realized the station's potential and suggested its acquisition, and since my arrival had made substantial progress toward a possible agreement with the owners of the station. On second thought I said to myself "What the hell" and did not send either the cable or the letter. As in other cases, there were too many cooks—the broth was spoiled. We did not get the station.[2]

In early July, I received word that President Truman was coming through Brussels on July 15 to attend a meeting of Allied leaders at Potsdam. However, no one was to be informed of this, not even Belgian officials. The developing drama was nothing short of comic. I was not permitted to mention the matter, although it was in all the Belgian papers. Keeley came in from Antwerp, where the President was to land, reporting that the burgomaster was hurt not to be notified nor given a chance to greet the President. The same was true of the governor of the province. The Prince Regent had asked if he could meet the President when he set foot on Belgian soil. I was forced to say that, embarrassed as I was, I had received no instructions and could not make such arrangements. I cabled Secretary Byrnes requesting that I be permitted officially to inform the Belgian Government. This cable remaining unanswered, I continued to send others. On July 13 I cabled as follows:

American Ambassador has received no reply to his message of yesterday. In view of the fact that everyone in Belgium knows of the arrival of the President, including the approximate time and point where he will land, Belgian authorities are extremely mystified that no word whatever has been given to them with reference to this matter. They ask if they are to be regarded as a conquered country. They say that other heads of state such as Queen Wilhelmina of Holland have made private trips through the country, but in each case the Government has been notified and has had someone present to represent Government upon arrival. This privilege they request be given them tomorrow. They are not suggesting any official welcome nor any publicity whatever.

If President is willing to leave the matter to the Ambassador's judgment, latter will arrange an official contact without publicity which will satisfy the Belgians.

In reply to that message, I received the following:

TOP SECRET
Please deliver immediately the following message to Ambassador Sawyer from the Secretary of State.

Your message of one three July confidential communication to Belgian Foreign Office authorized. You may explain that security considerations prevented earlier notification.[3]

On the morning of July 15, the day of the President's arrival, I left at seven o'clock for Antwerp, having just received the cable informing me that I could notify the Belgian Government. I had already taken the bit in my teeth, however, and notified them on my own authority. It was a clear morning and the arrival was spectacular. Planes were flying overhead, ships were all over the harbor; soon we could see in the distance the dark hull of the cruiser *Augusta*. She docked on schedule at exactly 10:00 A.M. Meanwhile, General Eisenhower, Admiral Stark, General Lee and other officials had arrived. The dock was alive with dignitaries. I had told Keeley to bring the governor and the burgomaster, ignoring my lack of instructions. We could see the President sitting on the deck. When the gangplank was laid down, Eisenhower and Stark said I should go first, as protocol demands, since an ambassador is the President's personal representative in a foreign country. Both the President and Secretary Byrnes greeted me warmly.

We talked frankly about many things. I told the President I thought the time had come to stop playing Santa Claus to Europe, and that UNRRA was a waste of money, with which he agreed. I voiced the opinion that the liberated areas should not suffer while we made gigantic efforts to take care of Germany; the time had arrived to look first after ourselves and then after our friends. He said he was in complete accord. He said he would not let anyone tell us what to do, including the Russians. I told him of the Belgian sensitivity to his "secret" arrival and asked that he stop in Brussels on his way home. He said he had been invited to four or five capitals but he had decided to take his plane at Potsdam and fly directly back to Washington. This would avoid many complications. He asked if I would like to bring anyone on board ship. I said Mrs. Sawyer was on the dock with Mr. Keeley. He asked that they join us. At 11:15 the President walked down the gangplank followed by Secretary Byrnes and me, General Eisenhower and Admiral Stark. As he stepped ashore he was met by M. Vanderbosch, representing the Prince Regent, following which he met the governor and the burgomaster. President Truman, Byrnes, and I then climbed into an open car and drove to the airport near Brussels. I had suggested quietly to Van Acker that he be at the airport when Truman arrived. He showed up with the mayor just as the President was about to take off. I ran to the plane and told the President that the Prime Minister was there. He said to "wait until I put on my coat." He then came down out of the plane and shook hands with Van Acker. Everyone was satisfied.[4]

Although the war had ended, it could not be forgotten. It had left wreckage everywhere, both physical and psychological. The atrocities of the Germans were constant topics of conversation. Of the greatest significance for Americans was the cold-blooded murder of United States soldiers by ss troopers at Malmedy. In commemoration of this massacre the people of that region had erected a monument. I was asked on July 22 to help dedicate this shaft. Among other things, I said:

> At a time when the American Armies were fighting gallantly to save Belgian soil from the invader, German Storm Troopers here committed one of the most senseless and brutal mass murders of their horrid history.
>
> During the last war I was with the Army of Occupation in Germany. I observed then a most curious phenomenon. Within a few months after the hostilities had ceased there spread among the American soldiers a feeling of resentment and ill will toward our recent Allies and a feeling of tolerance, if not outright friendliness, toward our recent enemies. It was explained in part as a result of the normal irritations which are bound to result from the effort of several allies to cooperate; and also it was said to be due to the skillful and continued campaigns by the Germans to ingrati-

ate themselves with the British and the American Armies of Occupation.

Strange to say, within two months after the end of hostilities in this second great war brought on by Germany I see evidence of a recurrence of the same state of mind. Once more we hear from those who are solicitous about our recent enemies and who talk about possible difficulties, disagreements and trouble with our recent Allies.[5]

From Malmedy we went to Luxembourg. There I heard unpleasant rumors about the actions of our military. The manager of Radio Luxembourg had been ordered out of his own home. Since December there had been thirty-five houses requisitioned in Luxembourg and left unoccupied, although thousands of Luxembourgers were returning home from concentration camps. This, like many other unfortunate developments during the war, was due largely to one arrogant and stupid officer, who enjoyed throwing his weight around. I threw my weight around when I interviewed him and the situation changed immediately. That day I went with Bech, Mrs. Sawyer, and Waller to visit the city of Trier, where I had served with the Army of Occupation in the First World War. I saw for the first time in twenty-six years the castle which had been my headquarters. We crossed the old Roman bridge and drove through the streets of the city.

On July 26, Colonel Owen, in charge of important prisoners of war at Mondorf, called on me. When I said I would like to visit the prison, he said it would be arranged for August 2. Mondorf was heavily guarded with charged wire stockades; soldiers with machine guns were stationed every fifty yards. As we came through the gate the Germans stood silently at attention. There were many whom I recognized, Albert Kesselring, Wilhelm Keitel, Karl Doenitz, and others. Hermann Goering was walking in the distance. In Goering's room the cards were all spread out on a little table for a game of Napoleon solitaire. When Goering was first brought in, he came with a suitcase of codeine pills. He had been taking forty daily. By the time I was there he had been reduced to fourteen. At first they had denied him any pills at all and he had gone immediately into a coma. At that time he weighed 375 pounds. I did not see Joachim Von Ribbentrop, but was told that he maintained he did nothing but carry out Hitler's orders. Hanns Frank, the former guillotiner of Poland, had tried to commit suicide, and was very contrite, saying that he deserved to be shot. Franz Von Papen had written a letter, apparently trying to establish the fact that he was deranged. I was impressed by these men. They looked intelligent and exhibited great physical strength and vigor, although they were thin. Their faces showed strain. They had no comforts. Each had an iron cot, a table and one chair, no sheets and no mirror.[6]

During the summer, we tried to see more of Belgium. On August 6 we visited Ghent. The Burgomaster told me that I was the first American ambassador to come officially to that city and presented me with a document giving me the freedom of the city. From the city hall we were taken on board a lovely yacht and toured the harbor and the canals for about two hours. That afternoon we went to a beautiful orchid garden where Mrs. Sawyer was shown the "Elizabeth Sawyer" orchid. At the cathedral, we saw the large blank space formerly occupied by the famous "Mystic Lamb," a painting by the Van Eyck brothers. Several times during a succession of wars, it had been stolen from its original location, and more than one hundred years ago one of its panels had been lost. This painting was one of Belgium's great treasures. I realized that to return this masterpiece would be a ten-strike and said then and there that I would get it back. The following day I cabled Eisenhower:

May I suggest an action which I believe will go far to promote good will in Belgium and which, unlike most of the other things we do, will not cost us one dollar.

Yesterday I was in Ghent and there was asked if it was not possible to secure the return to Ghent of the Van Eyck triptych (*Agneau Mystic*) which was stolen by the Germans and is now reposing, if not deteriorating, in some salt mine in southern Germany. I assume that well-known art treasures such as this, stolen from countries like Belgium, will eventually be returned to them. Is it not possible to take the initiative in this matter without waiting for demands from the respective governments for what they are obviously entitled to?

If we could assume with proper publicity that on a certain date the art treasures of Belgium would be returned to her, and particularly this famous painting, it would be an event of major importance in the maintenance of good relations between the U.S. and this country.[7]

Several days passed with no reply. I then called Eisenhower by phone and explained my desire to have the "Mystic Lamb" returned immediately to Belgium. He said that matters of this sort were regularly referred to a mission whose duty it was to identify the art treasures, ascertain the proper owners, and arrange for their return. Since there were approximately a hundred people in this mission and a great number of stolen treasures, it would take many months for this to be accomplished. I reiterated that the return of the "Mystic Lamb" would be a marvelous piece of propaganda for the United States. Eisenhower then said that this was the only painting in Europe with which he was personally familiar—he would skip the routine and order its return by special plane at once.

The "Mystic Lamb" was flown in secretly at night and moved to the palace, where, on September 3, on behalf of General Eisenhower, I presented it to the Belgian Government. It was received by the Prince Regent and the Minister of Public Instruction. The painting remained on exhibit in Brussels for many months and was eventually returned to Ghent. Four days after this ceremony, Acting Secretary of State Dean Acheson sent me the following telegram:

You are commended for your initiative and the part you played in bringing back to Belgium *Agneau Mystique*, the Triptych by Van Eyck . . . It is gratifying to us to see the benefit this has had upon public opinion in Belgium and the help it will give to our relations with the Belgians.[8]

The real significance of my action in this matter was that I obtained results without spending Uncle Sam's money.

I was greatly assisted in recovering this painting by Ambassador Robert Murphy, then stationed in Germany. Among my most fortunate and rewarding experiences was knowing Robert Murphy. He was good-humored, frank, clear-headed, realistic, and dedicated. He was by far the ablest State Department representative whom I met. Among other things he told me of the mission of Ed Pauly who had been sent over as a special representative to handle matters of supply and rehabilitation. Although Pauly was at that time located in Moscow, he was trying to tell General Lucius Clay what to do in Germany. Murphy said Clay did not think that German problems should be settled in Moscow. This sentiment made a great hit with me.[9]

Though my life in Brussels was a busy one, I did find time occasionally to play golf. One day at the La Zoute golf course near Ostende, I heard explosions every ten or fifteen minutes. This part of the country had been heavily mined by the Germans; the Belgians were demining it. As I started to play, my caddy pointed to the ninth hole and said, "A man was killed there yesterday afternoon." I asked if he were joking, and he said, "No, a mine went off." As a matter of fact, a mine went off about a quarter of a mile away while we were playing. We could see a great cloud of smoke and dust. A fairly narrow fairway had been cleared and was marked off with white paint and tape. Balls traveling into the areas still mined were not retrieved. It was the most curious game of golf I ever played. The course was rough but the game was not dull. As can be imagined I kept carefully in the fairway. The caddy said, probably untruthfully, that I was the only player who had not lost a ball.[10]

During my travels that season I frequently visited Antwerp. While there were places of historic moment in Antwerp, the most interesting exhibit was its Burgomaster, C. Huysmanns. He was a gaunt, picturesque figure, who talked with the utmost, and at times embarrassing, frankness. He said that he was probably the result of an illegitimate liaison. He was a tense, extremely caustic but funny man of seventy-three, both mentally and physically alert—as he still is at age ninety-five. He gave a luncheon for me where he was very gay, drank quite a bit of wine and finally, at my suggestion, did not give his intended speech but let me look it over and reply to it. He had known Stalin personally for twenty years and said Stalin was not a Communist but a plain Georgian peasant whose fundamental concept was anything but Communistic. He himself had been accused of being a Communist, but was not. I was told that Huysmanns would like to be the first president of the new Belgian Republique, which he envisioned.

During the fall and winter and spring this assignment had been exciting and satisfying. By midsummer, however, I was becoming slightly bored. I was also being urged home by important business enterprises which needed my supervision and an extensive law practice to which I had always intended to return; and I wanted to get back to my children.

Perhaps it is a weakness of non-career ambassadors to weary of diplomatic routine. This is not however the major criticism of non-professionals. We hear frequently about their folly or ineffectiveness. Why should we have any so-called political appointments? My appointment was obviously political. When it was announced, commentator H. V. Kaltenborn took occasion to berate President Roosevelt. I may be forgiven, however, if I note that when Kaltenborn himself was in Brussels during the Battle of the Bulge, he came to my office after a visit with Spaak and took back everything unpleasant he had said.[11] I have great respect for experience—between two men who are equally talented the one with experience obviously is the better man. But "political appointments" are not necessarily bad. There have been numerous political appointees who have done very well and who have stayed on as career ambassadors. The important consideration in any appointment should be the quality and ability of the man who is to get the job. A career man is not necessarily one of great ability—a political appointee is not necessarily a fool. I am aware of cases where political appointees have made fools of themselves. This was not because they were political appointees, but because the President had thrown to the winds the question of fitness.

I had advised President Truman when he came to Belgium in July that I wished to resign and followed some weeks later with the following letter:

Brussels, August 9, 1945

Personal and Confidential

My dear Mr. President:

When you took the oath of office as President, I cabled to you my resignation as Ambassador to Belgium and Minister to Luxembourg. You were gracious enough a short time thereafter to say you were glad I was in your official family, and that you desired me to remain.

At this time, I wish, however, to request that within the near future you permit me to terminate my service at this post.

My wish to resign is based upon the feeling that, with the war and its ending behind us, my activities will soon become routine and largely social; I prefer under those circumstances to be back in the States. I have greatly enjoyed my experiences here and hope that I have rendered some service to the Government and to President Roosevelt and to you.

Respectfully yours,
CHARLES SAWYER [12]

Meanwhile, I had become party to a development of world importance. The United States had produced an atomic bomb. Essential to the making of this bomb was uranium. To secure an adequate supply of it was vital. It was found in various parts of the world, but the largest known uranium deposit was in the Belgian Congo. This was owned by the Societe Mue-niere, a branch of the Belgian Societe Generale. General Leslie Groves, head of the "Manhattan Project" which had produced the bomb, sent a representative to me early in the summer. I was approached with great secrecy and informed that the general wished my help in securing access to this Belgian uranium. In this effort I was highly successful. I contacted the head man of the Societe Mueniere—Monsieur Sengier, who proved to be one of our greatest friends. After extended nego-tiations, contracts were signed on October 27, 1945, giving us the entire uranium production of the Belgian Congo mines for the next ten years. At the urging of Groves and me, Sengier was decorated by the President.

At this time I was also able to be of help to Belgium. President Truman, in a gesture of generosity, had ordered all lend-lease obligations cancelled. He had not known, or had then forgotten, that under reverse lend-lease we owed the Belgians some ninety million dollars for food, transportation, and services furnished to American military forces. The Bel-gians were making no progress in getting payment and had organized a delegation to go to Washington to plead their cause. As I was visiting with Spaak on September 5, he re-quested most insistently that I accompany this delegation, and I agreed to go.

When I arrived in Washington I found our State Depart-ment magnificently indifferent to the Belgian request for pay-ment. One day Spaak, Gutt, Baron Boel, and other delegates— men of great eminence in Europe—met with Willard Thorpe, an Assistant Secretary of State. I attended the meeting. Thorpe said the department greatly regretted its inability to give the Belgians an early answer to their request, but mean-while perhaps they would like to hear a talk on the attitude of our government toward the economic development of other countries. He then introduced a Professor Walker, of whom I had never heard, who undertook to instruct these outstanding international businessmen on how to run their country, including the need to get rid of cartels. Since some of his listeners represented the Belgian Societe Generale, one of the biggest cartels in Europe, his talk was not too well received. When he finished, M. Gutt rose and said that they had listened with great interest to these "bedtime stories," but they would like to know when they were to get their money.

I was so incensed by this cavalier treatment that I left the room, went straight to the White House and asked to see the President. I poured out my anger. I said that the State Department was so busy trying to force the British to borrow four billion United States dollars that they apparently had no time for the Belgians, to whom we owed ninety million dollars. I pointed out the importance of our uranium dealings with Belgium: no country in the world was more needed as a friend. I said that I thought the treatment accorded to the delegation by our State Department was outrageous. The President agreed and said he would see that something was done. Within a few days the whole thing was settled and the ninety million dollars paid. At a later time Spaak was most compli mentary about the help which I had given them.[13]

During the weeks I was in this country I saw the President several times. I told him I would like to follow up on my letter of resignation. He asked me, and I agreed, to stay on as ambassador until the first of the year. It was understood, however, that I might return to the United States before January first. During our conversations the President said he hoped I would accept an appointment to the Senate to succeed Harold Burton, whom he had appointed to the Supreme Court. I said I did not wish this appointment and had told friends who had mentioned the matter to tell Governor Lausche that I was not interested.[14]

Mrs. Sawyer and I returned to Europe on the *Queen Mary*.

The weather was so foul the ship could not dock at Southampton. We were taken off in a tender, as mine sweepers circled around us. The storm had washed loose a number of mines which had floated ashore the day before.

As my term of service drew to a close, I was reluctantly obliged to tell my many friends that I was leaving. I called upon the Prince Regent, Van Acker, Spaak, and my colleagues in the diplomatic corps to give them the news. All seemed greatly surprised and regretful. I myself was unhappy. On October 30 I went to Luxembourg. The roads were if anything worse than when I had gone to Bastogne just after Von Runstedt's offensive. I saw Du Pong and Bech. They seemed shocked upon hearing about my plans to leave. The following day I called on the Grand Duchess and Prince Felix. They also seemed greatly upset when I said I was saying "good-bye." They were so complimentary about my service that it was almost embarrassing.

My second day in Luxembourg was one of the most enjoyable I have ever spent. Bech and I dined alone at a little country inn, after driving through miles of colorful forest and over the rolling hills of his small nation. We consumed much too much of the superb food and drank a bottle of fine old Riesling. Bech described his recent visit to Poland. At one spot he had commented on the peculiar character of the soil. He was told he was walking on the ashes of thousands of human beings who had been cremated there. In some places the ashes were six to seven feet deep. A careful scrutiny revealed the truth of what he had been told. He saw mountains of shoes, including many tiny ones, and piles of spectacles with other vestigia of those who had been tortured and burned. Never in his life had he been exposed to a scene of such horror.

We talked about the atom bomb. He said, "This is the first time in the world's history that a nation with only peaceful intentions has the means to destroy anyone who threatens war." I said that some American scientists and columnists were clamoring that we give the secret away. He replied that everyone in Europe hoped that this great source of peace and strength would not be shared with anyone. I said I doubted that it would not be.

Learning to know Bech had been a privilege. He was probably the ablest diplomat in Europe, although he represented one of the smallest countries. He had the greatest friendliness for the United States. Indeed, his son Charles had endeavored to join our U.S. Air Corps. He was the best raconteur to whom I ever listened. His stories of the American Embassy in earlier years were always entertaining and sometimes excruciatingly funny. While in San Francisco he had received a redwood salad bowl from Edward Stettinius, our Secretary of State. After his return from San Francisco he came in one day to tell me about it, saying that he planned to fill it with Russian salad and add French dressing.[15]

Early in November I called upon the Prince Regent. He had purchased a present for me in Portugal—a necktie. The trouble was, he had opened the package hurriedly before I arrived and the tie was missing; but he would find it and send it to me. He expressed great sadness about my plans to leave and said, "You are the most highly regarded of any American ambassador since Brand Whitlock." I said he was very kind, and he said, "No, I am telling the truth."

On the night of November 10, Mrs. Sawyer gave a party for prominent Belgians and American officials. It began at 9:30 P.M., and an hour later there were about 375 people in the dining room. When they later moved into the large ballroom, the French Ambassador remarked that guests usually wear out only one carpet. Normally a diplomatic reception is over no later than midnight. Our guests finally left about 2:00 A.M. having drunk 110 bottles of champagne and 22 bottles of whisky. Apparently the party had been a success.

On November 12 I went to Bruges to attend the presentation of the Michelangelo statue of the Christ Child which I had been able to recover for the Belgians. In the church I saw the blank spaces from which paintings had been torn and where this statue had stood. The Germans had told the Belgians they did this to prevent the Americans from stealing them and selling them to Jews.

I had met Churchill several times in Brussels. A most impressive thing in the appearance of this greatest man of our time was his completely unblemished and babylike skin—in spite of his well-advertised and extensive use of alcohol and tobacco. In a recent book about Churchill, he was quoted as saying to a lady friend: "I have a cuticle without a blemish." In this, as in many other things, he was right. Pierre Dupuy, the Canadian chargé d'affaires, told a most amusing story of entering Churchill's room in London. The Prime Minister was in bed with his wife's red dressing gown around him, a towel or napkin or some such thing around his head and a bottle of cognac on the night table. He was dictating to two secretaries at the same time. This was at 10:00 in the morning.

On November 15 Churchill came to Brussels and addressed a meeting of the Royal Academy. He ended with several sentences in French, although I had been told that he knew no French. The following afternoon I attended a reception given for him at the Grande Place. It was here that little Belgian girls sang English songs and General Erskine wept. Churchill also had tears in his eyes.[16]

On November 17, Mrs. Sawyer and I lunched with the Prince Regent and de Staercke. It was sad to realize that this was the last time we would be in the palace. The Prince Regent gave me the necktie he had lost and gave my wife a little jade statue. De Staercke talked amusingly of the recent Churchill reception; he described Churchill, tired of shaking hands or perhaps inebriated, slouched in his chair coughing and belching, to the dismay of those around him.

The time for my departure was at hand. One thing, however, I decided to do before I left. General Hume had come in from

Vienna and had talked in a most interesting and revealing way about Displaced Persons' camps. There was such a variety of rumors that I felt it would be helpful to the President if I could visit some camps myself and report to him first hand. I, therefore, decided to go to Le Havre by way of Frankfurt. I called General Bedell Smith who said he would be most happy to arrange for me to visit some of these camps. He was concerned only that I get to Frankfurt before dark, as the field was small and was not as yet equipped for night landings. I was at the airfield on time, as was the plane; but the lieutenant pilot was missing. When he finally did show up, my own air attache said he thought it was too late to take off. However, the lieutenant said he could make it to Frankfurt before dark. We took off. Within a short time after we were in the air a heavy fog closed over the land and it grew darker and darker. As I sat watching the lieutenant and the sergeant in the cockpit I sensed that something was wrong. I walked up and asked if we were having trouble. They reported that we had no lights, and the radio was not working. We could not go back to Brussels —it was enveloped in fog. We were flying blind in the dark at 165 miles an hour, without lights or ground contact. There was nothing I could do. I sat back and waited for what might happen. All of a sudden the plane turned abruptly to the left; this was a little scary but I felt it was a good omen. It seemed we had established contact with Weimar. We were definitely off our course but at least this gave us some idea of our position. As we headed for Frankfurt the clouds broke a little and I could see a few lights on the ground. Although this boy had never landed in Frankfurt, he had, fortunately, done a lot of night flying. General Smith had been told I was in the air and had arranged for some meager lights at the air strip. They proved adequate. The lieutenant brought the plane down without a mishap, although we were only about eight feet away from a building when we stopped. He was a little nervous and so was General Smith, who was waiting to meet me.

I spent the next day exploring camps. Although I had some months before visited a camp that held refugees of many religions and nationalities, most of the DP's here were Jewish. The camps were well run—but there were problems. In one large camp they had refused to do any kind of work and would not even wash their own dishes. However, after a smart and tough American Jewish captain was put in charge, the DP's did cooperate. I visited four camps and found only one where they seemed to be happy. Here young Jews, men and women, were working cheerfully and were in fine spirits. They had been notified that they would be sent to Palestine. They had something to look forward to.

I left the second night. General Smith made good on his earlier promise to furnish transportation when I needed it. He sent me from Frankfurt to Paris as the sole official passenger on what had been Hitler's special train. The cars had been made especially for Hitler. I myself slept in his bedroom. It had all sorts of gadgets—bullet-proof windows and an elaborate washroom. During the following day, as we sped through France, I had a wonderful view of the countryside. I arrived in Paris in the late afternoon. I took another train to Le Havre, where I met my wife. We left for home that night on the ss *George Washington*. My foreign service had ended.[17]

13 Secretary of Commerce

I RETURNED from Belgium with relief. It was good to be home again, back with my children, in familiar surroundings and free from public responsibility. In a short time I had picked up my law practice. In an even shorter time I had picked up a new business enterprise—a sports arena. Cincinnati had no large, modern arena. To build one would be of great benefit to Cincinnati sports fans and would add measurably to the city's attractiveness. I knew the venture had its risks. Every arena in the country had gone through bankruptcy and was in the hands of government authorities or bondholders. But I was willing to take a chance—as were the others who became associated with me. In the case of each prospective investor, I said I did not want his money unless he could afford to lose it. We tried three locations before we found a subsoil which would carry the enormous weight of the building. We had problems in securing title to the property. We had opposition from local nearby residents. We had problems in design. I sent our architect to every large arena in the country and he finally came up with a plan for seat banks with a slightly concave line, which gave every customer a marvelous view of the entire floor. After

171

three years and spending three million dollars we completed
the Cincinnati Gardens in 1949. By that time I had become
Truman's Secretary of Commerce. I came from Washington
for the opening, to be introduced to the assembled throng as
"the secretary of the Chamber of Commerce." This was not too
auspicious a beginning. After our first big event, the Maxim-
Charles heavyweight fight, things looked promising, but the
rosy prospect quickly faded. As time went on it was clear that
this arena would go the way of the rest. I lost everything I had
put into it. But I have no regrets. As one great sports character
said, and he had seen arenas all over the world, it is "the finest
there is." [1]

At that time my investments in entertainment seemed to be
ill-fated. For years I had been a major stockholder in a Cincinnati amusement park known as Coney Island, located on the
Ohio River about ten miles upstream from the center of the
city. Coney Island owned a boat known as the *Island Queen*, a
very large "side wheeler" with a dance floor on one deck that
held more than four thousand people. Throughout the day and
early evening the *Island Queen* would steam slowly up and
down the river between Cincinnati's public landing and the
amusement park, on its top deck a Calliope playing loudly
enough to be heard for miles in all directions. It had been our
custom, following the regular summer season, to send the
Queen on a trip down the Ohio River. She would stop at
Madison, Indiana, and at Louisville, Kentucky, and other river
cities, where thousands of dancers would swarm aboard. In
1947 we decided to change the program and send her on a trip
up, instead of down, the river. I myself was somewhat concerned that the pilot would not know the upper river and
might run her aground or snag her keel. What did happen was
far, far worse. One morning about 9:30, while docked at
Pittsburgh, after a great night of dancing and hilarity aboard,
the *Queen* was rocked by an explosion. A devoted employee
who lived aboard the *Queen* had been welding a step on the

stairway to the dance deck. The flame from his welding torch went through the thin steel into a large tank of fuel oil. He was among the fourteen who were killed by the blast. Many more were injured, and there was never another *Island Queen*. There was an odd aftermath to this tragedy. One member of the band was asleep on a lower deck when the explosion occurred. He leaped up, dove into the river, and swam to shore, leaving a roll of bills under his mattress. Many weeks later, when the blasted and broken hull of the *Island Queen* was raised for removal, he climbed aboard and, under the sodden mattress, found his money intact. Coney Island recovered from the loss of the *Island Queen*. In spite of floods and other handicaps it came to prosper. Year by year we add to its attractions and its attractiveness and year by year the people of this area indicate in mounting numbers that they enjoy it.

I have been happy with my investments, varied and for the most part profitable. My great profit, however, has been the continued contact with American business. My knowledge of business was not gained by reading about it, but from wide experience. It has confirmed my belief in the great contribution which American business makes to our society.

In the fall of 1947, after I had picked up the threads of my private life, I was offered another opportunity for public service. On October 10 I received a letter from Harry B. Mitchell, president of the U.S. Civil Service Commission, asking if I would serve on the Loyalty Review Board. The nation was then greatly concerned about the loyalty of federal employees. Communist activities within the government had been uncovered and it was necessary to deal with this threat. However, fairness demanded that charges of disloyalty should be carefully reviewed. To accomplish this, the Loyalty Review Board had been created.[2] Since I felt this to be a matter of importance and was told it would take but little time, I decided to accept. The meetings I attended were devoted to a discussion of the scope of our program. Should our meetings be public or private? Should confrontation of witnesses be permitted? Should a transcript of all board proceedings be made? Should minority reports be permitted? Should panel members make public statements concerning the proceedings? Should the board files be kept secret? What rules of evidence should be followed? One troublesome issue was the list of subversive organizations published by the Attorney General. Should we undertake to grade or characterize or eliminate some of these organizations? I expressed my views in a letter to the chairman:

> If we were to undertake any such task we would run counter to the wish of the Attorney General, and would probably incur his vigorous opposition; we would be embarking on a sea of endeavor which would be almost limitless. We shall have enough to do if we carry out the work laid down in the directive. I am not concerned about possible criticism which would follow a statement that we had accepted the decision of the Attorney general.[3]

An amusing sidelight concerning my expense accounts occurred at an early date. The amount of $6.83 was deducted from one of my bills, to which, however, I was given an offset of $1.50. I was not permitted to charge $2.00 for taxi fare unless I could prove there was no other means of transportation available at the time; and $4.83 was deducted because I had used a bedroom instead of a lower berth. I was told that I could reclaim the amount charged—

> On a subsequent voucher with a statement to the effect that the accommodations actually used were the lowest first-class accommodations available at the time your tickets were purchased or reservations were made. The amount of deduction was computed by subtracting the cost of two lower berths at $5.05 each from the amount of $14.30, which represents the cost of accommodations actually used. This difference of $4.20 is subject to a fifteen per cent Federal tax, making the total deduction $4.83.
>
> The extra subsistence to which you are entitled, in the amount

of $1.50, has been added to the voucher to offset the deductions mentioned above. In computing the per diem allowance for continuous travel of more than twenty-four hours, the calendar day (midnight to midnight) is the unit, and for fractional parts of the day at the beginning or ending of such continuous travel, one-fourth of the rate for a calendar day is allowed for each period of six hours or fraction thereof.[4]

Would that such a meticulous check applied to Americans were applied by Uncle Sam to foreign recipients of our unrestrained generosity!

My activities on the board were short-lived. Early in May 1948 I was called to the telephone and told that President Truman wished to talk with me. After a brief greeting he said that Averell Harriman was leaving the Cabinet to handle the aid program known as the "Marshall Plan" and he would like very much to name me Secretary of Commerce.[5] I scarcely knew what to say. I managed to thank him for the offer, by which I was greatly complimented; but I had been out of public life for so short a time that I wanted to think it over. Would he mind if I postponed my answer for one day? If I accepted, once again I would have to adjust from private to public life, dissolve my law partnership and turn over control of a number of business enterprises. Yet, to be offered a cabinet post was a great honor; and I was fond of Truman. The following morning I called the President and told him I would accept.

I flew to Washington for a meeting with Averell Harriman, came back to Cincinnati for the wedding of my daughter Jean, and returned to present myself before the Senate committee which was to pass upon my appointment.[6] Following the President's call I had thought about my approach to this new assignment. I was a Democrat and thoroughly in sympathy with Democratic doctrine. I did not, however, share the view of many in the Truman administration and in the earlier Roosevelt administration that the businessman was a God-given whipping boy. The government spent great sums of money and energy attacking American business, but little of each in promoting it. Businessmen had become cautious, if not timid. Should we not have a Secretary of Commerce who was an unashamed partisan of business? I also gave thought to another matter. A President has problems in choosing the members of his Cabinet. Sometimes he makes a poor choice but is stuck with the appointee. In such a case, his usual course is to suffer for several months or years and then, with "great reluctance" and a letter of high appreciation, accept the appointee's resignation for "urgent personal reasons." Occasionally he is able to kick the inept official upstairs. I determined that Truman would not face that problem and would be proud of his Department of Commerce. I would try to run the best outfit in Washington, which everyone, Congressmen and the public, would be bound to respect.

As I reviewed my experiences in Belgium, it occurred to me that there were some specific contributions I could make. I would add my voice to the demands of those who discouraged the creation of new agencies. Also, my contacts with foreign aid in Europe had left me disgusted. It was incredibly wasteful and frequently ignored our own interests. My predecessor was embarking on a program of giving away our money on a scale never before imagined. I might help indirectly to reduce the waste and inefficiency and perhaps the amount of foreign aid. I had other hopes and plans. It is well to say here that but few of them were realized.

Upon my arrival in Washington, I told a group of reporters that Averell Harriman had left Washington to help Western Europe; perhaps I could help the United States of America. We were taking care of the rest of the world; why not take some care of ourselves? This approach seemed to interest them.[7] The Commerce Department I found to be a vast and somewhat disorganized operation. Its building, designed by Herbert Hoover, was known as "Hoover's Folly" and was the

Ambassador Sawyer's visit to Louvain in the Spring of 1945. Behind the mace carrier, left to right: Cardinal Van Roey, Ambassador Sawyer, Monsignor Van Waeyenbergh.

General Eisenhower's visit to Brussels, September 16, 1945. Left to right: General W. Bedell Smith, Mrs. Sawyer, General Eisenhower, the Burgomaster, Ambassador Sawyer, Prime Minister Van Acker. Behind Mrs. Sawyer is Colonel John Sherman.

Ambassador Sawyer with the Prince Regent following the presentation to him of Chief Commander Degree of the Legion of Merit, April 27, 1945. At the right is Colonel John Sherman, American head of SHAEF mission to Belgium.

General George Patton's visit to the U.S. Embassy in Brussels, November
7, 1945. Left to right: Colonel John Sherman, Ambassador and Mrs.
Sawyer, General Patton, Colonel Robert Pflieger.

Mr. Sawyer being sworn in as Secretary of Commerce, May 6, 1948. Background, left to right: Jesse Donaldson, Postmaster General; William Foster, Undersecretary of the Department of Commerce; Attorney General Thomas Clark; General Marshall; John Snyder, Secretary of the Treasury; John Sullivan, Secretary of the Navy. Administering the oath of office is Mr. Justice Harold Burton.

largest structure in Washington. On my first visit I repeated the experience of one or two of my predecessors and became lost trying to find my own office.[8]

Averell Harriman was gracious in his reception and offered to help in any way that he could. I saw nothing of him thereafter. It was soon clear that I was on my own. The two top men in the Department were William Foster and David Bruce. Although Harriman was leaving, I had assumed that I would have the advice and help of the experienced men under him. I had been in my office about one hour when Foster came in to announce that he was going to Europe with Harriman. I was surprised and somewhat dismayed and urged him to stay for at least a short time. After two hours of discussion I gave up. Shortly thereafter David Bruce, Assistant Secretary for Foreign Affairs, reported that he was leaving—he also was joining Harriman.[9]

Foster and Bruce were not the only ones seduced. Many other Commerce employees were asked to join the ECA—and did. Quite a few of those who left wanted to retain their status in the department. This I refused. I would not permit them to enjoy this junket in Europe and when the fun was over or when they had tired of it, return and pick up where they had left off. This was not my idea of what was fair to the hard-working and loyal employees who had stayed behind and carried on. In spite of my edict many of them left, hoping that I would weaken later. When they tried to return and asked to be allowed to reacquire their earlier status I refused.

This was my first direct experience with the lure of the "give-away" agencies. The opportunity to help the unfortunate; to demonstrate Uncle Sam's generosity; the emotional uplift in assisting other peoples to do what we think they should do; the chance to see foreign countries and play an important role in their rehabilitation; the chance to travel and learn other languages; the opportunity for one's children to benefit from foreign contacts—all made it easy for ECA to recruit a vast organization. Nor was the agency's appeal lessened by the astronomic amount of money it had to dispense. When General Marshall first appeared before Congress, he said that if he were not given all the money he requested he might as well be given none. Congress, however, did what it has done ever since—it reduced the amount requested; and the agency did what it has done ever since—it accepted the reduction. This reduced, but still vast, amount accomplished within a short time all of the original objectives of the "Marshall Plan," leaving a far-flung organization free to devise arguments for keeping itself alive.[10]

Though some people left, I had a very large organization to worry about. The Department of Commerce then included, among other agencies, the Coast and Geodetic Survey, the Bureau of Foreign and Domestic Commerce, the Patent Office, the National Bureau of Standards, the Weather Bureau, the Inland Waterways Corporation, the Bureau of the Census, and the Civil Aeronautics Administration. While I was Secretary, the Bureau of Public Roads, the Maritime Administration, and the Maritime Board were added.[11]

Although Harriman had dipped into the department's senior staff to form ECA, plenty of good men stayed on. Few of them knew much about me. One of the first things they learned was that I disapproved of smoking. I had been a smoker, a heavy smoker, who used and inhaled everything—cigars, cigarettes and pipes. Since one cigarette would raise my normal pulse by twenty beats, I realized it was not good for me. Many times I gave up smoking for Lent or some other short period. However, when I was Lieutenant-Governor of Ohio I came to a final decision. Alone one evening, sitting in front of the fire in Columbus and smoking a cigarette, I noticed that I was unusually nervous and my pulse was very fast. I asked myself— "What are the arguments in favor of this habit?" There was only one—I enjoyed it. I then asked: "What are the arguments against it?" There were several. It was expensive, obviously bad for my health, a bad example for my young children, and so forth. The cigarette I had between my fingers I threw into the fireplace and said I would never smoke again. I never have.

Like the reformed drunkard I became intolerant of tobacco and developed a particular aversion to pipe smoking. I was therefore unfavorably impressed when an amazing number of pipe smokers turned up at the conference table on my first day in office. At that time I said nothing. Two days later Bernard Gladieux, my executive secretary, came in. In his hand was a pipe. He asked me if things were going well; I said, "Yes!" He asked if there was anything at all that I did not like. I said, "Yes—these damned stinking pipes!" He was shocked, turned white, and with obvious embarrassment put his pipe into his pocket. From then on there was no smoking in my meetings. Gladieux was a fine executive and had passed the word around. Once or twice I referred to the fact that no one was smoking and said that I appreciated it. I added that I did not feel sorry for them—it was good for their health and they were so anxious to get out and drag on their pipes or cigarettes that they finished their business in half the usual time.

My nonsmoking regime perhaps also helped me to move through work at a rapid pace. I had taken over a big job. In my first speech I indicated how I intended to get it done:

I left Cincinnati because I was convinced that the work of the Department of Commerce is vital to the national welfare. It is vital because its primary function is to help American business, and I am one of those who believe that the success of American business is essential to the successful operation of our social, economic, and governmental systems. . . . We have embarked upon an effort to aid the recovery of Western Europe. It is a serious and stupendous undertaking, and a prime factor in its successful accomplishment must be the maintenance of a sound and strong American economy. We shall continue to help Europe with all the intelligence and energy we possess, but we cannot do it without a recognition of the interdependence of that problem with the maintenance of our own financial stability.[12]

There were shortages of everything. One of my earliest efforts was to organize groups of businessmen who would arrange "voluntary agreements" within industries producing commodities in short supply. Here I encountered the prejudice against "WOCS"—workers without compensation. The businessmen on these committees were top executives who gave their time for nothing. That very fact encouraged anti-business critics to claim that they would get inside information of benefit to themselves: a man engaged in a business must be barred from helping prepare agreements for that business.

This view had once been expressed by President Truman, during his years as Chairman of the Senate Committee investigating government contracts. It seemed highly desirable to explain my point of view to him. To me it was folly when dealing with steel, to look for someone who knew nothing about steel. When I pointed out that this operation must employ men who knew a great deal about a business rather than those who knew nothing he agreed to my program, in spite of strong opposition from the Department of Justice and others.

The Voluntary Agreements Program was then my pet enterprise. It was a way to avoid government control and still make full use of our supplies and our talents. Its intent was to combine control and freedom—and it worked.[13] Coupled with this program, I sought out new sources of those commodities in short supply. As soon as I took office I had representatives in Europe looking for steel; I also organized extended domestic scrap drives.

As part of my program to give prestige to businessmen and to secure their help, I enlisted the aid of the Business Advisory Council. This group had been created under President Roosevelt to advise the Secretary of Commerce. It was a select group and membership was regarded as an honor. In suggesting new members for the Council, I paid no attention to politics. When Averell Harriman later commented that I was putting too many Republicans on the Council, I said that I did not know their politics and didn't care to. The Council was drawn from big business and small business, but its members represented successful business, and in many cases that was big business. This made it subject to attack from those who made political capital out of attacking businessmen. Congressman Emanuel Celler, chairman of the House Judiciary Committee, questioned the fact that Council meetings were closed to the public and to the press and that everything occurring there was "off the record." The reason for this was clear; completely frank discussion of business and government problems would not occur if the press and the public were present. Celler was particularly distressed by a meeting of the Council at Sea Island, Georgia. He telegraphed me there demanding that we tell his committee what this secret conclave of businessmen on "an island in the Atlantic" was plotting against the American people. As most people know, "Sea Island" is not an island. I did not answer his telegram nor his following letter. A few days later Celler called to ask why I had not answered his telegram or letter. I liked the chairman and he and I were good friends. I said he was playing politics and I did not propose to give him any help. Meanwhile, he had subpoenaed before his committee the records of the Council. I called President Truman to ask him to tell "Manny" to "lay off." The President complied promptly with my request. Celler returned the records and for some time thereafter gave us no trouble.[14]

I was not long in office before I was confronted by my first security problem. On May 18, ten days after I had been sworn in, I received a letter from Republican Congressman Fred L. Crawford of Michigan, demanding that I request the resignation of John C. Virden, director of the Office of Industry Cooperation.[15] The letter was given to the press before I received it. Crawford's demand was based upon the fact that Virden's daughter had been employed in the Washington office of TASS, the Russian news agency. I tried to phone Crawford, hoping that a verbal explanation might satisfy him; he would not take my call.

On May 20 I wrote to him, refusing his request. I gave *my* letter to the press. I departed from the policy of obsequious treatment of congressmen. Was Mr. Virden unfit to do the work he was doing? Did he become unfit because his daughter, against his wishes and to his great regret and dismay, had associated herself with a Communist group? I pointed out Virden's distinguished service in this country and in Europe, his high position in industry and in his community. Virden himself had been a vigorous antagonist of the Communist ideology. I closed my letter as follows:

He disagrees violently with his daughter's decision, has undertaken unsuccessfully to persuade her to follow a different course, and has had no contact with her for several months. It is obvious, however, that the exposure of this difficult family situation by the publication of your letter presents a problem to Mr. Virden which is nothing short of tragic. I shall ask him to remain, but if he feels that he does not wish to have his personal family affairs the subject of further public discussion, I shall acquiesce in his decision.

He did not resign and Crawford said no more.[16]

I received many letters of congratulation from "liberals" for my handling of the Virden case. Later, when I closed other loyalty cases by dismissal, I was severely criticized by these same individuals. I particularly recall hearing from Dean Erwin Griswold of the Harvard Law School and Professor Arthur M. Schlesinger, Jr.[17] Shortly after my arrival in Washington Attorney General Tom Clark alerted me to charges that William Remington, employed in my department, was a member of a Communist spy-ring. I decided to interview Remington. I found him an extremely intelligent, quiet, somewhat sarcastic young man, well-informed and effective in his work. He had come to play an important role in export control. I decided to watch him and create a situation in which his disloyalty, if it existed, would be revealed. Some weeks later this opportunity came. The Russians were eager to get oil which we had in the Black Sea and were willing to exchange certain products, including manganese. I arranged for this matter to come to the attention of Remington. In a short time, in a subtle and unobtrusive way, he had managed matters so that he personally would deal with the Russians. It was then clear to me that the stories of his Communist connections were probably true. Other evidence confirmed my suspicion. I ordered him investigated by my security board, which decided against him. I fired him.

He appealed his case to the Loyalty Review Board. This Board, to which I had briefly belonged, reversed my decision and ordered me to reinstate him and pay his back salary, amounting to over ten thousand dollars. I could not return him to his former delicate and important position. With some misgivings I placed him in a spot where we hoped he could do no harm. He was, however, a drag on the taxpayer. He was later convicted of perjury in his testimony before a Federal grand jury and sent to the penitentiary. There he was stabbed to death by a fellow prisoner.[18]

Among other security problems was Edward U. Condon, chief of the Bureau of Standards. From his college days Condon had been a radical. He had participated in the development of the atomic bomb at Los Alamos, where he had been a difficult man to handle. Indeed, he had deliberately refused to obey orders and had incurred the great displeasure of his boss General Leslie Groves. In Washington he continued to flaunt his contempt for security measures and his sympathy for Russia. He and his wife made a point of attending receptions at the Russian Embassy. He was often under attack from Congress. However, he was a brilliant scientist and, as head of the Bureau, was doing an outstanding job. I decided not to discharge him. I had some misgivings, I must admit. His public statements criticizing our security methods made my decision difficult; but I felt that he was not disloyal. On one occasion he stated to me that he might as well live in Russia. I said to him, "Dr. Condon, don't be stupid. If you had done and said in Russia the things which you have done and said here, you would be dead!" He smiled and said, "You are probably right." [19]

Almost as touchy as the problem of security was the problem of export control. Congress had given the Secretary of Commerce final authority to decide what things should be shipped out of this country. These decisions involved not only our commercial needs but questions of foreign policy. As many government programs dealt with these matters, action was handled by an interdepartmental committee upon which were representatives from State, Defense, Interior, Treasury, and other departments. It met continually and employed a far-flung organization of subordinates; it was into this committee that William Remington had penetrated before I became Secretary of Commerce.

There were many differences of opinion. The State Department was inclined to favor the interests of other countries; the Defense Department usually supported the Commerce Department in an effort to promote and protect the interests of the United States. I recall a violent disagreement over exporting materials for building a steel mill in Yugoslavia. The controversy came up from subordinates to the department heads. Louis Johnson, Secretary of Defense, and I, opposed the shipment. Dean Acheson, Secretary of State, favored it. Johnson and I thought it was a mistake to put American money and materials into a steel mill for which there was little need, and which in case of war could immediately be used by our enemies. The State Department believed that this risk should not outweigh the need to improve the economic status of Yugoslavia. We could not agree, and the matter was taken to President Truman. Dean Acheson is a very persuasive man; Truman sided with him and authorized the shipment.[20]

Export control was not confined to Iron Curtain countries. The United States was strongly urged to ship quantities of steel rails to India. The Indian Minister of Industry called on me, explained his nation's needs and the enthusiastic support he had received from our State Department. He asked if I would approve the shipment. I said that I would approve it after India had shipped to us certain quantities of manganese. We had practically no manganese and the only large reserves not controlled by Russia were in India and Brazil. The minister gave me several reasons why this could not be done until they had the rails. I said that we would ship the rails when we got the manganese. When he saw argument was useless he agreed to ship the manganese. After it arrived I carried out my agreement to release the rails.

Late in the summer of 1948, congressman Walter C. Ploeser undertook to embarrass me by making public a letter critical of our export policy. The congressman disclosed his "great amazement" that in 1947 Sweden had imported two hundred eighty-six thousand tons of steel from the United States. I replied, "You can relax. Shipments for the current year are only twenty-eight thousand tons for the first quarter and nineteen thousand tons for the second quarter; furthermore, we have imported nine thousand tons of steel from Sweden and currently are running at a higher rate than that." I heard nothing more from Ploeser.

In September a Senate Investigations Subcommittee blasted the Office of International Trade in my department. Immediately I replied:

Another show has opened on the Hill.

The charges are unworthy of attention except that they are so misleading.

1. The story—"Nails had been exported as 'shoe tacks'."
   The facts—The nails were never exported.
2. The story—"A man under suspicion was granted permission
   to export a million dollars worth of goods."
   The facts—His license had been canceled before any use was
   made of it.
3. The story—"An employee of the office admitted favoritism in
   granting two export licenses."
   The facts—The Subcommittee failed to notify anyone in the
   Department. The day the information came to us, not
   through the Committee, the employee was removed from
   office.

Since I have been Secretary of Commerce I have not received
from the Committees investigating export control one single con-
structive suggestion. If the Senators have such suggestions, I
welcome them. If they have not, I can only conclude that the sole
reason for parading these stale "revelations" in public is the fact
that this is an election year.[21]

As the year wore on, my contacts with Congress became frequent. Congressional respect for the department increased and
my relations with members from both parties became friendly,
even cordial.

I tried to develop in the public mind my concept of the
function of the Department of Commerce. On October 26 I
made a speech in Boston and reminded my audience:

The Department of Commerce was created and should operate
to help American business. It should recognize that a businessman
is likely to know much more about his own business than a
Government employee or economist, well-intentioned and well-
read as the latter may be.

As a small boy I was fascinated by the picture of Atlas, the
giant who carried the entire world upon his shoulders. I was
fascinated, not only by the immense load he was carrying, but by
the mystery—what was he standing on? What supported the man
who was supporting the world?

America today is in the position of Atlas. What are we standing on? We have nothing to stand on but the strength and solidity of our own economy. The richness of our resources, our marvelous productive system, the efficiency of our methods of transportation, distribution, and marketing of goods, the ability of our workers and the intelligence of our technicians and the skill and experience of the managers—these, and nothing else, are the substructure which carries the entire load.[22]

Earlier, I had made known my objections to the program of creating new agencies. The House Committee on Interstate and Foreign Commerce had asked my views on establishing a National Science Foundation. I told the committee:

In setting up any new agency it is important to examine the existing agencies in the same field. Ones already active here include the Smithsonian Institution, Atomic Energy Commission, National Bureau of Standards, Weather Bureau, etc. The Government is no newcomer in the field of scientific research and in setting up the National Science Foundation it is important to avoid overlapping of functions and confusion between the equally vital departments of Government.[23]

This was my first chance to slow down or modify the program of creating new agencies. Every new problem called for a new agency. The routine is unchanged, even today. First the President picks an administrator—an outstanding, dedicated, and usually not too modest soul—who is persuaded to make the sacrifice of his personal interests to undertake this "challenging" task. When the administrator arrives in Washington he begins to recruit his subordinates. Two are essential: an executive secretary and counsel. Then he must pick a staff. This is not too difficult—there are always many government employees or those out of work who are willing to aid the cause. Housing must be secured, usually at the expense of some permanent department. This accomplished, secretarial help is gathered. Meanwhile, the new administrator is beset by reporters; he gives out interviews on what he expects to do; he calls in advisors, frequently professors with no practical experience in business or government, who also must have secretaries and who also must meet the press. The new agency has not even begun to function when it finds the need to expand its originally assigned duties. This will require greatly enlarged space and additional personnel. Immediately and inevitably its activities overlap with those of existing departments.

My conservative approach and my defense of business were particularly annoying to commentators and columnists, most of whom were of the liberal persuasion. But as time went on commentators who had been critical became friendly. Some of them I came to know well and favorably. Elmer Davis, among others, was extremely critical of my action in discharging William Remington. I called him on the telephone and asked what he knew about the facts. He admitted that he knew nothing and offered to take part of his next broadcast to elaborate on my side of the case. I thanked him but, perhaps foolishly, declined his offer. Not one commentator among those who had criticized me had called to ask why I had acted. No columnist ever called me and the only commentator who called about a prospective story was Fulton Lewis. He was planning to make a statement on the air that night and wished to know what I had to say about it. I said that his statement was incorrect. He thereupon said he would state the facts I had given him when he went on the air—and he did. Drew Pearson made many nasty statements about me. While I had never undertaken to answer any columnist or commentator, one of Pearson's columns was so bad that I asked the President what he would advise me to do. Truman said: "Do not answer him. You will get the s.o.b. off of page eight onto page one."

I took part frequently in panel discussions on radio and television. These were interesting and edifying experiences. I remember my first "Meet the Press," run then by Martha Rountree and Lawrence Spivak. It was great fun. In a later television appearance I encountered Victor Riesel, the labor columnist who had attacked me unrestrainedly because I had not stopped the shipment of critical materials to China. During this interview I was able to demonstrate that I had done the very things he said I had not done.[24]

The most dramatic event of the year 1948 was the Presidential election. As a confidant of Truman I was privileged to see his impressive performance from the inside. Many frightened Democrats were suggesting some other candidate. Jimmy Roosevelt was talking about Eisenhower. Truman, however, was calm and unperturbed. One day after luncheon he told me of the stir in Missouri when he attended the funeral of Kansas City's boss Pendergast. He had been urged to stay away; this might cost him his political future. Newspapers publicly warned him not to attend. Truman ignored them. He said to me, "All of the papers in the state threatened me with annihilation if I attended the funeral. Pendergast never asked me to do a wrong thing because he knew I would not do it if he had asked me. However, he had been my friend and I felt that I should attend the funeral—which I did. After that I ran for the Senate and fought like hell and was elected." He then added, "I am going to do the same damn thing this year and get elected." He said this in June, before he began his famous whistle-stop tours across the country, the unexpected result of which is now a fantastic bit of political history.

Following Truman's victory, businessmen began to worry that the President's policies and program would bring on a depression—and Drew Pearson predicted that within sixty days I would be out of the Cabinet. Neither of these frightening developments took place.[25]

14   Business—
Large
and Small

THE YEAR 1949 opened on a "timely" note. The Bureau of Standards had discovered a new way to measure time. Time had been based upon the rotation of the earth upon its axis; but the earth is an imperfect timekeeper—it is gradually slowing down. There are also irregularities in its rotation, altering the length of each day. Atomic timekeeping, because of the constant nature of atomic action, does not suffer from changes due to temperature, pressure, and age. The Bureau produced the Atomic Clock. I said: "At the threshold of the Atomic Age, science now gives us atomic time—time, let us hope, for world peace and progress." [1]

The non-scientific activities of the department got off to an equally promising start, in which I was greatly aided by the members of Congress. In January I appeared before the Senate Committee to urge the extension of Public Law 395, embodying the voluntary agreements program. I was delighted to have my recommendation supported by the unanimous vote of both houses.[2] I received another vote of confidence from Capitol Hill in a matter of greater importance when a renewal of the Export Control law was also unanimously approved.

Truman's surprising victory over Dewey had amazed, and

in some quarters dismayed, many people who assumed that business would be punished and times would be bad. I believed that this pessimism would produce the very results that were feared. Businessmen would reduce their purchases, restrict their operations, cut down the number of their employees. I knew that the economic condition of the country was sound. If businessmen could be assured that they had nothing to fear from the Truman administration, there would be marked improvement in their psychology and in business. I discussed the problem often and at length with Truman. He decided that I should undertake a nation-wide tour to explore economic conditions and prospects with business leaders. We also decided that these discussions should include labor leaders and city and state officials. I traveled thousands of miles, mostly by air, and interviewed thousands of people. I went first to New England, then to Detroit, Lansing, Cleveland, Cincinnati, Memphis, Birmingham, Savannah, and Buffalo. In October I resumed my survey, going to Chicago, Pittsburgh, Miami, Jacksonville, New Orleans, Houston, Dallas, Fort Worth, Oklahoma City, Kansas City and Omaha and other cities.[2]

At Mobile, Alabama, the newspaper printed a hair-raising account of my driving escapade in the middle of their fair city. I had left a meeting with businessmen to go on the air at a radio studio six blocks away. As I rushed to my car, a reporter stopped me and began to ask questions. I invited him to join me. The man who was to take me to the radio station climbed into the driver's seat but could not start the car. I left the back seat, told him to move over, started the car, and took off after my motorcycle escort. We went around curves, through red lights, and amused and angered many citizens. I was a boy going to a fire. I pulled up at the curb with one minute to spare. As I left the car, the reporter, somewhat shaken, climbed out after me. I told him he could talk as we went up in the elevator. He said: "Never mind—I have my story."

My first report to the President noted: "There was no view

in any area that the time had come for major pump-priming or special public works activity by the federal government." Then, as now, theorists in and out of government felt that some such program was badly needed.[4] Later I reported the almost universal demand for tax relief and reduction of federal expenditures, the need to liberalize depreciation allowances, and a liberal interpretation of Section 102, dealing with accumulated earnings. The small businessmen, in particular, should be permitted to retain a larger share of earnings for working capital. There was agreement by labor with management that we should maintain a prosperous and growing American business. The emphasis was not upon the responsibility of the federal government to create work; the emphasis was upon measures to make private business operate profitably and give employees steady work at good wages. Only a few of the problems of the small businessman could be solved by government. This did not require the creation of any new bureau as had been repeatedly suggested. The troubles could be cured or greatly alleviated by certain changes in the tax laws. Owners of small businesses had to be given more leeway to keep and reinvest their early profits. They also needed some way to enable their companies to survive them. The small businessman, if he had been successful, would at his death leave a property subject to the attack of the Internal Revenue Service. That Service would give his stock a high value, because of his success, but it would be impossible, or at least difficult, for his executors to sell it to anyone except a competitor. His only hope was to merge during his lifetime with a company whose stock was listed on a major exchange.[5]

Almost everyone I had met on my trips had been cooperative. Businessmen and labor representatives discussed matters in a calm, unemotional, objective way. State and city officials also were helpful, with one exception. Early in my trip I met with the governors of the New England states to discuss the problems of that area. One governor, Sherman Adams, indicated indifference, if not disdain, and finally stalked out of the

meeting. He later stalked out of the White House—but not
with disdain.[6]

As we moved into 1949, I had become settled in the routine
of my job and had time to work on the application of some of
my ideas. I was especially intrigued by the Point IV Aid
Program, the plan to share American technical know-how with
other nations of the world. It had been the fourth point in
Truman's inaugural address. This suggestion met with great
favor; but I feared it would develop into another extravagant
give-away program and tried to keep this from happening. On
April 24 at Cape Henry, Virginia, I spoke at a celebration of
Captain John Smith's landing and talked about the Point IV
program. The President had read and approved my speech. I
began with a reference to John Smith and emphasized the fact
that most of our early settlers were financed by businessmen
who risked their fortunes, as these adventurers risked their
lives, on uncertain but potentially profitable business ventures.

The things which the President suggests we should share with
others are, for the most part, the fruits of American business. This
makes clear that what is contemplated under Point IV of the
inaugural address is in large measure an extension to other parts
of the world of what American businessmen and their associates
and helpers have done here in America.[7]

I was emphasizing the need for American business participation in our overseas aid program. As I was giving my speech at
Cape Henry, an assistant secretary of state was in New Orleans
advocating the opposite view—this was an opportunity to recognize our obligation to underdeveloped countries and to give
away American money in large amounts. The possible activity
of American business was not mentioned.

Later I amplified my position before the House Committee
on Foreign Affairs.

I wish to point out briefly what I regard as the practical and
common sense approach and discuss in particular the part which
may be played by American business.

I listed what American businessmen had already done, without any prodding by Government:

Oil wells and pipelines in Venezuela, Saudi Arabia, Indonesia, Burma, and many other countries; the mining or processing of aluminum, cooper, lead, zinc, tin, tungsten, vanadium, and iron ores in Latin America and South Africa; lumbering and wood processing in Newfoundland, British Honduras, Costa Rica, and the Gold Coast; the operation of sugar plantations and mills in Cuba, the Dominican Republic, and Haiti; the development of hydroelectric power in Mexico, Uruguay, and Portugal.

To talk about Point IV is easy; to make it work will not be so easy. If the President's suggestion is to be fruitful, two things must be accomplished. First, we must obtain the freely given consent and cooperation of the countries affected. We should not force our money, our techniques, or our ideas upon other countries. Our effort should be to create a climate where American businessmen and their dollars are eagerly desired. . . .

We cannot expect to transplant American techniques, root, stem, and blossom, into every part of the world; some of our techniques will thrive only in a highly developed industrial society. In many areas of the world people are still cultivating the soil with hoes. What they need is plows—not tractors and flame cultivators. Technical progress in underdeveloped areas involves more than blueprints and engineers: it involves sensible human beings.[8]

Later that year I saw how the program was being run. Thomas McDonald, Chairman of the Bureau of Public Roads, perhaps the leading road builder in the world, was happy and excited by the arrangement he had made with Emperor Haile Selassie of Ethiopia. Ethiopia was to pay 17 million dollars for our help in rebuilding their roads and bridges. The program was proceeding beautifully, to the satisfaction of everyone, when a young representative of the Point IV Program went to the Ethiopian authorities and told them it was not necessary to pay for the help of our technicians; the Point IV Program was designed to give this help for nothing. This suggestion upset the Ethiopians, or at least bewildered them, and indicated clearly that different parts of our government were working at cross-purposes. However, like anyone else, the Ethiopians would take Uncle Sam's money if they could get it, and they did. My conservative suggestions were not followed; within a short time the Point IV Program was in vigorous and direct competition with all the other give-away efforts.

In June, I spoke to the Canadian Chamber of Commerce at St. Andrews and mentioned, for the first time, my great interest in the St. Lawrence Seaway.

Among the resources with which the people of Canada and the United States have been blessed, none is more impressive than the great system of waterways along our common border. As the early explorers pushed their way through the Great Lakes, looking in vain for a Northwest passage to the Indies, they could not foresee that these Great Lakes would some day become the busiest waterway in the world.[9]

Although the Seaway and Power Project had been advocated by Presidents of the United States for thirty years and had been recommended by President Truman in six separate messages to Congress, the Canadians had done all the work. I pointed out our shrinking resources in the Mesabi Range and the importance of the Quebec-Labrador iron ore to the American steel industry. A St. Lawrence Seaway would give us a source of ore, free from the wartime hazards of Atlantic transportation. I asked the question, "What has been stopping us?" We had been stopped by representatives of various United States seaports who felt that the St. Lawrence Seaway would have a disastrous effect upon their harbor traffic. Some influential Senators were bitterly opposed. Also, coal companies believed that water transportation would hurt them. The miners' unions felt the same way. When I spoke at St. Andrews, I could not know that within a short time President Truman would give me the job of pushing the St. Lawrence Seaway legislation through Congress.[10]

There were at this time men in Washington who claimed they could put any businessman in touch with "the right parties" in the government. This they were willing to do for 5 per cent of the amount of whatever contract was obtained. There was great discussion of this activity—and great criticism. It occurred to me that the Commerce Department might replace these "five percenters." On August 25, I pointed out that the average small businessman lacked the knowledge to deal effectively with federal agencies. He did not know where to start or what to do. Then I announced that "Commerce Department employees will do the five percenters' business but will do the business for nothing." [11]

I was beginning, even at this early date, to get special assignments from Truman. On August 30 he wrote to me on the subject of transportation, pointing out that various Federal programs were being administered by different agencies, each concerned with only a limited sector; a unified and coordinated Federal Program for transportation was clearly essential. He asked me to prepare a report, to be ready by December first, outlining the transportation issues which needed to be resolved. He also requested my views on the desirability of my conducting, on a continuing basis, broad studies relating to federal transportation policies and programs. This assignment involved an enormous amount of preparation and work, many contacts with other departments and the uninterrupted endeavor of a large number of my own employees. We met the deadline: the report was in the hands of the President on December first. Regrettably nothing came of it at that time, but I have been told that subsequent surveys have made continuing use of its findings and recommendations.[12]

On several occasions I had voiced my feeling that Mexico and the other Latin American countries had been neglected. We seemed interested only in more remote places. Early in the fall it was suggested that a trip to Mexico by the Secretary of Commerce might be in order. Life in Washington was a little dull; I leaped at the offer. On October 19 I arrived in Mexico City where I was met by high officials and an eighty-piece band. I visited Chapultepec Park and was shown through the castle that had served as a palace for Maximilian and Carlotta. From its terrace I could see Popocateptl and the Sleeping Lady (Ixtaccihuatl), both of which were at that moment entirely free of clouds. I attended cocktail parties and a dinner and was taken to the Rancho del Artista. The following morning my tour continued at the 400-year-old Iglesia Hospital de Jesus and the National Palace. At the Palace of Fine Arts I addressed the annual meeting of The American Society of Travel Agents, accompanied to the stage by President Alemán. I spoke about foreign travel; in 1949 the people of the United States had spent 114 million dollars in Mexico, nearly a fifth of the total amount our travelers had spent over all the world. I mentioned the Point IV Program, our desire to cooperate with Latin America and our wish to make private investment in Latin American enterprises.[13] After this I returned the President's courtesy and called on him at his office, where he personally opened the door with his own key. That evening I was the honored guest at a banquet given by the Chamber of Commerce of Mexico. The next morning I visited a modern steel plant and met the governor at the Municipal Palace. Here, in the Hall of the Cabildos, where the councilors of the city have met for hundreds of years, I was entertained with Mexican music and presented with a medal of honor and a hand-written parchment scroll.

I had enjoyed myself immensely. The next day I took off for Acapulco. There I spent the night at the home of my friend Romulo O'Farrill, a beautiful residence on top of a rocky hill commanding a view of the Pacific on one side and the harbor on the other. Before dinner I made a circuit of the harbor aboard President Alemán's yacht. I was to leave the following morning at ten o'clock but was persuaded to go fishing at 6:30 A.M., on the promise that a sailfish would be "planted" for me in the ocean. After an early breakfast we boarded a cabin cruiser at the Club de Pesca and moved rapidly out to a point several miles off shore. At 8:40 A.M. the bait boy gave me the rod. Within fifteen seconds the bait was struck; in twenty minutes I had a beautiful sailfish along side. I had caught many sailfish in the Atlantic, but this Pacific fish was my biggest catch—approximately one hundred pounds. I boarded President Alemán's yacht, which had been circling at a distance, and returned to the dock. I took off from the airport on schedule and returned to Washington.

My law practice had acquainted me with the problems of businessmen as they deal with the government, especially the problems they encounter in dealing with several government agencies. I felt it was time to try to clarify the businessman's role and the role of government, and to reconcile the attitudes of the Department of Justice and the Federal Trade Commission. I had discussed these matters with the President. On November 25 he gave me another assignment:

I feel that it would be desirable to explore the means of increasing the effectiveness of Federal efforts with respect to monopoly and restraint of trade, including improvements in programs and administrative arrangements and needed revisions in legislation. I should like to have you consult with the Attorney General and the Chairman of the Federal Trade Commission and take the leadership in setting up an inter-agency group to develop proposals for my consideration of these matters. The Economic Council is, of course, interested in this subject in its advisory capacity to me on general economic policy. I am sure you will want to consult with the members in developing a proposed program of action.

I explained the job I was about to undertake with this statement:

Heretofore, Government efforts in this field have been confined primarily to prosecuting those guilty or suspected of unfair trade practices. This is a different approach.

A major task of the new group will be to propose sound factual underpinning for Government policies in this field. As part of the Commerce responsibility, I am releasing today a comprehensive study prepared by my Department, at the request of the Celler House Monopoly Committee, showing the degree of concentration of output in each industry in the United States engaged in manufacturing in the year 1947. This study marks the first time since before the war that such data have been made available. I have sent this material to Chairman Celler for use in connection with the current inquiry of his Committee.[14]

This report had involved a tremendous amount of work. I was pleased to prepare it, however, because it enabled us to work with facts, instead of fantasies. We classified all manufacturing activities based upon the "Census of Manufacturers." We showed the proportion of output concentrated in the top four companies, the top eight companies, the top twenty companies, and the top fifty companies in each industry and the corresponding proportions for 1935. This study made some interesting disclosures. In 1935 the first four companies in the tin can and tinware industry controlled 80 per cent of the business; in 1947 they controlled 77 per cent. In 1935 the top four manufacturers of domestic laundry equipment had 56 per cent of the market, in 1947, 39 per cent. The four big linseed oil mills had 87 per cent in 1935; in 1947, 74 per cent. The first four tire companies in 1935 had 80 per cent; in 1947, 76 per cent. For most industries concentration at the top had diminished—not increased.

Within a short time I had organized "the President's Committee on Business and Government Relations." I should have realized that this effort was doomed to fail. Not only was my pro-business approach unpopular, but like a fighting family which promptly unites when an outsider comes on the scene— the agencies which had quarreled with each other promptly joined forces to keep the Commerce Department from getting into the act. At our very first meeting it was clear that all my fellow members were opposed to the President's proposal, except Lowell Mason, acting chairman of the F.T.C. I made repeated efforts to discuss our assignment and lay out a program. My only success was to secure agreement on a form of questionnaire, sent to thousands of businessmen and others, including such questions as:

Under present Federal laws against monopolies, restraints of trade, and unfair competition, what new procedures, if any, are needed in order to:
   (a) increase public understanding,
   (b) promote voluntary compliance,
   (c) bring about more effective enforcement, or otherwise make these laws more effective in promoting competition? What changes in existing procedures are needed for these same purposes?

The response to the questionnaire was extensive, informative, and could have been extremely helpful if I had been able to arrange for its use. It was soon lost in the limbo of good intentions come to naught. Time after time I tried to hold meetings. With one excuse or another, the others failed to attend. The President and I had accomplished nothing.[15]

In December of that year I spoke to the Outdoor Advertising Association of America. I dealt with distribution costs, always a favorite target for the radical.

Some months ago a friend who owns an orange grove in Florida, but lives in New York, complained to me that he sold his oranges cheaply in Florida but paid a high price to get them in New York. "Someone in between was making an inordinate profit." I asked —"Why don't you make this profit yourself?" He did not follow my suggestion; but he did get the point. Many things were done with his oranges between Florida and New York City.

I also talked about advertising. The nation's great increase in purchases and the resulting increase in employment were in large measure due to advertising. I was so convinced of advertising's importance in stimulating the growth of our economy that I set up an Advertising Advisory Committee for the Department of Commerce. That committee functioned effectively during my tenure, but was abandoned after I left office.[16]

All cabinet members give many talks—too many, in fact. One of my "too many" talks was made before the Public Relations Society of America, where the performance of the chairman was a public relations classic. I was the guest of honor and the only listed speaker. After an excellent and prolonged dinner the chairman said that he would like, before my talk, to make some awards. His comments were lengthy and each recipient responded *in extenso*. He then introduced every person at the head table and offered an elaborate tribute to each. At eleven o'clock I was introduced to a groggy and somewhat irritated audience. I asked if they wished me to say good night and let them go home; they were gracious enough to shout that I go on. I told one or two stories of similar experiences that seemed to put them in good humor, and they stayed on cheerfully until I concluded. The subject of my talk was "A New Liberalism for the Next Half Century." This speech developed a point which I had been making for some time:

> The idea of accepting a relatively modest profit in order to sell more goods to more people is one of the most progressive ideas in the world today. I will go further—I will say that this idea is the only really radical idea in the modern world—and the United States is the only country in the world in which that idea is the main principle of economic action.[17]

Many men in politics didn't share my views. The most prominent of these was Henry Wallace. While I thought Wallace's political ideas were fuzzy, I liked him very much and agreed to debate with him on a radio program called "American Forum of the Air." Our subject was "How Can We Keep America Prosperous." When this debate between the progressive Wallace and the conservative Sawyer was publicized, his followers made a particular effort to pack the auditorium of the Department of Commerce. As the debate began the applause was all for Wallace, but after a few managed efforts the audience became less vociferous. Wallace announced that the country was in bad shape. I said we were not in bad shape; we were exceedingly well off. We should compare our situation with any other period of our own history or with that of any other country of the world. In countering Wallace's claims of approaching disaster, I said that we should "stop scaring everybody, including consumers, into the idea that we are going to have a depression." To which Wallace commented, "That sounds like a Republican to me." I replied: "It doesn't make any difference what my answer sounds like. I am telling you the truth." [18]

What sounded to Wallace like Republican sentiment was the point of view of a conservative Democrat. But I am a Northern conservative, and do not agree with the position of most Southern conservatives on the racial question. While civil rights was not a major issue in 1949, I did have an opportunity to end one small bit of segregation. The Washington National Airport operated under my supervision and control. The Airport is in Virginia, which had a law *requiring* segregation. I was apprised by the airport manager that Negroes were being refused admission to the restaurant at the airport because of this law. I issued orders to ignore the law and permit anyone to come into the restaurant. A few Negroes came, behaved well, and no one complained. [19]

The pace of events picked up in 1950 and I was hard pressed to keep up with my work. Fortunately, I enjoyed excellent health. Indeed, I had been seriously ill only once, in the 1920's. One day, on Long Island, I had picked up my four children (there were then only four), two on each arm, and paraded up and down the beach. Then I ran the two miles to our summer home. Later, when I told my wife that I wasn't feeling well, she said I deserved not to feel well after showing off on the beach. Her chiding turned to concern as my temperature rose, and the doctor we called diagnosed my illness as pneumonia. I was in bed for four weeks that beautiful fall on Long Island. I have had two operations, one of them while in Washington, during this same year of 1950. One night in March, shortly after returning to my home in Georgetown from a Democratic dinner, I began to suffer pains in my side. The next morning I saw my doctor. He confirmed my suspicion that I had a gall bladder condition and recommended that I have the annoyance removed. I left for Cincinnati that afternoon, and the following morning was returned from the operating room minus my gall bladder and my appendix. The next day the surgeon, Dr. Reed Shank, was in surgery when he received a message that he was wanted on the telephone. He asked who wanted him and the messenger said, "The President." He said, "The president of what?" The messenger said, "The President of the United States." Dr. Shank, in appropriate language, told the messenger to tell the joker where to go; but when it developed that it was the President, he took the call. Truman, considerate as usual, was trying to find out how I had come through the operation.[20]

I was soon back in Washington and back at work. At Minneapolis I made a speech on the subject of "Size." Many people were worried about big business—as was I. It did seem that these giant enterprises were too big. But what to do about it?

A few months ago, on a farm in central Ohio where two of my sons were employed, a tremendous skeleton was plowed up. It was the bones of a mastodon. Full grown, this beast stood fourteen feet high, weighed six or eight tons, and with his great curved tusks looked as if he could handle all comers. Conditions in that distant era were favorable for mastodons. With plenty of warm sunshine, cool water, and lush prairie grass, this huge hairy beast could get by and even prosper. What was it, twenty thousand years ago, which caused the death of this big animal?

Was it disease? Was it weakness caused by sloth and idleness, because, being so large, he didn't need to fight? Was it the result of a battle with another beast stronger and more alert—or a battle with many smaller, weaker beasts, individually more alert and in combination stronger? Did he die because he was so big he could no longer function—or because he needed so much to eat that food was no longer available? Did he lose the desire to live? We will never know; we do not have the facts. We do know that he did not die by government decree.

If the sponsors of the Sherman Act believed that this law would prevent business enterprises from getting bigger, they were mistaken. Business units have grown to stupendous size. Today all but the smallest of the Standard Oil subsidiaries are larger than the parent company which was broken up.

What can we do about size? If we attack size in business, shall we ignore it in other fields—labor, for instance? Is a big co-op a menace or a blessing?

We have heard it said—"Let an enterprise be big enough to be efficient, but no bigger." What is efficient? How do you calculate the efficiency of a firm producing many different items, some whose market may be declining, some whose market may be expanding, and others for which there is as yet no market at all?

What are the symptoms of a business malfunction? Is it failing to maintain or raise our standard of living? Is it considering the welfare of its employees? Is it earning money for its shareholders? Is it contributing its share of taxes for the support of the government? Is it doing its part in time of war? These questions should be asked and answered.[21]

Probably the most important of all my appearances before congressional committees occurred that spring, on April 24, when I appeared before the House Public Works Committee to support House Joint Resolution No. 271, approving the agreement between the United States and Canada relating to the Great Lakes-St. Lawrence Basin. The President had asked me to coordinate the efforts of those trying to promote the St. Lawrence Seaway and in particular to arrange and direct the

presentation of our case to Congress. Hearings in earlier years
had been perfunctory and brief. I arranged for detailed presentations both in the Senate and in the House and coordinated
the testimony of everyone who was to appear. We still had
bitter opposition from representatives of New York City, Boston, Galveston, Baltimore, and other ports, who felt that the St.
Lawrence Seaway would reduce, if not destroy, their city's
overseas commerce. I myself made many appearances before
the committees of both houses. I pointed out that if war should
come this Seaway would be the only safe route to an adequate
supply of iron ore.

Without enough iron ore, our steel industry, our economy, and
our military posture would decline disastrously. The hard fact is
that our steel industry is facing a rapidly growing dependence on
foreign iron ore.

As time went on the prospects for the Seaway improved.
Conditions had changed, and the point of view of one important individual had changed. George Humphrey, later Secretary of the Treasury under Eisenhower, had for many years
opposed the Seaway project. Now he favored it. He was the
head of the M.A.Hanna interests who now owned valuable
reserves of iron ore in northeast Canada. The Seaway would be
a great help to them. The result of our efforts was the legislation which authorized the Seaway.[22]

In the year 1950, we took the Seventeenth Decennial Census. In ancient Rome censors called people together in the
open squares of towns and cities to inquire about their wealth
and their health. On the basis of this information they levied
taxes and drafted men into the Roman Army. In the United
States the Census Bureau gathers information to be used as an
index of opportunity and progress. The Census Bureau does
not exist just to count noses. Every day it is collecting information. It plays an important part in business planning. An
automobile manufacturer wants to know how many families

have moved from the city to the suburbs where they will need two cars. How many families living on farms have two cars? I began early to prepare for the 1950 effort. The Bureau of the Census planned to use the first computer, called UNIVAC, which the Bureau of Standards in my Department had helped Remington Rand to build. Remington Rand had employed General Leslie Groves, whom I had known when he was head of the Manhattan Project. Groves invited me to come to Philadelphia to see the computer's first public demonstration. After the obligatory speeches, including one by me, we were conducted into the room housing the amazing invention. The console was like a large pipe organ keyboard, and one of the scientists present sat down to play. We waited silently as his fingers moved skilfully over the keyboard—but nothing came out. He tried again and again. We waited. Still nothing came out. In great embarrassment, those in charge finally announced that the computer would not work. The meeting adjourned, and I went back to Washington. But the computer did work when we needed it, after 132,000 census takers had moved out across the country. Within four weeks, a record time, the job was done.[23]

In the spring Philadelphians were celebrating "Stephen Girard Day." I was asked to talk:

A week ago I saw a letter to a Pennsylvania businessman from one of his agents in France: "The period we now live in is so rich in Extraordinary Events and Commerce in Europe subject to so many sudden changes that it is impossible for us to give you such information as might serve to guide your future Commercial operations in this quarter . . ." A similar letter from Holland concludes: "The State of Affairs here is actually a crisis." A letter from Montevideo tells about the impossibility of procuring dollars —the Government has prohibited their exportation.

These letters should not spread discouragement about the present conditions of our foreign trade. They were written in 1810–1811 to Stephen Girard, merchant and world trader of Philadelphia.[24]

I continued in various ways and places my defense of American business. Early in the spring I was asked to address a graduating class of a business college which one of my sons was attending. I did not address myself wholly to the youthful audience in front of me.

Young people have been led to believe that business is something to be tolerated and not encouraged. They have been taught that business is a low order of activity, engaged in for the purpose of making money by selfish people who have little or no regard for the general welfare. They have been given the impression that businessmen must be carefully and continually watched to see that they don't violate the law; perhaps the best thing which could happen would be the discovery of some plan by which businesses and businessmen could be relegated into the background of history.

That doctrine did not originate in nurseries or kindergartens; it has been taught in our colleges.

You should believe that business is a blessing, a business career is attractive, and your greatest contribution in business will be your willingness to work and work hard.[25]

15 *War in Korea*

IN LATE spring of 1950 we were at war in Korea. It was not called war, but it was. As the Korean action began, I placed an immediate embargo upon all United States exports to that country—4 P.M. June 28. Shortly thereafter, the President delegated authority to me, under the Defense Production Act of 1950, to decide production priorities and to allocate materials and facilities.[1] To administer this program, I formed a National Production Authority. My first problem was to get men, men who understood manufacturing and distribution—in other words, businessmen. I had available a great reservoir of business talent in the Business Advisory Council and called a meeting of the Council, which every member attended. It was a thrilling and heartwarming response. I chose one member, General William Harrison, to head the new Authority and began to recruit men to help him.

Before a congressional committee, I took the opportunity to point out the contribution of businessmen to the defense program.

I would like to add a word with reference to the attitude of American businessmen in this emergency. The businessmen of this

Secretary Sawyer presenting the final count of the Seventeenth Decennial Census to President Truman at the White House, November 2, 1950. Left to right (standing): Dr. Roy V. Peel, Director, Bureau of the Census; A. Ross Eckler, Deputy Director, Bureau of the Census.

Secretary Sawyer with Greek Minister Spyras Markesinis in Athens, November, 1952. Left to right: (partly obscured person unidentified); Charles R. Hook, Chairman Armco Steel Corporation; Langbourne M. Williams, Jr., President, Freeport Sulphur Company; Secretary Sawyer; Leland Barrows, MSA Mission Chief in Athens; Minister Markesinis; interpreter.

Secretary and Mrs. Sawyer with Miss Margaret Truman aboard the *Ile de France* at ceremonies marking the return of the liner to Atlantic service, New York, July 28, 1949.

Secretary Sawyer at the opening of the Canadian International Trade
Fair in Toronto, May 30, 1949. Left to right: The Right Hon. C. D.
Howe, Canadian Minister of Trade and Commerce; The Hon. Harold
Wilson, then President of the British Board of Trade, later Prime Minis-
ter of Great Britain; Secretary Sawyer.

Secretary Sawyer receiving the Freedoms Foundation award
from Mr. Don Belding, President of the Foundation, "for
outstanding achievement in bringing about a better understanding of the American way of life." In the background
is the Department of Commerce flag.

Secretary Sawyer meeting with the Advertising Council, April 11, 1951.

country are not only willing but anxious to cooperate with the Government and with other groups of our population to whatever extent necessary and to make whatever sacrifices are demanded by considerations of public security and the general welfare. It is not only desirable but necessary to utilize that feeling and not discourage or dissipate it.[2]

Unfortunately, some enthusiastic government officials were demanding production far beyond what was reasonable or possible. I recall particularly Assistant Secretary C. Girard Davidson of the Department of the Interior. He had a definite anti-business attitude and continually insisted that I force the steel people to increase their output. Commenting on these demands, I said:

You don't increase capacity by turning on a faucet. It takes two things—men and materials—each of which must be taken from an economy working at virtual capacity and already suffering shortages of both men and materials.

The difficult task facing the Administrator is to draw a proper balance between military demands of great variety, civilian demands of greater variety, and the demands of current use and new productive capacity which are in direct conflict.[3]

Export control was bound to become an issue during the Korean conflict. I was continually questioned about shipments to China. In November, on television, I pointed out the drastic reduction in shipments to China and also made the point that it was unwise to shut off these shipments completely. We were receiving valuable imports from China, specifically tungsten. We imported from China 3.9 million pounds in 1948; 4.590 million in 1949; and 6.6 million through July 1950.

Lawrence Spivak questioned me on "Meet the Press." I replied, "We are far better off than we were before World War II. We had practically no shipping before World War II. We had twenty-three hundred ships in mothballs before the Korean invasion began. The Inchon landing was accomplished by ships we took out of mothballs." Spivak also asked, "Will we have wage and price freezes quickly?" My answer was, "You are getting them now. The freeze in automobiles was issued last night." On this same program I was asked about the discharge of security risks. I replied that I had discharged many. Congress had paid me a most unusual compliment in allowing me alone, among all the department heads, to discharge employees for security as well as disloyalty reasons. I was quizzed about homosexuals, and said that I had ordered long ago that they were to be fired.[4]

In October I sent to the President a Progress Report on N.P.A.:

Your order was signed at 4:30 P.M., on Saturday, September 9, and on the morning of Monday, September 11, I established the National Production Authority in the Department of Commerce.

It is obvious that this prompt action was only possible because the necessary preparatory work was undertaken immediately when you sent your message to Congress, many weeks ago, requesting the power to impose these controls. During the entire summer, an extended series of conferences was held between myself, officials of the Department, diversified industrial groups, and my Business Advisory Council. We canvassed the measures necessary for economic mobilization, the type of organization needed, and the availability of personnel to staff such an organization.

I am proud to say that in these few weeks we have arrived at the point reached by the Office of Production Management when Pearl Harbor was attacked, a year and a half after beginning consideration of these same problems. This was possible because we have been able, in line with your policy, to use the existing agencies.[5]

Later that fall, *Business Week* had this to say:

President Truman has turned over to his Secretary of Commerce the task of doling out priorities and allocations for most industrial raw materials and practically all components.

That means headaches all around. But Sawyer is the man in all Truman's Cabinet who can come closest to keeping business happy. When he joined the President's official family, he made it

clear that his idea of the job was to represent the businessman in
Washington. It is generally conceded that he has stuck to this job.
At the same time, he has been given more power than any other
Cabinet member now holds.[6]

An article in this same issue of *Business Week* contained this
interesting statement:

Senator Lyndon Johnson of Texas is taking a page from the
Harry Truman story as a guide for the Senate's new preparedness
subcommittee.
He couldn't have chosen a better bible for a congressional
investigation—or for political success.
The committee was Truman's springboard to the vice-presi-
dency, and finally to the White House.[7]

I had felt and stated on numerous occasions that we were
neglecting Latin America. We had been giving money by the
billions to Western Europe and other parts of the world; we
had been niggardly in the treatment of our neighbors. I had
tried to indicate some interest in that area by my trip to
Mexico the year before. In 1950 I was to make a Columbus
Day speech at Miami and decided to take time for a short trip
through the Caribbean before arriving there. In Puerto Rico
we were housed in La Fortaleza, the Governor's Mansion,
where we enjoyed a delightful dinner party the night of our
arrival. I was impressed by Governor Luis Muñoz Marín, an
experienced and sophisticated man, who was obviously doing
much for Puerto Rico. And how much he has done since! But
the high spot of the trip was our stay in the Dominican
Republic, which we visited after a brief stop at St. Thomas.
My impression of the Dominican Republic was favorable. I
was aware of the ruthless character of Trujillo and his regime,
but, at least superficially, the country was in good shape. The
people should not have been happy—but they were. (This
happy attitude I found on a later trip through Spain where
another dictatorship was running the country.) The hospitals

were excellent, roads, bridges, and buildings were being built and improved, large monuments were being constructed. Trujillo himself could not have been more gracious. On our first night he arranged a concert by a famous violinist followed by a very late supper party where I saw tables literally "groaning with food." I was impressed by the good-looking women— beautifully gowned and extremely intelligent. The strong economy built up by Trujillo needed and received little help from us. I received no request for preferential treatment for their sugar, one of our large imports from the Dominican Republic, although it was pointed out that there was serious discrimination against them in favor of Cuba. One reward of this trip was the privilege of seeing the "bones of Columbus" in the Santo Domingo Cathedral, oldest in the New World, and the ruins of the palace built by Columbus' son Diego. Three days later I was shown the "bones of Columbus" in a cathedral at Havana, Cuba. From the Dominican Republic we went to Haiti. I arrived there the day after the election of President Colonel Paul Magloire. He had received 98 per cent of the votes. He laughed when I told him the two per cent were probably mistakes. Our last stop was Cuba. I had planned to see Nicaro, the nickel works of The Freeport Sulphur Company. Those of us concerned with supplies of strategic materials had been greatly interested in Freeport Sulphur's development of this nickel deposit. I wanted to visit the plant and had arranged to land there. Shortly before I left Haiti, however, I received word that landing would be impossible; the best I could do was to view it from the air. This we did, circling several times. This valuable asset was later expropriated by Castro. My trip to Cuba was made most enjoyable and impressive chiefly through the efforts of Ambassador Luis Machado, one of the ablest foreign representatives ever to be in Washington. I met most of Cuba's official family, and was impressed by President Carlos Prío Socarrás, later deposed by Batista. He was extremely handsome and dynamic, and was painstaking in his efforts to make my trip informative.[8]

In 1951, as our war effort increased, we became acutely conscious of Communist efforts to get information. Early in 1951, I made it the business of the Commerce Department to provide guidance for state and local officials, representatives of business and private citizens who wished to know what information should be released and what should be withheld or given only limited distribution. As examples:

A major railroad had been asked to provide minutely detailed information on the physical layout of its system and an analysis of the flow over its lines. The stated purpose of the inquiry was to construct maps of that and other rail systems. The railroad questioned whether or not such a set of maps might constitute strategic intelligence of importance.

A city official had received a number of requests from unknown persons for detailed information concerning fire, police, and water department operations.

A major oil company wished advice on whether or not to publish a book showing the location of its storage facilities throughout the world.

A maker of electronic equipment asked whether a proposed radio broadcast of technological aspects of his products would be a security violation.

I had become proud of the National Production Authority. Its task was immense, but it was working smoothly, far more so than its predecessors. In a speech in Boston, I dwelt upon our successful effort to organize activities within existing agencies

During World War II there existed the idea that you can accomplish miracles by setting up great new agencies with new names and new staffs. In an effort to avoid this error, President Truman, at an early stage of our defense activity, announced that where possible mobilization would be directed by the existing agencies of government.

Controls over materials were given to me as Secretary of Commerce and I promptly set up the National Production Authority within the Department. It has functioned continuously and effectively since September. It has not pleased everybody—it was not expected to. Benjamin Franklin in *Poor Richard's Almanac of 1758*, said: "To serve the Public faithfully and at the same time please it entirely is impracticable." [9]

I sent Truman a copy of this speech and received the following gracious and amusing note:

Thanks a lot for the copy of your speech for tonight. I am more than happy to have it and, as I told you, the first thing you know, you may hear some of it over a national broadcast.[10]

While the National Production Authority was functioning well, we were not free of conflicts of opinion. Occasionally I was in disagreement with some of my very good friends. Stuart Symington, later a senator but then chairman of the National Security Resources Board, disagreed with my encouragement of aluminum facilities in Canada. Domestic producers had put tremendous pressure upon Symington to halt or slow down the Canadian development. I strongly disapproved of this attempt. C. D. Howe, Canadian Minister of Trade and Commerce, at that time the most powerful and important figure in Canada, was greatly worried about Symington's attitude. A "Statement of principles for economic cooperation" had been publicly signed in October of 1950 by our Secretary of State and the Canadian Ambassador. The first principle read:

In order to achieve an optimum production of goods essential for the common defense, the two countries shall develop a coordinated program of requirements, production, and procurement.

I assumed that we meant what we said. I was involved because I was allocating to Canada critical materials and equipment to be used in the building of ALCAN—aluminum in Canada. On February 7 before the Committee on the Study of Monopoly Power I said:

My opinion is that we should get all the aluminum we can, as fast as we can, as cheaply as we can, and from wherever we can.

I propose in the future — as in the past — to carry out the spirit of the cooperative understanding with Canada. I might add that we have found them on their part to be more than cooperative with us and their requests of us have been modest in the extreme.[11]

My interest in newspapers had been evident when I was still quite young. However, I had never felt that newspapers should be allowed to print everything. I discussed this matter at Columbus on March 8 in a speech to the Ohio press. I pointed out the difficulty or the impossibility of controlling the press by law or executive edict, and then suggested a possible solution, closing with those paragraphs:

In the newspaper field, as in others, activities and programs are far less organized than the public believes. We hear statements that "business" should do this or that, the Republican or Democratic Party should do this or that, "labor" should do this or that, "the farmers" should do this or that; the assumption being that there is some hierarchy at the top which issues orders.

Those in the inner councils of either business or political parties know how humorously inaccurate this is.

However, it may not be too much to hope that some unified effort will be made by the newspapers of this country to meet the problem of information in relation to security. I can speak for many government officials with whom this matter has been discussed when I say that they give out information because of the bitter criticism which will follow the discovery that information is being withheld. If the initiative were to come from the press, it would make the task of the public official much easier.[12]

This suggestion bore no fruit. Meanwhile I had persuaded the President to authorize a survey of what would appear to be harmful disclosures. My Office of Technical Services came up with a report which shocked the President and other public officials, including the Secretary of Defense, Robert Lovett. As a result the President issued a "security order" and was immediately charged with an effort to muzzle the press.

In October, before the Poor Richard Club in Philadelphia, I dwelt again on the problems involved in an effort to restrain the release of information.

Every honest newspaperman in Washington knows that there are two kinds of news rivalry: one, the rivalry to get news; the other, rivalry among public officials to give out some bit of sensational information to make a headline or to prove that the agency involved is more alert and more entitled to Congressional appropriations than some competing agency.

I quoted from William Philip Simms, who said: "The United States is a spy heaven," a description he had heard from a Japanese Embassy official "smilingly" just before Pearl Harbor. "All a foreign spy needs to do is sit comfortably in his embassy and read American publications; he doesn't have to risk his life." I quoted Henry McLemore, who said:

Why any foreign power should go to the trouble and expense to spy on this country is a mystery to me. Given time, the United States will reveal everything but the hat and glove sizes of the Secretary of State, the midnight password at Oak Ridge, and the list of foods to which President Truman is allergic. This country goes right ahead blabbering and blubbering everything it knows. The next thing you know, the men who are entrusted with our top secrets will be wearing sandwich boards announcing our very latest developments to the last detail.[13]

In October I wrote the President a letter suggesting a "panel for information" in the office of the President to consist of publishers, editors, broadcasters, and commentators who would discuss with government officials the problems of releasing information. Of this proposal, also, nothing materialized.

From childhood I had practiced economy. I had foolishly hoped to promote it while in government. As an exercise in futility one should spend a week in Washington, walk up and down the limitless corridors of our great public buildings, and look into the adjoining rooms. The routine is the same in all the departments—individuals at their desks, turning papers, and groups around tables, talking and smoking. Graphs and charts are produced in endless profusion; reports flow continually from one room and building to another; views are written and rewritten; directives are drafted; and thousands of studies recommend a further study of the problem. Every objective observer agrees that our federal establishment is greatly overmanned. I myself believe that a greater volume of far better work would result from a 25 per cent reduction in the number of government employees. I am well aware of the difficulty of its accomplishment. Since the days when we began to get rid of the "spoils system" we have created a body of laws and regulations designed to keep federal employees on the job, whether we need them there or not. In the fall I discussed "saving taxpayers' money."

One hears frequent suggestions about streamlining government and increasing efficiency. It is well for us to face reality. Some savings can result from improved efficiency; large savings will not be made except by the drastic method of eliminating or reducing functions. The temptation to undertake new and laudable enterprises is almost irresistible, but a nation, like an individual, cannot do everything it would like to do.

With any specific suggestion along this line, there will arise a howl of protest and anger from every affected individual or group throughout the country.

In connection with the budgets presented to me, one of the recurring items is "within-grade salary increases." This means that automatically the employee gets an advance. Almost no supervisor will face the loss of time and effort necessary to prove an "unsatisfactory" rating which is required to prevent the automatic raise.

Congress has been fine in giving credit to my Department for its endeavor to economize, and for that reason I have suggested to my subordinates that a particular effort be made to operate within the amounts appropriated, and if possible come up with a surplus. I was told that a surplus gives the impression that the original request was excessive and the agency head, a poor administrator. Instead of being rewarded for his success in economy he will be penalized by reduced appropriations for the following year.

It is well known that toward the close of the fiscal year extraordinary efforts are made to discover ways of spending any surplus.

The remedy for this disturbing procedure lies partly with the administrative heads and partly with Congress. I have stated to my bureau heads that I will not tolerate any such practice. As a result the amount of $6,220,000 of funds available to the Department of Commerce for the past fiscal year was saved. These funds will be returned to the Treasury as required in the case of all unexpended balances.

In the current year we sold, instead of giving away, public documents for $1,009,000. We saved in the Civil Aeronautics Administration over $3,000,000 through improvements in operation. In the Patent Office, savings of over $123,000 were brought about through reductions in printing costs alone.[14]

In March 1951, the President wrote to me from Key West, enclosing a copy of the document known as the "Rockefeller Report." He asked for my comment. Its title was moving— "Partners in Progress." It began:

We peoples who are still free face two threats. One is military aggression and subversion. The other is hunger, poverty, disease, and illiteracy.

As a result of its findings, *the Advisory Board feels that strengthening the economies of the underdeveloped regions and an improvement in their living levels must be considered a vital part of our own defense mobilization.*

As I read this wordy, maudlin, visionary, and completely impractical program my concern developed into alarm. On March 16 I wrote the President at length:

My dear Mr. President:

I have your note of March 9 with enclosed copy of the Rockefeller Report.

The novel and perhaps most important aspect of the report is its recommendation of a speedy centralization of foreign economic activities into one new "over-all" agency.

The second important aspect of the report is the all-inclusive nature of the task which it envisions. The following outline is arresting: "Our concept of economic development, it will be seen, carries with it land and other reforms, where the people feel them needed, a living wage, fair and rising labor standards, full participation in the benefits accruing from increased wealth or income, the removal of discriminations based on race, color, nationality, religious belief, caste, or sex. It also includes freedom of speech, freedom from want, the right of trial by jury, the right to work, the right to self-organization, the right to strike, the right to vote. It also includes training in democracy to enable all of the people to take active part in public affairs. With these rights go inherent responsibilities and duties."

The organizational suggestion is fundamentally unsound, and is based upon an idea current in connection with mobilization—that the solution of any problem is to organize a new agency. It runs completely counter to your idea and practice in connection with mobilization. It is expensive; it is inefficient.

The report refers to a "people to people" program, and states that the United States does not stand for "the perpetuation of regimes merely because they happen to be in power." If these phrases are not meaningless, they indicate that we would undertake through this economic agency to develop the underprivileged countries regardless of the wishes of the government in power. This concept is certainly fraught with peril.

The report is a recital of most of the economic and some of the social-political problems which beset the world. Its assumption is that we have a responsibility and an opportunity to solve them. The real questions are—"How do we balance the demands of our own economy, now tightly stretched, with the financial burden which the suggested program would entail?" "How much harm will be done by promising things we can't or don't perform?"

In view of the statement that the strategy must be "both global, embracing every part of the world, and total, with political, psychological, economic, and military considerations integrated in one whole," I am sure that we have not sufficient resources in this country to implement it.

One of the intriguing but disconcerting things about this report is the number of new agencies suggested. First of all is the "United States Overseas Economic Administration"—"a unified agency with a new point of view." Within this agency an Assistant Administrator would work with all international agencies and voluntary groups. Another Assistant Administrator would be "a man of recognized business experience who would be charged with securing the cooperation of private enterprise, removing obstacles to the investment of private capital in these areas, and facilitating in every possible way the maximum use of private capital and private initiative. . . ."

There are envisaged several Land Development Projects—the East Andean, the Tigris-Euphrates, the Jordan Valley, etc.

We are to have many Joint Commissions. These would be the vehicles through which the Overseas Economic Administration would work out national development plans. It is to be noted that these Joint Commissions "would in no way preclude the establishment of other types of mixed commissions or United States participation in regional commissions."

The report also recommends "Institutes" which "stand out when contrasted with other types of U.S. governmental assistance programs." These regional Institutes would apply to the Middle East, Africa, South Asia, and Southeast Asia.

There is suggested the prompt creation of a new "International Development Authority" in which all free nations will be invited to participate. Local or regional authorities, similar to the Port Authority in New York, will be used.

An "International Finance Corporation," as an affiliate of the International Bank, is also contemplated.

If it be asked, "What, then, would I suggest?"—I am glad to be specific. *First*, a decision that no new overall agency needs to be created; *second*, a setting up within the State Department of a section devoted to foreign economic problems, headed by "a man of proven administrative capacity with vision and understanding"; *third*, a survey by him of all present foreign economic activities, including those undertaken jointly with United Nations

Organizations, and a prompt effort to wipe out duplication; *fourth*, a reaffirmation of the fiscal authority established by Congress in the National Advisory Council; *fifth*, renewed effort by the State Department to increase the number of treaties of friendship and commerce which will make American private investment abroad more attractive; *sixth*, a worldwide application of the cooperation already achieved between the State Department, represented by Assistant Secretary Miller, and the Department of Commerce, in connection with the problems of investment and business operation in South American countries.

These suggestions would not involve the enormous sums of money which are so casually referred to in this report, and would permit the integration of this new program with the Point IV program which is now carried on in the State Department.

There is one final, undramatic but important, consideration. Such a new agency cannot be set up in the immediate future. The terrific demand of mobilization for personnel has already produced an intolerable situation in some of the existing agencies and has put a tremendous drain upon the supply of both business and professional men who are already occupied with some other government job or in private business. Furthermore, the security clearances required make the recruiting process extremely difficult and slow.

The Department of State is undertaking diligently with the help of other interested departments to set up machinery for handling the Point IV program. It is taking a minimum of 100 days to process individual employees to handle this program, a great deterrent to its early activation. If the handling of a $35,000,000 program is proving to be a problem, what will happen to a program which sets $500,000,000 as its initial expenditure?

I received the following reply from the President.

I appreciated most highly your detailed analysis of the Rockefeller Report and I am giving the whole thing the most careful consideration.

I'll talk with you further on the subject before final action is taken on the Rockefeller Report. I think your analysis was a good one.[15]

That same month, while I was busy setting up a National Shipping Authority within the Commerce Department, Chairman Celler of the House Judiciary Committee renewed his attack on the Business Advisory Council. He had addressed a letter to my solicitor and another letter to Walter White, executive director of the council, to appear before his committee to testify. I thought it preferable that I appear personally, which I did. I was never permitted to deliver my statement— Celler adjourned the meeting without letting me speak. In my statement I had outlined the history of the Council, the manner in which it conducted its affairs, the manner in which it was financed, the speakers who had appeared before its meetings. I mentioned its great contribution in connection with the mobilization for Korea. I outlined the names of its distinguished members who had served the Government. It was a lengthy and extremely impressive list. I had said:

This brief recital of what Council members have done in the way of public service does not carry the implication that they are immune from investigation. They would be the last to make any such claim, as would I. I have stated repeatedly to you and other Chairmen of Congressional Committees my feeling that Congress has a right to investigate the Executive Branch and that I would at all times give what assistance I could.

May I be permitted, however, to say that it is becoming increasingly difficult to persuade businessmen to participate in Government activities and to help with the problems which are facing Federal officials, and a feeling by them that this participation will in itself subject them to investigation and possible censure is bound to have a discouraging effect. In particular, may I request that if your investigation shows, as I believe it will, that this group has over the years been a very helpful adjunct to the Department of Commerce and has made a great contribution to public service generally, during World War II and after it, you will, in whatever report you make, say so. This will be encouraging to businessmen generally and this group in particular, and will help to correct an impression that Congressional investigations never result in anything but criticism.

I sent a copy of this statement to the President. On June 29 the President wrote to Celler:

I have just had a communication from my Secretary of Commerce enclosing a copy of a statement which he prepared for your Committee. I hope you will read that statement with care and insert it in your record.

Charlie has done a bang up job as Secretary of Commerce. I believe if you will get all the facts you will find that he deserves a pat on the back and I hope you will give it to him.

He also wrote me on June 28:

I read your letter and statement with a great deal of interest.

I think that our friend Celler will not bring in an unfavorable report.[16]

Celler did not bring in any report.

Senator Paul H. Douglas suggested the establishment of a committee on "Ethics in the Federal Government," and asked for my opinion. I replied:

I do not favor the establishment of any more commissions or agencies in the Federal Government. I am not one of those who believe that the solution of every problem lies in the organization of another alphabetical agency.

It is clear that the ethical standards of a public official will be determined by his own instincts as to what is and is not proper. If he does not know that it is improper for him to accept a gift no finding or supervision by a commission will educate him.

There are public officials who will not accept a cigar on the theory that they might be compromised. This, it seems to me, indicates too insecure a sense of rectitude.

I note your reference to Federal employment of persons with "strong industry connections." I am not aware how ethics is involved in this matter, but to say that Charles Wilson or Eric Johnston should not be urged to give their talents to public service because of "strong industry" connections is nonsense.

We are endeavoring to secure the services of experienced businessmen for temporary duty in the various divisions of the National Production Authority. Our problem is not to keep these men from seeking opportunities where they can benefit themselves; our problem is to get them to come in the first place and to keep them for a reasonable time after they are here.

I note the reference to discussion of Government business outside of office hours and at social gatherings. I, myself, and many other top-level officials in Washington—and for that matter many others at lower levels—have worked many hours at night, and on Saturdays and on Sundays, in my office, and out of my office—at home. Would a Government official be required to stop this work, or would he, after a certain hour, if not in his office, be prevented from talking about his work with anyone outside of Government? Who is to say what is an office hour and what is not? Much legitimate and important business would be stopped if none of us could work after five o'clock in the afternoon, either in or out of our offices. This certainly applies, if I may add the compliment, to many hard-working Members of Congress.

The adoption of a code of ethics, while harmless, will do but little good. Any man who must look up his code of ethics to find out what is proper or improper for him to do is too innocent to be around Washington.

I also raised the question of ethics in Congress.

Heretofore my comments have referred to activities in the Executive Branch of the Government. I might refer to legislative activities.

The Executive Branch is at the mercy of the Legislative Branch. Congressional committees can investigate my Department with complete abandon. There is no machinery known to me by which my Department can investigate Congress. This puts the Congress at an advantage, but it puts upon it an obligation, perhaps involving ethical considerations.

Is it proper or improper to disclose statements and information of a secret nature given in executive session before a Congressional committee by representatives of the Executive Branch who have carefully withheld such information from general circulation?

I might put one other question, particularly applicable to the operation of the National Production Authority. The officials of

NPA receive many Congressional requests for action. In view of the preferred position of Members of Congress, how insistent should they be and how far should we go to comply with their requests?

I present these last particular matters with a certain hesitancy; but you have invited general comment. I feel free to ask these questions because I, personally, have been very well treated by the Committees of Congress.

I received the following note from Truman:

I have seen your letter to Senator Douglas on ethics. It is a jewel.

I'll venture to say that he'll not answer the questions on page four and five which, in my opinion, are very pertinent.[17]

That summer I was much involved with the purely administrative machinery of my Department. On August 8 I announced an extensive reorganization. My object was to consolidate functions and delegate operating responsibility to key personnel. Seventeen major offices and ten major bureaus in the Department which had reported directly to me were placed under the control of the Undersecretary for Transportation and certain assistant secretaries. I said:

Never in its history has the Department of Commerce contained such a wide variety of essential activities. I am confident that this reorganization will enable the Department to make even greater contributions than before to our economic progress and national defense.

I was concerned with the state of small business. I had been a small businessman myself. But I was also concerned about the alleged "friends" of small business. They were determined to set up a new agency to care for small business. This I opposed. Its actual contribution would be negligible; its cost would be high. The Department of Commerce was better equipped than any new agency to solve the problems of small business; it was already deeply involved in this endeavor. Furthermore, small business was hardly on the rocks. As a matter of fact, the number of small business firms had grown from 3.3 million in 1939 to 3.9 million in 1950. I took occasion to point out that:

there is no formula, no panacea for strengthening small business. Small business can be kept strong and prosperous by maintaining a prosperous and growing economy. Small business is the first to suffer when times are bad.

The Government cannot by any device furnish the energy, the brains, the ambition, the good judgment, and the managerial genius which is required to make a business successful. We can try to eliminate the handicaps and the discriminations and the unfair practices. In the last analysis success depends upon the individual, as it always has in the past.[18]

But my ideas were old-fashioned. We must have action—to save small business. Senator Sparkman, in particular, took up the cause. And before long we had a "Small Defense Plants Administration." Telford Taylor, a close friend of Truman, was appointed Administrator. He was brilliant, persuasive, and ambitious and began immediately to grasp for power and personnel. My letter of December 17 to the President is self-explanatory.

I received only this morning from Mr. Telford Taylor a copy of a letter which he wrote to you on December 1 suggesting the transfer of certain functions, personnel, and money from the Commerce Department to the Small Defense Plants Administration. While I'm sure that no action would be taken by you in this matter without consultation with me, in view of the time that has elapsed since you received the letter, I hasten to send you my comments.

The small business activities of my Department are varied and extensive and have been carried on effectively for many years. They are closely enmeshed with various other activities of the Department. To undertake to pull apart this experienced organization and to lift out certain personnel and transfer the personnel and the money from the permanent Department of Commerce to an agency whose life ends on June 30 of next year would have a damaging effect upon the Department morale and would certainly impair government service to the small businessman.

It may be well to point out that the functions of the SDPA are confined to manufacturers. The individuals throughout the Department who are interested in and working for small business do not confine their activities to manufacturers, who make up only about one-tenth of the total business in the country. Here again, not only will the practical problem of separation be extremely difficult but it will result in a serious impairment of the service rendered to small business other than manufacturing.

It was clear to me upon the passage of this legislation that certain problems of coordination and effective organization would be presented when the activities of this agency got under way. Realizing this, I prepared and sent to you on September 7 a memorandum suggesting "a practical assignment of responsibilities under the Small Business Amendment to the Defense Production Act." Upon a review of this document, I still feel that its suggestions were sound and if followed would give the Administrator plenty to do and would not upset present arrangements.

I did not confine my cooperative effort to this memorandum but offered to transfer and did detail on a non-reimbursable basis to Mr. Taylor's agency, nine employees of the Commerce Department who were, we thought, qualified to be of help to Mr. Taylor and his agency. I agreed temporarily to carry these employees on the Commerce Department payroll even though they were working for the SDPA. In addition to this, at his request, we loaned Mr. Taylor on November 14 four employees, three of whom are still with the SDPA.

I addressed another letter to the President on December 20:

I do not wish to labor the point, but a transfer of functions and personnel and money from Commerce to the Small Defense Plants Administration is a typical example of the thing which you and I have been trying to prevent, to wit: a raid on permanent agencies in an effort to build up temporary agencies.

It is difficult to thwart this effort at all points, but certainly there is every reason to prevent it where we can—and this is where we can.[19]

It was clear even in 1951 that the increasing air traffic into Washington required an additional airport. At my suggestion Del Rentzel, Undersecretary for Transportation, began an extended but secret investigation of a possible site near Washington. After a survey of every available area, we decided upon a location in the vicinity of Burke, Virginia. It was adequate and conveniently located. I requested the National Park and Planning Commission to give me an opinion of its practicability. After extended analysis of the need for a supplemental airport at a reasonable distance from central Washington and from the existing airport, the Commission said:

Under these circumstances, it would seem that to deny any location in Fairfax County would be to prohibit the National Capital from having anywhere within reasonable time distance the major airport which its commercial and governmental needs so obviously require. It is fortunate indeed that the Burke locale, which meets these requirements, is in a portion of the County that should be able to adjust itself to the new factors for development which the airport will bring about.[20]

No sooner was the Burke story out than opposing pressures began to mount. Only a fraction of the capacity of Baltimore's Friendship Airport was being used and Baltimore insisted that its airport should serve Washington. My very good friend Senator Tydings of Maryland was most active and demanding. On the other side, certain residents of the Burke area began to object and enlisted the services of their Congressman, Howard W. Smith, a man of great influence. I did not give up, but held meetings with all sorts of groups and individuals and requested the Attorney General to proceed immediately with the acquisition of the land, the cost of which was estimated at approximately 14 million dollars. Actual condemnation proceedings were filed on June 13. However, the opposition grew and my effort was finally thwarted. Years later, at a cost many times the cost of the Burke project, the Dulles Airport was built far, far away from the center of the city.[21]

During this time, I continued to worry about the expansion of foreign aid and the proliferation of government agencies. As I watched the original Marshall Plan expand and divide itself into other cells which broke loose and also expanded and divided, I became even more concerned and sought ways of stopping the process. On August 10, I wrote to the President:

It has been slightly more than four years since you appointed a "Committee on Foreign Aid," the Chairman being your then Secretary of Commerce. This Committee was asked to determine the limits within which the United States could safely and wisely extend aid to Western Europe.

I am writing to suggest the desirability of appointing a similar committee to bring this earlier report up to date and to suggest, in view of the changes which have occurred, including the birth and activation of the Point Four program, that this report cover not only aid to Western Europe but to other parts of the world.

This action will be timely, not only because of the passage of four kaleidoscopic years and the changes which have ensued, but because numerous reports—the Gordon Gray report, the Rockefeller report—and growing activity in Congress point to the desirability of reviewing and programming this vastly important matter.

It will be of great benefit for you to fit within a framework of realistic idealism the demands of emotional persons who think the solution of every world problem is for Uncle Sam to give something away.[22]

Nothing came of this suggestion. Others were giving him different advice.

In the late summer bills were introduced providing for a study of administrative arrangements needed to handle foreign aid. I addressed a letter to Senator Tom Connally, chairman of the Senate Foreign Relations Committee:

I am well aware that some eminent citizens and some organizations have taken the position that we need a new, over-all inde-

pendent unit at Cabinet level to administer foreign aid. I respectfully suggest that this plan is unsound, will create serious if not
insoluble administrative and foreign relations problems, and in
the long run will produce an unbearable drain upon the taxpayers.

We shall certainly always need a Department of State, Defense,
Justice, Treasury, etc. The existing departments, in other words,
deal with problems which are inherent in government and obviously permanent. To assume that we must now include in the
regular government operation as a permanent feature aid to the
other nations of the world involves an attitude of superiority
which neither our experience, resources, or wisdom can justify.
Nor will it do to say that if the need for this agency comes to an
end the agency will come to an end. It will not work that way. It is
as certain as the rising of the sun that once this permanent agency
is established as a department of the government, we will never get
rid of it. Once we have created this "Old Man of the Sea," we shall
have him upon our backs forever.[23]

We did get a new name for the old agency, which, with
changing alphabetical designations, seems headed for permanent status.

I had for some time considered the possibility of working
out a plan for the prompt use of commercial airplanes in the
event of a full-scale war. Finally, on December 17 the Secretary of Defense and I jointly approved an agreement to provide for the rapid and orderly phasing of commercial four-en-
gined aircraft into the military air-transport system. Under the
program a sound balance would be maintained between essential civilian requirements and strategic military air-transport
requirements. Our joint statement said, "This is the first time
in the history of the civil air industry that a completely coordinated plan for its mobilization has been attempted in
advance." [24]

Toward the close of the year I wrote to the President,

You may be interested in seeing the number of men it takes the
Department head to do his job.

COMPARISON OF EMPLOYMENT
FOR OFFICE OF SECRETARY
OF GOVERNMENT AGENCIES
(EXCLUSIVE OF INDEPENDENT OFFICES)

	No.
Department of Commerce	299
Department of Agriculture	1,129
Department of Interior	424
Department of Justice	556
Department of Labor	400
Post Office Department	1,156
Department of State	1,182
Treasury Department	542
Secretary of Defense	571
Secretary—Army	1,164
Secretary—Navy	1,017
Secretary—Air Force	1,596

Source: Organization Chart of Federal Executive Departments and Agencies.

(U.S. Senate Committee on Expenditures in the Executive Departments.)[25]

Not only had I talked about economy—I had practiced it. By the fall of 1951 a record had been established in my personal executive office. I felt justified in telling the President about it.

The year 1951 had been a busy one. I had made a few good speeches and offered several good suggestions. Perhaps they were not so good. The speeches were forgotten and the suggestions appreciated but rarely followed.

16 On Being Advised Into Jail

THE YEAR 1952 climaxed my service as Secretary of Commerce. I was exceedingly busy. The problems and the difficulties mounted. I will not dwell upon the many absorbing and varied experiences of that crowded year. I will, however, describe three of them—the first two having to do with ships. These problems faced me because President Truman had put the Maritime Administration under me.

Late in the spring of that year I was able to close the file on the Dollar Line case, a controversy which had dragged on for nine years.[1] As the inheritor of the Maritime Commission's actions and responsibilities, I was confronted with a fascinating legal question, the complicated problem of dealing practically with a highly controversial matter and the difficulty of working with an intransigent Solicitor General whose conduct, as will be disclosed by our correspondence, was difficult to understand and should be intriguing to those who wonder about what goes on behind the scenes in Washington.

The Dollar Line originally operated steamships in the Pacific under the famous Captain Robert Dollar. Later it extended its passenger and freight service around the world. In

1928 a new company, Dollar Steamship Lines, Inc., was organized, borrowed large sums of money from the United States Shipping Board and was able to secure certain profitable ocean mail contracts. R. Stanley Dollar, son of the original Captain Dollar, was the president and controlling stockholder of this company and agreed at that time to be personally liable for the debts due the United States. However, it was not long before the company ran into trouble and this trouble continued. In 1938 a so-called "adjustment agreement" was made, by which there was sold to the Maritime Commission 92 per cent of the Dollar Steamship Lines voting stock and under the terms of which the Maritime Commission loaned 2 million dollars more to the shipping company for repair of its fleet. The agreement also provided that R. Stanley Dollar, and a company known as "Dollar of California" would be released from liability to the United States. The name of the company was changed to "American President Lines." As a part of this transaction the Reconstruction Finance Corporation also put up 2½ million dollars for working capital.[2] For various reasons, including the war, the company's operations thereafter became quite profitable and by 1943 all of its debts to the United States had been paid.

In July 1945 the Maritime Commission undertook a public sale of the stock, and $8,611,776.90 was offered for it. The Dollars, however, challenged the right of the Government to sell, insisting that the transfer was a pledge. Their debt having been paid they wanted their stock back. The Maritime Commission refused this demand, arguing that the stock had been turned over without reservations; the parties had treated the transaction as an outright sale and the Dollars had taken tax losses based on that understanding. In November 1945 the Dollars brought suit against the Maritime Commission in the U.S. District Court for the District of Columbia. This Court dismissed the suit. The decision was however reversed by the Court of Appeals and upon appeal, the Supreme Court held

that the plaintiffs were entitled to a trial but did not pass upon
the pledge or sale question. It did note that a decision would
be against the Maritime Commission only and not *res adjudi-
cata* against the United States.[3] The case was retried, and the
District Court again held in favor of the defendants. The Court
of Appeals again reversed the District Court, holding that the
stock had been pledged. A petition for certiorari was denied
by the Supreme Court.

The stock turned over in 1938 was now held by me. Meanwhile, on November 30, 1950, the President had sent me the
following letter:

> The Attorney General informs me that the Supreme Court has
> declined to review the recent decision of the Court of Appeals for
> the District of Columbia in the suit brought by the Dollar interests
> against members of the former Maritime Commission, ruling that
> the stock of American President Lines which you now hold on
> behalf of the United States was merely pledged by the Dollar
> interests.
>
> As you know, the United States claims outright ownership of
> this stock. Impairment of the Government's title to this stock
> would seriously affect the public interest.
>
> The Supreme Court, which has expressed no opinion on the
> merits of Dollar's claim, has specifically said that the judgment in
> this case is not binding on the United States.
>
> Accordingly, you are directed to continue to hold this stock on
> behalf of the United States. All appropriate action should be taken
> to assert and maintain the Government's rights as owner of this
> stock.[4]

This letter I turned over to the Department of Justice.

On January 31, 1951, the Court of Appeals directed the
District Court to enter a judgment in favor of the Dollars for
"effective possession" of the stock. Since sending the President's letter to the Department of Justice I had received no
word from them and was not even told of the order from the
Court of Appeals to the District Court ordering me to transfer

effective possession of the stock. Meanwhile, the Department of Justice itself had filed suit against the Dollars and others in the District Court for the Northern District of California in an effort to establish title to the stock in the name of the United States. The California Court issued a preliminary injunction against the transfer of the stock to the Dollars and forbade them to exercise or attempt to exercise any rights or privileges as owners. The Court of Appeals of the Ninth Circuit refused to lift this injunction. The situation was somewhat confused. On March 16, at about noon, I was called out from a meeting of some importance and handed an order of the District Court directing me to deliver the certificates of stock to the attorneys for the Dollar Line and to direct the transfer agent in San Francisco to see that the stock was transferred in accordance with the court order. The order also provided, in the alternative, that the clerk of courts should endorse the certificates and instruct the transfer agent if I failed to do so.

I was between hell and the ironworks. I had received an order from the President to hold the stock. I had an order from the District Court to deliver the stock. The Washington Court had decided in favor of Dollar—the California Court had decided against Dollar. I immediately addressed a letter to the Attorney General requesting instructions. Before the day was out the Solicitor General advised me in writing to deliver the certificates to the court—but to do nothing further.[5] This I did. The following morning the clerk of the District Court, as the alternative order had provided, endorsed the certificates in lieu of my endorsement and gave the specified instructions to the transfer agent. As was later pointed out in my solicitor's brief in the Supreme Court of the United States, the orders of the District Court had been carried out.

Some time prior to this the attorney for the Dollars had told the Attorney General that they intended to ask that I and other officials be cited for contempt. I was not informed and knew nothing about this until I read in the papers that Judge Clark of the Court of Appeals had told the Solicitor General that he might "be advising the Secretary of Commerce into jail." At that point I became decidedly interested. On March 17, an affidavit was filed, charging me and others with contempt. My solicitor in the Department of Commerce had taken no part in the litigation and had not been consulted. I called him in, said that I wished him to represent me personally and that I wished to comply with the order of the court. This instruction he conveyed to the Solicitor General—who never informed the court. On April 11, 1951, I appeared before the Court of Appeals to find myself charged with contempt for actions taken without my consent and against my express wishes and instructions. I immediately sent word to the Department of Justice that I was requesting the Dollar attorneys to return the certificates from California so that I might personally endorse them, even though they had already been endorsed by the clerk of courts. I said further that I did not wish to appeal from the order of the District Court; I wished to comply with it. In the absence of express direction from the President, I would not refuse to comply with a court order.

From here on ensued a most bizarre and mysterious performance on the part of the Solicitor General, Philip Perlman. I am still at a loss to explain his conduct. When I first learned of the Dollar Line situation, Perlman had already made statements for me and taken legal positions on my behalf, all without my knowledge. Perhaps this was understandable at that time. Perlman's later conduct, however, was not understandable. Following my appearance in court, I instructed my solicitor to write to the Solicitor General as follows:

Now that we are entering a new phase of this controversy, it seems appropriate to ask that your Department inform this Department in writing of all moves in this litigation, particularly those involving the name of the Secretary of Commerce. I mention this because our files do not indicate that this Department, or the Secretary personally, was informed of various appearances made

and appeals taken in his name, and the Secretary states that he has
no recollection of any oral clearance.[6]

The request that I be kept informed was not honored; my
instructions as to what I wished done in my behalf were
ignored and violated. Meanwhile Perlman prepared to appeal
to the Supreme Court and included my name among the appel-
lants.

On May 21, while in New York, I received a telegram from
C. Dickerman Williams, my solicitor, stating that Perlman said
I had no authority to comply with the court order. I called
Williams and instructed him to tell Perlman in writing that I
wished to comply at once. Following this, Perlman himself
called me from the office of the Clerk of the Supreme Court,
objecting to the instructions I had given Williams. I told him
that I wished to comply with the court order and did not wish
him to apply for a stay in my name. He said he would not
follow my instructions but would file my application anyhow.
This he did.

The situation was growing a little sticky. I wrote to
J. Howard McGrath, Attorney General:

> The litigation on its merits, of course, is something to be
> handled entirely by your office and I have no desire to interfere—
> or for that matter to participate—although I should like to have
> my Solicitor kept currently informed as to what is going on and
> notified in advance of any step involving the use of my name.
>
> With reference to the contempt proceeding, which is personal in
> nature, I should like to have whatever petitions, pleadings, or
> briefs are prepared or filed done on my behalf, personally, by the
> Solicitor of the Department of Commerce.

McGrath replied to this letter, pointing out the custom by
which the Solicitor General was in charge of all litigation
against Government officials, thereby in effect refusing to comply with my request.[7] Unpersuaded by McGrath's letter, perhaps written by Perlman, I instructed Williams to prepare a

separate petition to the Supreme Court. I felt that I should be permitted as a personal matter to make my position clear through my own counsel. Williams sent Perlman a copy of my proposed petition with supporting brief and asked for his comments. They came the following day.

I am somewhat surprised that you should attempt to pursue a course already expressly rejected by the Attorney General. I do not consent to the filing of your petition, and shall so notify the Clerk of the Supreme Court. In view of the fact that the Court has already indicated it intends to grant the petition, this effort, in addition to the objections outlined by the Attorney General, seems wholly unnecessary.[8]

On August 10, Williams wrote at length to Perlman explaining why we felt that a separate presentation should be made. He said:

Mr. Sawyer wishes me to say in all good humor but quite frankly that the position taken by your letter of July 17 is in his opinion unnecessarily and strangely arbitrary.

He outlined our reasons—

1. The personal character of the contempt proceeding.
2. The Solicitor General was employing arguments which did not apply to the only action which I had taken and the only action I had taken (with reference to endorsement) would not apply to anyone else. "It is confusing and not clarifying to have these arguments lumped together as if every argument applied to every individual." He pointed out further that I wished to be the judge of arguments made in my behalf.
3. The Solicitor General had failed even to mention arguments in my behalf which we deemed important: for instance, the argument that the head of a Department should be protected from contempt by following the advice of the Attorney General. Nor had this brief men-

tioned another important argument in my behalf, alternative performance by the Clerk of Court was as effective as performance by me.

4. The Department of Justice attorneys themselves were involved in the contempt proceeding and it was better for me to be represented by counsel who was not, himself, a co-respondent and whose office was not involved.

5. It would benefit the case generally to have a separate presentation on my behalf. The Dollars had claimed that there was a concert of action among the respondents. "All of those familiar with this litigation know that this is not true. Mr. Sawyer's personal participation in the case was confined to action which he took on March 16, 1951, and the only direct personal contact between him and the Department of Justice was his request on that day for advice with respect to the court order. There certainly was no conspiracy to violate the order of the District Court and Mr. Sawyer and the Justice respondents as well will be aided by a presentation which clarifies the distinctive roles of each individual. As a matter of fact, this clarification will present a convincing answer to the charge of conspiracy."

6. The immunity argument should be omitted. "The Court and public generally have assumed, contrary to the fact, that Mr. Sawyer was seeking to avoid responsibility on that ground.

"Over the course of years you have frequently, I am informed, expressly approved separate appearances on behalf of Government officers and agencies. The reasons stated in this letter would seem to me to establish that this is an appropriate case for such permission. However, my construction of the statutes is that an officer of the United States is required to accept Department of Justice representation in the Supreme Court only when involved 'as such officer.' Accordingly unless you care to reconsider and give your consent, I feel obliged on Mr. Sawyer's behalf to file a separate petition for certiorari." [9]

Following this letter McGrath called me from Chicago, where he was making a speech, to request that I hold up my separate petition until he could come and talk with me. This he did on August 15, accompanied by Perlman. McGrath said that my case should be presented in a manner thoroughly satisfactory to me. Perlman disagreed and said that I could not file a separate petition for certiorari. I replied that he might learn that I could. Williams, who was present, said that he had been told by the Clerk of the Supreme Court that separate petitions had frequently been filed. Perlman said this applied to briefs and not petitions. I said that would satisfy me as I was seeking only to secure a separate presentation of my argument. I also said I wished my solicitor to make a separate verbal argument. At first Perlman objected even to this. He left, however, saying that he would notify Williams as to whether or not my suggestion was acceptable. Later that afternoon he accepted it. This was on August 16. Williams promptly prepared a separate brief on my behalf and sent it to Perlman for comment.[10]

Over three months later, on November 26, Williams asked Perlman why he had not commented on the brief which had been in his hands for many weeks. Perlman replied he would not permit my brief to be filed until after the Department of Justice brief was filed. Williams said he did not recall any such reservation when Perlman consented to our filing a separate brief. Perlman said that made no difference. When Williams said the matter was up to Secretary Sawyer, Perlman said it was not up to Secretary Sawyer, it was up to him, Perlman. My brief was filed on January 11, 1952, and the Solicitor General never filed any brief on behalf of any other defendant.

My differences with the Solicitor General persisted. Some time during the year, at a dinner given by the President for the then Princess Elizabeth, McGrath said to me, "I suppose you

Secretary Sawyer on his way to appear before the Court of Appeals in the Dollar Line Case, April 23, 1951. Left to right. C. D. Williams, Solicitor of the Commerce Department; U.S. Attorney General J. Howard McGrath; Secretary Sawyer; Peyton Ford, Assistant Attorney General; Philip Perlman, Solicitor General.

Secretary Sawyer conferring with Philip Murray, head of the CIO, during the steel mills seizure. Immediately behind Murray is David McDonald, officer of the Steel Workers' Union; to his left Arthur J. Goldberg, then General Counsel for the CIO, later a justice of the Supreme Court and still later U.S. Ambassador to the United Nations. At Secretary Sawyer's left is C. D. Williams, Chief Counsel for the Department of Commerce.

Secretary Sawyer signing the order releasing the steel mills from government control. Beside this document is the original June 2, 1952, letter from President Truman terminating Secretary Sawyer's authority over the steel mills.

Secretary Sawyer in his office in the Department of Commerce. The white phone is a direct line to the White House.

know that we are discussing a settlement of the Dollar case." I
replied that I had not known but made no further comment.
From time to time I learned that the Solicitor General's efforts
at a settlement were making no progress. On May 25 I had
written to Stanley Dollar suggesting that he and I agree on a
public sale of the disputed stock, the proceeds of which would
be placed in escrow and paid to the party to whom the courts
would finally award ownership. In this letter I said that this
proposal "will preserve the right of each party to litigate this
matter to a conclusion, but will free the practical business
operation from the annoyance, burden, and handicap of the
litigation."

It will demonstrate the sincerity of what I have stated on several
occasions, that the Government had no desire whatever to continue
to operate this line, or as some have claimed, to "nationalize"
shipping, and would eliminate the confusion in the public mind
which arises from a mixture of the operating with the litigating
considerations.[11]

I had not consulted the Solicitor General before writing this
letter. I was certain he would oppose anything I suggested.
Dollar did not accept my offer. His lawyer proclaimed that my
letter was a trap to lure Dollar into a disadvantageous position.
I abandoned any further effort to get together with Mr. Dollar.
    Some time in December 1951 George Killion, president of
the President Lines, whom I had known for many years, called
on me to ask if I knew that the Department of Justice was
undertaking to negotiate a settlement with Dollar. I said that I
had heard of it. On February 8, 1952, Killion came into my
office to ask if I would be willing to talk with Dollar about a
settlement. I gave him no answer then; but I talked with
President Truman, telling him that I thought the case should
be settled and I might have an opportunity to settle it. However, I wished to be certain that the Attorney General would
get the proper instructions—in other words, instructions to

approve the settlement. The President said that any settlement I made would be a good one and the Attorney General would be so instructed.

On Friday, February 29, McGrath, at a Cabinet meeting, said that he would like to have me talk with Dollar about a settlement. I replied that I would not undertake to negotiate a settlement while his office was trying to do the same thing. He said that he would call off his negotiations and would like very much to have me go ahead. That same Friday, February 29, Killion called from San Francisco to ask if I would see Dollar. I said that I would. Killion stated that Dollar would call me on Sunday. This he did, asking if he might come in to see me on March 3. At 4:30 P.M., March 3, Dollar came in, accompanied by Killion. After a little while, Killion left. Meanwhile, I had invited Admiral Cochrane, head of the Maritime Board, to sit with me, as he did at every subsequent conference with Dollar or his counsel.

On March 7, at a cabinet meeting, Perlman, who was by then the acting Attorney General, asked how I was getting along with Dollar. I said nothing had been concluded; whereupon he said, "You must not make any agreement with him." I said that I had not made one as yet, but would probably do so. He seemed greatly disturbed. Immediately thereafter in a conversation with the President I repeated what Perlman had said. He said "Go ahead and make the agreement; I will approve it and instruct Perlman to carry it out."

On May 3, I addressed the following letter to Perlman:

Dear Philip:

As you know from my recent conversation and your talk with the President, I have been negotiating with the Dollar interests a settlement of the matters involved in the controversy between them and the United States Government. I am happy to say that agreement has now been reached on the enclosed draft.

I have a letter from R. Stanley Dollar stating that this draft is acceptable to him and that he will sign it when it is approved and ratified in writing by the Acting Attorney General of the United States; and upon the further condition that the Treasury Department shall issue tax rulings or enter into a closing agreement with respect to the tax consequences of the settlement agreement satisfactory to the Dollar interests.

As a first step in finally closing this matter, I would appreciate it if you would affix your approval to the two enclosed copies. The agreement has been read and approved by the President. Upon receipt of your approval the Dollar interests will ask for the indicated document from the Treasury Department and upon receipt of that, Mr. Dollar and I will sign the documents and proceed to close the matter out. The agreement involves, as you can see, the discontinuance and dismissal of all pending actions. This is, of course, a matter to be carried out by your office.[12]

Perlman replied saying that my proposed settlement was indefensible and he would not be a party to it. His letter was lengthy, repeating many things he had said before.

Perhaps more objectionable than any of these considerations is the fact that the Dollars, or those acting on their behalf, have been engaged for months in using pressures from a variety of sources to obtain a settlement that would mean many millions to them and their associates. They have not been content to let their case be adjudicated by the courts, and I do not believe that the various moves on their behalf will stand investigation. The Government is entitled to have its rights adjudicated; and not substantially given away by a "settlement."

I have written you at length because I still hope to convince you that you should drop the matter, and agree that it should again be handled by the Department of Justice, which is in charge of the litigation, and which still hopes that its every act will be vindicated.[13]

Two days later I answered him:

There appear to be four points made in your letter: first, that any settlement is improper; second, that the settlement that I have made is not the best one which could have been made; third, that if settlement is made, it should be handled by the Department of

Justice; and fourth, no settlement should be made until the pending litigation has been adjudicated.

With reference to the first point, practically everyone disagrees with you. The chief law officer of the Department of Commerce, Mr. C. Dickerman Williams; the Maritime Board headed by Admiral Edward L. Cochrane; I, myself; former Attorney General Howard McGrath; and the President; each of whom has or had a close and direct official interest in this matter, think a settlement is desirable. All feel that this litigation has gone on long enough; that unless settlement is made it will go on many months, if not years, longer; that the Government should as soon as possible get out of the shipping business, and that the Maritime Board should be able to devote itself to maritime affairs instead of litigation. From the standpoint of proving or disproving interesting legal points there may be a strong argument in favor of pursuing the litigation to its conclusion. From every other standpoint the desirable thing is to end it.

You state that the settlement I have made is not the best one which could have been made, that it is less advantageous than an offer previously made by the Dollars to the Department of Justice. My information is to the contrary, but in view of the fact that Justice had not kept me informed of the status of your negotiations, I have not been in a position to know what offers had been made by Mr. Dollar.

Your third point appears to be that a settlement should be handled by the Department of Justice. With this conclusion I do not agree. The really interested party here is not the Department of Justice but the Maritime Board, whose chief responsibility is the welfare of our merchant marine. This Board and the Administrator who is the Chairman of the Board, operate under me. The effort to dispose of this matter should properly rest with the Secretary of Commerce and not with zealous counsel moved by a laudable desire to prove a disputed point of litigation, or by considerations of personal pride. In private litigation the decision of the client is the final one. The lawyer advises his client but in the end follows instructions. The same situation should apply in Government.

You suggest that I drop the matter and let a settlement be handled by the Department of Justice. The Department of Justice undertook to make a settlement long before I did. That settlement was not made and Mr. McGrath asked me to undertake a settlement. I pointed out to him that negotiations had been pending between Dollar and the Department of Justice; that it was foolish to have two negotiations going on at the same time. He agreed with this and asked me to go ahead.

Following this conversation with the Attorney General I asked the advice and instructions of the President, who authorized me to do what I have done. As I stated in my letter to you, he has seen and approved the agreement which we arrived at.

You suggest that the matter should not be settled until pending litigation has been adjudicated. If by that you mean after all questions have been fully and finally passed upon by the courts, there would, of course, be nothing left to settle.

I note your statements about the repeated efforts of the Dollars to bring about a settlement. The only effort of which I know is the request by Mr. Dollar to come to see me to discuss a settlement. You speak of "pressures" from a variety of sources to obtain a settlement. There has been no pressure put upon me by anyone. If you believe that moves made by the Dollars should be investigated I suggest that you initiate an investigation promptly. No move made by me or Admiral Cochrane or Mr. Williams need fear any investigation.

The matter has now dragged on for many years and everyone involved in the actual operation as distinguished from the litigation wants it disposed of. It seems to me that you have misconceived your role in this matter.

The conduct of the litigation, of course, is your responsibility. Decisions of policy with reference to operation, etc., are my responsibility. I think the settlement in question is an excellent one from the standpoint of the Government and the Merchant Marine. You may disagree with this conclusion and of course are free to do so. I would appreciate it, however, if, having voiced your disagreement, you would approve of the settlement contracts as I have requested.[14]

By this time Mr. Perlman seemed almost beside himself. He did, of course, have many things on his mind, as we were at that time in the midst of the steel seizure matter.

On May 22 he sent a message to the Supreme Court asking in my name and the names of others for an immediate argument on the Dollar Line case. I wrote him a letter that same day:

I have just received a copy of your memorandum to the Supreme Court suggesting an "immediate argument" in the Dollar Line cases. It is difficult to believe that this suggestion is seriously intended. The Court plans to adjourn June 2nd, according to its May 12th announcement. The members of the Court must finish their work on a number of cases, some of them—such as the steel case—of the greatest importance. Apart from the steel case, which was exceptional and admitted of no delay, the Court has ended oral argument. The Dollar Line cases have been pending in one form or another for more than a year. In no one of them has any brief been filed except the brief filed in No. 247 by C. Dickerman Williams, Solicitor of the Department of Commerce, on my personal behalf. In No. 353 the Supreme Court has so far refused to hear the case at all, and there is pending only a second petition for rehearing of the Court's denial of certiorari more than a year ago. To imagine that the Court will at this late date accede to this unusual and sudden request is fantastic.

I might add that the filing of this memorandum by you is contrary to our earlier understanding that no court papers involving the use of my name would be filed without clearance from me or Mr. Williams.

In trying to explain your extraordinary action, I am forced to conclude that you believe it will somehow impede the carrying out of the settlement agreement which I have made with the Dollars, with the approval of the President. Yet you make use of my name in this effort. This memorandum having been filed without my approval or knowledge, I am asking that it be withdrawn at once. If this is not done, I shall make my attitude and wishes known to the Court directly.[15]

Shortly thereafter James P. McGranery was appointed Attorney General and he promptly approved the settlement. Under the terms of settlement a public sale was to be made to the highest bidder and the proceeds were to be divided fifty-fifty between the government and Mr. Dollar. The government received as its share $9,128,557.53. I was very happy about the settlement, as was everyone except Mr. Perlman.[16]

17 The
SS United States

I HAD some difficulties with the Solicitor General during 1952. That same year I took on another "general"—the Comptroller General—a powerful figure in the Washington bureaucracy. He is appointed for a fifteen-year term and cannot be removed. This leaves him free of control or dictation by the Executive. His function is to check on governmental expenditures. In 1952 the Comptroller General was Lindsay Warren, a former congressman.[1] He had a high opinion of his responsibilities and his powers. My collision with this worthy official involved the great ship ss *United States*. Some years before I became Secretary of Commerce, the Maritime Commission had contracted with the United States Lines Company to subsidize the building of a new liner. The arrangement contemplated its possible use as a military transport, able to carry soldiers in both arctic and equatorial waters. It had to be air-conditioned, able to cruise for thousands of miles without refueling, capable of making its own fresh water and carrying large supplies of oil. It must be very fast—fast enough to outrun and outmaneuver submarines. These and other military requirements greatly increased its cost.

The Maritime Commission and the United States Lines agreed upon a price, and construction of the ship began at Newport News. It was ready in 1952 and in April had completed a highly successful trial run. At this point I received a letter from the Comptroller General saying that the subsidy agreed upon earlier should be reduced by 4 million dollars. Warren charged no fraud, merely maintained that the Maritime Commission had made a bad bargain. He asked me not to release the ship to the United States Lines.[2] This suggestion, in my judgment, was outrageous and for the first time in history a cabinet member prepared to defy the Comptroller General. I asked the Solicitor General and my own solicitor to furnish legal opinions on the validity of the agreement. Perlman, the Solicitor General, would give me none. But my own solicitor and the general counsel of the Federal Maritime Board each furnished me with an extended opinion that the contract was valid and binding. Armed with these studies, I wrote the Comptroller General the following letter on May 6:

I have your letter of April 21, concerning the contract of the former Maritime Commission to sell the liner ss *United States* to the United States Lines Company, and have noted that your office "does not regard the subject contract as a binding and unavoidable agreement."

Inasmuch as the Attorney General has declined to give me an opinion and my own Solicitor and the General Counsel of the Federal Maritime Board have reached an opinion (a copy of which I furnished to your office on March 31st) exactly opposite to the one indicated by you, I should like very much to have a copy of the opinion of your Legal Department setting forth the reasons for the conclusion which you have reached.

In the absence of an opinion from the Attorney General it is my present intention to follow the opinion of the Solicitor of the Department of Commerce and the General Counsel of the Federal Maritime Board; but if your counsel clearly demonstrates the error of this opinion, I shall of course be open-minded in the matter. In view of considerations which I shall state below, I would appreciate it, however, if you would be kind enough to let me have very promptly a copy of your General Counsel's opinion.

I note your comment with reference to stripping this case to a simple and readily understandable position with reference to subsidies and charges to appropriate funds. From my standpoint the situation is already stripped to the simple fact that this ship is about to be put into commercial operation, and regardless of possible errors of judgment by the Maritime Commission and the variety of legal opinion, or lack of legal opinion, I must take action in the immediate future. This I intend to do.

The decision made by the former Maritime Commission was not made by me or by anyone under my control. It may or may not have been sound. That question, it seems to me, is beside the point. There is no suggestion that the contract was affected by fraud of any kind, and to me the opinion of my counsel that it is a valid and binding contract is persuasive.

If I should refuse to go through with this contract the United States would immediately have a ship on its hands and would be forced to try to make some prompt arrangements for its use. I prefer not to strain at a gnat and swallow a camel. From the standpoint of the taxpayer and his ultimate situation, and from a practical common sense standpoint, it seems to me more important for the United States to carry out its contract already entered into than that the Government be saddled with a ship which it cannot run and a lawsuit which it cannot win.

I note that you have stated time and again your wholehearted support of a strong privately-owned American merchant marine composed of the most modern and best equipped ships that can be built. That, of course, is my position. I would be happy to feel that you believe I can most effectively strengthen this position by going through with the program I have outlined above.[3]

Meanwhile, the ss *United States* went on her builders' trial run on May 14, and this second test was a tremendous success. The ship reached speeds far beyond our expectations. On June 7 I wrote a letter to Truman which contained this sentence:

If we are to permit the Comptroller General to issue orders to the Executive Departments in the manner undertaken here, it might be well to appoint him Assistant President and let him run the country.[4]

But I had opposition within the White House itself. Some of the President's staff thought that my position was unfortunate politically—it would be popular and helpful to Truman if I were to support Warren's claim and blackmail the United States Lines into paying more money. I was somewhat concerned that Truman, under pressure, might order me to withhold the ss *United States* from delivery.

On June 13 I wrote him a letter which I took personally to the White House.

There can be no doubt that any claim which the Comptroller General feels should be presented can be litigated to a conclusion in court; the delivery of the ship is in nowise an estoppel against the United States Government and will be no bar to the presentation and litigation of any proper claim.

Under the circumstances it seems to me there is no course open except for Admiral Cochrane to go through with the contract on June 20th in accordance with its terms. This he will do, with my approval, unless meanwhile I receive instructions to the contrary from you.[5]

I also felt that this item should be kept in proper focus. In an interview I said: "The United States has spent as much under ECA for ships and ship subsidies in Europe during the last three years as it has spent in sixteen years on its own Merchant Marine." As usual we were giving money away lavishly to foreigners while trying to beat down our own businessmen.

As the day approached when the transfer was to be made I was still nervous about the White House. I learned that more pressure was being put upon the President and arranged to discuss the matter with him personally.[6] I told him that I planned to release the ss *United States* exactly on schedule and asked him, as a favor to me, not to direct me to hold it. He agreed. In this, as in all other matters, he kept his word. The ship was to be turned over at 11:00 A.M. on June 20. Shortly before that hour I called Admiral Cochrane of the Maritime Administration to ask what was going on. He said there were transfers of documents at two places—Newark, New Jersey, where the United States Lines had its home office, and Newport News, where the ship itself was docked and where a press conference was to be held. I told him to stop the press conference and order the company to take over the ship. At five minutes after eleven, Admiral Cochrane entered my office, solemnly saluted, grinned, and said: "The ss *United States* has been turned over." I was just in time. Ten minutes later, one of my secretaries came in and told me that the President had released a letter blasting the United States Lines and the extravagance of this expenditure. He had kept his agreement with me; but he had yielded to those who urged him to play a little politics.[7]

Meanwhile, the Comptroller General had taken his arguments before a special committee of the House. On this same day I wrote a letter to Congressman Shelley, the committee chairman:

Upon receipt of General Warren's May 27th letter with reference to the United States Lines, I stated that I would not continue the correspondence. I did not, of course, anticipate the uncalled for and highly critical testimony which he gave before your Committee last Tuesday. You yourself, Mr. Chairman, characterized it as "wholly gratuitous." In fact, the Comptroller General himself said that he did not understand that the case of the ss *United States* was before your Committee. Nevertheless, he made his statement.

This statement was obviously for the purpose of creating a public impression that the Comptroller General, a knight in white armor, is defending the taxpayers from some nefarious plot to which I and the Maritime Board are parties.

His other purpose, perhaps, was to try to scare me into refusing to go through with the contract. I feel that the Government, like a private citizen who makes a contract, is bound by it. If a private citizen makes a bad contract he is not allowed three years later to say that he should not have made it and will not go through with it. The same should apply to the Government. Mr. Warren, however, apparently feels that the Government can repudiate and flout its obligations because some public official in his wisdom thinks its results are unfortunate.

I don't think the results are unfortunate. I think at this critical juncture in our history we are extremely fortunate—and not unfortunate—to have this great transport ship available. If a world war should engulf us tomorrow I challenge Mr. Warren to say that he would regard the existence and availability of this ship as unfortunate.

If the United States Lines owes money to the Government the Government should get it back. I don't want the taxpayer to lose one dime to which he is entitled. If, as Mr. Warren claims, the contract is illegal I am not only willing but anxious to have that established. This should not be done by the wholly arbitrary action of Mr. Warren or myself—it can be done sensibly and properly where it should be done—in court.

I had a ship on my hands—the biggest passenger ship ever to fly the United States flag. I had to decide what to do with it. Mr. Warren says that the transfer of this ship by the Maritime Board would give the buyer nothing more than a tainted title. Let him abandon histrionics and prove his point. If the title of the buyer is tainted, government lawyers should be able to prove it and get back this great superliner, which of course would still have to be operated and eventually disposed of.

What would the Comptroller General have had the Board do? Should it refuse to deliver this great ship and let it gather barnacles at Newport News while thousands of hopeful travelers, not knowing that a contract with the Government is worthless, were being told that their passages to Europe were cancelled and the ship could not sail? Should it remain at the wharf as a mecca to which enthusiastic advocates of a strong merchant marine could go to regard and admire but not use this "First Lady of the Seas"? Should we, having built this greatest ship of all time, make ourselves the laughing stock of the world by not being able to use it? Should we become an object of contempt and derision because bureaucratic involvement can thwart the patience and the genius and the hard work and the foresight of the architects, engineers, businessmen, and workers who have created this ship? Mr. Warren brushes off lightly the practical aspects of this situation, but I and the Maritime Board could not do so.

In my opinion the public interest referred to by Mr. Warren required me to deliver this ship. Mr. Warren has in effect dared me to turn this ship over to the United States Lines pursuant to the contract. Well, I have turned it over.

Four days later I had the following note from the President: "Thanks a lot for sending me a copy of your letter to Congressman Shelley. It certainly is interesting reading." and written in longhand below—"I had quite a kick out of it!" [8]

I stood on the bridge, as this great ship moved up New York Harbor. The veteran pilot by my side said there had never been such a reception. Every boat in the harbor was blowing sirens and whistles, fire boats were spouting water, thousands of people lined the piers and waved from windows. Within a few days the ss *United States* made its record run across the Atlantic, showing the world that we had the fastest passenger ship afloat. It was a high moment.[9]

18 *Steel*

BEFORE THE Dollar Line and ss *United States* affairs were settled, I was tossed into the most frustrating, but also the most fascinating, experience of my cabinet career, and the most controversial episode of the Truman administration — the steel seizure.

Negotiations between the steelworkers and the steel companies had begun in November of 1951. The union sought sizeable gains for its members and the President of the United States Steel Corporation insisted that a wage increase which violated the government's anti-inflation program would have to be handled in Washington. On December 18 the United Steelworkers of America-CIO gave notice of a strike, effective at midnight December 31. Two days later management and union representatives conferred in Washington with the Federal Mediation and Conciliation Service. The following day President Truman referred the dispute to the Wage Stabilization Board and asked the union to postpone its strike. From week to week the strike was postponed and the wage board's steel panel held public hearings in New York and Washington. On March 30 the board submitted recommendations which

255

included an initial wage increase of twelve and one-half cents an hour plus two and one-half cents an hour more on July 1, 1952 and two and one-half cents more on January 1, 1953. It also endorsed certain fringe benefits and approved a *closed shop*. These recommendations were accepted by the union but rejected by management. On April 1 no one was fooling around. The companies raised their wage offer to twelve and one-half cents, but the union held out for everything the Wage Stabilization Board had recommended. Negotiations were deadlocked and the union called a strike for April 9.[1]

On April 4, 1952, I had received the following note from the President:

Thanks a lot for yours of the second, enclosing a copy of your speech to be made on the seventh, in Detroit. I read it with a lot of interest and it also gave me some information which I need.

In the speech referred to I closed by saying:

Another thing can be done and I propose to do it. In 1949, when many within and out of Government were predicting a depression, I felt we would have no depression unless we scared ourselves into it. In that year I undertook a survey of opinion throughout the country to test the soundness of my belief. I propose again to take a trip throughout the country and examine conditions and receive opinions on the spot from those who are not too close to government in Washington.

It is wise for those of us in Washington occasionally to get out of our official chairs and move around through the country—not to tell the people what they should do or not do, but to find out what they think we should or should not do. I am certain that this survey will be of great benefit to me officially, and I am beginning the first leg of these trips today. It will take me to the Pacific Coast and back.[2]

I did not make the trip. As I was about to begin that speech I was called to the telephone by John Steelman, the top man in Truman's White House office. The President wished me to return to Washington immediately; the steel situation was getting bad and the President wanted to discuss it with me and "perhaps give me something to do." I asked if I might postpone my leaving until after lunch. He agreed that I could. After lunch I called Steelman. Things were chaotic and he asked that I stay put at least until the following day. He called me early that day and asked that I return immediately to Washington. The President wished me to take over the steel mills.[3]

I arrived in Washington about 11:00 A.M. on April 8. Shortly after lunch I called the President and arranged to see him at five that afternoon. Meanwhile, Steelman asked me to attend a meeting of mobilization advisers at 3:00 P.M. At this meeting were Robert Lovett, Secretary of Defense; John Snyder, Secretary of the Treasury; Manly Fleischmann, head of the National Production Authority; Roger L. Putnam, Wage Stabilizer; Governor Ellis Arnall, Director of Price Stabilization, and the Defense Department's Anna Rosenberg. Steelman outlined the situation as he saw it and Lovett made clear how seriously a steel shortage would affect the war in Korea. Arnall said that he had offered to the operators a price increase of $4.50 a ton, which they had refused to accept. He talked about the importance of standing by the Capehart Amendment, which determined how much price relief employers were to receive. The amendment would have permitted an increase of only $3.00 per ton. Anna Rosenberg said that it looked to her as if Arnall had violated principle when he offered $4.50. However, she grinned and said she did not think "a little violation" would be too serious. The conversation went on and on. I left, telling Steelman I saw no point in further talk. The President must tell me what he wanted done.

I met the President with Steelman later that afternoon. He said he was giving me the dirtiest job he had ever given anyone but he knew I could handle it. I said I was complimented but concerned. I asked if I would have a completely

free hand after I took over. He said that I would. I asked if
any commitments had been made to either side and Steelman
said that there had been no *real* commitments. I gathered from
his tone of voice that some encouragement had been given to
Philip Murray, head of both the Steelworkers' Union and the
CIO.

"Mr. President," I said, "this job will be tough enough as it
is and I hope that your talk tonight will not make it any
tougher." He said he certainly would not make it any tougher.[4]
That night, however, he did make it tougher by putting the
blame for the seizure entirely on management. The Presidential order was issued about nine o'clock and at ten-thirty the
President went on the air. Among other things, he said:

The steelworkers have had no adjustment in their wages since
December 1, 1950. Since that time, the cost of living has risen, and
workers in such industries as automobiles, rubber, electrical
equipment, and meat packing have received increases ranging
from thirteen to seventeen cents an hour. . . .

In other words, if the steel companies absorbed every penny of
the wage increase, they would still be making profits of seventeen
or eighteen dollars a ton. . . .

In the face of these facts, the steel companies are now saying
they ought to have a price increase of twelve dollars a ton, giving
them a profit of twenty-six or twenty-seven dollars a ton. That's
about the most outrageous thing I ever heard of. They not only
want to raise their prices to cover any wage increase; they want to
double their money on the deal. . . .

The plain fact of the matter is that the steel companies are
recklessly forcing a shutdown of the steel mills.

The following day he sent a message to Congress explaining
his action.

To The Congress Of The United States:
The Congress is undoubtedly aware of the recent events which
have taken place in connection with the management-labor dispute
in the steel industry. These events culminated in the action which

was taken last night to provide for temporary operation of the steel mills by the Government.

I took this action with the utmost reluctance. The idea of Government operation of the steel mills is thoroughly distasteful to me and I want to see it ended as soon as possible. However, in the situation which confronted me yesterday, I felt that I could make no other choice. The other alternatives appeared to be even worse —so much worse that I could not accept them. One alternative would have been to permit a shutdown in the steel industry. . . .

The only way that I know of, other than Government operation, by which a steel shut-down could have been avoided was to grant the demands of the steel industry for a large price increase. I believed and the officials in charge of our stabilization agencies believed that this would have wrecked our stabilization program. . . .

Accordingly, it was my judgment that Government operation of the steel mills for a temporary period was the least undesirable of the courses of action which lay open. . . .[5]

I had issued my seizure order as of midnight April 8. I designated the president or chief executive officer of each company as the operating manager for the United States and gave him authority to run the company. Managements and employees were ordered to continue their functions. The order provided for termination of possession when the interests of national defense permitted it. I sent a telegram to the president of each company instructing him to fly the United States flag, post the notice, and acknowledge his appointment as operating manager. I also sent a telegram to Philip Murray asking his cooperation. Murray immediately postponed the strike. A steel production loss was avoided, for the time being, and I told the press:

I neither requested nor wanted this job, but when our men at the front are taking orders in the face of great danger those of us further back can do no less.

I dislike as much as anyone to witness, let alone participate in, the seizure of property. We are, however, facing a situation of great peril where continued production of steel is essential to our national welfare.

The President has made his decision and has given me certain work to do in that connection, and I shall do it.

I hope that both industry and labor will accept the statements I make in good faith and will cooperate to the end that a solution of this problem may be reached and the continued production of the weapons needed for our defense may not be interrupted.[6]

Rarely has the country been so stirred. Resolutions for and against seizure and fourteen separate Presidential impeachment resolutions were introduced into congress; newspapers were charged with bias in reporting; businessmen said the government had yielded to the pressure of the unions. The Senate undertook to prohibit the use of any government appropriations for operation of the steel industry. Joint resolutions were introduced to ban payment of salaries and expenses to any federal official or employee operating the steel plants. This, of course, included me. I was threatened with a personal judgment running into millions of dollars—damages to the steel companies resulting from my seizure. The American Association of Newspaper Publishers voted to censure the President. Charles E. Wilson, Director of the Office of Defense Mobilization, resigned, claiming that the President had reneged on previous agreements regarding steel prices. The president of the United States Chamber of Commerce bitterly condemned Truman. Steelworkers quit, went back to work, and quit again. Drew Pearson, on the air one night, announced: "Four years ago I said that Sawyer would be out of the Cabinet in sixty days. Last week he was put in charge of all the steel mills in the country—How wrong can a commentator be?"[7]

Meanwhile I went right ahead. I invited executives of the major companies to meet with me and received assurances of their cooperation. The United Steelworkers also agreed to cooperate. While the steel executives went along with the

seizure, they were far from happy and insisted that the government had no legal right to take over their property. Several
suits were filed. One of these was the famous *Youngstown
Sheet and Tube Company vs. Sawyer,* before Judge David A.
Pine of the U.S. District Court. During the hearing of this
case, Judge Pine requested the Attorney General to secure a
statement from me, agreeing to make no changes in wage
schedules before the case was decided. I tried several times to
get such assurance to the judge. The Solicitor General, Phillip
Perlman, acting as my counsel, refused to pass this word on.
When I mentioned this to the President, he said he was surprised and would talk to Perlman. I was in Cincinnati on April
26 when my solicitor, C. Dickerman Williams, phoned to say it
was of the greatest importance that I get this message to Judge
Pine; on three separate occasions he had asked for such a
commitment. I told Williams to tell Holmes Baldridge, the
Assistant Attorney General trying this case, to assure the judge
that I would make no change while his decision was pending.
But the Solicitor General refused to let Baldridge deliver this
message. I then instructed Williams to set forth my position in
a letter to Baldridge. Only then did Perlman get word to the
judge.[8]

On April 29, Judge Pine granted a temporary injunction
against my seizure. Immediately, the men began to walk out.
There was little I could tell the reporters who wanted to know
what I would do.

I have seen Judge Pine's opinion but have as yet received no court
order. Meantime, I shall of course take no action which would run
contrary to the court's finding. Under the President's order I was
directed to run the steel mills—not conduct the litigation. Therefore, any appeal or decision with reference to a request for a stay
will be up to the Attorney General.

The next day, the Circuit Court of Appeals stayed the District
Court Order, to enable the government to file a petition for

certiorari with the Supreme Court. I was still in charge of the steel mills.[9]

There was a division of opinion as to what Truman should do. I felt that he should invoke the Taft-Hartley Law. On April 30 before the Court of Appeals reversed Judge Pine I had written to him:

Since you gave me the job of running the steel mills, perhaps I am justified in outlining my views and suggesting a course of action.

We are dealing today with an actual, and not a theoretical, problem. Judge Pine has declared the seizure unconstitutional and Mr. Murray has ordered his men out. No matter what the final judicial opinion may be, we are faced with the immediate problem of producing steel, which at the moment is not being produced except in about one-tenth of our steel plants.

In my opinion you should invoke the Taft-Hartley law. Some may strongly urge you not to take this course. I realize that it will be interpreted as your acknowledgement of its usability and that you may be charged with an anti-labor turn. I think these possible criticisms should be faced; in the long run, both from your standpoint and that of labor, I feel this course will be desirable.

If you appeal to Congress for the third time to enact legislation dealing with this problem you will be met immediately by the demand that you use the provisions of the Taft-Hartley Law. If you refuse to do this you will be in an interminable argument with Congress as to whether or not you have done everything within your power under the law to solve the immediate problem. If, after such a demand from the Congress, you finally do apply it you will be in a much weaker position than if you had done so originally.

This act will give an unquestioned legal basis to your right to get the men back to work and resume production of steel. It will enable the Board of Inquiry to present to the public and the workers the best offer which the steel companies will make. This has been gossiped about, but their complete offer has never been made categorically, or at least publicly, to anyone. It will stimulate them to make their best offer. It will also provide a period during which the parties may be brought together. If, at the end of the eighty-day period, the problem has not been solved, it will leave in the lap of the Congress, without any excuse whatever, the sole responsibility for whatever chaos may result.

You will then be in an impregnable position in stating to the Congress the need for some immediate legislation which will enable you to deal with this, and with similar situations.

The President did not agree with me then or later.[10]

Meanwhile, he made a further effort to bring labor and management to an agreement. At a meeting on May 2 in Steelman's office, I was strongly urged to issue an order changing the terms and conditions of employment. Perlman was of opinion that I should issue this order the following day. I said flatly that I would not do so and felt it unwise to make any statement of what I would or would not do while the matter was in the courts. We then discussed sending a telegram to Murray asking him to order the men back to work. I said this was fine if the men would go back. There was great risk, however, unless the President knew in advance that this request would be granted. Perlman thought it would and intimated that some advance commitment might be made to Murray. Putnam supported him—we would undoubtedly make some wage changes and there was no harm in saying so. I urged that no such prior commitment be made: it would embarrass the President and create a wholly unfair situation for the operators. In addition it would make a settlement impossible if Murray knew in advance what he was going to get. The discussion was lengthy. After some time Putnam said he had changed his mind and agreed with me; the others were still uncertain. I excused myself and left the meeting. The President called later in the day and said someone had told him that Cliff Hood, president of United States Steel Corporation, had said that he would not take the men back until he heard what the terms and conditions would be. The President was very angry: "I want you to fire that son-of-a-bitch right away and put a general in charge to run his mills." I replied:

"Mr. President, I think that would be unwise. Let's not take any impulsive action based on a ticker report. I recommend that before I do what you have indicated, I find out the facts." Truman was soon mollified and agreed that I was right.[11] A short time later the President decided to order the parties to get together and called a meeting for the following day. Meanwhile I suggested to the President that he talk with the men responsible for the mobilization effort. Heretofore he had discussed the situation only with his staff. I suggested that Lovett, Fleischman, Perlman, Steelman, and Snyder be invited. He agreed to this list and asked me to have them at the White House at quarter of seven that night. I called John Snyder and he suggested that we include Charles Murphy. I called Murphy who said he would come. It was then about six-o'clock.

Shortly thereafter, when everyone had arrived at the meeting, the President asked me to state its purpose. I said I hoped we could agree on what was to be said and done and by whom. Lovett pointed out the seriousness of the situation and said he felt it was desirable for me to be given authority to make a settlement. Steelman immediately broke in to say that he was afraid Lovett misunderstood the situation; mediation matters were in his, Steelman's, hands. Lovett retorted that he had not misunderstood the situation. Fleischman advised an effort toward a settlement but was cautiously noncommittal as to whether Steelman or I should handle the negotiations. Perlman's reaction was violently anti-management. He suggested that I should find out which executives had said they would not take the men back. Anyone who said that should be fired and an Army general put in his place. This sounded like Truman's statement to me; it was fairly clear that Perlman had been the source of that bit of information. I pointed out that Army generals know nothing about running steel mills. Lovett supported this line of reasoning and said that no threat of discharge should be made unless we were prepared to carry it out. Perlman orated upon the majesty of government. I said

that I also was anxious to maintain the government's position
but a certain amount of realism was desirable. Running a steel
mill was a complicated matter which should not be turned over
lightly to men of no experience. During our prolonged discussion, Lovett said it would be desirable for someone to shut up
the "goddamned mouth" of Arnall—addressing his remark to
me. I said that Arnall was not under me and I could not shut
him up; he was operating under Steelman. The latter laughed.
Later, I asked Steelman the flat question. Had any commitments been made to Murray? Steelman said no commitment
had been made. John Snyder repeated the question and received the same answer. Nothing was agreed upon that night.
But one remark of the President had been disconcerting. I had
asked that he say nothing at the meeting next morning that
would make it difficult to come to an agreement. He said that
his formal statement would satisfy me and then added, "Of
course, I don't know what I may say when I begin to talk off
the cuff." [12]

The next morning, before the meeting with labor and management representatives, I went to the White House at 9:30,
and found the President alone in his study. He said he was
anxious that the meeting go off well, and I said I also wanted it
to go well; but I was fed up with the whole thing. When the
Solicitor General, without consulting me, made statements in
court about what I was going to do, when other officials
continually told the press what should be done, I thought it
was time to ask him to put somebody else in charge. He
begged me not to "rock the boat" and undertook in every way
possible to mollify me. He said he could not get along without
me. He mentioned that he wanted to keep Steelman happy and
that the others were anxious to get into the act. I said there
was at least one difference between them and me—they wanted
to get into the act and I wanted to get out of it. He laughed
and then said—"That is exactly the reason why I want you to
stay in it." I was very fond of Truman and realized that he had

many and greater problems. I said I would talk with him again in a few days. He then said, "Is the meeting this morning in conformity with your wishes?" I told him that if I had been consulted I would have postponed it for a day or two until a definite agenda could have been arranged. He admitted that no program was planned. He said he wanted to make his statement, put John Steelman in charge, and then leave with me. I told him that I would be distressed if the meeting were allowed to close on a note of failure. He agreed with this completely. He said that he regarded me as his "ace in the hole"; if Steelman was not able to make progress he would call on me. I said I hoped the settlement job would not be handed to me so late that nothing could be done. Before we left the study, I said: "Mr. President, as I review my four years in your Cabinet, I think I have solved some problems for you—I hope I have created none." He said that was certainly true and told me he would see that I was not "left out on a limb" in this matter. Truman and I then went into the meeting where he urged the operators and the union to try again to settle their differences. After we had left the room, the President led me to his office and again urged me to stay and see the job through. He said he was going to do something nice for me in the future. I assumed he was thinking of an appointment to the Supreme Court, but I made no comment.[13]

While the Saturday meeting brought the two parties no closer together, the steelworkers did agree to return to work while the mills were under government control. On May 2 appeals for certiorari had been filed with the Supreme Court by the steel companies and by the government. On the afternoon of May 3 the Supreme Court agreed to take the case and set the hearing for May 12. The Court also granted the steel companies' request that changes in the terms and conditions of employment be prohibited before the Court had ruled on the case.[14] I dropped in at the White House for the Congressional Reception a little after 5:00 P.M. on May 12. While waiting outside, Mrs. Truman saw me through the door and asked me to come in where she and the President were having a brief rest. The President immediately asked what I had heard about the argument before the Supreme Court. He had received no report. I said things were not going too well for our side. He was disturbed. I told him that most of the questioning of Perlman had been hostile. Only Sherman Minton had tried to help him. He said, "Minton would do that," and confessed he would be terribly shocked, disappointed, and disturbed if the Supreme Court went against him. I said I hoped he would not take it too hard. He asked me if Perlman had filed a fine brief. I said I did not know; I had not been favored with a copy. He could not understand that; he had requested the Solicitor General to give a copy to each member of the cabinet. I said that I particularly should have received a copy, as I was the party whom Perlman was representing.[15]

I had been giving thought to what should be done when the Supreme Court handed down its decision. On May 21 I addressed a detailed memorandum of suggestions to the President.[16]

As we awaited the Supreme Court's decision, the stalemate continued. Unemployment was rising. House Republicans charged the Democratic leaders with stalling on the impeachment resolutions. The administration's united front was crumbling. Nathan Feinsinger, head of the Wage Stabilization Board, said the government had made every mistake in the book. Vice-President Alben Barkley made an impassioned speech to the steelworkers' convention and said he hoped the union would gain a victory.

By late May I had received so many complaints about damage to steel plants and equipment that I sent a telegram to Murray in Atlantic City where the steelworkers' convention was being held.

Production reports which I receive periodically from the steel companies under Government operation have contained information regarding sporadic damage in connection with the shut-down on April 29 by reason of the lack of necessary standby arrangements to safeguard equipment when the men left the plants. In the main, your suggestion with reference to protection of the properties was followed explicitly, but I feel it advisable for your information and in the interest of all of us to call your attention to the fact that this protection was not universal. I am sure you will agree that a proper preservation of steel-producing equipment is as much in the interest of the workers as the rest of us. I thought you might appreciate having this message and this information while you are meeting with the representatives of your union in Philadelphia. With kindest personal regards.[17]

Murray, perhaps egged on by friends in government, was angry because I had not granted a wage increase during the seizure. When he received my telegram he blew up and attacked me on the floor of the convention. He accused me of "unthinkable bias against the union." I discussed Murray's action with the President and on May 20 sent Truman a letter outlining what was going on.

On May 22 I received the following note from him:

Thanks a lot for your good letter of the twentieth regarding the Philip Murray Incident. I think you have handled it perfectly.

I had already known about the matters which you called to Mr. Murray's attention. I don't know why he had to make an incident out of it but you and I are acquainted with the men who head great organizations. They must be sure that they stand right with their organizations, even if it should take a little demagoguery.

HARRY [18]

Meanwhile, I had talked with the President about his plans in the event of an adverse decision and had urged him strongly not to defy the Supreme Court. He assured me that he would not. On June 2 the Supreme Court decided against us—six to three.[19] I called the President immediately. He had already heard of it. His comment was—"Well, you are now out of a job." I was out of a job and the men went out of the mills. The

President said he would like to talk with me and some others later in the day. He asked if I could meet at 4:30 in his study. I said I would be there. Meanwhile, Charles Murphy called to say that the President had directed him to draft a letter which would be on its way to me shortly. At 12:45, Murphy called back again to say that the letter was drafted and ready for the President's signature, but he had been unable to reach the Solicitor General. I was having lunch with the President and Truman told me at the table that he had signed and sent the letter (which was in my office when I returned). He also confirmed our appointment for that afternoon. The letter was as follows:

June 2, 1952

Dear Mr. Secretary:
In view of today's decision by the Supreme Court, you are hereby directed to take appropriate steps to relinquish immediately possession of the plants, facilities, and other property of the steel companies which have been in the possession of the Government under Executive Order No. 10340, of April 8, 1952.

I prepared the following telegram terminating the appointment of each respective president as my manager of his company.

In accordance with instructions from the President following the Supreme Court decision of today, I hereby terminate my possession of your plants and properties.
All instructions issued and appointments made by me are withdrawn, effective immediately. You are requested to post at places where you previously posted notice of taking possession by me, a new notice substantially as follows: The Secretary of Commerce has authorized a notice to whom it may concern that he no longer is in possession of this plant.[20]

At 4:30 o'clock we met in the White House Study: the President, James McGranery, who had just become Attorney General, Perlman, Steelman, Stowe, Lovett, Murphy, Joe

Short, and myself. Throughout the meeting Perlman kept going back to the Supreme Court decision. He discouraged using Taft-Hartley; he feared this action would be strongly attacked by the union. I interrupted to ask if the fact that it would be attacked was any reason for not using it. He admitted it was not. He continually reiterated that he did not know whether the men would go back to work or not; they had been very badly treated, and so forth. Steelman said very little. Stowe suggested opening a few of the mills in order that defense production could be kept going. I had already discussed this with Henry Fowler, the head of the National Production Authority, that morning, and he believed this attempt would result in nothing but confusion. Stowe said that he had been in touch with others who had a contrary view. I said I thought it important to clear this matter up and would do so promptly.

At the end of lengthy discussion the President asked for my opinion. I said there were two things to be done: the more urgent was to get the two parties to settle; the other was to obtain legislation which would enable the President to act. The Taft-Hartley Act should be considered as a means of getting the parties together and getting Congress to legislate. As to the first, a delay of two or three days might well be in order; Murray had indicated he would be glad to negotiate. The strike was already on—the important thing was to give the parties time to think. The temper of Congress could be learned from Rayburn, Barkley, McCormack, and McFarland. The President interjected that they did not know anything about the temper of Congress and had proved it; furthermore, the temper of Congress was very much anti-Truman and the Republicans could be counted on to oppose whatever was proposed. I then suggested that since he had promoted a bi-partisan policy with respect to foreign issues, he could take the same approach to the steel matter—call in some Republicans for consultation. This seemed to meet with everyone's approval, although the President doubted he would get much real cooperation. I said it was worth trying.[21]

As the conference broke up, the President said he would call us together the next night at eight o'clock. That night we met in the Cabinet Room. Those present at the previous day's meeting were there, plus Sam Rosenman, Clark Clifford, Secretary of Labor Maurice Tobin, David Bell and Henry Fowler. The President began by asking Lovett his opinion. Lovett spoke about the difficulty of getting Murray to make concessions. I interrupted to ask if Lovett felt that Murray could not be expected to make any concessions whatever. He said he did not intend to convey that impression, but wanted to talk about the difficulty of Murray's position. He mentioned the union shop. I interrupted again to ask, "Are you suggesting that Murray will not even concede the union shop?" He said "No," he was not suggesting exactly that. The President then called on McGranery, who discussed the Supreme Court's decision at length and said the minority opinion of the Chief Justice, from which he read, indicated clearly that the President was right. He said the matter had not been presented as well as possible —the Court had not been given sufficient evidence of the emergency. This was critical of Perlman, who immediately replied that there had indeed been such evidence before the court, affidavits from Secretary Lovett, from myself, from the AEC, and so forth. Next Murphy spoke. He had been in touch with Maybank and other senators. Maybank was prepared to offer a bill giving the President authority to seize any properties where defense production would be jeopardized during a period of national emergency. He said Maybank appeared anxious to help and some such bill would be offered as an amendment to the Defense Production Act.

The President then called on me. I said that, in the light of Murphy's statement, it might be well for the President to postpone for two or three days sending a message to congress, although I had on several earlier occasions urged him to send one. I said that it was still important to get the parties together; but there was no point in bringing them together if the union was expected to concede nothing and the operators were expected to concede everything. Only if both sides were to make concessions could we hope for a settlement. The President agreed.

Sam Rosenman said he would probably be thrown out of the room, but he thought the President should immediately invoke Taft-Hartley. He felt Murray had been badly treated. He did not like the act and knew the President did not like it; but we should use the only legal remedy left. During his talk he was interrupted by the President, by Murphy, and by Stowe, each of whom said that the union's agreement to postpone the strike for ninety-nine days precluded use of Taft-Hartley. Perlman maintained that the union would unquestionably resist its use. Rosenman said what I had said on the previous day—Perlman might be right, but that was no reason not to try it. Rosenman added, "If the court should hold with the union that the Taft-Hartley Act could no longer be employed that would clear the air so far as the President is concerned." Clifford's views were much the same as Rosenman's.

The President finally called on Tobin. Contrary to what everyone expected, and to the great credit of a fine public servant, the Labor Secretary said that the President should use the Taft-Hartley Act. Stowe then suggested, as he had earlier, that agreements be attempted with a few of the mills. Lovett pointed out that adequate national security depends upon many things in addition to weapons. A solution which would permit a few steel mills to produce weapons but would paralyze our transportation system and wreck our civilian economy would not contribute to national defense. The President supported this position, as did I.

Perlman asked to be heard again and promptly began once more to criticize bitterly the court's majority opinion. The President interrupted to say that the court had not considered

Secretary Sawyer debating with Henry Wallace in the Commerce Department auditorium, June 1950. The moderator is Theodore Granik.

Cartoonist's reaction to Secretary Sawyer's statement of the gross national product.

At the time of the steel mills seizure heads of big steel companies came to Washington. Left to right: Eugene Grace, Chairman, Bethlehem Steel Corporation; Secretary Sawyer; Ben Fairless, President, U.S. Steel Corporation.

Secretary Sawyer speaking at a dinner in Detroit, December 9, 1948, celebrating the production of the one-hundred millionth automobile.

At the Ministry of Commerce, Havana, Cuba, October 1950. Left to right:
Dr. Pedro Popes Dorticos, Cuban Sub-Secretary of Commerce, later
prominent official under Castro; Secretary Sawyer; Dr. Jose R. Andreu,
Cuban Secretary of Commerce, Dr. Luis Machado, Cuban Ambassador
to the United States.

The Truman cabinet presenting to President Harry S Truman the chair he used during his term of office. Left to right: Maurice Tobin, Secretary of Labor; Joseph Fowler, National Production Authority; Dean Acheson, Secretary of State; Charles Brannan, Secretary of Agriculture; Jesse Donaldson, Postmaster General; Averell Harriman, with ECA; President Truman; John Snyder, Secretary of the Treasury; Charles Sawyer, Secretary of Commerce; Oscar Chapman, Secretary of the Interior.

the matter carefully; he intended to fight this thing through; and in a somewhat emotional voice said that, if necessary, "they may have to take me for four years more." In the general discussion that followed, McGranery criticized Rosenman's statement that the real problem was to get steel—the real problem was the position of the Executive. He did not make clear what he had in mind. I asked the question, "What do you suggest that we do at this time?" He did not answer. Steelman asked Rosenman if bringing labor and management together should be postponed until Taft-Hartley had been invoked. Rosenman said he had not intended to suggest that. I said that, the strike being on, it might be well to wait a day or two before taking any action. The President, however, indicated that Steelman wanted to call the parties together. I got the impression that he would act the next day; which he did. I suggested that no votes were ever made after 10:15; we should let the President get to bed. He laughed, said again he was not tired, and wanted the discussion to go on as long as anyone cared to continue it. Shortly after this the meeting adjourned. As we were leaving, I remarked to the President that he could easily decide what to do in view of the unanimity of the advice we had given him. This was received with loud guffaws.[22]

On June 10 the President addressed a joint session of Congress. He requested authority to operate the mills temporarily until the parties reached an agreement. He suggested the legislation provide for changes in wages and working conditions during seizure. He also pointed out the need for a method of determining compensation for the owners. Part of his speech explained his failure to use the Taft-Hartley Law, which he believed would be unfair, harmful, and futile in this case. He concluded:

Whatever may have been the intention of the Court's majority in setting limits on the President's powers, there can be no question of their view that the Congress can enact legislation to avoid a crippling work stoppage in the steel industry. Mr. Justice Jackson referred to "the ease, expedition and safety with which Congress can grant" emergency powers of the type needed to handle this crisis.

The issue is squarely up to the Congress. I hope the Congress will meet it by enacting fair and effective legislation.

Nothing came of these suggestions. The strike went on until the matter was finally settled by agreement. Wages went up, as did prices.[23]

There have been many articles and books written about the Steel Seizure. Most of them deal with the legal aspects of the matter, which I have not undertaken to discuss. I began this treatise with a query—Why do people write books? Perhaps at this point I might add another one—Why do people who write books not do their homework? Dr. Richard E. Neustadt, now director of Harvard's John F. Kennedy School of Government, wrote a book on *Presidential Power—The Politics of Leadership*. It had a powerful title and I was told that President Kennedy kept it on his bedside table. After reading it, I began to have concern for the state of the nation. In this book, Professor Neustadt devoted much attention to a story about my failure or refusal to carry out the wishes of President Truman. The following are excerpts:

. . . A case in point is Secretary Sawyer's interesting behavior in his first weeks as administrator of the seized steel industry.

Having seized the mills in desperation to avert production losses, the White House wanted to be rid of them as fast as possible—which meant as fast as it could gain assurance that production would continue once they were returned to private hands. This called for some settlement of the labor dispute whose lack of settlement had led to seizure in the first place. The circle could be broken only if continued government control were made so unattractive in the eyes of both disputants that they would prefer agreement with each other. To that end a tactic was devised: the Secretary of Commerce, as administrator of the mills, was to put into effect a *portion* of the union's wage demands to which the men were automatically entitled under the existing rules of wage control (a so-called cost-of-living adjustment). At the same time, he was to ask the price controllers for the amount of price relief to which the companies were automatically entitled under "pass through" provisions of existing legislation (the so-called Capehart Amendment). Secretary Sawyer then was to announce that he would do no more. Management and labor would be faced by a *fait accompli* that satisfied neither the union's wage demands nor the company's price demands but put some things beyond dispute and foreclosed better terms for the duration. With this prospect before them both sides might conclude that more was to be gained from settlement than from continued government direction. So, at least, the White House hoped.

Within a week of seizure Truman had decided to proceed along these lines. He asked that Sawyer act at once and planned to call for bargaining by companies and union with his Secretary's action in the background. The President's intent was clear. There were no ambiguities. But Sawyer did not act. The Secretary of Commerce spoke for business in the Cabinet. Officially and personally Sawyer had no liking for the seizure. He had not wanted to administer the mills, and he had taken the assignment with distaste. He was evidently unhappy at the prospect of his signature on wage orders and price requests committing the steel industry. Although he did not refuse to act, he managed to immerse himself in preparations. Presently the District Court relieved him of embarrassment (and the government of opportunity) by denying his authority to run the mills. When the Appeals Court restored his powers, Sawyer reached the point of action only after he had won agreement from the President that in the public record his department should be seen to act on the advice of others. . . .

. . . When Truman urged wage changes on his Secretary of Commerce while the latter was administering the steel mills, he and Secretary Sawyer were not just two men reasoning with one another . . . Truman's status gave him special claims to Sawyer's loyalty, or at least attention. In Walter Bagehot's charming phrase "no man can *argue* on his knees." Although there is no kneeling in this country, few men—and exceedingly few Cabinet officers—are immune to the impulse to say "yes" to the President of the United States. It grows harder to say "no" when they are seated in his oval office at the White House, or in his study on the second floor, where almost tangibly he partakes of the aura of his physical surroundings . . . There is nothing in the record to suggest that Truman voiced specific threats when they negotiated over wage increases. But given his *formal* powers and their relevance to Sawyer's other interests, it is safe to assume that Truman's very advocacy of wage action conveyed an implicit threat.[24]

Dr. Neustadt is a brilliant man and writes well; this is fascinating reading. It has only one defect—it is pure fiction. If some bright assistant in the White House devised such a "tactic"— no one told me about it. If anyone, including the President, had suggested this I would have pointed out that I was having trouble enough trying not to offend either side. A tactic designed to irritate both sides would have brought chaos. Dr. Neustadt tells of the people with whom he consulted. Strangely enough he never contacted me. One might think that a careful playwright would talk to the party involved, even if he were the villain of the play. Perhaps I have done Dr. Neustadt an injustice. His failure to contact me may not have been an oversight. He may have realized that such a call would impair, if not eliminate, one illustration of the theory upon which his book was written. It would be unfortunate indeed if "presidential power" were to be destroyed by an effort to ascertain the facts.[25]

It is interesting to watch a fabrication persist. In August of 1963 a Roy Hoopes wrote a book on *The Steel Crisis* in which he said:

There was an added significance to Hodges' appearance. It should be recalled that when President Truman seized the steel mills in 1952, his Secretary of Commerce, Charles S. [sic] Sawyer, did not agree with the decision and did everything possible to obstruct the President's move. Although Kennedy's 1962 battle with the steel industry cannot be compared to Truman's seizure of the steel mills (which was eventually declared unconstitutional), it is significant that Kennedy had the complete support of his Cabinet—including his "spokesman" for business at Cabinet meetings, the Secretary of Commerce.

I wrote to Mr. Hoopes asking for data which would support his statement that I tried to obstruct the President's move. He replied and explained that he had relied completely upon what Neustadt had said in his book and had not undertaken to check the facts. He apologized for the incorrect impression given.[26] He, like Neustadt, had never contacted me.

19 *Barkley*

LATE IN the summer of 1952 I made my last foray into party politics. I had avoided political activity for some years and had not planned to attend the 1952 Democratic National Convention in Chicago. But I was persuaded to run as a delegate-at-large from Ohio, supporting the "favorite son" candidacy of Senator Robert Bulkley. Although Senator Kefauver campaigned hard in the state and took most of the delegates, I was elected, along with a few other Bulkley supporters.[1] Earlier in the year, President Truman had discussed with me the selection of a desirable Democratic nominee. At first he did not indicate a preference; perhaps he had none. Later, when I told him I would attend the convention, he said that he had been in favor of Stevenson, but Stevenson was too coy to be a good candidate. He was now for Barkley, and asked if I would quietly try to help the Vice-President and, at the proper time, convey the message that Barkley was his choice. The leading candidate was Kefauver, supported by the liberals in the party, including such personalities as Herbert Lehman of New York, Paul Douglas of Illinois, and "Soapy" Williams of Michigan.[2]

278

Barkley arrived on the first day of the convention, after the other candidates and their supporters had already been active among the delegates. To demonstrate his vigor at seventy-one, he and his young wife Jane walked the mile from the railroad station to the Blackstone Hotel. This produced some good publicity. However, having reached the Blackstone, he seemed lost, unable to decide what to do next. He called me at the Ambassador East and asked if I would come over and talk with him. We were joined by Les Biffle, Governor Lawrence Wetherby, and Senator Earle Clements. Barkley said that he was being pressured by the television networks to show himself. I asked why he hesitated. He replied that it was not dignified for the Vice-President of the United States to make such an active bid for the nomination. To my question, "You are a candidate, are you not?," he answered, "Yes, of course." I said that if he wanted the nomination, he had better work hard to get it. By all means he should make himself available for television. He then said, "Well, what about Jane?" I replied that she was the best looking woman around the convention; the more she showed herself, the better it would be for him. I urged him to accept every invitation and have Jane do the same. The others strongly supported me. He then said, "But I have no one to clear these engagements and make arrangements to carry them out." I said I would take care of this and telephoned Ludwig "Curly" Caminita, a smart and hardworking public relations man in Washington. Curly came that afternoon.[3]

I began my own efforts to promote Barkley. A number of his supporters assisted me and we met each morning at my suite to discuss the previous day's activities and plan for the day ahead. I was in constant touch with President Truman. At one point we had Barkley on twelve television shows, taped and live, national and regional, including Meet The Press. In each case we would arrange to have someone, either participating in the program or in the audience, ask Barkley how he kept up such a hectic pace when all the young men around him were tuckered out. We were proving that he was no "tired old man."

Within a short time Barkley and his wife were getting practically all the publicity. Kefauver, and Harriman, who was also a candidate, became alarmed at Barkley's progress. They were able to persuade two labor leaders to state that Barkley was too old. These men were both friends of mine from Cincinnati—Jack Kroll, head of the Political Action Section of the CIO, and George Harrison, President of the Railway Clerks' Union. The effect on Barkley was devastating. He was crushed; he was the victim of "base ingratitude," for he had backed labor unfailingly. How could they do this to him? He was not encouraged by the fact that other labor leaders were sticking with him—William Green, President of the American Federation of Labor, John L. Lewis, and Caesar Petrillo. They were not impressed by the attack on his age; they were as old, or older, than Barkley. I discussed the situation with President Truman, who said we should try to persuade Barkley to stand up against this attack. He made this interesting comment: "I don't know how he would stand up as President if he can't even stand up against two labor leaders."

I tried to make Barkley stand and fight. I said that he now had the only issue before a convention which, until this time, had none. "State that no two business leaders, or no two labor leaders can tell you that you cannot be a candidate and you will present a picturesque and understandable issue which will interest the convention and the country at large. It will, in my judgment, get you the nomination." He listened but was not impressed. He invited Kroll and Harrison to breakfast and undertook to persuade them to withdraw their statement. They refused. Following this breakfast meeting, Senator Clements and Governor Wetherby advised Barkley that he should back out. They helped him draft a withdrawal statement. The Vice-President refused to read the statement and "Curly" Caminita read it to the assembled newsmen.

That evening, as I was about to go to the convention hall, Barkley called from the Blackstone and said he had decided to go back to Paducah and wanted to talk to me. He and Jane were packing, planning to leave Chicago the next day. I urged him to reconsider. I said it was inconceivable that the Vice-President of the United States would leave Chicago like a dog with his tail between his legs. He persisted. I then asked if he would be willing, before leaving, to address the convention, not as a candidate, but as the Vice-President. He said that he would, if properly invited. I left him and immediately telephoned Truman, who liked the idea. I then telephoned Frank McKinney, Chairman of the National Committee. McKinney said he would arrange for Barkley to get an invitation. Sometime early the next afternoon Barkley phoned to say that the invitation had come and he was preparing to address the convention that night. I asked if I might come over and talk about what he was planning to say. When I arrived he outlined what he had in mind. He was bitter at the labor leaders and was planning to make a speech with the "dagger in the back" as his principal theme. He expanded on the unswerving support he had given to labor throughout all his years in Congress and his right to expect decent if not generous treatment from them. I pointed out that this kind of a speech was not in character. I took Mrs. Barkley into another room and urged her to suggest that he change his approach completely. Then I left. I did not see him again until he had made his speech.[4]

The speech was the big event of the convention. It was a typical Barkley effort—friendly, generous, orotund. He had the convention in the palm of his hand, tuned to a high pitch of frenzy. When he concluded, delegates from all parts of the hall came streaming to the rostrum to shake his hand. Members of my delegation asked if I was not planning to do the same; others were congratulating Barkley, did not I like his talk? None of them knew that I had arranged it. I finally did go to the platform, where Barkley put his arm around my shoulders and said, "I can't tell you how much I appreciate what you did for me."

That same night at least fifty top Democratic leaders came to a room in the convention hall to talk with him. The next morning many prominent Democrats visited my suite to say that they thought there was still a chance to nominate him. Among those who continued to work toward that end were John L. Lewis, William Green, and Caesar Petrillo. Some of Barkley's close friends also felt that the situation had changed and his chances were again good. I called the President. Truman asked me to be sure that Barkley would accept the nomination if it were offered him. I said, "Of course he will accept it—that is what he is here for." I phoned Barkley at the Blackstone and then called the President to say that Barkley said he "wanted to think about it." Truman said that if Barkley could not make up his mind he had better not be nominated. Perhaps the six words, "I want to think about it," lost Barkley the nomination. Barkley did try to revive his cause. I advised against this, for he no longer had the President's support. Some of his friends continued to urge him to run and he was nominated by Senator Thomas Hennings of Missouri. The result, however, was what I had expected—on the third ballot he received only sixty-seven and one-half votes. Adlai Stevenson was nominated and made a great speech of acceptance. Following the convention I received a most generous letter from Barkley:

I cannot let another day go by without expressing to you my deep appreciation of your efforts in my behalf in Chicago. I hope you realize that there is no man in America for whom I have a more profound respect and whose confidence I cherish to a greater extent than yours.[5]

During that final evening a fire broke out in front of the South Carolina delegation. For a few moments an atmosphere of horror overhung the convention. The hall was packed and a possible holocaust was beginning. The flames were soon extinguished, however, and Jimmy Byrnes, who had been threatening to leave the convention, got to a floor microphone to say that he wished all the delegates and the galleryites to know that he had not started the fire. This produced a laugh and ended the tension.[6] With the number of papers which accumulate in any political convention and the number of smokers who carelessly drop matches on the floor, it is really a wonder that this does not happen frequently.

I did not attend the 1956 convention as a delegate. I did attend as an observer, a refreshing and relaxing change. Truman was leading a forlorn hope for Harriman, an effort with which Chairman Paul Butler was not in sympathy. Butler showed his distaste for Truman by giving him a box with only four seats. One amusing incident of the 1956 convention was a call to me from A. B. "Happy" Chandler asking for my support of his candidacy for President. I had known him for many years. After explaining why he thought he would be nominated, he came up with this classic statement: "There are probably a thousand men better qualified than I, but they ain't runnin'." [7] That was my last convention.

20 *Farewell to Washington and to Truman*

By LATE summer the steel companies and the union had agreed, the Dollar Line case had been settled, and the ss *United States* was crossing the Atlantic regularly in record time as the new "Queen of the Seas." Shortly thereafter the American people chose the man who would follow Truman into the White House. It was not the candidate we had selected in Chicago.

The Republicans were coming in. But a few things remained to be done. In July, I had announced that the Commerce Department would prepare an exhaustive appraisal of business prospects for the coming years. We were assisted by a committee of outstanding economists, enlisted by Marion Folsom. An immense amount of work went into the report "Markets After the Defense Expansion," which was ready for distribution late in the year. In my foreword I wrote:

American businessmen are just as emotional as any other group. Like every other group they are susceptible to fear. Nothing generates fear like uncertainty. Even bad news is better than uncertainty. By whatever measure we can reduce uncertainty in the mind of the businessman we can contribute to a steadiness in

the business world which in itself is perhaps the most important—
at least one of the most important—factors in our future prosperity.[1]

I did not give up entirely on my effort to coordinate the
work of various government agencies dealing with business
competition. I continued to urge the Business Advisory Council to come up with a report on this subject, and towards the
end of 1952 was able to make public their study on "Effective
Competition." I said:

In a discussion of every program it is well to start with the
question, "What is our objective?" This applies with great force
to the question of competition. Competition is not an end in itself
but a means to an end. The basic job of our competitive business
system is to provide more and better goods and services for all of
us consumers at prices we can afford to pay. The test of competition is its effect upon the consumer.

The report itself stated:

The word COMPETITION, by itself, is inadequate as a standard
for interpretation and administration of the Antitrust Laws. There
are many kinds of competition. The "perfect competition" of
academic economics is too abstract to be of value.

The term EFFECTIVE COMPETITION, however, provides the basis
for a satisfactory standard. This concept describes a business
community which is characterized by ceaseless striving among
competitors, all endeavoring to expand their share of the market
—and the total size of the market, as well—by producing relatively
more and better goods and services at relatively lower prices;
provided that there must, of course, continue to be safeguards
against unfair or predatory competition.

Like many other reports upon which great time and effort and
thought have been spent, nothing came of it. However, it is
still, if I may say so, a persuasive document.[2]

In September the President's Airport Commission made its
recommendations, which in turn were placed in my hands by

the President. These recommendations dealt with almost all of the problems of air travel. Unfortunately, there was not time enough for me to act upon them.

During my service as Secretary of Commerce I had been burdened by the operation of the U.S. Barge Lines, a company created to stimulate commerce on our waterways. One of my earliest, and continuing, problems was to get money from Congress to buy tankers for its fleet. Government operation of this enterprise did not meet with my approval and shortly after taking office I began to seek some way to dispose of it. In the fall of 1952 I had reached an agreement of sale. After Eisenhower's election the buyers approached me and said they would be grateful if I would permit them to conclude the sale with my successor. I saw no reason to refuse. My successor and good friend Sinclair Weeks, however, was given the credit for getting the government out of the barge business.[3]

In the fall I resumed the trip which had been postponed by the steel seizure. I traveled to cities which I had not before visited: St. Louis, Colorado Springs, San Francisco, Los Angeles, Las Vegas, Salt Lake City, Denver, Oklahoma City, Lincoln, Nebraska, and Chicago. Again I found a feeling of optimism about our economic condition and again I found a desire on the part of everyone to cooperate. By this time, the survey for our study, "Markets After the Defense Expansion" was talked about and businessmen were greatly interested.[4]

Following this trip, I went to Europe. For four years I had been handling export control, had been in contact with our "give-away" programs and was interested in their economic effect at home and abroad. I discussed with Truman the desirability of surveying the European economy and our relation to it from a business point of view. We both realized that this trip and its resulting report would be coming late in his administration, but felt that it would probably be valuable to his successor, whoever he might be. The President by letter suggested the trip as a desirable complement to my final survey in the

United States. He hoped that our findings would put "particular emphasis upon and attention to our business relations abroad and to the effect of our policies upon growing business in other countries." It would enable me

to make helpful suggestions in connection with the operation of Point IV as it involves the question of private investment abroad and the responsibility imposed upon you by an Act of Congress for investigating and reporting to the Mutual Security Agency upon impediments to private investment abroad.[5]

On October 31, we sailed from New York on the ss *United States*. The mission included Andrew N. Overby, Assistant Secretary of the Treasury; J. Thomas Schneider, Assistant Secretary of Commerce; Hawthorne Arey, vice-chairman of the Export-Import Bank; Charles R. Hook, chairman of Armco Steel Corporation; Langbourne M. Williams, Jr., president of Freeport Sulphur Company and Henry Fowler, head of the National Production Authority. I was the chairman. We were to visit Great Britain, France, West Germany, Italy, Greece, Turkey, Spain, Switzerland, Belgium, and the Netherlands. We hoped to investigate business and economic conditions in each country and get some idea of prospects for the years immediately ahead. We planned interviews with representatives of American business in each of these countries and separate meetings with business representatives of the country itself. Each embassy was to brief us on economic conditions and furnish us with supplemental reports.[6]

We landed at Southampton and proceeded to London. The American Ambassador, Nelson Aldrich, was most gracious and helpful, and arranged a series of meetings with top British businessmen. The British were worried about increased competition in their overseas markets, especially from Germany and Japan. They felt that Britain must end inflation and build up reserves. They were also worried about United States tariffs and customs procedures, and particularly concerned

over United States gold policy. American investment in the
u.k. thus far had improved, not damaged, relations between
the two countries, although this was too frequently misunderstood in England. I was impressed, as I had been on previous
occasions, by these British businessmen and their unhurried
approach to their problems. They were able, shrewd and
friendly; and nothing interfered with their tea time. While in
London, I also talked at length with Peter Thorneycroft, my
counterpart in the British Cabinet.

Not all of my stay in Britain was given to business. Ambassador Aldrich and I were invited to attend the celebration of
the Three-hundredth Anniversary of Lloyd's of London, during which the Queen was to lay a cornerstone for the company's new offices. Thousands of people were on hand, straining
to catch a glimpse of the proceedings. From time to time
various guests were escorted to the Queen's side. I noted the
difference in applause accorded each guest and was pleased by
the fine response when my name was called. It was certainly
not for me, but for America and perhaps for the aid we had
sent to England. At a small supper party after the ceremony,
given by the Queen and Sir Winston Churchill, I met members
of the Royal Family, the Cabinet Ministers and the Archbishop of Canterbury. Queen Elizabeth was as lovely and
charming as I remembered her in Washington, when she was
still a princess. It was a very pleasant affair and I had an
opportunity to chat with almost everyone there. The Archbishop of Canterbury spoke glowingly of my daughter Jean
and her husband John Weaver, who had spent some time at
Lambeth Castle in 1948.[7]

From London the mission flew to Paris. Our plane almost
crashed coming into Orly Airport. The Commerce Department
had air representatives in Europe, and I had been assured that
competent pilots were available there. I had insisted, however,
on taking along my own pilot, Larry Doyle. It proved to be a
wise precaution. The pilot misjudged the approach at Orly,

and Doyle, who was also in the cockpit, brought the plane up rapidly enough to avoid an accident.

In Paris we found four United States "ambassadors," operating to the confusion and sometimes the amusement of the French. The real ambassador was James Dunn, a man of extended experience in the Foreign Service and extremely competent. Other "ambassadors"—William H. Draper, Jr., Livingston R. Merchant and David K. E. Bruce—were running their own independent operations. Thousands of Americans stationed in Paris were building up the resentment of Frenchmen dispossessed from their homes to make room for these well-paid interlopers. I talked with Ambassador Dunn and disclosed my views, which had not changed since my days in Belgium. He confided to me that his position had become almost intolerable. Representatives of ECA and other "giveaway" agencies could hold out promises of money, which he could not. The French of course were quite willing to take Uncle Sam's money, pretending that they were very happy with the great service rendered by the hoard of "do-gooders" we had sent over.[8]

Representatives of American business firms with whom we talked agreed that American aid, although important in the past, should not go on. Several said that the achievement of financial stability in France would bring in great flow of capital investment. While the immediate economic outlook presented problems, the economy was potentially stable and productive. On one point all American businessmen agreed—the U.S. Government should consolidate its agencies and reduce the number of American employees. Ambassador Merchant thought that the military campaign in Indo-China, with its huge drain on French resources, had influenced the French attitude toward NATO. As the risk of Russian aggression in Europe diminished, there was a strong desire on the part of Europe to be independent of the United States and the Western European nations were taking concrete measures to

strengthen their ties to each other. The far-reaching Schuman
Plan for a single coal and steel market had been signed in
March. The Coal and Steel Community, together with the
European Defense community, promised a basis upon which a
European Federation could grow.[9]

We flew from Paris to Bonn, the capital of the German
Federal Republic, where we saw an additional example of
United States extravagance—an entire town had been built,
and was being enlarged, to house Americans sent there to take
care of the Germans. I talked at length with federal officials in
Bonn. The Economics Minister, Professor Dr. Ludwig Erhard,
who later became Chancellor, wanted to make private American investment attractive. Foreign investment would help German industry to modernize its equipment. Western Germany
had an important role to play in Europe by becoming a strong
outpost against communism. His country had recovered
greatly since 1948 but needed to import more raw materials.
West Germany also had to find ways to export more to the
United States. Regarding a European Federation, Dr. Erhard
thought that economic integration of Western Europe should
precede political integration and that free convertibility of
currencies should also be a prerequisite. Dr. Fritz Schaeffer,
the Finance Minister, emphasized that the Federal German
Republic was America's first line of defense against communism in Western Europe and all the economic help which the
United States gave would be used to strengthen this barrier.
Walter Freitag, Chairman of the German Federation of Trade
Unions, told me that since 1945 the German trade unions had
fought successfully to reduce communist infiltration into the
union movement, but that final defeat of communism in Germany depended on a stable, viable economy. My most interesting meeting was with Konrad Adenauer. He was impressive
both physically and mentally and a refreshing example of the
finer qualities found in the German people. He showed an
understanding of our problems and disclosed a keen sense of
humor when speaking frankly of certain world figures.[10]

From Bonn we went to Dusseldorf where both American and German businessmen from all parts of the Federal Republic came to meet us. The German economy had made great strides toward recovery, although much remained to be done: there was still a low standard of living, a housing shortage, and heavy taxes. There were still refugees. But it was interesting to note that there was no German "balance of payments" problem. We pointed out that American businessmen wanted the Germans to let American profits be returned to the United States and that American investors had to be assured of a reasonable return, in dollars. On their part the German business leaders hoped that "trade, not aid" would prevail. I was greatly impressed by their strength, shrewdness, and drive. Our visit had been successful. It was obvious that the Germans considered it important; they had spent much time and effort preparing for it.[11]

We next went to Milan, the heart of the northern Italian industrial area. This region had expanded its production greatly since the end of the war and was now the most important Italian market for American and other foreign goods. The problems were overpopulation, unemployment, and high prices. Italian officials were convinced that the future of their foreign trade was bound up with the development of a wide, free trading area that included the major countries of Europe. During my stay in Milan I was able to see Leonardo da Vinci's "Last Supper" and the Rondanini "Pieta" of Michelangelo. This was his last and unfinished work. He was working on it only a week before he died. The thousands of his small chisel marks were fascinating to look upon and almost as thrilling as the completed work would have been. This sculpture, in Rome in a private family collection for centuries, had recently been purchased by the City of Milan. I was privileged to see it before it was put on public exhibition.

From Milan to Rome we flew through thick, unending fog. However, in the late afternoon, as we were about to come down, the clouds broke, the sun streamed from the west, and I caught my first glimpse of the Eternal City—the Seven Hills, the River Tiber, and the Colosseum. In Rome I was favorably impressed by the men we met, as I was by the officials of other governments. These, as well as my earlier contacts, made clear how foolish it is for Americans to adopt a condescending attitude toward the governments and peoples of other countries. Many are wiser than we and far more experienced.

The Italian economy as a whole seemed to be in a precarious state. There was need for tax reform and greater efficiency in business and in government, to care for a growing population which could no longer emigrate. Here also the American businessmen were, without exception, critical of our foreign aid program. Here as elsewhere officials of the government suggested, off the record, that our aid should stop. This state of mind was expressed sometime later in a book, *The Italians*, by Luigi Barzini.

After the war for instance everybody tried hard to find a suitable answer to the puzzling problem: why was the United States showering billions of dollars on their country? Communists were certain it was part of a master-plan to impoverish, starve, enslave, and destroy the Italian proletariat. Non-Communists could not make up their minds. Were the Americans mad? Many possible explanations were debated and discarded. At the end, most people said: "Why should they, who won the war, enrich us, who lost it? They must have their own reasons. Whatever they are, there is no doubt the Americans are serving their own interests. Therefore, there is no need for us to be grateful to them." [12]

We spent three days in Greece and were received elaborately by the King and Queen. He was tall, handsome, and, alone among all the kings I have seen or seen pictured, really looked like a king. The Queen was intelligent, vivacious, and extremely good-looking. We considered this visit important. The Truman Doctrine had been a unique venture in American foreign policy. From 1947, when Congress passed the Greek-Turkish Aid bill, until 1950, the United States had given approximately 659 million dollars to save these two countries from Communist aggression. I had wished to see the results at first hand. We were in Greece immediately after the election that made Marshal Papagos the Premier. I talked with several members of his cabinet and at length with my counterpart, an unusually brilliant man. He said that Papagos' majority was so great that he "could afford to do some unpopular things." We discussed at length the question of Uncle Sam's aid. He said that we were disgustingly extravagant, forcing aid on countries which really did not need it. When I asked him why he thought it was kept up, he said it was a question of *Cherchez la femme!* I was not certain what he had in mind, but on further questioning, he said it was the wives of our overseas administrators who kept promoting the cause. They were usually women who had few or no servants at home. When they were introduced into high social and governmental circles, given large houses and many servants, they could pass on to their husbands numerous reasons for not giving this up.[13]

Here our mission split. A seven-man party headed by J. Thomas Schneider went to Istanbul; I stopped briefly in Rome and then flew back to Paris. I wrote to the President from Paris on November 22:

While this mission will make a detailed and formal report when we get back home, I thought you might like a brief recital of what we have been doing. I, myself, and the others feel that this trip has been well worthwhile. We have been very much on the go. We have been in England, France, Germany, Italy, Turkey, Greece, and Switzerland. Today I flew into Paris from Rome. We flew over Elba and took about one hour to fly from Elba to Nice. It took Napoleon somewhat longer.

You might be interested in one or two definite impressions. None of the countries is as badly off as they claim. We have talked with many private citizens and public officials and checked with our own State Department and MSA officials and that opinion, I think, is unquestionably correct. They all have problems and some of them have special problems. If that were not true, this would be Heaven and not Western Europe. France certainly has a special problem in connection with Indo-China, and Germany certainly has a special problem in connection with occupation costs. Although they will not admit it publicly, they are fairly well reconciled to the ending of economic aid, except perhaps in Greece and Italy.

I, myself, think that economic aid to Greece should be continued. A new administration has gone in there, apparently of a stable character, and it would be unfortunate if, after great aid to governments which were weak and temporary, we should shut it off from a government of a different sort. You can count your decision to aid Greece as one of the great accomplishments of your administration. It has cost us far less than Korea and has maintained our position at a point in the world which is far more important. The aid has been extravagantly and, in some cases, stupidly administered; but the overall objective has certainly been accomplished. It is a tribute to your courage as well as good judgment.

We will go from Paris to Holland and Belgium and from there to Spain.

We shall not be home in time for Mrs. Sawyer and me to attend your cabinet dinner on December 4; this I greatly regret. Perhaps you would have time before we all leave Washington to have me come and lunch with you or at least talk to you personally about this trip. This will be in addition to our formal report. We might also have a post-mortem on the election and talk a little politics.

Please give my best to Mrs. Truman and Margaret.

On December 1, 1952, I received the following answer:

Thanks for your letter of November twenty-second.

I was much interested in your statements about the NATO countries. I rather think the Foreign Policy will be up in the air for some time and that there will be an attempt to cut off economic aid—we will see what the result will be. I'll talk with you about it when you return.

I am sorry you can't be present at the dinner on the fourth.[14]

From Paris we flew to Holland and Belgium. In each country we visited I tried to ascertain what was being done about the Benton-Moody Amendments of the 1951 and 1952 Mutual Security Acts. Congress, in a well-intentioned but child-like effort to improve the economies of Western Europe, had ordered the expenditure of 100 million dollars to "stimulate workers, and owners." I had suspected that this objective would prove difficult to accomplish; I had underestimated the extent of its failure. Nowhere were the ambassadors or the MSA representatives able to spend anything like their quota. In Brussels, although there were twenty-seven employees operating our give-away program, the head man admitted to me that, try as he might, he found it impossible to spend the money which he was required to spend under this amendment. I asked how he proceeded. He explained that he first tried to find failing businesses and then build them up. In other words, he was pumping Uncle Sam's money into the failures to help them compete against those businesses which were successful. Needless to say, the successful Belgian businessman was hardly delighted, and the recipients of our bounty made fun of us. Our representatives in other cities were doing the same thing.[15]

For many years Spain had intrigued me. I was entranced by her strategic location in Europe—the Mediterranean on one side, the Atlantic on the other and the Straits of Gibraltar between; her geography; her fascinating history, the Moors, Queen Isabella, Christopher Columbus, Philip II and the Armada, the Alhambra, the Prado; her literature; her art; her colorful people, gay and flamboyant and courageous; her bullfights. It was, therefore, no hardship to go through Spain to meet our ship at Gibraltar. From Brussels we went by train to Paris. While in Paris, I was asked by the State Department not to call upon Franco. Franco was a ruthless dictator; the United States should have nothing to do with him. When I asked where Europe would be today if Franco had been defeated and the Communists were in control of Spain and Gibraltar, I received no answer. I said that I would call on Franco if he invited me. Inasmuch as I was the first prominent United States official to visit Spain, and inasmuch as the State Department had shown its disinterest in, if not contempt for, the Spanish government, I was exceedingly well received. All officials from The Caudillo down laid out the red carpet. I was invited to call upon Franco and did. I expected to stay about fifteen minutes. He kept me for an hour. The approach to his retreat was spectacular. Men on horseback, heavily and gorgeously uniformed, sat rigidly at attention on either side of the road, as my car passed through a long entry way. I found Franco himself intelligent, clearheaded, and willing, even anxious, to talk. Upon my return, I recommended that we establish better contact with Franco and consider Spain in the development of our defense program.[16]

Before boarding ship we visited the fortress of Gibraltar. This was my first sight of it. Within this rock is a vast labyrinth of passages and rooms built by the British. Here I thought again of the situation if the Communists, not Franco, were in control of Spain.[17]

The entire mission spent the return trip drafting our report. Here are some of its observations:

There was an almost unanimous opinion that we have too many people and too many agencies in Western Europe . . . Confusion and wasted effort are the result . . . There are at the moment four men each with the title of "ambassador" in Paris . . . The situation is duplicated in practically every other country of Western Europe. The solution to this problem is the abolishment of emergency agencies whose task is either completed or can be absorbed by the regular departments . . . We still have MSA missions in countries to which we are not now giving and for some time have not given economic aid. There would seem to be no reason why these missions should not be terminated . . . This situation does not require another study employing a large staff to consider and report upon the problem. . . .

We met, of course, the tendency to place the burden of action upon the United States. It is clear to us and was clear to many of the men we met that the ultimate solution to the economic problems of Western Europe lies not in the United States of America but in Western Europe itself. . . .

In every country there was voiced an eager desire for private capital investment from America. . . .

It should be a fixed and clearly recognized permanent policy of the United States that all of our activities in any foreign country should be under the direct and effective control of the ambassador.

This report would make good reading today. It was widely read at the time and there were some indications that its recommendations would be followed. This did not greatly encourage me, for I had frequently seen my excellent suggestions go down the drain.[18]

My official life in Washington was at an end. It had been stimulating, fascinating, sometimes amusing, always different. I had moved in with the hope that I might render service to the business community. I had tried to blunt the anti-business philosophy prevalent in my own party. The results, not all that I might have wished, did not disappoint me. During these five years I had come to feel even more strongly the need for realism in Washington's atmosphere of theoretical liberalism. My prejudice against the size and extravagance of our foreign aid programs became more fixed. I left Washington with no regrets. I had not become afflicted with "Potomac fever," that lingering disease which causes so many appointees to stay on after their service and usefulness has ended.

Early in the year, before the Executives' Club of Chicago, I had commented upon the life of a Washington official. He "must expect criticism—

much of it uninformed; he must learn the difference between running the Government and running a business; his satisfaction must come, not from public approval or applause, but from the sense of a job well done; he must have a sense of humor about himself and his office.

One of the amazing things about official life in Washington is the jargon. You don't refer to your office—you refer to your "shop." You don't delay—you "drag your feet." You don't slow up a program—you "phase it out." You don't deal with this matter under a certain description—you handle it within a "frame of reference"; everything, of course, follows a "directive." You don't refer to a mistake in timing or a discrepancy between objective and accomplishment—you talk about "slippage" or "short fall." You don't say that there isn't enough of something to go around —you say it is "in short supply." You don't appoint a group to look into a certain problem—you employ a "task force." You don't refer to the matter at hand as a specific problem—it is an "ad hoc" detail. You don't conclude or end a job—you "finalize" it.

It is interesting and somewhat disconcerting to note a common impression that fine public servants are those who give out the best statements. I'm aware of the importance of words in influencing public opinion and their importance in the direction of policy. The public official, however, should be judged partly by what he says, but mostly by what he does. We occasionally hear references to great public servants which are laughable to those who know the facts. If I were asked, "How can the public identify good public officials?" I would say that the best officials are those who talk the least.[19]

I might have added that many officials in Washington, both in and out of Congress, do not always voice their real convictions. I have thought many times how interesting the results would be if congressmen were to vote secretly on the matters before them. This will never occur, but it would throw light upon the difference between what congressmen really believe and how they vote.

Being a cabinet member was a great experience. The prestige is high and the atmosphere different from anything outside of Washington. The relationship with other Washington officials, including cabinet colleagues, is interesting and in my case was extremely pleasant. Most cabinet meetings were routine. The President frequently called for comment on some matter, but did not ask for lengthy reports or discussions. Those who wished to discuss a particular matter would accompany the President to his private office after the meeting. I myself did this on many occasions. The functions of cabinet members have to a certain extent been taken over by the White House staff. The administrative job of the President is too much for one man. Not only is he responsible for the activities of his cabinet, but he is supposed to direct personally more than fifty independent agencies. The result is more and more reliance upon a small group of readily available men in the White House. When we view the maze of government operation and its millions of employees, the marvel is not that it functions imperfectly; the marvel is that it functions at all. Oxenstierna, Gustavus Adolphus' Chancellor, who taught his son always to remember "with how little wisdom the world is governed," would perhaps have been favorably impressed in Washington.

Most cabinet members work hard. I was always at the office by eight o'clock and rarely left before six. Many times I worked at night either at my office or at home. While I enjoyed my fellow cabinet members I also enjoyed my associates at the Commerce Department. I sought diligently the friendship and good will of all my employees, even those whom I rarely if ever met. Among the least rewarded and noticed Federal employees are the airport control tower operators who by day and by night guide planes in and out of airports and have in their hands the lives of the millions of Americans who fly. I sent a Christmas card to every one of these devoted men and women. I was told that never before had any Secretary shown the slightest interest in them, or even acknowledged their existence.

Washington social life is a part of the assignment. It is

elaborate, elegant, continuous, and demanding. Although there is generally believed to be a certain compulsion to attend social functions, this is probably not true. James Forrestal, for instance, rarely attended any. Once or twice the Secretary of Defense came to our house for dinner but stayed only a few moments, leaving his wife to carry on. There was no indication that his effectiveness was impaired by his disinterest in social events.[20] There are perhaps two reasons to yield to social demands. A cabinet member is often invited to the embassy of some foreign government. If the invitation is regretted, the host is hurt. It does not help to explain that a cabinet officer is very busy, particularly if he attended another embassy function a few days before. There is another reason for attending cocktail parties and dinners. Newspapermen, columnists, and commentators should not be charged with gluttony because they accept many invitations; they can overhear important bits of information and learn of important decisions. So can cabinet members. Shrewd diplomats have been aware for centuries of this possibility. Francois de Callieres, private secretary to Louis XIV, wrote in 1713:

It is in the nature of things that good cheer is a great conciliator, that it fosters familiarity and promotes freedom of exchange between the guests, while the warmth of wine will often lead to the discovery of important secrets.

The most riotous social activity of the Washington scene during my term was the vigorous, if not bitter, social war between two ambitious women, Perle Mesta and Gwendolyn Cafritz. Each one tried to outdo the other in elaborate entertainments. Mrs. Mesta usually seemed to be ahead, but occasionally it was a draw. Needless to say, both women tried to get the most prominent government officials to attend their parties. As I recall, President Truman never attended, while Vice-President Barkley was at almost all of them. Truman indicated a preference, however, as he later appointed Perle Mesta Minister to Luxembourg, where she did very well.[21]

My memories of individuals in the cabinet and elsewhere are vivid. I could extend this story inordinately if I were to talk about each of them. I might mention three. Shortly after my move into the Commerce Department, I was called by General Marshall, then Secretary of State, who wished to talk with me about a matter of mutual interest. I was a new member of the cabinet, but he insisted upon coming to my office. Needless to say, this impressed me. As time went on my high regard for him increased.[22] One day I received a call from Congressman John Kennedy who wished to talk about a Massachusetts problem. When he walked in I could hardly believe my eyes—he looked like a sixteen-year-old boy. As he talked it became clear that the mind in this young body was top-flight. My memory of Lyndon Johnson is that of a man in a hurry. No matter where I saw him, in the Congressional halls or committee rooms, he was always moving rapidly and forcefully, brushing aside interference. I might also add a further word about John Snyder. He and I were the conservative members of the cabinet. Our thinking was along the same lines. Snyder, like Truman, was a friendly and lovable personality; and strong. He had known Truman for many years and had great influence with him.

On January 5 I wrote my letter of resignation and received the following reply:

Effective at the end of my term of office, January 20, 1953, I accept your resignation as Secretary of Commerce, as you have asked me to do.

Since you took office in May 1948, you have done a great deal in bringing business and Government closer together, in administering the materials control program, in strengthening our national economy, and in preparing a plan for the businessmen to cope with the problems of post-defense markets. These are accomplishments of which we both can be proud. I want also to commend you for your skillful management of the Department of Commerce and its constituent bureaus in the performance of their far-reaching activities in behalf of foreign and domestic commerce, shipping, aviation, transportation, science, and invention.

I am grateful for your service during my administration and glad that it has been a satisfying experience for you. Please accept my good wishes.

Sincerely yours,

HARRY S TRUMAN[23]

During my years as Secretary of Commerce, there were occasional stories that Truman and I were not hitting it off too well. The truth is that my relations with Truman were of the very best. I had for him the highest regard and affection and my feelings have not changed.

In March 1952, during the Dollar Line controversy, he had sent me this handwritten letter:

Dear Charlie:

I've been somewhat upset because I couldn't have you and your family come to the President's House when you wanted to come after my personal invitation.

As you know Mrs. Truman's mother is hanging to life by a thread. For three months we have been expecting the worst.

Moving into the refurbished Executive Mansion has been a pain in the neck. It will take at least two months to find things. I don't know where my shirts, socks, neckties, underwear are parked. My study looks like an atomic explosion had taken place.

We'll have a cabinet luncheon on Monday and I'll show you what I'm up against.

About time I get accustomed to the damned place—I'll be moving out.

I hope you'll forgive my inhospitable act and that I may be the guide to your family through the House before I leave it.

Sincerely,

HARRY S TRUMAN

A few days later, some of my children and I did get a personally conducted tour of the White House. My answer of the fourth of April:

You cannot know how touched I was to receive your note of March 30th. It is one more bit of evidence to prove your extraordinary consideration of the feelings of those around you. Needless to say, the "personally conducted" tour last Sunday was thrilling to the children and to me. This will be as good an occasion as any for me to comment upon your valedictory at the dinner last Saturday night. [He had announced that he would not again be a candidate.] As I said to you yesterday—your statement marked the end of an epoch. Things will be different during the next four years—and I do not share your feeling that we can elect any Democrat. You could have won, I think; but nobody else can fill your place.

It will, however, be interesting to sit on the sidelines, so to speak, and watch the parade go by. I'm speaking of myself, not you—altho I imagine you will get enjoyment out of a certain detached observation of what goes on politically.

I am very proud and happy to have served in your Cabinet— and to have seen daily the courage, good judgment, and good humor with which you have served your country.

Respectfully,
CHARLES SAWYER

Truman's answer on the fifth:

Thanks a lot for your good letter of the fourth. I don't know when I received one that I appreciated more.

HARRY[24]

It would appear that these quotations from our correspondence would establish our friendly relationship. Truman's courage, and, I might truthfully say, his willingness to fight, are well known. An outstanding characteristic was his complete honesty—and everyone felt that he was honest, which is important. I disagreed occasionally with the things he did and told him so. This he did not resent. Presidents as a rule are not good administrators, and do not appoint good administrators. This was less true under Truman, by all odds the best administrator of all of our recent Presidents. Truman is a clear thinker. In many ways he is like Lincoln, whose outstanding characteristic was not his humility, not his compassion, not his sense of humor, not his almost poetical use of English prose, but the crystal clarity of his thinking. While Truman is not a great scholar, he is a far more talented man than most people realize. He understands music, enjoys it, and is widely read, especially in American history.

Some time after Truman and I left office he asked me to stop by Kansas City to talk about his *Memoirs*.[25] My son John and a fellow pilot flew me to Kansas City where Truman, characteristicly, was at the airport to meet us. As we went up in the elevator to his Kansas City office, an old farmer looked at him and said, "You look like Harry Truman"; whereupon Truman replied: "People have told me that before"; and said nothing more. Waiting at the office I found Howard McGrath, former Attorney General. We were all invited to luncheon, including my two pilots. After one or two cocktails, Truman turned to me and said: "What do you think of my speeches?" I said: "I don't like them. You are now an ex-President, your position in the world would be magnified and your influence in this country would be far greater if you were not so bitterly partisan. You asked for my opinion—that is it." At this point McGrath broke in and said that this would be completely out of character: President Truman must be partisan—the Democratic Party made him and the Democratic Party elected him President. I said, "No, the Democratic Party did not elect him President—he elected himself President." At which Truman laughed. He knew and I knew and so did McGrath that this was the truth. McGrath, it will be recalled, was the Chairman of the Democratic National Committee at the time of the famous election of 1948. I then added, "It might be interesting to ask Mrs. Truman what she thinks—I'd bet she will agree with me." The President grinned and said: "She does." About one week after this luncheon Truman spoke at a fund-raising

dinner in Washington and tore the Republicans limb from
limb. When my son John read an account of this speech, he
called me up and said: "It would appear that President Truman does not pay too much attention to the advice which he
gets from you."

21 Semi Public Service

I HAD now returned to private life. The excitement, the intense activity, were over. I practiced law, managed my business affairs, spent more time with my family, traveled some, and received a number of honorary degrees, thus acquiring a collection of beautiful colored hoods. I also, from time to time, ran across prominent figures from Belgium and Washington.

One winter, while in Palm Beach, Florida, I met Paul Henri Spaak. I was delighted to see him again and he seemed equally delighted to see me. I invited him to take a swim in the ocean. Before I picked him up, I had undertaken to buy him a pair of trunks at various stores on Worth Avenue. He is a very large man—especially around the waist. None of the shops had trunks big enough. At the Bath and Tennis Club I found a pair of enormous trunks which had belonged to some former member. However, they had no belt. I found a clothesline and cut off five feet of it. This held up the trunks and kept him modest and the two of us went into the surf. He, like Churchill, has a fair baby skin and as he waddled into the ocean he looked like a big kewpy doll. He said that *Life* Magazine would probably give five thousand dollars for a picture of him in this garb.

In 1954 I was approached by a group of prominent Cincinnatians who asked that I head the 1955 Community Chest drive. Since I would certainly be expected to take on this chore sometime, they suggested I might as well "do it now." I agreed and started out by visiting all ninety of the charities supported by the drive. My campaign was successful, and we "went over the top." However, I had been but a short time in charge of the drive when I became convinced that some effort should be made to cut down the multiple appeals which afflict the American public. Every ill that flesh is heir to has been organized to beg for money. There are too many appeals, too much work for devoted solicitors, too much money wasted on organization and occasionally, money going to wholly unworthy groups. Following my suggestion, we turned our Community Chest into a United Appeal, after persuading the Red Cross to join us. Later, other organizations took part, and the United Appeal, of which I was president for several succeeding years, has operated with great success.[1]

I had not been away from Washington for two years when I was asked to serve on the Overseas Economic Operations Task Force of the Hoover Commission. The commission, headed by the former President, was charged with examining the functions of the administrative branch and recommending changes.

Our task force dealt with Foreign Aid. Americans have for years been greatly concerned about other peoples. Earlier our missionaries wandered over the world seeing that others enjoyed religion of the type we recommend. Latterly we have enlarged our concern to include their political and social welfare. Beginning with UNRRA, we have encouraged almost beyond credibility the notion that we must care for the entire world. If other peoples are hungry, we must feed them; if they do not think right, we must change their thoughts; if their government does not suit us, we must help them get rid of it.

The failure of this concept to recognize the limits of our experience and wisdom and wealth has been hard for me to understand.

At the time this is written the level to which our aid has mounted is shocking. Over the years we have given aid to 116 separate countries, including Burundi, Cambodia, Chad, Cuba, Gabon, Ghana, Guiana (British), Hong Kong, Ivory Coast, Laos, Malaysia, Mali, Rhodesia-Nyasaland, Rwanda, Ryukyus, Surinam, Tanzania, Togo, Uganda, Viet Nam, and Zambia. We have sent to France 10 billion dollars; India six billion; Italy 6 billion; Japan 4 billion; England 9 billion; and Yugoslavia 2½ billion.

The nauseating waste of these programs; the effrontery of their sponsors—their supercilious stare at any uncouth oaf who questions the virtue or the success of foreign aid; the ingratitude and the insults from those we have aided; the encouragement we give to those who think our wealth is inexhaustible; the nonchalant attitude toward the vast amounts of money which we spend; the refusal to recognize that our imbalance of payments problems are due largely to this activity; the weakening of our foreign policy by using foreign aid to solve every difficult problem—all this seems not to impress government officials in either party as it does me and, I firmly believe, the majority of American citizens unconnected with government. When confronted with the unending stories of waste, extravagance, and mistakes, the sponsors of foreign aid dismiss them blandly with the statement that with such a large operation, waste and mistakes are to be expected.[2]

Our task force undertook with great seriousness to survey the activities of the Foreign Operations Administration (FOA) in all of its phases—programming, future commitments, offshore military procurement, defense support, organization, Point IV duplication, et al. FOA was to expire by law on June 30, 1955. In our innocence, we assumed that the end of the program was a possibility. Soon after we began our study, I received a note from our staff outlining a proposed plan for the coordination of foreign aid. This aroused my deep concern and I wrote back protesting the scheme.

I have your "proposed plan for the coordination of foreign aid."

I am strongly opposed to setting up any independent permanent agency for the handling of foreign aid. The assumption that foreign aid will go on forever is, I hope, incorrect; in any event, we should not commit ourselves to this idea by setting up a permanent agency to handle it. We began with ECA. When it was suggested that ECA should be abolished, its proponents and supporters were clever enough to see that MSA rose from its ashes. From the ashes of MSA arose FOA; the current suggestion would have OEA arise from the ashes of FOA.

It is true that this plan refers to a "small professional and clerical staff" and says that the Director of Overseas Assistance Affairs shall avoid the building up of any staff in his own office that seeks to do any of the work that can or should be performed by specialists in the Missions or in other governmental agencies. To suppose that this will be the actual practice is to ignore completely the teachings of experience.[3]

At a meeting in New York on October 15 Hoover gave emphatic approval to my position—to utilize existing agencies and not create new ones.

The task force received numerous reports. The Director of the Division of International Education said that a huge program in Thailand was training far more skilled workmen than that country could possibly employ. A building twice the size needed had been erected; its equipment even included cranes and milling machines. Fifteen crankshafts had been sent to Indonesian vocational schools. They had been ordered before the training program began and were rusting away. Our ambassador in Peru had said there was no need for a "Country Director of Agriculture"; nevertheless, one arrived, and his staff soon included twenty Americans and twenty-five Peruvians. He immediately requested $170,000 for a new office and hired the best public relations man in Latin America to publicize his work.

From a modest beginning in 1949, under ECA, our aid program in India had grown enormously. Why ECA ever moved into India was a puzzling question, since ECA had been created to restore war-torn Western Europe. However, they were in India and were treated with indifference, if not contempt, by Prime Minister Nehru. Loy Henderson, Assistant Secretary of State for Administration, told us that until 1951 he had felt Nehru was friendly to the West, but things had changed as had Nehru, and we should slow down our efforts until Nehru demonstrated his intention to work with us. It was refreshing to have so competent an authority speak frankly about Nehru—In Washington it was sacrilege to criticize him. I felt that this idolatry was overdone. I continued to feel the same way; the man who uttered the sententious pronouncement that at no time or place could war or force be justified and six months later overwhelmed little Goa rated more critical appraisal. I had once sat next to Nehru at a luncheon where, during a frank discussion, he had said to me, "I am not a statesman—I am an agitator." One confidential report from India stated:

I am convinced that if Congress did not appropriate one dollar more for economic development or technical assistance for India the program would continue to roll for at least two years at or about its current rate of activity. For example, of some $800,000 for industrial technical assistance programmed with '54 funds only $398,000 has been expended and now we are picking up the balance for reobligation for a program in 1956 which cannot be completed for two or three years. I am told the '54 amounts are valid through 1957. This situation undoubtedly exists in other areas.[4]

Cornell University had signed a contract with the University of Burma for a program of training in aerial photography.

This would enable the Government of Burma to use the photographic equipment they had already received under our technical aid program. Georgetown University had arranged with Yugoslavia and Turkey to teach English to trainees coming to the United States so that they could understand our language. Syracuse University had contracted with FOA to make training films for agricultural programs in Iran. These deals, a few out of many, might suggest why so many universities were such strong supporters of give-away programs. One report explained that these contracts had been let to colleges and universities as "fishing expeditions" to help FOA find new projects.

We discovered what vast amounts of money we were giving the French to support their forces in Indochina. One memorandum to us asked how much of our 745 million dollars might be salvaged. Little did we realize what would be the extent of our later involvement in that area, or to what fantastic figure this already swollen total would rise. We could not then conceive what epochal crises would grow out of our attempt to extend our influence and our aid into that Asian morass.

In April 1955 we were furnished with a copy of *The Shield* —published monthly by the FOA Service Organization; it gave a revealing picture of agency activities. We learned of regional conferences of FOA directors held in Washington. Representatives from Latin American missions alone numbered twenty-one. One article asked "Is Cancer Your Pet Phobia?" References were made to soft-ball leagues, bowling teams, and a spring dance in the Chantilly Ballroom at the Hamilton Hotel. On the front page was a message from Governor Stassen, then head of FOA, complimenting the entire staff for the energy and general excellence with which they had approached *"the difficult assignment of preparing for the Congressional presentation"* of the President's 1956 Mutual Security Program. They had faced with resolution the task of discovering new ways to spend money.[5] Among the few bright spots revealed by our investigation was the performance of the Export-Import Bank, which was operated on a sound basis by a very small staff.

The vast amount of material brought to us was not designed to discredit the program, although it certainly had that effect. It indicated, overwhelmingly, the waste and extravagance and impractical thinking of those who had been handling foreign aid. During the fall we began drafting our report. On October 22 I outlined my views to the chairman, Henning Prentiss:

Congress apparently has the idea that the FOA effort should be wound up. The first sentence of your Report should indicate clearly the feeling of the group that FOA should be wound up, definitely and finally, and that dealing with foreign aid should be, from now on for the most part, on a liquidating basis. There are, of course, certain spots where aid will continue and certain spots where it should be continued for military reasons.

The theory of the Marshall Plan was to restore the Western European countries to their status at the beginning of World War II. This was accomplished promptly.

But the horde of ECA employees who had meantime been brought together immediately began to agitate for a continuance of this endeavor. The primary excuse given was to fight Communism—but any excuse was sufficient. Even then were evident such ideas, still perpetuated in FOA, as the need to raise the labor standards of the rest of the world, to tell them how to do business, to eliminate cartels, and, in general to direct their lives and economies from the eminence of our position as a very rich and a very wise nation.

We should certainly re-examine our policy of aid to India, whose Foreign Minister treats our Secretary of State with indifference, if not contempt, and who gives great acclaim and honor to the Foreign Minister of Communist China. In my judgment, some firm indication of our distaste for Nehru's indifferent attitude toward us would react to our advantage and to the advantage of the world, including India.

Our chief emphasis should be on Latin America. In view of the world situation, it is obvious that great benefit to us lies in keeping the countries of the Western Hemisphere in a harmonious and friendly relationship.

I do not agree that loans are preferable to grants. Let us not fool ourselves into thinking we are doing anything but giving away our money. Sound loans should be made by lending agencies already set up, such as the Export-Import Bank and the International Bank. Each of these agencies has operated sensibly and skillfully and constructively.

One fundamental error lies in the belief that the more money spent, the more good is done. This error continually permeates the thinking on the subject of aid as it does on the subject of military strength. The question is not how much money is spent, but what results are obtained. What has really been accomplished in the areas where our aid has gone?

We feel that efforts to control the economic life and the thinking of other countries are unwise. This is chiefly exemplified in the so-called Benton-Moody amendment which was aimed theoretically at increasing productivity, but which undertook to regulate or eliminate cartels, set labor standards, and in many other ways impose our thinking upon other countries. This is much too large an order.

With reference to Asia, we view with skepticism the idea that spending money in order to raise the standards of living of Asian countries will have a deterrent effect upon the march of Communism. We can pour money into Asia as one would pour water upon a sandy beach, with exactly the same effect—it would disappear with no change in the beach.[6]

The task force generally took this approach, but the eagle-eyed foreign aiders had been watching us. They could not stop us from stating our beliefs, but they could work on the main Hoover Commission, which had but little time to check our findings and whose staff was generally sympathetic to their programs. While our investigation was going on, FOA undertook to reorganize its office, reassigning functions and personnel. One member of the FOA with a sense of humor said that this was done to receive a higher "Hoover rating."

When the Report of the task force had been watered down by the Hoover Commission, we were informed:

The Commission wishes to express its appreciation for the devoted service of the Task Force. We have not adopted all of their recommendations as to policies, but in our Report we affirm and expand their recommendations leading to more effective and economical administration.[7]

The Commission did approve a few of our suggestions:

Industrial projects should not be undertaken in countries which do not already have an industrial background. In these countries there is little local capital available for participation and the vast background of transport, marketing, technical and executive skills is lacking.

The original relatively modest concepts of the Point IV Programs of technical cooperation have been enormously expanded. Its activities now cover not only imparting American industrial training but also furnishing professors to Universities, bringing large numbers of persons to the United States for industrial and professional training (often short-term visitors), in labor relations, agriculture, commerce, trade, public administration, even including aid to so highly developed a nation as "The Netherlands" in "social psychology" and "human relations practice." This service is not only over-expanded, but duplicates services by other Departments of the Government. Its organizational concept needs complete reorganization. It is divided into a multitude of projects (probably over 2,000) and is spread over more than fifty-five countries and overseas territories.

As all the countries in the original North Atlantic Treaty Organization have the highest degree of technical proficiency, the technical assistance by American personnel in these countries should cease.

No economic aid should be granted for projects or undertakings where private investment capital is available for such project.[8]

The Commission did note our task force statement that on June 30, 1955, there would be approximately 7.9 billion dol-

lars of an unexpended balance in the foreign aid account.
Certain Commissioners supported the task force report. One
was Joseph P. Kennedy who wrote:

Surely, after almost ten years, the time has come to apply some
brakes to this overseas spending program. We believe, therefore,
that the Commission should recommend substantial reductions in
expenditures for this purpose. By no other means will the growing
trend toward permanent foreign spending be halted.[9]

The task force had devoted much time and thought to
objective examination of foreign aid. It was for the most part a
wasted effort. FOA was terminated on June 30, 1955, as required by Congress. In its place arose a new agency—the
International Cooperation Administration, headed by my good
friend and later law partner John Hollister. It had the same
offices, personnel, and facilities as FOA. However, one suggestion of the task force had been followed, and ICA became a part
of the State Department. As I had recommended, the chief of
mission in each country was now charged with coordinating
the activities of all United States agencies in that country,
including economic and technical assistance missions.

On May 31, 1955, I received a citation expressing the
sincere appreciation of the Commission on Organization of the
Executive Branch of the Government for the "notable contribution Charles Sawyer had made" to the work of this Commission as a member of the Task Force on Overseas Economic
Operations, referring to my "wonderful help, advice and assistance." This was—if ever there was—malarkey.

After the Commission's report had been published I was,
however, able to voice my opinions to Senator Mansfield:

Pursuant to your request when I was in Washington the other
day, I am writing to give you some of my current views on the
matter of foreign aid.
There is great duplication of effort. FOA is doing things which
permanent departments are doing, and, in many cases, have been

doing for a long time. In my judgment, the permanent departments are doing them better. The organizational involvement of
FOA is a labyrinth. Apparently it is functioning with difficulty. A
week ago Mr. Stassen called a meeting in Paris of his many
country representatives. Although the representatives showed up,
Mr. Stassen did not. Neither did Mr. Fitzgerald, whom he had
arranged to send in his place.

I supported President Truman's original suggestion of the Point
Four program and still feel that assistance of a strictly technical
nature given by technicians who know what they are doing can be
a worthy and helpful indication of our interest in the welfare of
others. The technical aid program as now administered, however,
has become simply another economic aid program which should
be abandoned.

As to foreign investment by American businessmen, no wander-
ing hordes of FOA employees or any other government agency can
do for American businessmen what they can do much better for
themselves if the climate for their investments is good. The only
real service which can be rendered in this field is to persuade
other countries who would like to have Americans invest their
money that they must make that investment attractive. In my
opinion this will not occur until the other countries of the world
realize that we are no longer a nation of suckers.[10]

I did not fret long over the unsatisfactory results of our
work and in spite of this experience I accepted other *pro bono
publico* assignments from time to time. Shortly after I left the
Commerce Department, I told a friend in Detroit that I was
going to Hot Springs to attend a meeting of the Business
Advisory Council.[11] He asked if my successor, Sinclair Weeks,
would be there and I said that I thought not: Weeks was
attending a trade fair, or several trade fairs, in Europe. My
friend laughed and said that he had an amusing story to tell
me. The day before Weeks was to take office, my friend had
seen him in New York, where Weeks had recounted with pride
how he had just stopped at the dock two men I had sent to
attend trade fairs in Europe. Even before he took office he

"was able to cut off some of the extravagances of the preceding Democratic Administration." I was happy to note that Weeks' attitude had changed.

Fairs are a help to international trade, but they also demonstrate dramatically the power of a competitive economy. International Fairs are regulated by the *Bureau International des Expositions,* in Paris, established in 1928 to coordinate plans and reconcile dates for prospective World Fairs. The 1928 Convention which set up the bureau described the types of expositions and the length of time each should run. The United States never signed the Convention but we do consult and work with the BIE. In the fall of 1959 where and when the next United States International Fair would be held had to be decided. Los Angeles, Washington, and New York—each had plans for a fair in the sixties. The City of Seattle had already started work on their "Century 21 Exposition." Senator Magnuson had persuaded Congress to appropriate 9 million dollars for this fair, and the State of Washington and the city of Seattle had committed additional millions.[12]

During the closing days of the Congressional session, Senator Fulbright proposed that a Presidential commission decide the issue. The New York Senators, Javits and Keating, charged that this move was to prevent New York from holding the fair. When they threatened to talk the resolution to death it was withdrawn. President Eisenhower then took the matter in hand and appointed a committee to recommend a date and a site. Although the committee could not prevent any city from moving ahead with its plans, it was hoped that its recommendation would prevail. On October 8, 1959, I was asked if I would serve on this committee. I said that I would. The next day I received a note from the President:

1 am glad you are willing to serve as a Member of the 1964 World Fair Site Committee and I hereby appoint you in this capacity.

It will be the duty of the Committee to consider appropriate

sites for the Fair and to submit its recommendations to me and I
know you will be able to contribute greatly to this task.

With best wishes.

Sincerely,

DWIGHT EISENHOWER

Harry A. Bullis, chairman, and Aksel Nielsen were the Republican members of the committee. I was the Democrat.[13]

Seattle had already contacted the BIE; New York and Washington were planning to do so. European countries were also
planning fairs and applying to BIE for approval. It was clear
that the committee should act fast. We issued invitations to
New York, Los Angeles, Washington, and Seattle to present
their arguments in Washington on October 23. But suggestions
were not confined to formal presentations by these cities.
Many individuals addressed us, and I recall one who proposed
a Saint Lawrence Seaway Floating Fair that could move
through the Great Lakes, thus promoting the seaway and also
giving several different areas a whack at the publicity and the
income.

Seattle made its presentation first. Their concern was that
another fair might be held at or near the same time as theirs,
which was planned for April to October 1962. They asked that
a reasonable period lapse after "Century 21" before another
fair was held. New York was represented by the Governor, the
Mayor, Commissioner Robert Moses, and other leading men.
It was the world's most cosmopolitan city. The year 1964
would mark the Three-hundredth Anniversary of its naming.
Senator Javits also mentioned experience; and Commissioner
Moses said they would not repeat their earlier mistakes of
1939. These comments made a hit with me. Los Angeles
bragged about its weather: "You can ski down the mountain-
side, bathe in the desert sun, and enjoy exhilarating seabreezes
in the course of almost any single afternoon." Washington
would combine a World's Fair and a permanent urban development project. World's Fairs are temporary. "They open in

the spring, close in the fall, and last for two seasons at most."
Washington planned permanent uses for the exposition buildings and other facilities. The exposition grounds could easily
become a city. An ideal site was already chosen. Their presentation by architect Gruen was a spell-binding effort.

As we listened, I became growingly aware of the time and
thought and money already involved. The importance of our
decision became apparent, as did the need for prompt action. I
believed that New York had one great advantage—experience.
They would not repeat earlier mistakes. The real competition
was Washington: their project was thrilling. However, it
finally became our unanimous feeling that the effort to combine an international exposition with the creation of a new city
was too large an order. We reported on October 30, recommending New York. We said that an international exposition
of the first magnitude in the United States during the mid-six-
ties would be very much in the national interest. No city in the
country had held such an exposition for a quarter of a century.

It happens, also, that the year 1964 is especially appropriate in the
case of New York, since it will mark the 300th anniversary of the
establishment and naming of that city, and also the fifteenth
anniversary of its becoming the home of the United Nations.[14]

Newspapers throughout the country noted that the committee had acted more rapidly and at less expense than any other
committee in history. The President promptly approved our
selection. As early as November 3 columnists were saying that
our report came as a sharp jolt to some White House aides
who had indicated that Washington was all but a cinch. I
received several letters repeating this and replied to one from
a staff reporter on the Washington *Post*.

There is not the slightest basis for the report that the White House
made an effort to influence the decision of the Committee; nor is
there any basis for the report that the Committee first voted for

Washington. The Committee waited until all of the presentations had been made and then arrived at its decision.[15]

Some years later, when the New York World's Fair was in full swing, I received an invitation from Robert Moses to attend a luncheon in honor of General Eisenhower. The fair corporation wished to present a medallion to Aksel Nielsen and to me, the surviving members of this committee. In accepting this medal I stated that New York's earlier experience was the influencing factor in my decision to approve their application and I quoted Moses' promise that New York would not repeat the mistakes made in 1939. Since the Fair has closed, I have questioned how thoroughly that commitment was met.

In 1958 the Committee for Economic Development established a Commission on Money and Credit. I was asked by CED chairman, Don David, to serve on this commission. I replied that I was unqualified—all I knew about money and credit was that it was nice to have some of each. David urged me to accept; the committee was seeking a broad spectrum of social and economic opinion and hoped to have some "level headed" members. What he really wanted, I was sure, was a prominent Democrat, who need not be particularly well qualified, but would contribute to a proper political "mix." I agreed to give the matter serious thought. I had misgivings, but on February 28 I wrote:

After prayerful consideration, fraught with some doubts, I have decided to accept your invitation to become a member of the Commission on Money and Credit, which the CED is creating.[16]

The commission membership was a cross-section of businessmen, labor union officials, farmers, bankers, and lawyers. Its chairman was Frazar Wilde—head of the Connecticut General Life Insurance Company. The staff was headed by Bertrand Fox of Harvard, with the brilliant Eli Shapiro, from the Massachusetts Institute of Technology, as his deputy. There was an advisory board of outstanding economists, willing to voice their opinions and so certain of their views that they were sometimes amusing and sometimes shocking. Occasionally they revealed a distinctly anti-business point of view. It soon became clear that the economists felt that this was to be their report. The commission members would sit and listen to endless and sometimes bitter discussions. At an early point I suggested that we meet without our advisors. My suggestion was adopted, for one meeting.

I was disturbed from the beginning by the assumption that the commission should concern itself with practically every one of the nation's economic and social problems. Repeatedly, I reminded the members that we were charged with considering "money and credit." With both liberal and conservative positions represented on the commission, conflicting views soon developed on the relative importance of providing full employment, preventing inflation, and stimulating growth. I felt we should recognize this conflict. As it turned out, we pretended there was no conflict. Soon after we began our meetings I prophesied, with tongue in cheek, the kind of wording which would duck this issue many months later:

As between growth, price stability and maximum employment, it is impossible to establish permanent priority. Perhaps they are equally important as long-term objectives. From time to time, however, due to circumstances then facing us, one of them may well move ahead of the others—only time and the wisdom of our public officials at the moment will give a clear answer to this problem.

In a more serious approach, I said: "My concern with reference to the product of the Commission's activities is that neither time nor available money will permit as extended theoretical discussion as the present suggested program undertakes." [17] We held dozens of sessions, as month after month slipped by. We discussed at length suggested amendments to the Employment Act of 1946 and the Federal Reserve Act. There was considerable debate over the proper percentage level of unemployment. I felt and said that we were overly impressed by percentages. Some members and advisors were obsessed with the need for maintaining a specific rate of growth. Here again, I felt that we were being wholly theoretic and unrealistic. Growth was certainly desirable; but growth of a certain percentage gained by pumping money into the nation's economic arteries would, in the long run, create a sick, not a healthy, economy.

After two years of meetings and discussion chairman Wilde asked each of us for his views. My letter set forth my thinking:

Several Position Papers have said, although there has been evidence that the saying was not taken too seriously, that we do not want to suggest change merely for the sake of change. With this I agree. Nor should we proceed on the assumption that somehow or other, if the recommendations of this Commission are followed, the result will be a perfect mechanism where everything works smoothly and public officials always exercise good judgment.

If the functioning of the present financial structure has been reasonably good, the Report should say so. If there are places where it has not worked well, we should suggest change. We should not toss out agencies or systems merely because they are not consistent with other agencies or systems—we should not casually suggest changes in operating activities which have been achieved after long argument, pressures from contending forces, and concessions in the legislative body. We do not live in a perfect world and this Commission cannot create one.

In suggesting remedies for current problems, we should be sure that the remedy is not worse than the disease. I have seen some evidence of an inadequate exploration of the consequences of Task Force suggestions.

Furthermore, we should keep in mind the distinction between defects in structure and defects due to bad judgment on the part of human beings. Errors of judgment will not be corrected by tinkering with the structure.

Regarding monetary policy, I wrote:

Whatever improvement in coordination is desirable should not be undertaken by creating another agency. Such a program implies that the new agency will be wiser than the existing ones and there will thereafter be no need to coordinate the actions of the coordinating agency with those being coordinated.

I have grave doubts about the experiment with an automatic discount rate formula, where the discount rate varies automatically with the short-term money market rates. This assumes that our judgment as of today in fixing the automatic rate is superior to the judgment which will be shown from time to time by the Board as circumstances require.

The idea that the President or a Congressional group, such as the Joint Economic Committee, should be empowered to change tax rates impresses me as unrealistic. It would certainly enable the President to "put his teeth into his responsibility." I think it more important that the President use his brain rather than his teeth. If any suggestion could produce more confusion and conflict between the executive and legislative branches, I haven't thought of it.

With reference to the flexible expenditure policy, this is sound. For that reason it probably is well to suggest it. How to make it work, however, is a different matter. As is well said, "Care must be taken that countercyclical use of expenditure programs does not interfere with their long run efficiency." Once you start a building, you can't stop when it is half built.

There is no adequate treatment of the psychological element in a buoyant economy. When businessmen and consumers alike feel that economic prospects are good, each group will spend money and thereby stimulate growth. When either or both groups feel that prospects are bad, they will hold back, thereby retarding growth. Should there not be in our discussions a place for consideration of this matter? How far will steps to promote growth produce the desired result if they bring fear into the mind of the businessman and the consumer?

With reference to unemployment, we will always have some. The lazy, inefficient worker is bound to have trouble getting a job. For the hardworking, efficient worker the situation depends wholly upon demand. If people are willing to buy and businessmen are willing to build, the demand will reduce unemployment.

In connection with the matter of unemployment, I am not too much intrigued by percentages. The four per cent figure seems to be merely a compromise between three per cent and five per cent.

There is nowhere a recognition of the fact that there are some things which government simply cannot do; unfortunately, we shall probably always have in a free society a substantial amount of unemployment; prices may fluctuate, as may growth. There is too much of the thought that somehow or other, by using percentages, "built-in" formulae and "vigorous" government action by wise and dedicated men, perfection can be achieved. It is foolish to be too hopeful; perhaps, at the risk of being unpopular, we should say so.

Chairman Wilde wrote to me on November 8: "Your comments on our Position Papers are terrific! Your letter is a refreshing breeze." [18]

I had not prepared footnote dissents to be added to the published report, which would have made my personal position clear. I did, however, forward to our staff a few comments:

I wonder . . . if the word "reasonable," which is applied to price level stability, and which did not appear originally in our outline, cannot be eliminated or applied equally to "economic growth" and "low level unemployment." In each case we should deal with what is reasonable.

I would omit altogether reference in paragraph three to the President's Commission on National Goals. In my judgment this was one of the wordiest and most unimpressive documents I have seen in many a day. I say this in spite of the fact that many of my good friends were members of the Commission.

In Paragraph III of Chapter II reference is made to the need for vigorous antitrust policy to encourage competition and to discourage further increase of downward price rigidity. Why not mention labor and refer to the downward wage rigidity?

I note, with some amusement, the statement, "the need for speaking out will be something of a political liability to the President."

Why can we not say that a fruitful result would come from a more efficient operation in foreign aid areas and, if necessary, a reduction in the amount we are giving away? The exact opposite of this statement occurs in Paragraph 59, which states that the large U.S. foreign military expenditures and grants and loans for economic development "cannot be reduced" without a sacrifice of the objectives these programs are designed to secure. This statement is simply not true. I believe, and so does everyone else who has investigated this matter thoroughly, that the amounts which we have spent upon foreign aid of both kinds can, by efficient operation, be substantially reduced without in any wise sacrificing the objectives of the foreign aid programs. Both President Eisenhower and President Kennedy have recognized this."

I had pointed out earlier the implication that we were recommending a program which would last forever:

With reference to the entire Report and as a part of the introduction, I would suggest we make it clear that we are not undertaking to plan for an indefinite economic and monetary future. It is true that the Report, in one or two places, implies that we are really dealing with "the sixties." I think, however, it could be stated specifically that we are recommending changes to be applied during the next ten years.[19]

Soon after our report was issued, the commission went to the White House. We met in the Cabinet Room. President Kennedy, when he saw me, graciously suggested that these were familiar surroundings and I should feel at home. He was much impressed by the sections of the report which proposed that the President be given authority to raise and lower taxes. Indeed, he made this recommendation part of a message to Congress, and, as I had predicted, Congress turned it down. The report was an immense effort by sincere men to analyze, and suggest changes in, our entire economic and social system. Its influence has not been easy to ascertain. It has not yet produced any noticeable modifications in public or private credit systems.

From time to time I was asked to, and did, participate in other semi-public activities, but they were not important enough to call for specific description.

As a last word on an old subject, and at the risk of over-emphasis, I will quote a letter I sent from Italy in 1963 to Congressman John Rooney, the congressional watchdog over expenditures by the State Department.

My dear Congressman:

This afternoon I saw the United States Information Service at work.

About three o'clock I was walking along a street here in Florence and noticed a brass sign—UNITED STATES INFORMATION SERVICE. I wandered in to see what we were doing in Florence to present the image of the U.S.

Nowhere in the entrance way was there any indication as to where the U.S.I.S. was located. I took a self-operating elevator, in which there was no indication of our floor. I let myself out at the third floor, finally found a young woman who could speak English and was told that the U.S.I.S. was one floor up.

I walked up the old stone steps and saw the sign U.S.I.S. outside an oaken door. I pushed the bell repeatedly. After several minutes I turned to the elevator and was about to take it down when the door slowly opened and a sleepy caretaker looked out. I said I was a U.S. citizen who wished to look at our establishment. He regretted that he could not help as the Director was out. Then I asked: "When will the Director return?" He said he was not sure but thought it would be fairly soon. I asked about other employees and he said no one was in. I then walked in to see for myself. I looked into nine rooms filled with maps, unopened packages, books, pamphlets and furniture—but no human being was present.

In years gone by you and I have discussed the need to save the taxpayers' money and the drain we suffer from these foreign agencies. You would have been shocked, but not surprised.

Sincerely,
CHARLES SAWYER[20]

22 Concerns of a Conservative Democrat

THAT IS it. That is my story. I will say no more about myself; except that I remain a Democrat, a conservative —and concerned.

I am not concerned about being a Democrat. The Democrats will probably be running things in Washington for some time. Nothing, of course, is guaranteed. The Republicans may be lucky; they may get some breaks. They will probably not take advantage of them. Republicans are not very bright; they drive people out of their party—they want no extremists. We Democrats will take anybody into our party. Republicans could, if they tried, find several issues. If I were asked, "Well, what are they?" I would reply, "I am not talking—I am taking the 'Fifth.'" It would be a crime for a Democrat to try to educate Republicans. The Democrats, however, will not stay in power forever; no party stays in forever.

Nor am I concerned for us conservatives; we seem to be growing in numbers and in influence—even among students. Eventually reality gets a hearing.

I am concerned, but not unduly, by riots in the streets, student demonstrations, the dollar drain, the imbalance of payments, and inflation. All of these and similar distressing experiences have happened before. Thomas Jefferson, for instance, had trouble with the students at the University of Virginia.[1]

However, I am greatly concerned by two developments which have not happened before.

"God blessed Noah and his sons, and said unto them, be fruitful and multiply, and replenish the earth." This was probably good advice, to Noah. But we have more than replenished the earth. We should add perhaps, but not multiply. Many years ago Thomas Malthus warned that man's ability to propagate was greater than his ability to get the means of subsistence. He felt that the English poor laws with their system of dole and bounties for large families aggravated the problem. Only war, pestilence, famine, and misery could prevent disaster. Today the spectre which frightened Malthus has grown into a genie of far more frightening proportions. We can never put him back into a bottle. But he demands heroic treatment.

We fight unemployment and poverty. We fight for more schools at all levels. We are being gradually suffocated by automobile fumes and our cities strangled by traffic. In the not too distant future, traffic will not be slow, it will be stopped. There will scarcely be room to stand, let alone to move around. These alarming problems and countless others have one cause —too many people.

We augment the problem at the beginning and at the end of life. A group of doctors has extended the application of the Hippocratic Oath to the well being of the fetus; and dedicated doctors often prolong life beyond the point where the life in question is of any value to the individual or to society. We might hesitate to suggest legalizing euthanasia, but it would be much in order if doctors would extend their concern to preventing instead of preserving the fetus.

We furnish food, medicine, and help of various kinds to peoples in all parts of the world. It is of course more pleasing to talk about feeding hungry babies than to talk about fewer babies; but the benefits we confer increase the populations and aggravate the real problem. Instead of giving "the better life" we should first give contraceptives and advice as to birth control.

It is said by some that science will furnish the answer to over-population. By using nuclear and solar power we can extract what we will need from the air and the water, and feed people from algae farms and yeast factories. But will life be worth living if all human beings cling like mollusks to a vast, drab megalopolis?

The prospect is horrifying. In the words of one demographer, "during the second half of this century, there will be a greater increase in world population than was achieved in all the millennia of human existence up to the present time." There is a normal tendency to postpone drastic action as long as possible. People are not moved when they are told that in seven hundred years, if the world's 3 billion population continues to grow at the current rate, there will be one square meter per person on the planet's surface, including the oceans. Why worry about what will happen in seven hundred years? But worry we should.[2]

Of course, the Bomb could solve the problem, and probably will. This brings us to my second great concern. Scientists, out of their curiosity and their arrogance, have drawn aside the curtain and peered into the realm of the Creator—they have discovered and made effective the means of our destruction. This awesome power was temporarily the sole property of the United States. That is no longer true. Russia, France, England, China, and perhaps others, share the secret. It is possible that the nuclear holocaust will not come upon us immediately, but as more and more nations possess the Bomb, some Hitler, Castro, or Mao will go berserk and set the world afire. There is probably no way to prevent this—there may be a way to postpone it. Treaties will not do it. Treaties are regarded by

Communists as traps for the innocent. The threat of massive retaliation may keep Russia cautious—and perhaps other possessors of the Bomb.

I am concerned, and greatly, that the bomb may come from either of two places—China and Cuba—specifically, Mao and Castro. What are we doing and what can we do about either or both of these menacing figures? As for China, the solution is far from easy. Within two years the Chinese will be able to attack any country in Asia; in less than ten years they will be able to launch missiles against us. Mao and associates are tough, dedicated, and quite willing to sacrifice millions of Chinese if necessary. They are not afraid of an exchange of bombs some time in the future. They are not ready now—but time is on their side. Will we act or will we sit like a hypnotized bird facing a deadly approaching snake and watch the Chinese build their nuclear strength to the point where it will destroy us? Confrontation at any time is not pleasant to contemplate; but it is better now than later.

It has been suggested that we bomb their missile sites. Almost two years ago, comment was made upon this possibility by blunt, but worried French editor, Pierre Boutang:

The United States does not have the moral and political force to wage the just war, the war operation to forestall a danger immeasurably greater than any humanity has heretofore known. The publicly known doctrine of Communist China makes it imbecile and criminal to run, voluntarily, the risk of conceding them the weapon of universal terror. The operation that would annihilate that risk for perhaps twenty years would cost several thousand times fewer victims than those of a China possessed of nuclear armament; fewer, indeed, than the Vietnam War is costing. We are at the beginning of 1966, more than thirty years after the lost chance of destroying Hitler's death machine. I reflect with sadness on the condition of our world thirty years from now, if the Americans are as cowardly and stupid as the French Government then proved itself to be.

There are of course many who are frightened and terribly

upset even by the suggestion that this might be done. However, it could well happen as a development of our current war in Vietnam. Our worry there seems to be that we will blunder into a war with China. If we have committed no blunders up to this time, we should perhaps commit one now and blunder into a war with China. We could at least win a respite, if not an end, to the Chinese threat. Up to this time the benefits of the war in Vietnam are not too clear. We are fighting not to win but to bring about negotiations. We have apparently forgotten the famous statement of Will Rogers: "We have never lost a war or won a conference." We have of course been getting practice and in war, as in other matters, practice is helpful. At the moment we are the only great nation achieving that benefit unless, perchance, Russia is testing its weapons. If we should blunder into a war with China while we have vastly superior nuclear power, the war in Vietnam might prove to be a blessing.

It is argued that—

Bombing the missile sites would bring in the Russians. On the contrary, they would be greatly relieved; they would not need to do it themselves. The Russians might protest violently, but we underestimate their self interest and their good judgment if we believe they would do more.

Our action would shock world opinion. Of what importance is world opinion compared with our survival?

The Chinese might rebuild their powers of destruction. If they begin to rebuild, we can destroy them again.

This would cause the Chinese to hate us. It would seem less important that the Chinese hate us than that we are around to be hated. Furthermore, hatreds, like international agreements, are short lived. Recently Germany and Japan were greatly hated, and were great haters. Today they are among our friends. The Chinese are a wise and a patient people. They have lived a long time, and they are realists. We do not hate the Chinese. Why should they hate us?

It is said that if we are nice to China things will change—the mean old leaders will die, the young ones will be different. There is no evidence to support this hope, and if we have taught the present leaders a lesson, if we have shown that we mean business, succeeding leaders will be more anxious to avoid a conflict than to seek one.

And what of Castro? I am concerned that Castro might launch a missile attack against us. I am also concerned that our treatment of Castro will tempt other centres of communism to annoy, harass, and even attack us in the belief that we do not really mean business, with possible consequences of devastating proportions. We go ten thousand miles around the world to fight communism; but we tolerate it ninety miles from our own shores. Khrushchev agreed to on-site inspection of the missile sites in Cuba. U Thant journeyed to Cuba to make arrangements for this inspection. Castro would not permit it; U Thant came back and suggested that we abandon it. We did the easy thing; we did not go through with a tough but necessary showdown with Castro. It is possible that the missiles were never sent away. But missiles are not Castro's only weapons, and we make no move to stop the dedicated communists he trains who are working like termites at the roots of democracy in the western hemisphere.

Why should Castro think we mean business when, as patriotic and courageous Cubans prepared with our blessing to regain the freedom which Castro had destroyed, our President made the chilling announcement that we would have no part in any effort to aid them? When these brave men made the attack we kept our word. Castro won and proclaimed a great victory. He then blackmailed us into paying millions for the release to this country of the patriots whose capture was on our conscience. As they were brought before our President at Miami he told them we would salute them as they march victoriously through Havana. How do we make good on that promise? Do we encourage and aid them? No! We run them down and gun them down and arrest them as, with great daring and meager resources, they try bravely to harass and undermine Castro. We will permit no effort to overthrow him to originate from our shores, or even from nearby islands.

Not only do we withhold an attack on Castro, we contribute to his support through the United Nations. In 1963 we stipulated that none of our money was to be used for aid to Cuba. As our Ambassador James Roosevelt recently stated, this was nothing but a "bookkeeping gimmick." Now we are not even imposing that condition. Recently, the United Nations contributed a large sum (of which our share was $840,000) to a so-called School of Technology in Havana. There communist military personnel are training Cubans for penetration into other countries, including the United States. How can Castro think we mean business?

There are compelling reasons for an effort to defeat communism on this side of the world. The closer communism approaches the greater its threat. Furthermore, communists claim that their onward march has never been stopped, cannot be stopped. To reverse the onward march of communism and prove that it can be stopped in the western world would be of great benefit, psychologically as well as practically.

Castro can be eliminated. We can move in on him with troops trained in Vietnam; and Guantanamo must be of some military advantage. With far less risk to our own troops, he can be bombed-out. Yet the easiest and least painful plan would be to strangle him. There are indications that even our half hearted attempts at this are having some effect. If we were to place a complete embargo upon Cuba it would speed the day of Castro's removal.

These moves might not have the approval of so-called "world opinion," but human events, including wars, are not decided by world opinion. Wars are not made by people who are hungry, underprivileged, weak, or frustrated. Wars are made by leaders who are, or think they are, strong and can win.

The future will depend, as has the past, upon the character, the ambition, the imagination, the decisions, and even the mistakes of a few men. To use only modern instances, Washington, Napoleon, Lincoln, Marx, Lenin, Hitler and Churchill will have their counterparts in the years to come—if there are to be years to come—as will Edison, Einstein, and Pope John. What will influence and what may we expect from the leaders of the future? The prospect is not encouraging.

Of course, there is always hope. Perhaps the dedicated, ruthless leaders of communism will decide to abandon their effort to communize the world by intrigue and by force. They may decide to mind their own business, promote communism within their own countries, and set successful examples which will amaze and persuade the rest of the world. China and Russia and other communist nations may join us in an honest effort to end the possibility of nuclear war. They may agree with us to destroy all nuclear weapons and permit the safeguards necessary to see that this agreement is carried out. Castro may admit that he has been wrong and of his own accord remove the threat to the western hemisphere and to us. These things may happen. The reader may speculate as to the likelihood.

I devoutly pray that the fate I foresee may be avoided; that the joy of life and its beauty and its glory and its awe and its mystery may not end. God in his wisdom may touch the hearts of the leaders of men—who knows? Perhaps, before it is too late, our children or their children will see the glorious dawn of a new day when hate will no longer rule men's minds, when the age-long hope of men for the good life will become a reality, "when man will stand upon this earth as on a footstool, and laugh, and reach out his hands among the stars." Perhaps. My concern I believe to be justified; but I could be wrong. On this encouraging note I close.

NOTES / INDEX

Notes

BY EUGENE P. TRANI

1—YANKEE FROM OHIO

1. Charles Sawyer based this manuscript on his extensive personal paper collection, which is now located in his home in Cincinnati. This collection will eventually be deposited in the Harry S Truman Library in Independence, Missouri. The Sawyer collection is made up of four different parts. The first contains material on the Sawyer family, Mr. Sawyer's youth, his college days, and his legal and business activities. The second contains papers on Sawyer's political career; files on the elections in which he participated, the local and state offices he held, and his service with the Democratic National Committee. Third are the papers from Sawyer's term as diplomat. These records are highlighted by copies of telegrams that Sawyer sent to Washington. These records also include letter files, topical files, and copies of the many public addresses made by Ambassador Sawyer.

The most important and most complete parts of the Sawyer collection are the records of his years as Secretary of Commerce. The records are well-organized and include complete speech files, testimony files, and files of public appearances on radio and television. Thus the researcher is able to locate the public statements of Secretary Sawyer with ease. But there is much more. There are reading files, which contain the day-to-day correspondence of the Secretary. The records also contain daily activity sheets and daily telephone listings, which indicate where the Secretary was, whom he saw, and with whom he spoke on the telephone. He also has files of correspondence listed by name, and these files are highlighted by the Truman files for the years 1948 through 1953. Throughout the files is confidential dictation made by the Secretary on important conversations, particularly with the President. The dictation, made immediately after Sawyer had returned to his office, is very important in clearing up some of the controversies that have existed about events in the Truman era. In particular, the Sawyer MSS have a good deal on the steel seizure, the Business Advisory Council, the SS *United States*, the Dollar Line, Secretary Sawyer's Economic Survey Trips in 1949 and 1952, his mission to Europe in 1952, and the Voluntary Agreements Program.

It is appropriate, in fact necessary, to describe the other primary materials available on Charles Sawyer, as his manuscript has been checked against other collections. Mr. Sawyer wanted to be sure that he had not gained a limited or incorrect view of the events in which he played a part. The Franklin D. Roosevelt Library in Hyde Park, New York has material, particularly on Sawyer and Ohio politics. This material includes the President's Personal File 4386 (Charles Sawyer), the files from Ohio, and also some material from Belgium and Luxembourg. The Harry S Truman Library in Independence has, of course, much material. PPF 1118 (Charles Sawyer), the many files of the aides of the President, and the records of the various cabinet-level departments, especially the records on the Department of Commerce in the Truman Papers, all contain a good deal of material on the events of Mr. Sawyer's Secretaryship of Commerce. These paper collections are cited in the notes and the reader should refer to the notes to see the extent of the material in the Truman Library on particular subjects.

Finally there is material in Washington, D.C. The Department of Commerce Library has a collection of Secretary Sawyer's speeches, statements, public letters, radio broadcasts, and statements before Congressional Committees. This is a useful collection, and the Library also has copies of the many documents published by the Department of Commerce between 1948 and 1953. There is also material in the National Archives. The General Records of the Department of State, in Record Group #59, contain the records from Sawyer's term as diplomat. The documents are in File 711.55 (United States-Belgium Relations); 711.50a (United States-Luxembourg Relations); 855.00 (Belgium Political Affairs); 850a.00 (Luxembourg Political Affairs); and 740.0011EW (European War Files). In the General Records of the Legislative Branch of the Government, in Record Group #46, there is material from Sawyer's nomination as Secretary of

Commerce, as well as the records of his testimony before the various Congressional Committees. Special permission is required to use the materials in Record Groups #59 and #46. Then there are the General Records of the Department of Commerce, in Record Group #40. Boxes #1130–1143, in File #105431, the General Correspondence of the Office of the Secretary of Commerce, contain the day-to-day records from the beginning of Sawyer's term until March 15, 1950. Record Group #40 in the National Archives also contains the records of the many agencies and bureaus of the Department of Commerce. The Department of Commerce records from 1950 to 1953 are located in the Washington National Records Center, and are not yet open to researchers.

I would like to thank the many officials of all the libraries consulted in the preparation of these notes. They were all most helpful and gracious on my trips. I have checked this whole manuscript and found Mr. Sawyer to be unfailingly correct on the details of his public career. To Mr. Sawyer I can only say that it has been a privilege for me to help in the preparation of this work. One final comment: on occasions Mr. Sawyer has omitted sections of letters and statements without so indicating. This has not been an attempt to select evidence, but only to omit unnecessary material. The complete text of all letters and statements can be seen in the various files of the Sawyer MSS.

2. "Cunners" are American wrasse, abundant on the rocky shores of New England, and are good though generally small food fish.

3. The "rock crop" is a phenomenon in areas where there are severe seasonal changes.

4. A loon is a fish-eating diving bird that is found in the northern part of the Northern Hemisphere.

5. Mr. Sawyer was born on February 10, 1887. It should be pointed out that Sawyer has long been interested in the history of the area in which he has lived for so long. He has an excellent library on early Ohio history and on the development of the Northwest Territory.

6. Theodore Roosevelt, *The Winning of the West* (4 vols.; New York: G. P. Putnam's Sons, 1889–96). These volumes were part of a number that Roosevelt wrote.

7. William Bunn Shattuc was Republican Congressman from Ohio from 1897 to 1903. For a brief biography of Shattuc, as well as the other Congressmen and Senators mentioned in this work, see *Biographical Directory of the American Congress 1774–1961* (Washington, D.C.: United States Government Printing Office, hereafter cited as USGPO, 1961).

8. Oberlin College gained a reputation as a champion of womens' rights and equality for the Negro in the pre-Civil War period. For

an account of Oberlin in this period, see Robert Fletcher, *A History of Oberlin College from Its Foundation through the Civil War* (2 vols.; Oberlin, Ohio: Oberlin College, 1943).

9. For more on Charles Hall, see page 80.

10. Sawyer has copies of these college papers, as well as much other material from his youth and days at Oberlin, in his personal paper collection, hereafter cited as Sawyer MSS, at his home in Cincinnati.

11. See Andrew Carnegie, *Autobiography* (Boston and New York: Houghton Mifflin Company, 1920); and his official biography, B. J. Hendrick, *The Life of Andrew Carnegie* (2 vols.; New York: Doubleday, Doran and Company, Inc., 1932). Carnegie discusses his love of books and his interest in libraries.

12. The Lamro, South Dakota, *Advocate* was a weekly newspaper that was published until June 22, 1911. Apparently the cash customer was not successful with his venture.

13. The Cincinnati Law School, now part of the University of Cincinnati, was founded in 1833. In 1897 there was a merger of the Cincinnati Law School and the Law Department of the University of Cincinnati. Henry Churchill King was President of Oberlin from 1903 to 1927. See Donald M. Love, *Henry Churchill King, of Oberlin* (New Haven: Yale University Press, 1956).

14. Charles Sawyer to John Dittgen, October 6, 1910, in Files on Annexation Fight, Political Records, Sawyer MSS.

15. The Madisonville *Citizen* was published on October 14, October 21, October 28, and November 4, 1910. Copies are in Files on Annexation Fight, Political Records, Sawyer MSS.

16. Campaign card, Files on 1911 Election, Political Records, Sawyer MSS. Henry (Harry) T. Hunt was Mayor of Cincinnati from 1912 to 1914.

17. Madisonville *Reporter*, November 3, 1911, clipping in Files on 1911 Election, Political Records, Sawyer MSS.

18. Cincinnati *Enquirer*, clipping in Files on 1911 Election, Political Records, Sawyer MSS. In this election Sawyer ran against Jules Zeiner, and the final results were Sawyer 1986, and Zeiner 1351. In the Sawyer MSS, there is much material on this election.

2—BEGINNINGS

1. In the Sawyer MSS, there are extensive papers from Sawyer's terms on the Cincinnati City Council.

2. The Democratic convention in 1912 was a long affair. It took Woodrow Wilson forty-six ballots to gain the nomination. The first session of the convention was on the afternoon of June 25, 1912, and Wilson did not get the nomination until July 2, 1912. A

detailed treatment of the convention is in Arthur Link, *Wilson: The Road to the White House* (Princeton: Princeton University Press, 1947), the first volume of Link's definitive biography. Judson Harmon was Governor of Ohio from 1909 to 1913. William Jennings Bryan had been Democratic presidential nominee in 1896, 1900, and 1908. James Beauchamp (Champ) Clark was Democratic Congressman from Missouri from 1893 to 1895 and again from 1897 to 1921: he was Speaker of the House from 1911 to 1919. Wilson was Governor of New Jersey at the time, having been elected in 1910. Newton Baker was Mayor of Cleveland from 1912 to 1916, and was to be Secretary of War from 1916 to 1921.

3. The final results for this election were Sawyer 2889, and Albert R. Hoffman 1715. See the Files on 1913 Election, Political Records, Sawyer MSS.

4. Sawyer, at this stage in his life, found Judge Shattuck too conservative, because Sawyer was an out-and-out Progressive. He vigorously supported the fourth Ohio constitutional convention, which assembled in 1912, to change the constitution, and publicly defended the changes from attack. As one illustration of his activities and attitudes, see Daniel J. Ryan, "Influence of Socialism on the Ohio Constitution," *North American Review*, CXCVI (November, 1912), 665–72; and especially Charles Sawyer, "The Ohio Constitution: A Reply and a Rejoinder," *North American Review*, CXCVII (February, 1913), 275–79. Sawyer wrote that "the writer of the above article [Ryan] has given the impression that the new constitution of Ohio was fathered by fanatics and obtained by fraud. Some facts pointing to the absurdity and falsity of his idea should be brought before your readers." He concluded his letter by noting: "We have not been captured either by pirates or fanatics, but are learning, as the citizens of other states are learning, that our forebears did not perform a vicarious act of legislation for all generations to come when they framed our organic law sixty years ago." A detailed treatment of the 1912 constitutional convention is in Hoyt Landon Warner, *Progressivism in Ohio: 1897–1917* (Columbus: Ohio State University Press, for the Ohio Historical Society, 1964).

5. The legal papers from Sawyer's early career are in Legal Records, Sawyer MSS.

6. See the clippings in the Files on 1915 Election, Political Records, Sawyer MSS.

7. Such planks as regulation of privately owned utilities were typical of the Progressives of this period. Final results for this election for Mayor of Cincinnati were George Puchta 57,414, and Sawyer 35,144. By 1915 the Progressive impulse was on the wane. See the Files on 1915 Election, Political Records, Sawyer MSS.

3—OVER THERE AND BACK

1. General John Pershing had been on the Mexican border because of Francisco "Pancho" Villa, who in 1916 stopped a train in northern Mexico and killed 16 Americans and then later crossed into Columbus, New Mexico, where his men burned the town, killing 19. Pershing chased Villa without success, and was eventually recalled by Wilson. The best treatment of these events is C. C. Clendenen, *The United States and Pancho Villa: A Study in Unconventional Diplomacy* (Ithaca: Cornell University Press, 1961).
2. Sawyer Diary, May 13, May 28, June 6, June 30, July 2, and August 9, 1917, Sawyer MSS.
3. James Middleton Cox was Democratic Governor of Ohio from 1913 to 1915 and from 1917 to 1921. He was the Democratic nominee for the presidency in 1920, but was defeated by Warren G. Harding, also of Ohio.
4. Sawyer Diary, September 6, September 18, September 23, December 19, and December 31, 1917, Sawyer MSS.
5. Branch Rickey was for many years connected with various baseball clubs. He died in 1965.
6. Sawyer continued to keep his diary while overseas: see the diary in the Sawyer MSS.
7. George Patton wrote a good deal of poetry. For more of the poetry, as well as a general biographical picture, see Harry H. Semmes, *Portrait of Patton* (New York: Appleton-Century-Crofts, Inc., 1955).
8. Theodore Roosevelt, Jr., after his service in the war, was Assistant Secretary of the Navy from 1921 to 1924, Governor of Puerto Rico from 1929 to 1932, Governor General of the Philippines from 1932 to 1933, and a Brigadier General in the Second World War until he met his death in action in 1944.
9. Francis E. Warren was Republican Senator from Wyoming from 1890 to 1893 and then again from 1895 to 1929.

4—BACK TO FAMILY, THE LAW, AND POLITICS

1. Anne is now Mrs. John Greene and lives in Dayton, Ohio; Charles Jr. was a businessman in Cincinnati until his death on September 7, 1967; Jean is now Mrs. John Weaver and lives in San Francisco; John lives near London, Ohio, where he has extensive farming interests—he was recently elected President of the new Cincinnati professional football team in the American Football League; and Edward is a stock broker in Cincinnati.
2. Mr. Sawyer joined the firm of Taft, Stettinius and Hollister in 1956 and is now the senior partner of that firm.

3. William E. Borah was Republican Senator from Idaho from 1907 to 1940. Leonard Wood was Chief of Staff of the United States Army from 1910 to 1914. He was to become Governor General of the Philippines after the election of Harding and served until 1927.

4. For the nomination of Harding, see Andrew Sinclair, *The Available Man: The Life Behind the Masks of Warren Gamaliel Harding* (New York: The Macmillan Company, 1965).

5. Procter's role in the 1920 nomination fight is described in Randolph Downes, "The Rise of Warren Gamaliel Harding," a manuscript that will shortly be published by the Ohio State University Press. For more on Procter, see Herbert Feis, *Labor Relations: A Study Made in the Procter and Gamble Company* (New York: Adelphi Company, 1928).

6. Much of the legal papers for this trial are in Legal Records, Sawyer MSS.

7. The resulting book was Samuel Engle Burr, *An Introduction to Progressive Education (The Activity Method)* (Cincinnati: C. A. Gregory Company, 1933).

8. For Sawyer's relationship with Crosley, see the papers in Legal Records, Sawyer MSS.

9. John M. Pattison was Democratic Governor of Ohio from January 8, 1906 until his death on June 18, 1906. He had been Congressman from Ohio from 1891 to 1893.

10. Smith, who was Governor of New York from 1919 to 1921 and from 1923 to 1929, was defeated by Herbert Hoover in 1928. The best discussion of the election is E. A. Moore, *A Catholic Runs for President* (New York: Ronald Press Company, 1956).

11. Akron *Beacon Journal*, clipping in Files on 1930 Election, Political Records, Sawyer MSS. The 1920's for Sawyer were largely years of political inactivity, but of intense activity in business and law. Beginning with 1930 he represents the conservative wing of the Democratic party.

12. Final election results before the recount were William E. Hess 46,825, and Sawyer 45,546. After the recount the results were Hess 46,347, and Sawyer 45,761.

13. The 1932 Democratic convention was held in Chicago. Governor Albert C. Ritchie of Maryland was not a serious candidate for the nomination. Baker, former Secretary of War under Wilson, was the "ideal candidate" as far as Sawyer was concerned, for the two shared many beliefs. Eliot A. Rosen contends in a recent article, "Baker on the Fifth Ballot? The Democratic Alternative: 1932," *Ohio History*, LXXV (1966), 226–46, that Baker would have been nominated on the fifth ballot had not FDR won it on the fourth ballot. Mr. Sawyer indicates that such a feeling did not exist at the convention. Thomas Walsh was Democratic Senator from

Montana from 1913 to 1933. As it turned out Governor George White of Ohio received the votes of the Ohio delegation on the first ballot and then the move to Roosevelt began. White was Governor of Ohio from 1931 to 1935 and before that had been Congressman from 1911 to 1915 and from 1917 to 1919.

14. William Gibbs McAdoo, Wilson's son-in-law, was Secretary of the Treasury from 1913 to 1918 and was to be Democratic Senator from California from 1933 to 1939. In the 1924 convention in New York City, where Smith blocked his nomination, McAdoo led on more than 100 ballots until the Democrats finally chose John W. Davis of West Virginia as a compromise candidate. John Nance Garner was Democratic Congressman from Texas from 1903 to 1933 and then Vice-President from 1933 to 1941. The best description of the nomination of FDR and Garner is in Frank Freidel, *Franklin D. Roosevelt, The Triumph* (Boston: Little, Brown, 1956).

15. FDR was Assistant Secretary of the Navy from 1913 to 1920, was elected Governor of New York in 1928, and re-elected in 1930.

16. Bulkley served as Democratic Senator from Ohio from 1930 to 1939. He also had been Congressman from Ohio from 1911 to 1915.

17. See letters urging Sawyer to become a candidate, in Files on 1932 Election, Political Records, Sawyer MSS.

18. The final election results were Sawyer 1,240,667, and Lee B. Palmer 1,151,245. There is much material on this campaign in Files on 1932 Election, Political Records, Sawyer MSS.

19. Sawyer has complete files from his term as Lieutenant Governor of Ohio in the Political Records, Sawyer MSS. These papers include correspondence, speeches, and clippings.

20. Raymond Moley was one of the members of the first Roosevelt "brain trust" and was Assistant Secretary of State in 1933. For Moley's description of the events of the period, see Raymond Moley, *The First New Deal* (New York: Harcourt, Brace & World, 1966).

5—MORE POLITICS, BUSINESS, AND LAW

1. These letters are in Files on 1934 Primary, Political Records, Sawyer MSS.

2. Davey served as Democratic Congressman from Ohio from 1918 to 1921 and from 1923 to 1929.

3. CS to Franklin D. Roosevelt, File for Letters from 1933, Political Records, Sawyer MSS.

4. Joseph D. Schrembs was Archbishop of Cleveland from 1929 to 1945.

5. Final primary election results were Davey 215,227, Sawyer 193,080, and Pickerel 183,909. Davey went on to win the election in 1934 and served as Governor of Ohio from 1935 to 1939.
6. Mr. Sawyer held the controlling interest in the Lancaster *Eagle-Gazette* until 1967.
7. For the legal papers relating to these cases, see Legal Records, Sawyer MSS.
8. Luke Lea was Democratic Senator from Tennessee from 1911 to 1917.
9. See the two telegrams from M. H. McIntyre to CS, May 23, 1935, stating that the President would participate in the event by pushing a switch in the White House, and asking the exact time this should be done. The telegrams are in President's Personal File 4386 (Charles Sawyer), Franklin D. Roosevelt Library, Hyde Park, New York.
10. The Reds won the World Series in 1940 over the Detroit Tigers, 4 games to 3. The visitor was Francis Spellman, Archbishop of New York, who died in 1967. Spellman became a Cardinal in 1945.

6—POLITICS

1. One of the many to express sympathy was FDR. See FDR's telegram to CS, July 8, 1937, PPF 4386, Roosevelt Library.
2. James Farley was Postmaster General from 1933 to 1940, and Chairman of the Democratic National Committee from 1932 to 1940. Hopkins was Administrator of Federal Relief, 1933 to 1935, Works Progress Administrator from 1935 to 1938, and was to become Secretary of Commerce from 1939 to 1940. All the while he served as one of Roosevelt's most trusted advisers. See Robert E. Sherwood, *Roosevelt and Hopkins: An Intimate History* (New York, Harper & Brothers, 1948).
3. William Lemke, Union party candidate for President in 1936, was elected as a Nonpartisan to Congress in 1932 on the Republican ticket in North Dakota. He served as Congressman from North Dakota from 1933 to 1941, and then Republican Congressman from 1943 to 1950.
4. The final Ohio results were Roosevelt 1,747,140, and Alfred Landon 1,127,855; and Davey 1,539,461, and John Bricker, 1,412,773.
5. There were letters from Ohioans, and others, to FDR, urging that Sawyer be considered for various cabinet posts. See Official Files 3A and 25A, Roosevelt Library. Daniel C. Roper was Secretary of Commerce from 1933 to 1939, Harold L. Ickes was Secretary of the Interior from 1933 to 1946, and the Attorney General was Homer S. Cummings, who served from 1933 to 1939.

6. There is a copy of this speech, delivered in Columbus, on January 8, 1938, in Files on 1938 Election, Political Records, Sawyer MSS.

7. Atlee Pomerene was Democratic Senator from Ohio from 1911 to 1923.

8. Final results for the primary were Sawyer 450,902, and Davey 419,942. There is a good deal of material on this primary in Files on 1938 Election, Political Records, Sawyer MSS. The primary and the general election that followed are described in Carl Wittke, ed., *The History of the State of Ohio:* Volume VI, Harlow Lindley, compiler, *Ohio in the Twentieth Century: 1900–1938* (Columbus: Ohio State Archaeological and Historical Society, 1942). Because of his primary fight, Sawyer was receiving national publicity. See, for example, Charles Sawyer (Portrait), "Ohio Jewelry," *Colliers* (May 14, 1938), 14–15, 25–28.

9. Sawyer is certainly correct that FDR hoped to avoid a primary fight by getting both Davey and Sawyer to pull out. It should also be pointed out that the President wanted to "put" Charles West somewhere. West was Democratic Congressman from Ohio from 1931 to 1935. In this period FDR grew to like West, and after his bid for the Senate failed in 1934, the President appointed him Under Secretary of the Department of the Interior, where he served from August 5, 1935 to May 10, 1938. But Harold L. Ickes, the Secretary of the Interior, had opposed the appointment and was anxious to dump West. Finally in 1938 Ickes was successful. When Sawyer refused to pull out, FDR appointed West to the United States Processing Tax Board, where he served until 1940. For Ickes' comments about West, see *The Secret Diary of Harold L. Ickes* (3 vols.; New York: Simon and Schuster, 1953–1954).

10. The final results for the 1938 election were Bricker 1,265,548, and Sawyer 1,147,323. Sawyer did well considering the landslide the Republicans gained in the state legislature. The Republicans elected 27 to the Senate in contrast to 8 Democrats, and 100 in the House to only 36 Democrats. Senator Robert Bulkley was also a loser in this election. There is much material in the Files on 1938 Election, Political Records, Sawyer MSS. Bricker's side of the election is described in some detail in Karl B. Pauly, *Bricker of Ohio* (New York: G. P. Putnam's Sons, 1944).

11. CS letter to party officials, File for Letters from 1940, Political Records, Sawyer MSS.

12. Alvin Victor Donahey was Democratic Governor of Ohio from 1923 to 1929 and Senator from Ohio from 1935 to 1941.

13. Paul McNutt was Democratic Governor of Indiana from 1933 to 1937, United States High Commissioner to the Philippine Islands from 1937 to 1939 and 1945 to 1946, and Federal Security Administrator from 1939 to 1945.

14. James Byrnes was Democratic Congressman from 1911 to 1925 and then Senator from South Carolina from 1931 to 1941. Thereafter he was to hold many important positions.
15. Henry A. Wallace had been Secretary of Agriculture since 1933.
16. Alben Barkley was Democratic Congressman from Kentucky from 1913 to 1927 and Senator from 1927 to 1949 and 1955 to 1956. He was to be Vice-President from 1949 to 1953.
17. Claude Wickard to cs, File for Letters from 1940, Political Records, Sawyer MSS. FDR was also quite pleased with Sawyer's actions at the convention. See the letter exchange, FDR to cs, August 3, 1940, and cs to FDR, August 13, 1940, PPF 4306, Roosevelt Library. Sawyer wrote that he had backed the President for a third term because of "a feeling that I was doing the right thing both as a Democrat and as an American citizen."
18. cs to Ed Flynn, File for Letters from 1940, Political Records, Sawyer MSS. There is a large file on FDR's Ohio Inspection Tour, in early October, 1940, which Sawyer helped arrange. The tour covered Western Pennsylvania and Ohio. See the File, OF 200xxxx, Roosevelt Library. Sawyer later cabled FDR: "Willkie in Cincinnati ball park last night Republicans expected 50,000; prophesied 30,000 actually had about 12,000. Things still look all right." cs to FDR, October 17, 1940, PPF 4386, Roosevelt Library. See also OF 5596, Roosevelt Library, for more material on Ohio, Sawyer and the 1940 election.
19. cs to Flynn, File for Letters from 1940, Political Records, Sawyer MSS. Flynn was Chairman of the Democratic National Committee from 1940 to 1942.
20. Boies Penrose was Republican Senator from Pennsylvania from 1897 to 1921.
21. Andrew May was Democratic Congressman from Kentucky from 1931 to 1947.

8—AMBASSADOR AND MINISTER

1. Brand Whitlock was American Minister to Belgium from 1913 to 1919 and then Ambassador from 1919 to 1922. He published *Belgium: A Personal Narrative* (2 vols.; New York: D. Appleton and Company, 1919).
2. For a day-to-day account of Sawyer's term as Ambassador to Belgium and Minister to Luxembourg, see *Diary of Charles Sawyer Ambassador to Belgium: 1944 and 1945* (2 vols.; Lancaster, Ohio: Privately Published, 1961), copies of which are deposited in the Truman Library. Pictures of the diplomats appointed to the liberated countries appeared in *Life* (November 13, 1944), 42.

3. Eamon de Valera was Prime Minister of Ireland from 1932 to 1948.
4. cs to Spaak, November 3, 1944, Belgian Records, Sawyer mss.
5. fdr to Prince Charles, Belgian Records, Sawyer mss. In addition to the large amount of documents in the Belgian Records in the Sawyer mss, there is some material in of 14 (Belgium) and of 2547 (Luxembourg), in the Roosevelt Library, and further material in the Truman Library.
6. *Sawyer Diary*, November 8, 1944. Eisenhower was Commander in Chief of Allied Forces in Western Europe.
7. Hughe Knatchbull-Hugessen, British Ambassador to Belgium and Minister to Luxembourg from 1944 to 1947, wrote *Diplomat in Peace and War* (London: Murray, 1949), in which he devoted two chapters to his term in Belgium and Luxembourg.
8. Clemente Micara became a Cardinal in 1946, and served as Vicar for Rome from 1951 until his death in 1965.
9. Mikhail Grigorevich Sergeev was Russian Ambassador in Belgium from 1945 to 1946 and then Minister to Luxembourg from 1946 to 1950.
10. Raymond Brougere was referring to the Hitler-dominated puppet government of Southern France at Vichy, which was headed by Marshal Henri-Philippe Pétain, the hero of World War i. The American Ambassador to the Vichy government was Admiral William D. Leahy, who told his own story in *I Was There* (New York: McGraw-Hill Book Company, 1950). The best single study is William L. Langer, *Our Vichy Gamble* (New York: Alfred A. Knopf, 1947).
11. These problems, as well as others, are dealt with in the accounts of Belgium at the close of the war. See, for example, Jan-Albert Goris, *Belgium* (Berkeley and Los Angeles: University of California, 1945), particularly the article by Paul Van Zeeland, "Belgium in the Postwar World"; and Adrien de Meeüs, *History of the Belgians* (New York: F. A. Praeger, 1962, translated from the French by G. Gordon). Finally, for the contemporary scene, see *Belgium*, a monthly magazine published by the Belgium Press Association, Inc., which was affiliated with the Belgian government.
12. There does not seem to be much secondary material on the problem of Belgian collaborators. On other countries full studies have been made. See, for example, Henry L. Mason, *The Purge of Dutch Quislings* (The Hague: Martinus Nijhoff, 1952), a work that certainly illustrates the difficult problems presented by the collaborators.
13. cs to Joseph C. Grew, March 15, 1945, and Grew to cs, March 29, 1945, File on Joseph C. Grew, Belgian Records, Sawyer mss. Grew was Under Secretary of State from 1924 to 1927 and again

from 1944 to 1945. He was also Ambassador to Turkey from 1927 to 1932 and Ambassador to Japan from 1932 to 1942. For a detailed study of Grew, see Waldo Heinrichs, *American Ambassador: Joseph C. Grew and the Development of the United States Diplomatic Tradition* (Boston: Little, Brown and Company, 1966).

14. Hubert Pierlot was Prime Minister from 1939 to 1945, and Spaak was Minister of Foreign Affairs from 1936–38, 1939–45, 1946–50, 1954–57, 1961–, and was Prime Minister from 1938–39, 1946, and 1947–50. A good biography of Spaak, discussing his service in government, is Jacob Herman Huizinga, *Mr. Europe* (New York: F. A. Praeger, 1961).

15. *Sawyer Diary*, November 15–21, 1944.

16. See *Sawyer Diary*, November 25, 1944, for a further description of Breendonck.

17. In the 1919 World Series the Chicago White Sox lost to the Cincinnati Reds. Later members of the White Sox were barred from further play in baseball when they admitted "throwing" the series.

18. Walter Bedell Smith had great admiration for Eisenhower; see Bedell Smith, *Eisenhower's Six Great Decisions: Europe, 1944–1945* (New York: Longmans, 1956).

19. *Sawyer Diary*, November 10–11, 1944.

20. Georges Theunis was Belgian Ambassador to the United States from 1939 to 1944. He had been Prime Minister from 1921 to 1925 and 1934 to 1935.

21. This story is also related in Knatchbull-Hugessen, *Diplomat in Peace and War*, p. 220.

22. *Sawyer Diary*, November 24, 1944.

23. See Edmond Leclef, ed., *Le Cardinal Van Roey et l'Occupation Allemande en Belgique* (Brussels: Goemaere, 1945).

24. *Sawyer Diary*, November 30, 1944.

9—BATTLE OF THE BULGE

1. CS to Secretary of State, November 14, 1944, copy in November, 1944 cable folder, Belgian Records, Sawyer MSS.

2. *Sawyer Diary*, January 17, 1945. John Winant was Republican Governor of New Hampshire from 1925 to 1926 and 1931 to 1934, Chairman of the Social Security Board from 1935 to 1937, Ambassador to Great Britain from 1941 to 1946, and then United States Representative to the United Nations from 1946 to 1947.

3. *Sawyer Diary*, January 23, 1945.

4. *Sawyer Diary*, December 14, 1944. Patton died on December 21, 1945.

5. *Sawyer Diary*, December 23, 1944.

6. A good secondary account of the Battle of the Bulge is Robert E. Merriam, *Dark December: The Full Account of the Battle of the Bulge* (Chicago: Ziff-Davis Publishing Co., 1947).

7. *Sawyer Diary*, December 31, 1944.

8. Burnet Rhett Maybank was Democratic Senator from South Carolina from 1941 until his death in 1954. Richard B. Russell has been Democratic Senator from Georgia since 1933.

9. Sawyer has long been disturbed by the extravagances of foreign aid and programs such as UNRRA. He wrote an interesting article, "Foreign Aid" (Privately Published, 1956), which is a good summary of his beliefs on the subject. He concluded this article by writing: "Before our nation is bankrupt and we have made enemies of the countries of the free world by trying to help them, Congress should cut down and not extend foreign aid. This should be done sensibly and step by step if the facts can be obtained. If the facts are withheld the Congress should make an arbitrary cut. This process should be repeated year after year until foreign economic aid except in emergencies is ended." For further discussion of Sawyer's views on foreign aid, see Chapter 21—Semi Public Service—of this book.

10. CS to Secretary of State, December 13, 1944, copy in December, 1944 cable folder, Belgian Records, Sawyer MSS.

11. CS to Secretary of State, January 11, 1945 (#32) and January 17, 1945 (#54), copies in January, 1945 cable folder, and CS to Secretary of State, February 2, 1945, copy in February, 1945 cable folder, Belgian Records, Sawyer MSS.

12. CS to Secretary of State, January 2, 1945, copy in January, 1945 cable folder, Belgian Records, Sawyer MSS.

13. *Sawyer Diary*, January 29, 1945.

14. CS to Secretary of State, February 3, 1945 (#110), copy in February, 1945 cable folder, Belgian Records, Sawyer MSS. Van Acker was Prime Minister from 1945 to 1946.

15. CS to Secretary of State, February 12, 1945 (#141), copy in February, 1945 cable folder, Belgian Records, Sawyer MSS.

16. *Sawyer Diary*, February 13 and 14, 1945.

17. Eisenhower to George Marshall, Belgian Records, Sawyer MSS. Marshall was Chief of Staff of the United States Army from 1939 to 1945. A good study of Marshall is Forrest C. Pogue, *George C. Marshall* (2 vols.; New York: Viking Press, 1963–65).

18. CS to Secretary of State, February 14, 1945 (#154), February 22, 1945 (#198), and February 26, 1945 (#222), copies in February, 1945 cable folder, and CS to Secretary of State, March 15, 1945 (#316), copy in March, 1945 cable folder, Belgian Records, Sawyer MSS.

19. *Sawyer Diary*, June 2, 1945.

10—PEACE

1. *Sawyer Diary*, February 9 and 10, 1945.
2. *Sawyer Diary*, March 5, 1945.
3. *Sawyer Diary*, March 12 and 14, 1945.
4. *Sawyer Diary*, November 7, 1945.
5. Clement Attlee became Prime Minister of Great Britain in July, 1945, and was to hold that position until 1952. Attlee told his own story in *As It Happened* (London: William Heinemann, Ltd., 1954). cs sent a long telegram with his reflections on Attlee to the Secretary of State, March 13, 1945 (#299), copy in March, 1945 cable folder, Belgian Records, Sawyer MSS.
6. cs to Secretary of State, April 28, 1945 (#569), copy in April, 1945 cable folder, Belgian Records, Sawyer MSS.
7. cs to Secretary of State, May 4, 1945 (#601), copy in May, 1945 cable folder, Belgian Records, Sawyer MSS.
8. cs to Archibald MacLeish, August, 1945, copy in dispatch files, Belgian Records, Sawyer MSS. Sawyer continued to convey his ideas on relief to Washington even after he returned to private life. See cs to Truman, February 6, 1946, and Truman to cs, February 8, 1946, OF 426, Truman Library.
9. *Sawyer Diary*, April 10, 1945. Eduard Beneš was President of Czechoslovakia from 1935 to 1938, headed the government-in-exile in London during the War, and then was President again from 1946 to 1948. Thomas G. Masaryk was President of Czechoslovakia from 1918 to 1935.
10. cs to Secretary of State, March 20, 1945 (#344), copy in March, 1945 cable folder, Belgian Records, Sawyer MSS.
11. This trip was summed up in a long letter from cs to Secretary of State, "Visit to Liberated Areas of Germany," March 29, 1945, copy in dispatch files, Belgian Records, Sawyer MSS. See also *Sawyer Diary*, March 24 and 25, 1945. Gordon Browning was Democratic Congressman from Tennessee from 1923 to 1935, Governor of Tennessee from 1937 to 1939, and again from 1949 to 1953, and acted as deputy head of the Belgium-Luxembourg military missions until January, 1946.
12. cs to Secretary of State, Personal for the President, April 14, 1945 (#500), and cs to Secretary, For the President, April 18, 1945 (#517), copies in April, 1945 cable folder, Belgian Records, Sawyer MSS. Sawyer also sent a handwritten note to Truman, dated April 27, 1945, in which he spoke of the "enthusiastic reaction in Belgium to your discharge of the duties of the Presidency." cs to Truman, April 27, 1945, PPF 1118 (Charles Sawyer), Truman Library.
13. *Sawyer Diary*, April 20, 1945.

14. The ceremony was on April 27, 1945. See *Sawyer Diary*, April 27, 1945, for the details.
15. Eisenhower to cs, May 8, 1945, Belgian Records, Sawyer mss.

11—BELGIUM AND HER KING

1. The best secondary account of this whole problem is E. Ramón Arango, *Leopold III and the Belgium Royal Question* (Baltimore: Johns Hopkins University Press, 1961). See also *Belgium*, Volume vi, Number 7 (August, 1945), an issue devoted to the possible return of Leopold iii.
2. The Queen was killed near Küssnacht in Switzerland on August 29, 1935.
3. *Sawyer Diary*, April 3, 1945.
4. *Sawyer Diary*, April 3 and 6, 1945.
5. cs to Secretary of State, May 8, 1945 (#617), copy in May, 1945 cable folder, Belgian Records, Sawyer mss.
6. *Sawyer Diary*, May 8, 1945.
7. *Sawyer Diary*, May 12—May 17, 1945.
8. *Sawyer Diary*, May 18 and 19, 1945.
9. *Sawyer Diary*, June 24, 1945.
10. cs to Secretary of State, June 18, 1945 (#810), copy in June, 1945 cable folder, Belgian Records, Sawyer mss.
11. cs to Secretary of State, July 9, 1945 (#912), copy in July, 1945 cable folder, Belgian Records, Sawyer mss. See E. Ramón Arango, *Leopold III and the Belgium Royal Question*, which has chapters on "The Government's Case Against Leopold," "Leopold's Defense: The Report of the Commission of Information," and "The End of the Royal Question."
12. cs to Secretary of State, July 15, 1945 (#945), and July 16, 1945, copies in July, 1945 cable folder, Belgian Records, Sawyer mss. James Byrnes was Secretary of State from 1945 to 1947. He had served on the Supreme Court from 1941 to 1942.
13. *Sawyer Diary*, July 21, 1945.
14. cs to Secretary of State, August 11, 1945 (#1033), copy in August, 1945 cable folder, Belgian Records, Sawyer mss.
15. The election took place on March 12, 1950: the final results were 2,933,392 (57.68%) for the King; 2,151,881 (42.32%) against the King.

12—ADIEU LA BELGIQUE

1. *Sawyer Diary*, June 29, 1945.
2. cs to Grew, cable and letter not sent, File on Joseph C. Grew, Belgian Records, Sawyer mss.

3. cs to James Byrnes, July 12 and July 13, 1945, and Byrnes to cs, July 15, 1945, Belgian Records, Sawyer mss. See also *Sawyer Diary*, July 13, 14, and 15, 1945.
4. See "Log of the President's Trip to the Berlin [sic] Conference" (July 6, 1945 to August 7, 1945), written and compiled by Lieutenant William M. Rigdon, u. s. n. (No place, no date), a copy of which is in the Truman Library. This account has several excellent pictures of the stopover in Belgium. The visit is also mentioned in Harry S Truman, *Memoirs* (2 vols.; Garden City, New York: Doubleday and Company, Inc., 1955 and 1956), in Volume i—*Year of Decisions*; William D. Leahy, *I Was There*; and James F. Byrnes, *Speaking Frankly* (New York: Harper and Row, Publishers, 1947). For a general treatment of the conference itself, see Herbert Feis, *Between War and Peace: The Potsdam Conference* (Princeton: Princeton University Press, 1960).
5. Speech delivered at Malmedy, July 22, 1945, copy of which is in the Belgian Records, Sawyer mss.
6. *Sawyer Diary*, August 2, 1945.
7. cs to Eisenhower, August 7, 1945, copy in August, 1945 cable folder, Belgian Records, Sawyer mss.
8. Dean Acheson to cs, September 7, 1945, Belgian Records, Sawyer mss. Dean Acheson was Assistant Secretary of State from 1941 to 1945, Under Secretary of State from 1945 to 1947, and was to be Secretary of State from 1949 to 1953. See Dean Acheson, *Morning and Noon* (Boston: Houghton Mifflin Company, 1965).
9. Robert Murphy was Special American Representative in North Africa, 1940–43, and then United States Political Advisor in Germany from 1944 to 1949. He later served as American Ambassador in Belgium and Japan. See Robert Murphy, *Diplomat Among Warriors* (Garden City, New York: Doubleday and Company, Inc., 1964), for Murphy's account of his participation in the diplomacy of World War ii.
10. *Sawyer Diary*, May 23, 24, and 25, 1945.
11. *Sawyer Diary*, December 10, 1944.
12. cs to Truman, August 9, 1945, and Truman to cs, August 22, 1945, of 554, Truman Library.
13. See *Sawyer Diary* for September, 1945.
14. Harold Burton was Republican Senator from Ohio from 1941 to September, 1945, and served on the Supreme Court from 1945 to 1958. Frank Lausche was Democratic Governor of Ohio from 1945 to 1946 and from 1949 to 1957. He has been Senator from Ohio since 1957.
15. *Sawyer Diary*, October 30 and 31, 1945. Edward R. Stettinius was Secretary of State from 1944 to 1945.

16. *Sawyer Diary*, November 15 and 16, 1945.
17. Letter of resignation from CS to Truman, December 14, 1945, and
    Truman to CS, January 21, 1946, accepting Sawyer's resignation
    effective January 1, 1946, OF 554, Truman Library, and File on
    Truman, 1946, Belgian Records, Sawyer MSS. Sawyer was suc-
    ceeded as Ambassador to Belgium and Minister to Luxembourg
    by Admiral Alan G. Kirk.

13—SECRETARY OF COMMERCE

1. The Cincinnati Gardens has remained for nineteen years one of
   the most highly praised arenas in the country. It is used by sports
   teams (for example the professional basketball Cincinnati Roy-
   als), and for conventions and shows.
2. Harry B. Mitchell to CS, October 10, 1947, Loyalty Review Board
   Files, Sawyer MSS. For an explanation of the duties of the Loyalty
   Review Board, see Tom C. Clark, Attorney General, to Seth W.
   Richardson, Chairman, Loyalty Review Board, May 27, 1948,
   Loyalty Review Board File, 1947–50, OF 2E, Truman Library.
3. CS to Seth W. Richardson, Loyalty Review Board Files, Sawyer
   MSS.
4. See Loyalty Review Board Files, Sawyer MSS, for complete information on expenses.
5. W. Averell Harriman was appointed United States Special Representative in Europe under the European Cooperation Act of 1948.
6. The hearing for Sawyer's nomination was held on April 29, 1948,
   before the Senate Committee on Interstate and Foreign Commerce. The nomination was not controversial and the hearing was
   a formality. The transcript of the hearing is in the General
   Records of the Legislative Branch of the Government, in Record
   Group #46, in the National Archives, Washington, D.C. The
   hearing is noted in the *Journal of Executive Proceedings of the
   Senate*, Volume XC (80th Congress, Second Session, 1948). The
   transcript of the hearing was not published by the Government
   Printing Office.
7. This statement was repeated in Sawyer's press conference of May
   10, 1948; for a copy of the transcript, see Press Conference
   Transcript Files, Department of Commerce Records, Sawyer MSS.
   See also Memo from CS to all employees, May 6, 1948, Box
   #1130, File #105431, General Correspondence of the Office of the
   Secretary, General Records of the Department of Commerce, in
   Record Group #40, National Archives. This memo was Sawyer's
   statement to the employees of the Department on taking office.
8. Herbert Hoover was Secretary of Commerce from 1921 to 1928.
   An interesting account of Hoover's term as Secretary, which certainly indicates many of the problems that Secretary Sawyer

faced, is Joseph Brandes, *Herbert Hoover and Economic Diplomacy: Department of Commerce Policy, 1921–1928* (Pittsburgh: University of Pittsburgh Press, 1962).

9. See Foster to Truman, May 6, 1948, and Truman to Foster, May 20, 1948; and Bruce to Truman, April 29, 1948, and Truman to Bruce, May 7, 1948, Box #16, of 3, Truman Library. Foster's resignation was effective May 31, 1948, and Bruce's resignation was effective May 8, 1948.

10. George Marshall was Secretary of State from 1947 to 1949 and then Secretary of Defense from 1950 to 1951. For a monograph on the Marshall Plan, see Harry B. Price, *The Marshall Plan and Its Meaning* (Ithaca: Cornell University Press, 1955). A fine treatment of Marshall as Secretary of State is Robert H. Ferrell, *George C. Marshall* (New York: Cooper Square Publishers, Inc., 1966).

11. For the most detailed account of the yearly activities of the Department of Commerce, see the 36th to the 41st *Annual Report of the Secretary of Commerce* (Washington, D.C.: uscpo, 1948–53). These reports break down the Department by bureaus and list the activities of each bureau for the year. See also *United States Government Organization Manual: 1949* (Washington, D.C.: National Archives, 1949).

12. Speech, "Strengthening the United States Economy," June 14, 1949, before the Advertising Federation of America, Cincinnati, copy in Speech Files, Department of Commerce Records, Sawyer MSS.

13. There are, of course, difficulties connected with such an arrangement. See Michael Reagan, "Serving Two Masters: Problems in Employment of Dollar-a-Year and Without Compensation Personnel" (Ph.D. Dissertation, Princeton University, 1959). But Secretary Sawyer was able to overcome the difficulties in working with the Voluntary Agreements Program. He established a working relationship with the businessmen based on mutual confidence. See the Voluntary Agreements Program Files, Department of Commerce Records, Sawyer MSS.

14. The Business Advisory Council remained part of the Department of Commerce until the Kennedy Administration, when it became known as the Business Council. Much of the material in the Truman Library on the Business Advisory Council is in Boxes #76 and 77, Personal Correspondence Files, Papers of Lou E. Holland. See also the BAC Files, Department of Commerce Records, Sawyer MSS. The day-to-day files of the BAC are in the possession of the Business Council, Washington, D.C. Emanuel Celler has been Democratic Congressman from New York since 1923.

15. Crawford to cs, May 18, 1948, John C. Virden File, Department

of Commerce Records, Sawyer MSS. Crawford was Republican Congressman from Michigan from 1935 to 1953.

16. CS to Crawford, May 20, 1948, John C. Virden File, Department of Commerce Records, Sawyer MSS. Virden eventually resigned in September, 1948, for personal reasons unrelated to the controversy. See the clippings on the whole case in Box #17, OF 3, Truman Library. There was a good deal of public attention given to this controversy. See, for example, "Their Sisters and Their Cousins," *Time* (May 31, 1948), 14.

17. For all the letters, see the John C. Virden File, Department of Commerce Records, Sawyer MSS.

18. The Remington case was also quite controversial. There is a good deal of material on Remington in the Department of Commerce Records, Sawyer MSS. See also "Clean Bill," *Newsweek* (February 21, 1949), 22–23. Tom C. Clark was Attorney General from 1945 to 1949.

19. There is a folder on Condon in Box #873, OF 252K, Truman Library. There is also material on Condon in the Department of Commerce Records, Sawyer MSS. Condon remained with the Department of Commerce throughout the whole controversy, resigning for personal reasons in August, 1951. For the public controversy, see Edward Condon, "Science and Security," *Science* (June 25, 1948), 659–65; Henry A. Wallace, "Case of Dr. Condon," *New Republic* (March 15, 1948), 10; J. T. Klapper and Charles Y. Glock, "Trial by Newspaper," *Scientific American* (February, 1949), 16–21; and Leonard Engel, "Attack on Condon," *Nation* (March 13, 1948), 303. There were other security problems in the Department of Commerce: one was Michael Lee, chief of the Commerce Department's Far Eastern Division. For details of this case, see Michael H. Lee File, Department of Commerce Records, Sawyer MSS.

Security was thus a problem that troubled Secretary Sawyer and Sawyer spelled out his beliefs on the subject in a speech he gave: "Are Our Federal Employees Loyal?" August 30, 1948, before the Forty-ninth Annual Encampment of the Veterans of Foreign Wars, St. Louis, copies in Box #16, OF 3, Truman Library, and Speech Files, Department of Commerce Records, Sawyer MSS. After describing that some hoped that the loyalty investigations would "prove the failure of the Government loyalty program," the Secretary pointed out that the result showed the complete success of the program. Sawyer then talked about Condon, Virden, and especially Remington. He noted: "I have been asked why he [Remington] was not suspended immediately when it was known that he was under investigation. Investigation is not proof, it is not even a charge of any kind. To discharge or suspend a man because he is being investigated would obviously be the height of injustice. Under our scheme of government a man is presumed to be innocent until he is proved guilty." Taking this stand took courage and there was much reaction, some of it quite unfavorable. The General Correspondence of the Office of the Secretary, File #105431, Record Group #40, National Archives, contains many critical letters. For example, Jesup Jones, Alexandria, Virginia, to CS, July 31, 1948, in which Jones wrote: "You stinking Pinko. So Remington is not necessarily guilty of treason spying or anything else, eh? Well *who* the H—— is then. Is Stalin? Youre an American? or claim to be I seriously doubt if you have one single drop of red American blood in you." The majority were more grammatical. For general studies of the whole problem of loyalty, see Eleanor Bontecou, *The Federal Loyalty-Security Program* (Ithaca: Cornell University Press, 1953), and Ralph S. Brown, Jr., *Loyalty and Security; Employment Tests in the United States* (New Haven: Yale University Press, 1958).

20. See File on Steel Mill in Yugoslavia, Department of Commerce Records, Sawyer MSS. Louis Johnson was Secretary of Defense from 1949 to 1950.

21. Walter C. Ploeser to CS, August 7, 1948, and Sawyer statement, Department of Commerce Records, Sawyer MSS. Ploeser was Republican Congressman from Missouri from 1941 to 1949. Sawyer was particularly interested in foreign trade. See Charles Sawyer, "The Need for An International Trade Organization," *Department of State Bulletin* (July 10, 1950), 70–71, for the Secretary's views. Assistant Secretary of Commerce Thomas C. Blaisdell, Jr. was Director of the Office of International Trade and thus in charge of the Department's activities in this field. See Boxes #7–12 of the Blaisdell Papers, Truman Library, for an indication of scope of those activities. See also, Thomas C. Blaisdell, Jr., "The European Recovery Program, Phase Two," *International Organization* (September, 1948), 443–54.

22. Speech, "The Place of the Department of Commerce in Government," October 26, 1948, before the Conference on Distribution, Boston, copy in Speech Files, Department of Commerce Records, Sawyer MSS.

23. Testimony on H. R. 6007 and S. 2385, The Proposed National Science Foundation Act of 1948, June 1, 1948, before the House of Representatives Committee on Interstate and Foreign Commerce, copy in Testimony Files, Department of Commerce Records, Sawyer MSS.

24. See Files on Television and Radio Appearances, Department of Commerce Records, Sawyer MSS.

25. There was much support, particularly from businessmen, that Truman keep Sawyer in the cabinet after the 1948 election. See, for example, Earl McGavin, Vice-President, W. T. Smith Lumber

Company, Chapman, Alabama, to Truman, December 21, 1948, Box #17, OF 3, Truman Library. McGavin wrote: "I had not known him before his appointment but as a member of the Business Advisory Council for the Department of Commerce I have been impressed by his aggressive leadership and his able representation of American business." For an article on the 1948 election in Sawyer's home state, see Richard O. Davies, "Whistle-Stopping Through Ohio," *Ohio History*, LXXI (1962), 113–23.

14—BUSINESS—LARGE AND SMALL

1. Speech, "Remarks at Demonstration of World's First Atomic Clock at National Bureau of Standards," January 6, 1949, Washington, D.C., copy in Speech Files, Department of Commerce Records, Sawyer MSS.
2. Testimony on s. 547, Public Law 395, January 25, 1949, before the Small Business Subcommittee of the Senate Committee on Banking and Currency, copy in Testimony Files, Department of Commerce Records, Sawyer MSS.
3. There is a good deal of material on these trips in 1949. See the material in the Files on the Economic Survey Trip, 1949, Department of Commerce Records, Sawyer MSS. In Boxes #557–59, File #83057, in the General Records of the Department of Commerce, Record Group #40, National Archives, there are 24 folders on "Secretary's Fact Finding Survey, 1949." In both the Department of Commerce Records, Sawyer MSS, and the Library of the Department of Commerce in Washington, D.C., there are complete sets of the speeches that Sawyer made on this survey trip. The trip, as well as Sawyer's constant support of business, made him well known to the American public. Periodical articles began to appear in 1949 and 1950, stressing the Secretary's relationship with businessmen. See, for example, "Charles Sawyer: A Voice for Business That Gets a Hearing in the Cabinet," *Business Week* (January 1, 1949), 6; Bruce Catton, "Real Mr. Sawyer," *Nation* (December 31, 1949), 637; "The Cabinet: Good-Times Charlie" (Cover Story), *Time* (January 30, 1950), 15–17; and Beverly Smith, "Truman's Most Surprising Adviser," *Saturday Evening Post* (September 23, 1950), 24–25.
4. CS to John R. Steelman, August 26, 1949, August–September, 1949 File, OF 172, Truman Library. In this letter to Steelman, who was the Assistant to the President, Sawyer described the first part of his trip. Sawyer's letter noted: "My most significant impression from these trips and discussions is that the people generally have an abiding faith in the soundness of our business economy. I was reassured by the repeated expression of belief of

businessmen, labor, and government officials that our business structure is solid and that our economy can look forward to more new growth and progress." This was Sawyer's firm conviction, one he stated privately as well as publicly. He hoped that the government would do all it could to encourage business, but at the same time not interfere with its operations. For a private pronouncement see CS to Steelman, July 7, 1949, File on President's Economic Report to Congress, July, 1949, OF 396, Truman Library. Sawyer had been asked to comment on the Economic Report by Steelman, and the Secretary wrote: "As I have been asked to comment, however, I will do so frankly . . . The greatest danger today is continued pessimism on the part of businessmen. Where possible, the Message should reassure them." For a public statement, see *Will Business Get Better or Worse? An NBC Radio Discussion by Paul H. Douglas, Charles Sawyer, and Theodore O. Yntema,* July 24, 1949 (Chicago: University of Chicago Roundtable, 1949), a copy of which is in the Department of Commerce Library in Washington.

5. Sawyer completed his report in a letter from CS to Steelman, December 23, 1949, copy in the Department of Commerce Library in Washington, as well as in the Files on the Economic Survey Trip, 1949, Department of Commerce Records, Sawyer MSS. Sawyer wrote that "Discussions with business leaders, labor representatives, and government officials in all sections of the country disclosed their belief that our economy is essentially sound." Because of his activities, especially his trips of 1949, the White House looked more and more to Sawyer for all relationships with business. In May, 1950, a Small Business Act was submitted to Congress. The essence of the bill was that investment in small business would be encouraged by tax incentives and also that insured loans would be available for the small businessmen. This bill would not have created any new agencies, but worked through existing ones, particularly the Department of Commerce. Sawyer was assigned the job of getting the bill through Congress, but the outbreak of the Korean War postponed the bill. For a detailed description of the efforts of all involved, especially Sawyer, see the three volumes on "Small Business President's Program in the 81st Congress (1949–50)," Boxes #8 and 9, Files of Stephen J. Spingarn, Truman Library. Spingarn was Administrative Assistant in the White House in 1950. For the White House position on responsibility for this Small Business Act, see Memo of Spingarn, May 20, 1950, Small Business Folders, Murphy Files 27, Truman Library. Spingarn wrote: "I emphasized that the Secretary of Commerce had been charged by the President with the responsibility for executive branch presentation and coordination of testi-

mony." For some interesting secondary accounts of the problems of small business, see John H. Bunzel, *The American Small Businessman* (New York: Alfred A. Knopf, Inc., 1961), and Harmon Zeigler, *The Politics of Small Business* (Washington, D.C.: Public Affairs Press, 1961).

6. Sherman Adams was Republican Congressman from New Hampshire from 1945 to 1947 and then Governor of New Hampshire from 1949 to 1953. He became Presidential Assistant under Dwight Eisenhower and resigned in September, 1958, because of his relationship with Bernard Goldfine.

7. Speech, "American Business and World Development," April 24, 1949, at Memorial Service in Tribute to the First Landing of Permanent English Settlers, Cape Henry, Virginia, copy in Speech Files, Department of Commerce Records, Sawyer MSS. Sawyer's great concern about foreign aid, which he evidenced while Ambassador to Belgium, stood out in his years in the cabinet, both in his speeches and in private communications with the President. See CS to Truman, October 31, 1949, Box #16, OF 3, Truman Library, in which Sawyer wrote that the Democrats could win the election in 1952 if it was a time of prosperity and confidence. In stressing the expense of foreign aid, he wrote: "If a billion dollars or more could be saved at this point it would have a very beneficial effect both here and abroad."

8. Testimony on H.R. 5615, Authorizing United States Participation in the Effort to Assist Underdeveloped Areas of the World (Point IV), October 4, 1949, before the House Committee on Foreign Affairs, copy in Testimony Files, Department of Commerce Records, Sawyer MSS.

9. Speech, "Canadian-American Cooperation," June 8, 1949, before the Seventy-eighth Annual General Meeting of the Canadian Manufacturers Association, St. Andrews-by-the-Sea, New Brunswick, Canada, copy in Speech Files, Department of Commerce Records, Sawyer MSS.

10. Sawyer was given the job of presenting the St. Lawrence project to Congress in 1949. See Memo from Charles Murphy, Administrative Assistant to the President, to Truman, April 13, 1949, St. Lawrence, 1948–49 Folders, Murphy Files 26, Truman Library. Murphy wrote: "In accordance with your instructions, I have talked with the Secretary of State about transferring to the Secretary of Commerce the responsibility for taking the lead in presenting the St. Lawrence project to the Congress."

11. Sawyer statement, August 25, 1949, Department of Commerce Records, Sawyer MSS.

12. The Secretary's Report, "Issues Involved in a United and Coordinated Federal Program for Transportation," as well as the related correspondence, is in Folders on 1949, OF 173, Truman Library.

The correspondence is Truman to cs, August 30, 1949, cs to Truman, December 1, 1949, and Truman's public statement, December 12, 1949.

13. Speech, "Progress in the Americas," October 20, 1949, before the Nineteenth Annual Convention of the American Society of Travel Agents, Mexico City, Mexico, copies in Box #16, OF 3, Truman Library, and Speech Files, Department of Commerce Records, Sawyer MSS. Miguel Alemán Valdés was President of Mexico from 1946 to 1952. The Emperor Maximilian ruled Mexico from 1864 to 1867.

14. For the formulation of this idea, see OF 172, Truman Library, especially cs to Truman, October 17, 1949, Truman to cs, October 19, 1949, and the drafts of the letter from Truman to cs, November 25, 1949. See also Sawyer statement, December 5, 1949, Department of Commerce Records, Sawyer MSS.

15. See the material on the President's Committee on Business and Government Relations, Department of Commerce Records, Sawyer MSS.

16. Speech, "Salesmanship and Prosperity," December 1, 1949, before the Fifty-fourth National Convention of the Outdoor Advertising Association of America, Inc., Detroit, copy in Speech Files, Department of Commerce Records, Sawyer MSS.

17. Speech, "A New Liberalism for the Next Half Century," December 5, 1949, before the Second Annual Dinner of the Public Relations Society of America, New York, copies in Box #16, OF 3, Truman Library, and Speech Files, Department of Commerce Records, Sawyer MSS.

18. For the text of the debate, see Charles Sawyer, Henry A. Wallace, and Theodore Granik, "How Can We Keep America Prosperous?" *The American Forum of the Air*, Volume XII, Number 26 (June 27, 1949) (Washington, D.C., Ransdell, Inc., Printers and Publishers, 1949). After terms as Secretary of Agriculture from 1933 to 1940 and Vice-President from 1941 to 1945, Wallace was Secretary of Commerce from 1945 to 1946, and ran as presidential candidate on the Progressive ticket in 1948.

19. Secretary Sawyer was particularly interested in the Negro and American business. For the details of this interest, see the Papers of Emmer Martin Lancaster, Adviser on Negro Affairs, General Records of the Department of Commerce, in Record Group #40, National Archives. These papers cover the period from 1940 to 1953 and are concerned with insurance companies, lending institutions, banks, small business, and the Conferences on the Negro in Business.

20. See PPF 1118, Truman Library for a later telegram from Shank to Truman, March 7, 1950, and a letter from Truman to Shank, March 8, 1950. Truman wrote: "I am very fond of Charlie

Sawyer, and am most anxious to know how he gets along with his serious operation. His voice sounded strong and I imagine he is getting along all right."

21. Speech, "Size," April 13, 1950, before the Annual Banquet of the Minneapolis Chamber of Commerce, Minneapolis, copy in Speech Files, Department of Commerce Records, Sawyer MSS. These tours and speeches really made friends for Sawyer among American businessmen. After this Minneapolis speech, Harry Bullis, Chairman of the Board of the General Mills, Inc., wrote to Steelman that "I believe that I speak for the majority of American businessmen when I say that we believe Secretary of Commerce Charles Sawyer is the best Secretary of Commerce since Herbert Hoover." Bullis to Steelman, April 14, 1950, Box #16, OF 3, Truman Library.

22. Testimony on H. R. 271, Approving Agreement between the United States and Canada Relating to Great Lakes—St. Lawrence Basin, April 24, 1950, before the House Public Works Committee, copy in Testimony Files, Department of Commerce Records, Sawyer MSS. See the St. Lawrence, 1951 Folders, Murphy Files 27, Truman Library for the role of the Department of Commerce in the St. Lawrence presentation. For example, see the Memo from Murphy to Truman, January 15, 1951, in which Murphy wrote: "You will recall that in the last Congress you designated the Secretary of Commerce to take the lead in arranging for consideration of the matter by the Congress and presentation of the Administration's views. I suggest that this arrangement be continued. The Department of Commerce has done and is continuing to do some good work on this subject . . . I think it would be very helpful if you could, at the Cabinet meeting this afternoon. . . . Indicate that the Secretary of Commerce has been designated by you to take the lead in presenting the matter to the Congress for the Administration, and that you would like for all of the appropriate agencies and departments to cooperate with him for that purpose." Getting the Seaway Bill through Congress was no easy matter, and Sawyer was called on for further testimony. See Charles Sawyer, "Testimony on Question of St. Lawrence Seaway," *Congressional Digest* (June, 1952), 178–79. For the best secondary accounts of the fight, see William R. Willoughby, *The St. Lawrence Waterway: A Study in Politics and Diplomacy* (Madison: University of Wisconsin Press, 1961), and Carleton Mabee, *The Seaway Story* (New York: The Macmillan Company, 1961). George Humphrey was Secretary of Treasury from 1953 to 1957.

23. See Box #28, OF 3B, Truman Library, for presidential participation in the Census of 1950. Truman issued a proclamation on

March 18, 1950, stating it was the duty of everyone to cooperate with the census takers, and complimented Sawyer upon completion of the census.

24. Speech, "Balancing World Trade," May 24, 1950, at World Trade Week—Stephen Girard Day Dinner, Philadelphia, copy in Speech Files, Department of Commerce Records, Sawyer MSS.

25. Speech, "Business and Politics," June 20, 1950, at Annual Commencement Exercises of Miami-Jacobs College, Dayton, Ohio, copy in Speech Files, Department of Commerce Records, Sawyer MSS.

15—WAR IN KOREA

1. Sawyer's role in the Korean War was related to the economic field. He was in charge of keeping the economy on the move and making sure that the war effort was well-supplied. The conduct of the war, both militarily and diplomatically, was not a matter for cabinet discussion. Such a policy on the part of the President had some interesting results. In the case of the dismissal of General Douglas MacArthur in 1951, for example, the cabinet was not consulted. Sawyer admired MacArthur, whom he thought was without question the ablest general on either side in World War II. Sawyer believed that Truman as Commander-in-Chief had to have the final word in his dispute with MacArthur, and Sawyer has stated that MacArthur as a soldier had no right to criticize Truman. Sawyer thus agreed with Truman that the President probably made the only possible decision when the President decided to relieve the General of his command. *BUT* Sawyer also believed that MacArthur's ideas about refusing to give the Communists a sanctuary behind the Yalu River were absolutely correct. Sawyer's views were, of course, never made public. For secondary accounts of this fight, see John W. Spanier, *The Truman-MacArthur Controversy and the Korean War* (Cambridge: Harvard University Press, 1959), and Trumbull Higgins, *Korea and the Fall of MacArthur: A Précis in Limited War* (New York: Oxford University Press, 1960).

2. Testimony on Defense Production Act of 1950, July 25, 1950, before the House Committee on Banking and Currency, copy in Testimony Files, Department of Commerce Records, Sawyer MSS.

3. Sawyer statement, October 2, 1950, Daily Reading File (Truman, 1950), Department of Commerce Records, Sawyer MSS. Davidson was Assistant Secretary of the Department of the Interior from 1946 to 1950.

4. See Files on Television and Radio Appearances, Department of Commerce Records, Sawyer MSS. Because of his position in the

war effort, Sawyer's public statements became quite important. See, for example, "Executive Opinion: Commerce Secretary Says: The U.S. Can't Relax Now," *Business Week* (October 23, 1950), 30–36; "The Coming Controls: An Interview with Charles Sawyer, Secretary of Commerce, and William H. Harrison, Administrator, National Production Authority," *U. S. News & World Report* (November 10, 1950), 32–39; Charles Sawyer, "Mobilization and World Trade," *United Nations World* (November, 1951), 47–49; and finally Sawyer's published testimony in 1952: *Defense Production Act: Progress Report—No. 17* (Hearing before the Joint Committee on Defense Production, Congress of the United States, Eighty-second Congress, Second Session, to Hear Charles Sawyer, Secretary of Commerce; Thomas H. MacDonald, Commissioner, Bureau of Public Roads; and Vice Admiral Edward Cochrane, Administrator, Maritime Commission, on January 15, 1952) (Washington, D.C.: USGPO, 1952). In all of these statements Sawyer stated the position of his department and of the government and the goals they hoped to achieve. The secondary literature on the home front of the Korean War is building up. For general accounts, see Richard S. Kirkendall, ed., *The Truman Period as a Research Field* (Columbia: University of Missouri Press, 1967), and Barton J. Bernstein and Allen J. Matusow, *The Truman Administration: A Documentary History* (New York: Harper and Row Publishers, 1966). The Kirkendall volume is a series of essays describing primary material available on the Truman Administration as well as existing secondary literature. More specialized treatments are Marver H. Bernstein, *Regulating Business by Independent Commission* (Princeton: Princeton University Press, 1955); George Katona and Eva Mueller, *Consumer Attitudes and Demand, 1950–1952* (Ann Arbor: University of Michigan Press, 1953); Wilfred Lewis, Jr., *Federal Fiscal Policy in the Postwar Recessions* (Washington, D.C.: The Brookings Institution, 1962); and Herbert Rosenberg, "ODM: A Study of Civil-Military Relations During the Korean Mobilization" (Ph.D. Dissertation, University of Chicago, 1957).

5. CS to Truman, October 3, 1950, Daily Reading File (Truman, 1950), Department of Commerce Records, Sawyer MSS.
6. "Executive Opinion: Commerce Secretary Says: The U.S. Can't Relax Now," *Business Week* (October 23, 1950), 30.
7. "Watchdog Johnson Follows Truman Path," *Business Week* (October 23, 1950), 24.
8. Speech, "The Rediscovery of America," October 12, 1950, before Inter-American Cultural and Trade Center Committee, Miami, copy in Speech Files, Department of Commerce Records, Sawyer MSS. For details of the trip, see File on Caribbean Trip, October 5–12, 1950, Department of Commerce Records, Sawyer MSS. Luis

Muñoz Marín was Governor of Puerto Rico from 1949 to 1965. Rafael Leonidas Trujillo ruled the Dominican Republic from 1930 until his assassination in 1961. See Program of concert given in Sawyer's honor by Trujillo, October 8, 1950, Department of Commerce Records, Sawyer MSS. Carlos Piantini was the violinist. Paul Magloire served as President of Haiti from 1950 until 1956. Luis Machado was Cuban Ambassador to the United States from 1950 to 1952. Carlos Prío Socarras was President of Cuba from 1948 until 1952.

9. Speech, "Mobilizing Our Strength," January 10, 1951, before the Eighty-second Annual Banquet of the New England Shoe and Leather Association, Boston, copy in Speech File, Department of Commerce Records, Sawyer MSS.

10. Truman to CS, January 10, 1951, Truman File, 1951, Department of Commerce Records, Sawyer MSS.

11. Sawyer statement, February 7, 1951, Department of Commerce Records, Sawyer MSS. William Stuart Symington was the first Secretary of the Air Force from 1947 to 1950, Chairman of the National Security Resources Board from 1950 to 1951, Reconstruction Finance Corporation Administrator from 1951 to 1952, and has been Democratic Senator from Missouri since 1953.

12. Speech, "The Press—Freedom's Business," March 8, 1951, before the Ohio Newspaper Association, Columbus, Ohio, copy in Speech Files, Department of Commerce Records, Sawyer MSS.

13. Speech, "Freedom and Safety," October 9, 1951, before the Poor Richard Club and United Businessmens' Association, Philadelphia, copies in Box #16, OF 3, Truman Library, and Speech Files, Department of Commerce Records, Sawyer MSS. Robert Lovett was Secretary of Defense from 1951 to 1953.

14. Speech, "Government Economy—Its Prospects and Possibilities," October 19, 1951, at the Ohio State University, Columbus, copy in Speech Files, Department of Commerce Records, Sawyer MSS.

15. Truman to CS, March 9, 1951, CS to Truman, March 16, 1951, Truman to CS, March 26, 1951, as well as a copy of the Rockefeller Report, OF 20-U, Truman Library. There is also much material on the Rockefeller Report in the Department of Commerce Records, Sawyer MSS. Nelson Rockefeller was Assistant Secretary of State, 1944–45, Chairman of the International Development Advisory Board, 1950–51, and has been Republican Governor of New York since 1959.

16. Sawyer testimony prepared for delivery before the House Judiciary Committee, Truman to Celler, June 29, 1951, and Truman to CS, June 28, 1951, Department of Commerce Records, Sawyer MSS.

17. CS to Paul Douglas, July 23, 1951, and Truman to CS, Department of Commerce Records, Sawyer MSS. Sawyer's letter to Douglas appeared in "Ethics and Public Morals," *U. S. News & World*

Report (August 10, 1951), 39–40. Douglas was Democratic Senator from Illinois from 1949 to 1967.

18. Sawyer statement, August 8, 1951, Department of Commerce Records, Sawyer MSS.

19. CS Memo to Truman, September 7, 1951, CS to Truman, December 17, 1951, and CS to Truman, December 20, 1951, Department of Commerce Records, Sawyer MSS. John J. Sparkman was Democratic Congressman from Alabama from 1937 to 1946 and has been Senator from Alabama since 1946.

20. See the records on the selection of an additional airport for Washington, D.C., Department of Commerce Records, Sawyer MSS. Rentzel was Under Secretary for Transportation from 1950 to 1951, and before that he had been Administrator of Civil Aeronautics.

21. Millard Tydings was Democratic Congressman from Maryland from 1923 to 1927 and then Senator from Maryland from 1927 to 1951. Howard W. Smith was Democratic Congressman from Virginia from 1931 to 1967.

22. CS to Truman, August 10, 1951, Department of Commerce Records, Sawyer MSS.

23. CS to Thomas Connally, August 23, 1951, Department of Commerce Records, Sawyer MSS. Connally was Democratic Congressman from Texas from 1917 to 1929 and Senator from Texas from 1929 to 1953. He was Chairman of the Senate Foreign Relations Committee from 1949 to 1953.

24. The report which eventually followed was "Report to the Air Line Presidents on Civil Aviation Mobilization, March 26, 1952, Presented Jointly by the U.S. Department of Commerce and Department of Defense," copy in Department of Commerce Library.

25. CS to Truman, November 9, 1951, and Truman to CS, November 13, 1951, OF 264, Truman Library.

16 — ON BEING ADVISED INTO JAIL

1. For the material on the Dollar Line in the Truman Library, see OF 810, as well as Box #3, Files of Rear Admiral Robert L. Dennison, and File #145, Papers of J. Howard McGrath. Sawyer himself has much material in the Files on the Dollar Line, Department of Commerce Records, Sawyer MSS. Dennison was Naval Aide to the President from January, 1948 to January, 1953. McGrath was Attorney General from 1949 to 1952.

2. The early difficulties of the Dollar Line are noted in "Coast Shipping Blues Lifting; Maritime Commission's Subsidy Grant Gives Hope for Rehabilitation of Dollar Line," *Business Week* (January 15, 1938), 40–41; "Maritime Commission Takes Over Captain Dollar's Shipping Empire," *Business Week* (August 27,

1938), 23; and "Dollar Lines Get Set," *Business Week* (October 15, 1938), 21–22.
3. Clinton M. Hester, representing the Dollars, asked Truman to defer the sale of the stock. See Hester to Truman, September 5, 1945, OF 810, Truman Library. But the Attorney General, Tom Clark, felt that the Maritime Commission was fully justified "in maintaining its present position." He indicated his agreement with the Maritime Commission in a letter to Truman, November 6, 1945, OF 810, Truman Library. There was a good deal of support for the Dollars, in particular by Senator Pat McCarran. See McCarran to Steelman, May 10, 1947, OF 810, Truman Library. McCarran was Democratic Senator from Nevada from 1933 to 1954. For the earlier decisions, see *Circuit Court of Appeals, District of Columbia, No. 9168, R. Stanley Dollar v. Emory S. Land, Chairman, U. S. Maritime Commission,* deciding there should be a trial, and *Supreme Court of the United States, No. 207–October Term, 1946,* which was decided on April 7, 1949, affirming the judgment of the Court of Appeals, remanding the case to the District Court.
4. Truman to CS, November 30, 1950, copy in OF 810, Truman Library.
5. Sawyer to McGrath, March 16, 1951, and Philip Perlman to CS, March 16, 1951, Files on the Dollar Line, Department of Commerce Records, Sawyer MSS.
6. C. Dickerman Williams to Perlman, Files on the Dollar Line, Department of Commerce Records, Sawyer MSS.
7. CS to McGrath, June 14, 1951, and McGrath to CS, June 19, 1951, File #145, McGrath Papers, Truman Library. These letters are also in the Files on the Dollar Line, Department of Commerce Records, Sawyer MSS.
8. Perlman to CS, July 17, 1951, Files on the Dollar Line, Department of Commerce Records, Sawyer MSS.
9. Williams to Perlman, August 10, 1951, Files on the Dollar Line, Department of Commerce Records, Sawyer MSS.
10. Williams to Perlman, August 16, 1951, File #145, McGrath Papers, Truman Library. This letter tells of the compromise worked out by the two men.
11. CS to Stanley Dollar, May 25, 1951, copy in Files on the Dollar Line, Department of Commerce Records, Sawyer MSS.
12. CS to Perlman, May 3, 1952, copy enclosed in CS to Dennison, May 23, 1952, Box #3, Dennison Files, Truman Library.
13. Perlman to CS, May 5, 1952, copy enclosed in CS to Dennison, May 23, 1952, Box #3, Dennison Files, Truman Library.
14. CS to Perlman, May 7, 1952, copy enclosed in CS to Dennison, May 23, 1952, Box #3, Dennison Files, Truman Library.
15. CS to Perlman, May 22, 1952, copy enclosed in CS to Dennison,

May 23, 1952, Box #3, Dennison Files, Truman Library. All of the above letters are also in the Files on the Dollar Line, Department of Commerce Records, Sawyer MSS.

16. The best treatment of this whole controversy is in Charles Sawyer, *Settlement of the Dollar Line Case. A Report by the Secretary of Commerce to the President of the United States, December, 1952* (with letter from Sawyer to Truman, December 18, 1952) (Washington, D.C.: USGPO, 1952). In this report, Sawyer recounts the whole controversy and the actions he took. For the President's comments on the Dollar Line in conversations with Sawyer, see the "Confidential Dictation of the Secretary on the Dollar Line," in the complete Files on the Dollar Line, Department of Commerce Records, Sawyer MSS. Sawyer would return to his office after talking with the President and make this dictation. Some of the dictation is also in the Files on the Steel Seizure, Department of Commerce Records, Sawyer MSS. James McGranery was Attorney General from May 26, 1952 until January 20, 1953.

17—THE SS UNITED STATES

1. Lindsay Warren was Democratic Congressman from North Carolina from 1925 to 1940, and Comptroller General from 1940 to 1954.

2. Warren to CS, April 21, 1952, Files on the SS *United States*, Department of Commerce Records, Sawyer MSS.

3. CS to Warren, May 6, 1952, Files on the SS *United States*, Department of Commerce Records, Sawyer MSS. See also Opinion to Secretary of Commerce, Federal Maritime Board, and Maritime Administrator, from Solicitor, Department of Commerce and General Counsel, Federal Maritime Board, March 25, 1952. "Binding Effect of the Vessel Sales Contract (MCc61974) between the U.S. Maritime Commission and the United States Lines Company Covering the Sale of the Large Passenger Vessel (SS *United States*)." A copy of this opinion is in the Folders on the Merchant Marine, Box #3, Dennison Files, Truman Library.

4. CS to Truman, June 7, 1952, Folders on the Merchant Marine, Box #3, Dennison Files, Truman Library. The complete text of this letter was as follows.

"My dear Mr. President:

"I am happy to answer your letter of June 5th with reference to the SS *United States*. You have not received a report of the results of the review of the contract with the United States Lines Company because the Maritime Board, with my concurrence and following the instructions in your letter of March 30, 1950 that the legal aspects of the awards be examined, felt that the first question was to determine whether the formal contract which was made with the company by the former Maritime Commission was a valid and binding one.

"As you will doubtless recall, you have never received from the Attorney General an opinion with reference to this contract and recently, in reply to my request for a legal opinion as to its validity, the Acting Attorney General declined to give it.

"In the case of the two passenger ships completed about a year ago for the American Export Lines, Inc., that company agreed to a redetermination of the vessel sales price, but only with the reservation that, should the new price be beyond what they could accept, they would have the right to reject the price, return the ships to the Government and terminate the contract. The new price has been given to them and they have stated that if they are forced to a final answer on that price, their only answer can be to reject it and to return the ships to the Government.

"This American Export Lines case is to be the subject of a review in the near future by a special subcommittee of the House Committee on the Merchant Marine and Fisheries headed by Congressman Shelley to determine the need for further administrative action or additional legislation to carry out the intent of the Act. These hearings are to begin Monday morning. I will forward to you for your information a statement of the testimony to be given by Admiral Cochrane. It is to be hoped that some basis may be found in that hearing for a solution which will obviate the return of these two ships to the Government.

"Following the work on the American Export ships, a great deal of technical work has been done on the review of the sales price of the ss *United States*. While this work is well under way, it has been impeded to some extent by the great burdens placed upon the Maritime Administration and the Administrator by the demands of the war in Korea.

"With reference to our meeting on May 25th and the results of it, the Board undertook to discuss with General Franklin, President of the United States Lines Company, and his counsel, the import and effect of the letter from the Comptroller General and asked whether or not, in view of the questions raised, the United States Lines was willing to reconsider the purchase figure fixed in the original contract. I am enclosing herewith a copy of a letter of June 6th addressed by Admiral Cochrane to President Franklin setting forth what had been done. Admiral Cochrane is now awaiting a reply to that letter. I shall inform you promptly upon receipt of definitive word from the United States Lines Company.

"With reference to a future course of action, in my judgment if the Company refuses to renegotiate, Admiral Cochrane has no legal course open except to go through with the contract as it was made. There is no charge or indication of fraud in connection with it and if it should develop that the United States has any claim against the United States Lines Company, as indicated by the Comptroller General, suit can be filed and the whole matter determined in court. Following that course the Government will lose nothing in the end by carrying out its agreement entered into in good faith.

"There has been some recurring suggestion that the Administration should hold a club over the head of the United States Lines Company in connection with earned but unpaid operating subsidies and future subsidies to force them to make concessions with reference to this construction subsidy contract. Admiral Cochrane feels, and I agree with him, that this is an immoral and unwarranted attitude for the Government to take; that this use of monies admittedly due to force an operator into abandoning his legal rights is not in keeping with ordinary concepts of fair play nor the traditions which have governed the relationship between the Government and its citizens since our republic was founded.

"We have already, as we interpreted your instructions of March 30, 1950, held up earned operating subsidies in very large amounts and it seems to me that this question should be resolved promptly and these subsidy payments released. The proper way to settle respective claims in dispute between the Company and the Government is in the courts where evidence can be presented and the issues heard in detail.

"With reference to the claims of the Comptroller General both as to the facts in this case and his powers over the Executive Branch of the Government, it may be of interest for you to see the letter from Hoyt Haddock, Executive Secretary of the National Maritime Union, to Joseph Curran, its President, which I mentioned to you yesterday on the telephone. I am enclosing a copy herewith. If we are to permit the Comptroller General to issue orders to the Executive Departments in the manner undertaken here, it might be well to appoint him Assistant President and let him run the country.

"As stated above, the delivery of this ship by Admiral Cochrane will not prevent the Comptroller General or the Attorney General from presenting and litigating any claim which they wish to make against the United States Lines Company. If, as I suspect, the Comptroller General feels that he might not be successful in court, that is no reason why we should by any act of ours make it appear that our position was wrong and his position was right, in the absence of any hearing or court decision on the matter. As you stated in your letter to me, my Counsel has advised that the contract is legal and binding. The same advice has been given by the General Counsel of the Maritime Administration. For us to refuse to follow our own Counsel and yield to the threats of the Comptroller General would not only be an act of cowardice but would arrogate to him an authority which in my opinion will not be given to him if the matter is brought to trial in the courts. Personally, I would welcome, as I am sure you would, a complete and final adjudication by the courts of the rights of the respective parties to this controversy and the scope of authority of the Comptroller General with respect to executive action in the maritime field."

On June 10, 1952, John M. Franklin wrote to Admiral E. L. Cochrane, stating that the company would not "agree to the reopening of the contract and to pay more for the ships." See the letters from Cochrane to Franklin, June 6, 1952, and Franklin to Cochrane, June 10, 1952, copies in the Folders on the Merchant Marine, Box #3, Dennison Files, Truman Library.

5. CS to Truman, June 13, 1952, Folders on the Merchant Marine, Box#3, Dennison Files, Truman Library.

6. There certainly was great pressure on the President. See, for example, Truman to CS, June 13, 1952, Folders on the Merchant Marine, Box #3, Dennison Files, Truman Library. In this letter the President regretted the fact that the United States Lines Company would not renegotiate the price. But Truman would go no further than to indicate his dissatisfaction, particularly after he received a legal opinion from the Attorney General. See the Opinion of Francis P. Kelly to the Attorney General, R.E.: SS *United States,* June 14, 1952, in the Folders on the Merchant Marine, Box #3, Dennison Files, Truman Library. This opinion was probably crucial in the President's decision to follow Sawyer's advice. Kelly wrote: "I conclude that, all things considered, the best course of action is to deliver the SS *United States* to the United States Lines on the scheduled delivery date of June 20, 1952. This is not to say that I am by any means happy over the circumstances under which the contract with respect to the sale of this ship was executed; I feel that there is some merit in the criticisms of the Comptroller-General. That there is also much to be said in the way of practical and legal consideration that supports the delivery of the ship on schedule. Even more important, on the record as I have seen it, there is no evidence of bad faith or fraud on the part of the Maritime Commission or of the United States Lines."

7. See the letter from Truman to James McGranery, June 20, 1952, Folders on the Merchant Marine, Box #3, Dennison Files, Truman Library.

8. cs to John Shelley, June 20, 1952, Truman to cs, June 24, 1952, and a copy of the Statement of Warren before the Subcommittee of the House Committee on Merchant Marine and Fisheries, June 17, 1952, are all in the Folders on the Merchant Marine, Box #3, Dennison Files, Truman Library. John Shelley was Democratic Congressman from California from 1949 to 1964, when he became Mayor of San Francisco.

9. Sawyer was right that the case could be legally settled after the delivery of the ship and in fact this was the approach that Truman accepted. For the final settlement, see the Folders on the Merchant Marine, Box #3, Dennison Files, Truman Library, or the complete files Sawyer kept in the Department of Commerce Records, Sawyer mss.

18 — STEEL

1. For background material on the events leading up to the strike, see the *New York Times*, November, 1951–April, 1952.

2. Truman to Sawyer, April 4, 1952, Files on the Steel Seizure, and speech, "Where are We Headed," April 7, 1952, to the Economic Club of Detroit, Detroit, copy in Speech Files, Department of Commerce Records, Sawyer mss.

3. For the development of the idea to take over the steel mills, see the extensive material in the Truman Library.

4. Sawyer's talk with the President is described in a Memo of Harold L. Enarson, April 8, 1952, Files of Memos and Statements, Box #5, Papers of Harold L. Enarson, Truman Library. Enarson was Special Assistant to the President from 1950 to 1952. John Snyder was Secretary of the Treasury from 1946 to 1953.

5. Statement of Truman, April 8, 1952, and Message to Congress, April 9, 1952, David H. Stowe Papers, Truman Library. These documents are located in many other collections in the Truman Library, as well as in the Files on the Steel Seizure, Department of Commerce Records, Sawyer mss. See also Harry S Truman, *Memoirs*, Volume ii — *Years of Trial and Hope*, for the President's position on the seizure and the events of this whole controversy. Stowe was Administrative Assistant in the White House from 1949 to 1953.

6. Sawyer statement, April 8, 1952, Files on the Steel Seizure, Department of Commerce Records, Sawyer mss. It should be pointed out that Sawyer's seizure order also called for the managers to keep separate books for the period of government control.

7. Charles Wilson had resigned before the President had taken over the mills. He resigned because Truman ignored his advice on certain recommendations. See "Charles E. Wilson's Own Story of Break with Truman; Interview," *U. S. News & World Report*

(May 2, 1952), 11–14. For the President's side, there is his account in *Memoirs*, Volume II—*Years of Trial and Hope.*

8. See the Files Relating to the 1952 Steel Seizure, Papers of Holmes Baldridge, Truman Library, which contain most of the pertinent legal documents, as well as four interesting letters from Baldridge to Mrs. Nancy Dixon Bradford, the author of "The 1952 Steel Seizure Case" (M.A. Thesis, University of Southern California, 1967). The letters, from October 9, October 29, undated, and December 22, 1964, contain Baldridge's description of the government's case. In the undated letter, Baldridge notes that on the first day of argument counsel for United States Steel indicated that the company would not insist upon an injunction against the seizure order, provided the government would agree not to raise the wages of the steelworkers during the period of seizure. According to Baldridge's account, counsel for the majority of the other companies followed the lead of United States Steel, but the offer fell through, because Baldridge had no authority to make such a commitment. Perlman refused to grant Baldridge permission. Only after this did Sawyer's position reach Judge Pine. Truman supported Secretary Sawyer on this point, for when Sawyer saw the President and told Truman of Williams' letter to Baldridge, the President indicated that he agreed completely with Sawyer's view. See the letter from Williams to Baldridge, April 26, 1952, as well as Sawyer's "Confidential Dictation of the Secretary re The Steel Strike," April 28, 1952, Files on the Steel Seizure, Department of Commerce Records, Sawyer MSS.

9. Sawyer statement, April 29, 1952, Files on the Steel Seizure, Department of Commerce Records, Sawyer MSS. The legal documents are located in these files in the Sawyer MSS, as well as in many of the collections in the Truman Library. The legal aspects are also treated very thoroughly in Alan F. Westin, ed., *The Anatomy of a Constitutional Law Case: Youngstown Sheet and Tube Co. v. Sawyer* (New York: The Macmillian Company, 1958).

10. CS to Truman, April 30, 1952, copy in Files on the Steel Seizure, Department of Commerce Records, Sawyer MSS. The President was not willing to use Taft-Hartley, for reasons that are described in Harry S Truman, *Memoirs*, Volume II—*Years of Trial and Hope.* Surprisingly the White House staff was at least preparing arguments for the use of Taft-Hartley. See especially the Stowe Papers, Truman Library, for preparation of these arguments. For the President's position as the act became law, see R. Alton Lee, *Truman and Taft-Hartley: A Question of Mandate* (Lexington: University of Kentucky Press, 1966).

11. Sawyer dictation, May 3, 1952, Files on the Steel Seizure, Depart-

ment of Commerce Records, Sawyer MSS. This dictation contains a description of the meeting, as well as Sawyer's conversation with the President.

12. Sawyer dictation, May 3, 1952, Files on the Steel Seizure, Department of Commerce Records, Sawyer MSS.

13. This meeting with the President is treated at length in Sawyer's dictation, May 3, 1952, Files on the Steel Seizure, Department of Commerce Records, Sawyer MSS. For a copy of Truman's speech of May 3, 1952, see Murphy Files 20, Truman Library. For an account of the negotiations, see Notes by David H. Stowe, "The Bargaining Conferences of May 3 and May 4, 1952," Files on the Steel Strike, Stowe Papers, Truman Library.

14. For a discussion of the legal decisions, see Alan F. Westin, *The Anatomy of a Constitutional Law Case.*

15. Sawyer dictation, May 13, 1952, Files on the Steel Seizure, Department of Commerce Records, Sawyer MSS. Sherman Minton was Associate Justice on the Supreme Court from 1949 to 1956.

16. CS to Truman, May 21, 1952, Steel Companies 272, OF 897, Truman Library. The complete text of this letter was as follows.

"My dear Mr. President:

"Enclosed herewith is an outline of suggestions as to what action might be taken depending upon which way the cat jumps in the Supreme Court. This may be helpful as a basis for your plannings.

STEEL ACTIONS UNDER POSSIBLE COURT DECISIONS

I. Seizure upheld.
  A. With no restrictions attached.
    1. Secretary of Commerce will order new terms and conditions of employment promptly. Draft order is ready in the Commerce Department following recommendations of the Director of Economic Stabilization as cleared by the Acting Attorney General. In addition, the order will include a procedure for hardship appeal by companies claiming inability to operate under new terms and conditions. (Several small marginal companies have already claimed that bankruptcy will result if the complete new scale is put into effect.)
    2. Continue present operating set-up with such modifications as may be required.
    3. Be alert for possible settlement opportunities.
  B. With changes in terms and conditions of employment prohibited.
    1. White House should have legislation already prepared for transmittal to Congress to provide statutory basis for

making changes in terms and conditions of employment.
See items 2, 3, and 4 of attached outline of proposed
legislation.

2. and 3. Same as A2 and A3.

II. Seizure voided.

A. With direct indication that Taft-Hartley Act should be
used.

1. The President should be prepared to invoke Taft-Hartley
immediately and simultaneously to request Union not to
strike during initial period of fact-finding.

a. Have Board of Inquiry selected and ready to operate.

b. Have the complete steel case record ready for immediate reference to the Board of Inquiry.

c. Have arrangements completed with the Department
of Justice for prompt initiation of request for injunction, if needed, including advance preparation of
brief and all affidavits needed to support the injunction application.

2. At the same time Taft-Hartley is invoked send message
to Congress or arrange for introduction of necessary bill
which will provide a statutory basis for seizure during
periods of national emergency. A rough outline of proposed legislation, including provisions for compulsory
arbitration, is attached.

3. Have ready appropriate notice of termination of Government possession (This is being prepared in Commerce.)

B. With no indication as to line of action to be pursued by the
Executive Branch.

1. Be prepared to invoke Taft-Hartley and take other steps
as outlined under II A 1, 2 and 3.

2. The Attorney General should be prepared to meet all
arguments directed to its inapplicability.

III. Period of no decision. (For example, case remanded to lower
court for full trial on the merits.)

A. Re-examine possibilities of bringing about settlement.

B. Secure opinion from Attorney General as to legality of imposing changed terms and conditions of employment as-
suming no stay by either trial court or Supreme Court,

OUTLINE OF PROPOSED LEGISLATION

1. Authority to the President to seize plants by such department or agency as he may designate in an event de-
fined as follows:
'Whenever during the existence of national emergency
declared by the President of the United States or by

joint resolution of Congress a threatened or actual strike
or lockout affecting an entire industry or a substantial
part thereof engaged in trade or commerce among the
several states or with foreign nations, or engaged in the
production of goods for commerce, or of any product,
essential for purposes of defense, imperils, in the opinion of the President, the national security, he may . . .'

2. Appointment by the President of an ad hoc Board con-
sisting of three members from the general public. Members shall have no personal interest in the dispute.
Matter of Senate confirmation to be left to Congress.

3. Board shall have power to decide controversy, the decision to be put into effect at once by the agency in
possession of the plants.

4. Seizure shall be lifted when both parties accept Board's
decision."

No other member of the cabinet seems to have prepared alternatives for the President.

17. cs to Murray, Files on the Steel Seizure, Department of Commerce Records, Sawyer mss.

18. cs to Truman, May 20, 1952, and Truman to cs, May 22, 1952,
Files on the Steel Seizure, Department of Commerce Records,
Sawyer mss. The complete text of the Sawyer letter of May 20,
1952, was as follows.

"My dear Mr. President:

"Following up our conversation of last evening, I am enclosing
herewith a copy of the telegram which I sent to Philip Murray. It
seems clear to me that this telegram in itself was no provocation
for the remarks which he made. As a matter of fact, the telegram
was restrained in view of what actually happened. For instance,
production reports to me indicated that: (a) At Wheeling Steel
the men walked off the job leaving molten steel in many furnaces,
coke in the ovens and blast furnaces on blast. Jones & Laughlin
suffered damage to coke ovens which may keep them under repair
until late June. For a time there was serious danger of explosions
at their blast furnace in Pittsburgh. The cooperation at their
Aliquippa Plant, on the other hand, was excellent; (b) At the
Babcok & Wilcox plant, Beaver Falls, the men walked out and left
the equipment untended and unguarded. They did this on the
orders of the grievance committee which had somehow or other
got into the plant; (c) United States Steel had a varied experience. For the most part apparently the men cooperated but at
Clairton the leaders forced the men to leave the job and seriously
endangered equipment. At Gary and South Chicago the men

stayed in the plant and performed properly although the local leaders were on the radio urging them to walk off. At Geneva the men walked off without notice. The following paragraph is quoted from a report last week from my production man which, as you can see, was the basis for the telegram which I sent to Murray: 'Since the danger of another strike is not past, and the newspapers this morning indicate that Murray feels that he has no recourse but to call another strike if the Supreme Court action upholds Judge Pine, some message to Mr. Murray by you would seem to be in order. . . . Mr. Murray has an opportunity this week to tell his people either quietly or in open meeting that it is to the interest of defense and their own welfare to cooperate.' My telegram to Mr. Murray was not released to the public by me or anyone in my office prior to his blast at me. It was intended to be purely personal and friendly. I have been curious as to the real basis for his attack. Apparently, he and his associates have been led to believe that I, against the advice of everybody else, refused to put the new wage rates into effect as soon as the mills were seized.

"Reports which have come to me indicate that some other government official or officials have passed the word on to the Union that I was prejudiced against them. I have no apologies to make for my action in this matter; I am certain that I acted impartially and wisely and, of course, with your full knowledge of what I was doing.

"The Union leaders and some Government officials have assumed that all that was required was for me to issue an order raising wages. Suit was filed against me, as you will recall, the day after I took over. If during the few days while the suit was pending before Judges Holtzoff and Pine I had issued such an order the Company heads might have refused to carry it out, on the theory of irreparable damage which was eventually sustained by Judge Pine and temporarily at least by the Supreme Court. It would then have been necessary for the Attorney General to file contempt proceedings all over the country and have the case tried in several jurisdictions. Mr. Perlman was so anxious that the matter be tried in the District of Columbia that he urged me not to leave the District for fear that I might be served with summons in some other jurisdiction; I complied with his request.

"As you will recall my stating to you, the matter of increasing wages for thirty two different classes of employees, each being paid under a different wage scale, required some time for its effectuation. The contemplated order which Mr. Putnam submitted which you and I discussed provides for a delay of ten days for the Companies and the Union to work out the details. In other words, the issuance of an order by me would not of itself have produced money for the men. On the other hand, if some of the operating heads had complied with the order and the men had begun to receive their money it is easy to imagine the chaos which would have resulted when Judge Pine decided the case against us. Furthermore, it was contemplated at all times that the pay raise would date back to April 8th and delay, therefore, was of less real significance. Those who feel the increase should have been made effective immediately apparently labor under the delusion that the pay raise would have remained effective regardless of the intermediate decisions of the lower courts and the stay issued by the Supreme Court of the United States.

"I know that you meant what you said to the two groups meeting in the White House on May 3rd, 'Mr. Sawyer has been the operator under the present circumstances, and he's been fair and decent in this matter. We are going to continue to be fair and decent.'

"I do not intend to answer Murray or get into any controversy with him or his associates—I have not answered the many criticisms I have received from individual businessmen and business groups. I knew that this was no 'popularity contest' when you gave it to me and you did, too; the penalty for trying to be impartial, as usual, is that you please neither side.

"This letter is long but I thought it might be well to give you some of the background of my thinking and acting."

19. See *Opinion and the Dissenting Opinions in the Case of the Youngstown Sheet and Tube Company, et. al., petitioner, v. Charles Sawyer, and Charles Sawyer, petitioner, v. the Youngstown Sheet and Tube Company, et. al.* (Washington, D.C.: USGPO, 1952). The Court's decision is discussed at length in Alan Westin, *The Anatomy of a Constitutional Law Case.*

20. Truman to CS, June 2, 1952, and CS telegram to Steel Presidents, June 2, 1952, Files on the Steel Seizure, Department of Commerce Records, Sawyer MSS.

21. Sawyer dictation, Files on the Steel Seizure, Department of Commerce Records, Sawyer MSS. Short was Press Secretary for the President from December, 1950 to September, 1952. Sam Rayburn was Democratic Congressman from Texas from 1913 to 1961, and was Speaker of the House much of the time from 1940 to 1961. John McCormack has been Democratic Congressman from Massachusetts since 1928. Ernest McFarland was Democratic Senator from Arizona from 1941 to 1953, and later served as Governor of Arizona from 1955 to 1959.

22. Sawyer dictation, Files on the Steel Seizure, Department of Commerce Records, Sawyer MSS. Maurice Tobin was Secretary of

Labor from 1948 to 1953. Sam Rosenman was Special Counsel to President Truman from 1945 to 1946, and then served as a close adviser to the President.

23. A copy of the Truman speech before the Joint Session of the Congress on the Current Steel Dispute, June 10, 1952, is in Murphy Files 15, Truman Library. The strike was eventually settled at a White House Conference on July 24, 1952, with an agreement between Fairless and Murray.

24. Richard E. Neustadt, *Presidential Power: The Politics of Leadership* (New York: John Wiley & Son, Inc., 1962), pp. 22–35.

25. This controversy is an extremely important one, and calls for further discussion. There is much secondary material on the steel seizure, most of it seemingly inaccurate. From a constitutional point of view, with the necessary background material, see Alan F. Westin, *The Anatomy of a Constitutional Law Case*. This study examines the seizure case and its trip through the courts to the Supreme Court decision. It does not deal with the formulation of the administration's position. From a similar standpoint, there are many articles that appeared in the law school journals, shortly after the case was decided: Edward S. Corwin, "The Steel Seizure Case: A Judicial Brick Without Straw," *Columbia Law Review*, LIII (January, 1953), 53–66; Paul G. Kauper, "The Steel Seizure Case: The Congress, the President, and the Supreme Court," *Michigan Law Review*, LI (December, 1952), 141–82; and Donald Richberg, "The Steel Seizure Cases," *Virginia Law Review*, XXXVIII (October, 1952), 713–37, are only three of the numerous articles of this type that appeared in 1952–54.

It is the general treatments, the studies that examine the behind-the-scenes formulation of the government position, that are inaccurate and unsatisfactory. The two "standard" accounts of the steel seizure are Richard E. Neustadt, *Presidential Power: The Politics of Leadership*, and Grant McConnell, *The Steel Seizure of 1952* (University, Alabama: published for the Inter-University Case Program by the University of Alabama Press, 1960). Neustadt, Special Assistant to President Truman at the time of the seizure, helped McConnell with the preparation of the latter work. For reasons that are discussed in this chapter of Secretary Sawyer's autobiography, these studies are inaccurate. Their conclusions have until now been accepted and repeated. Other sources are Harold Enarson, "The Politics of an Emergency Dispute," in Irving Bernstein and others, eds., *Emergency Disputes and National Policy* (New York: Harper and Row, Publishers, 1955); John L. Blackman, Jr., *Presidential Seizure in Labor Disputes* (Cambridge: Harvard University Press, 1967); Leslie Lloyd Donald Shaffer, "Presidential Intervention in National

Emergency Labor Disputes, 1952–1960" (Ph.D. Dissertation, University of Illinois, 1963) ; Nancy Dixon Bradford, "The 1952 Steel Seizure Case" (M.A. Thesis, University of Southern California, 1967) ; Mark K. Hammond, "The Steel Seizure of 1952," *Current History*, XXIII (November, 1952), 285–90; John Carl Cabe, Jr., "Government Intervention in Labor Disputes from 1945 to 1952" (Ph.D. Dissertation, University of Illinois, 1952) ; and Robert Louis Berg, "Presidential Power and the Royal Prerogative" (Ph.D. Dissertation, University of Minnesota, 1958). The sources either rely on the Neustadt and McConnell studies or go into no detail on this aspect of the steel seizure. The best and most accurate study of the seizure was done under the direction of Clarence H. Osthagen, Assistant Secretary of Commerce. It is "The 1952 Government Seizure of the Basic Steel Industry," a 146-page document submitted to Sawyer by Osthagen with an accompanying letter of October 28, 1952, Files on the Steel Seizure, Department of Commerce Records, Sawyer MSS.

Sawyer's contention is upheld by examining the events of April and May, 1952. Sawyer took charge of the mills on April 8, 1952, and hoped that further negotiations would bring a settlement. That the President wanted continued negotiations can not be in doubt. At Truman's press conference on April 10, 1952, Merriman Smith asked: "Do I understand correctly that you will not order the w. s. b. recommendations put into effect while this collective bargaining is going on?" President Truman answered: "I will cross that bridge when I get to it, Smitty. But I want this negotiation to be successful and I think it can be." A week later the President was asked if it was up to Secretary Sawyer to decide about a raise in wages. Truman replied: "It is not. The thing has to be decided by the President of the United States in the long run. The buck always comes to my desk and I meet it. But I am not ready to comment on it now." The President still hoped for negotiation. (See the President's Press Conferences #s 294–306, April 10, and April 17, 1952, Truman Library. The press conferences also appear in *Public Papers of the President of the United States: Harry S Truman; Containing the Public Messages, Speeches, and Statements of the President, January 1, 1952 to January 20, 1953* (Washington, D.C.: USGPO, 1966).

On April 23, 1952, Secretary Sawyer sent a letter to Roger L. Putnam, Director of the Economic Stabilization Agency, asking Putnam to prepare "recommendations, coming within the scope of your functions . . . for changes in terms and conditions of employment which you believe I should put into effect. . . ." (CS to Putnam, April 23, 1952, Files on the Steel Seizure, Department of Commerce Records, Sawyer MSS). Presently the seizure case was before Judge Pine, and upon the advice of the solicitor of the Department of Commerce and with the agreement of the President, Sawyer decided not to act until Pine had reached a decision. (See Sawyer dictation, April 28, 1952, Files on the Steel Seizure, Department of Commerce Records, Sawyer MSS).

After Pine's decision against the President and the stay that was granted by the Court of Appeals, Truman seemed ready to act. He told the negotiators who met in the White House on May 3, 1952 that "You should know that if you cannot reach agreement, here and now, the Government will have to establish fair and reasonable wages and working conditions for the employees during the period that the plants remain under Government operation." He mentioned that Putnam's recommendations were available and he would act in cooperation with Secretary Sawyer on Monday, May 5, 1952. (See Putnam to CS, May 3, 1952, and Truman speech, May 3, 1952, copies of both in Murphy Files 20, Truman Library).

BUT, in the meantime the Supreme Court acted, staying the decision of Judge Pine, and at the same time ordering Sawyer to "take no action to change any term or condition of employment while this study is in effect unless such change is mutually agreed upon by the steel companies." (For the Supreme Court order, see Alan F. Westin, *The Anatomy of a Constitutional Law Case*).

26. Roy Hoopes, *The Steel Crisis* (New York: J. Day Co., 1963), p. 138. For the Sawyer-Hoopes correspondence, see Files on the Steel Seizure, Department of Commerce Records, Sawyer MSS.

19 – BARKLEY

1. Actually Sawyer was on the Steering Committee of the Convention, which organized and reviewed the convention proceedings, session by session. See Frank E. McKinney, Chairman of the Democratic National Committee, to CS, June 14, 1952, Department of Commerce Records, Sawyer MSS.

2. Estes Kefauver was Democratic Congressman from Tennessee from 1939 to 1949 and Senator from 1949 to 1963. Adlai Stevenson was Governor of Illinois at the time, having been elected in 1948. Herbert Lehman was Governor of New York from 1933 to 1942 and then Democratic Senator from New York from 1949 to 1957. G. Mennen "Soapy" Williams was Democratic Governor of Michigan from 1949 to 1960.

3. See Alben W. Barkley, *That Reminds Me* (Garden City, New York: Doubleday & Company, 1954). Barkley mentions that when he arrived in Chicago he had neither a professional publicity man or a public relations man and he notes that Sawyer sent him "an

able gentleman, Ludwig Caminita, Jr.," p. 235. Earle Clements was Democratic Congressman from Kentucky from 1945 to 1948, Governor of Kentucky from 1948 to 1950, and then Senator from 1950 to 1957. Lawrence Wetherby was Governor of Kentucky from 1950 to 1955.

4. In the transcripts of Sidney Shalett's interviews with Barkley, from which *That Reminds Me* was written, Barkley describes his feelings about this incident. In response to Shalett's question: "That was almost a knife in the back, wasn't it?", Barkley answered: "Well, I never did call it that, of course. I felt that it was something that I did not deserve after my whole lifetime record in behalf of labor and so forth . . . So frankly I felt offended. I felt grieved. . . . I just feel that my record in the House and the Senate, as Vice-President of the United States in advocating the cause of Labor deserved better treatment than I got at their hands." See the transcripts of Shalett's interviews, Box #1, Truman Library.

5. Barkley to cs, Department of Commerce Records, Sawyer mss. Thomas Hennings was Democratic Representative from Missouri from 1935 to 1940 and then Senator from 1951 to 1960.

6. James F. Byrnes was at the time Democratic Governor of South Carolina, a position he held from 1951 to 1955. Byrnes tells the story of his whole career in *All in One Lifetime* (New York: Harper and Row, Publishers, 1958).

7. A. B. Chandler was Democratic Governor of Kentucky from 1935 to 1939, Senator from 1939 to 1945, and Governor again from 1955 to 1959.

20 — FAREWELL TO WASHINGTON AND TRUMAN

1. "Markets After the Defense Expansion," a Report Designed, as originally announced in July, 1952, by Secretary of Commerce Charles Sawyer, "to Inform the Business Community on Factors Affecting the Level of Civilian Demand after the Present Defense Program has reached Its Peak," (Washington, D.C.: uscpo, 1952, with Foreword by Charles Sawyer), copy in Files on the Business Advisory Council, Department of Commerce Records, Sawyer mss. Marion Folsom was Chairman of the Board of Trustees of the Committee for Economic Development and was later to serve as Secretary of Health, Education and Welfare from 1955 to 1958.

2. "Effective Competition," Report to the Secretary of Commerce by his Business Advisory Council with a letter of Comment from the Secretary of Commerce of December 18, 1952 (Washington, D.C.: Department of Commerce, 1952), copy in Files on the Business Advisory Council, Department of Commerce Records, Sawyer mss.

3. Sinclair Weeks was Republican Senator from Massachusetts in 1944 and then Secretary of Commerce from January 21, 1953 to November 10, 1958.
4. See File on the Economic Survey Trip, October 4–19, 1952, Department of Commerce Records, Sawyer MSS.
5. Truman to CS, September 20, 1952, Files on the European Mission, 1952, Department of Commerce Records, Sawyer MSS.
6. The Files on the European Mission are broken down by cities visited and include letters, memos, telegrams, and activity sheets.
7. "London, November 5–8, 1952," Files on the European Mission, 1952, Department of Commerce Records, Sawyer MSS.
8. "Paris, November 8–12, and November 22–27, 1952," Files on the European Mission, 1952, Department of Commerce Records, Sawyer MSS.
9. Sawyer spent November 23, 1952, in Brussels and got the same reaction. "Brussels, November 23, 1952," Files on the European Mission, 1952, Department of Commerce Records, Sawyer MSS.
10. "Bonn, November 12–13, 1952," Files on the European Mission, 1952, Department of Commerce Records, Sawyer MSS. These files are quite interesting as they contain State Department accounts of Sawyer's visits. See, for example, Carl H. Boehringer, Commercial Attache, to Secretary of State, November 24, 1952, "Report on Visit to Bonn, November 12–13, 1952, of Mission Headed by S of C Sawyer," in the Bonn Folder. Konrad Adenauer was Chancellor of the German Federal Republic from 1949 to 1963, and was succeeded by Ludwig Erhard, who served until 1966.
11. "Dusseldorf, November 13–14, 1952," Files on the European Mission, 1952, Department of Commerce Records, Sawyer MSS.
12. Luigi Barzini, *The Italians* (New York: Bantam Book, 1965), pp. 174–75. See "Milan, November 15–17, 1952," and "Rome, November 18–19, 1952," Files on the European Mission, 1952, Department of Commerce Records, Sawyer MSS.
13. "Athens, November 19–21, 1952," Files on the European Mission, 1952, Department of Commerce Records, Sawyer MSS. The King and Queen of Greece were Paul I and Frederika. Marshall Alexander Papagos was Premier of Greece from 1952 to 1955.
14. CS to Truman, November 22, 1952, and Truman to CS, December 1, 1952, Department of Commerce Records, Sawyer MSS.
15. "Brussels, November 23, 1952," Files on the European Mission, 1952, Department of Commerce Records, Sawyer MSS.
16. "Madrid, November 27, 1952," Files on the European Mission, 1952, Department of Commerce Records, Sawyer MSS. Of particular interest in this file is Lincoln MacVeagh, American Ambassador in Madrid, to Secretary of State, December 5, 1952, "Call of Secretary Sawyer on the Spanish Chief of State, Confidential." Francisco Franco has been leader of Spain since 1939.

17. "Gibraltar, December 1, 1952," Files on the European Mission, 1952, Department of Commerce Records, Sawyer MSS.

18. "Report, 1952, by Secretary of Commerce Charles Sawyer to the President on the Economic Survey of Europe by a Presidential Mission," with letter from Sawyer to Truman, December 15, 1952, Files on the European Mission, 1952, Department of Commerce Records, Sawyer MSS.

19. Speech, "On Being a Public Official," February 1, 1952, before the Executives' Club, Chicago, copies in Box #17, OF 3, Misc., Truman Library, and Speech Files, Department of Commerce Records, Sawyer MSS.

20. James Forrestal was Secretary of Defense from 1947 to 1949. See Walter Millis, ed., *The Forrestal Diaries* (New York: The Viking Press, Inc., 1951), and for a biography, see Arnold A. Rogow, *James Forrestal: A Study of Personality, Politics, and Policy* (New York: The Macmillan Company, 1963).

21. For Perle Mesta's career, see *Perle: My Story* (New York: McGraw-Hill Book Company, 1960), with Robert Cahn.

22. Marshall was Secretary of State from 1947 to 1949.

23. CS to Truman, January 5, 1953, and Truman to CS, Department of Commerce Records, Sawyer MSS.

24. Truman to CS, March 30, 1952, CS to Truman, April 4, 1952, and Truman to CS, April 5, 1952, Department of Commerce Records, Sawyer MSS.

25. For some contemporary studies on Sawyer's leaving office, see "Truman Did Tolerate Two Outstanding Men," *Saturday Evening Post* (January 31, 1953), 10–12; and "Smilin' Through: Democrats' Washington Era Ends," *Newsweek* (January 19, 1953), 27.

21—SEMI PUBLIC SERVICE

1. There is a whole file, "Charles Sawyer: Campaign Chairman, 1955," in the Sawyer MSS.

2. See Charles Sawyer, "Foreign Aid" (Privately Published, 1956).

3. CS to Bernard S. Van Rensselaer, Staff Director, October 11, 1954, Files on Hoover Commission, Task Force on Overseas Economic Operations, Sawyer MSS.

4. John H. Nelson, Industrial Advisor with ICM Mission in India, to Van Rensselaer, May 20, 1956, Files on Hoover Commission, Task Force on Overseas Economic Operations, Sawyer MSS. The Nelson letter was only one of many such reports that the Hoover Commission saw. Van Rensselaer wrote an article, "How Not to Handle Foreign Aid," *Reader's Digest* (February, 1957), 25–30, based on his experiences.

5. *The Shield* (April 15, 1955), copy in Files on Hoover Commission, Task Force on Overseas Economic Operations, Sawyer MSS.

Harold Stassen, one-time Republican Governor of Minnesota, was at the time Director of Foreign Operations Administrations.

6. CS to Henning Prentiss, October 22, 1954, and Prentiss to CS, October 25, 1954, Files on Hoover Commission, Task Force on Overseas Economic Operations, Sawyer MSS.

7. See Files on Hoover Commission, Task Force on Overseas Economic Cooperation, Sawyer MSS.

8. Hoover Commission Report on Organization of the Executive Branch of the Government, "Task Force Report on Overseas Economic Operations," copy in Files on Hoover Commission, Sawyer MSS.

9. Statement of Joseph P. Kennedy and other commissioners, June 5, 1955, copy in Files on Hoover Commission, Sawyer MSS.

10. CS to Michael Mansfield, undated copy of letter, Files on Hoover Commission, Sawyer MSS. Mansfield was Democratic Congressman from Montana from 1943 to 1953 and has been Senator since 1953. John Hollister was Republican Congressman from Ohio from 1931 to 1937, Executive Director of the Hoover Commission from 1953 to 1955, and then Director of International Cooperation Administration from 1955 to 1957. For the views of the President on the Hoover Commission, see Dwight D. Eisenhower, *The White House Years* (2 vols.; Garden City, New York: Doubleday and Company, Inc., 1963 and 1965), especially Volume I—*Mandate for Change.*

11. Mr. Sawyer has been a member of the Business Advisory Council since he left the cabinet.

12. See the Files on the World Fair Site Committee, 1964, Sawyer MSS. Warren Magnuson was Democratic Congressman from Washington from 1937 to 1944 and has been Senator since 1945.

13. Dwight Eisenhower to CS, October 9, 1959, Files on the World Fair Site Committee, Sawyer MSS. James William Fulbright was Democratic Congressman from Arkansas from 1943 to 1945 and has been Senator since 1945. Jacob Javits was Republican Congressman from New York from 1947 to 1954 and since 1957 has been Senator. Kenneth Keating was Republican Congressman from New York from 1947 to 1959 and Senator from 1959 to 1965. Harry A. Bullis was former Chairman of the Board of the General Mills, Inc., and Aksel Nielson was President of the Title Guaranty Company of Denver.

14. Committee Report, October 30, 1959, copy in Files on the World Fair Site Committee, Sawyer MSS. See also Eisenhower to CS, November 6, 1959, Files on the World Fair Site Committee, Sawyer MSS.

15. Jerry Landauer, Staff Reporter, Washington *Post*, to CS, March 16, 1960, and CS to Landauer, March 21, 1960, Files on the World Fair Site Committee, Sawyer MSS.

16. Donald K. David to CS, February 18, 1958, and CS to David, February 28, 1958, Files on the Commission on Money and Credit, Sawyer MSS. The Committee for Economic Development is a non-partisan group founded to serve as a civilian advisory council for the nation in economic matters.

17. Sawyer comments, Files on the Commission on Money and Credit, Sawyer MSS.

18. CS to Frazar Wilde, November 3, 1960, and Wilde to CS, November 8, 1960, Files on the Commission on Money and Credit, Sawyer MSS.

19. CS to Bertrand Fox, Director of Research, March 27, 1961, Files on the Commission on Money and Credit, Sawyer MSS.

20. CS to John Rooney, File for Letters from 1963, Sawyer MSS. Rooney has been Democratic Congressman from New York since 1944.

22 — CONCERNS OF A CONSERVATIVE DEMOCRAT

1. Irving Brant describes Jefferson's difficulties with students at the University of Virginia in his work, *James Madison* (6 vols.; Indianapolis: Bobbs-Merrill Company, 1941–61), in Volume VI— *James Madison: Commander in Chief, 1812–1836.* Brant notes on page 455 that: "Jefferson expected that only earnest and intelligent young men, stirred by pride and ambition, would seek out such an institution. What he was confronted with, a few months after the school opened, was the uncontrolled carousing of undisciplined youths from wealthy families, who stormed out of classes, assaulted professors, got drunk in taverns and turned the dormitories into gambling houses. The situation reached a crisis at the end of September 1825, when a smoking stink bomb was thrown into Professor Long's house. The next night a masked mob of students surged through the grounds shouting, 'Down with the European professors!' They attacked Tucker and Emmet with a brick and a cane when the two courageous professors unmasked the mob leader. The next day sixty-five rioters sent a resolution to the faculty assailing these two professors because both laid hands on one student at the same time.

"Madison was at Monticello on the night of the riot and the Board of Visitors gathered there next day. They were presented with the resignations of Professors Long and Key and the threat of the entire faculty to quit unless discipline was established. Student Henry Tutwiler, afterward a professor, described the meeting that followed in the University Rotunda: 'At a long table near the center of the room sat the most august body of men I had even seen—Jefferson, Madison and Monroe. . . . Chapman Johnson . . . Cabell . . . Cocke . . . Jefferson arose to address the students. He began by declaring that it was one of the most painful events of his life, but he had not gone far before his feelings overcame him, and he sat down, saying that he would leave to abler hands the task of saying what he wished to say.'

"Johnson, one of Virginia's foremost lawyers, spoke with such firmness and deep feeling (aided by the effect of Jefferson's emotional upset) that when he called on the rioters to come forward and give in their names, nearly all did so. Jefferson then took the lead in establishing a disciplinary system and the two professors withdrew their resignations."

2. An interesting study of the population problem is Philip M. Hauser, *The Population Dilemma* (American Assembly, Englewood Cliffs, N.J.: Prentice-Hall, 1963).

Index

Acheson, Dean: commends CS on public relations, 160–61; and export control, 184–85; mentioned, 353n8

Adams, Sherman, 192–93, 360n6

Adenauer, Konrad, 290, 383n10

Advertising Advisory Committee, 200–201

Agneau Mystique. See "Mystic Lamb"

Albert I, 86

ALCAN, 214

Alcoa, 80

Aldrich, Nelson, 287, 288

Alemán, Miguel, 197, 198, 361n13

Ambassadors, Career: remuneration of, 104–5; CS' comments on, 162–63

Ambassador to Belgium and Minister to Luxembourg: and fellow foreign ambassadors, 90–92, 129; and concern over Belgian food problem, 93, 106–7, 117–24, 131; visit to Breendonck by, 96–97; and relations with Belgian Government, 106, 107, 108, 120, 148–49; visits to the front by, 109–10, 135–38, 351n11; and personal brush with

enemy, 113–14; and problem of UNRRA, 115–16; visits to displaced persons camps by, 136, 138, 169, 170; and Truman's stop at Belgium en route to Potsdam, 155–57; visit to Mondorf Camp for German High Command P.O.W.'s by, 158–59; recovery of "Mystic Lamb" by, 159–61; secures vital uranium contract with Belgium, 163–64; and U.S. reverse lend-lease obligations, 164–65

Anderson, Edward, 115, 117

Annapolis United States Naval Academy, 9

Antwerp, Belgium: defense of, 87, 111, 112, 115, 117, mentioned, 92, 131, 141, 155, 156, 162

Ardennes, Belgium, 98, 111, 117

Arey, Hawthorne, 287

Armour, Norman, 100

Armstrong, Col. John, 117

Arnall, Ellis, 257, 265

Astrid, Queen, 144, 152, 252n2

Atomic Bomb: acquisition of uranium supply for, 163–64, 165; mentioned, 124, 166–67, 183, 329–30

Atomic Energy Commission, 187, 271

389